I0819557

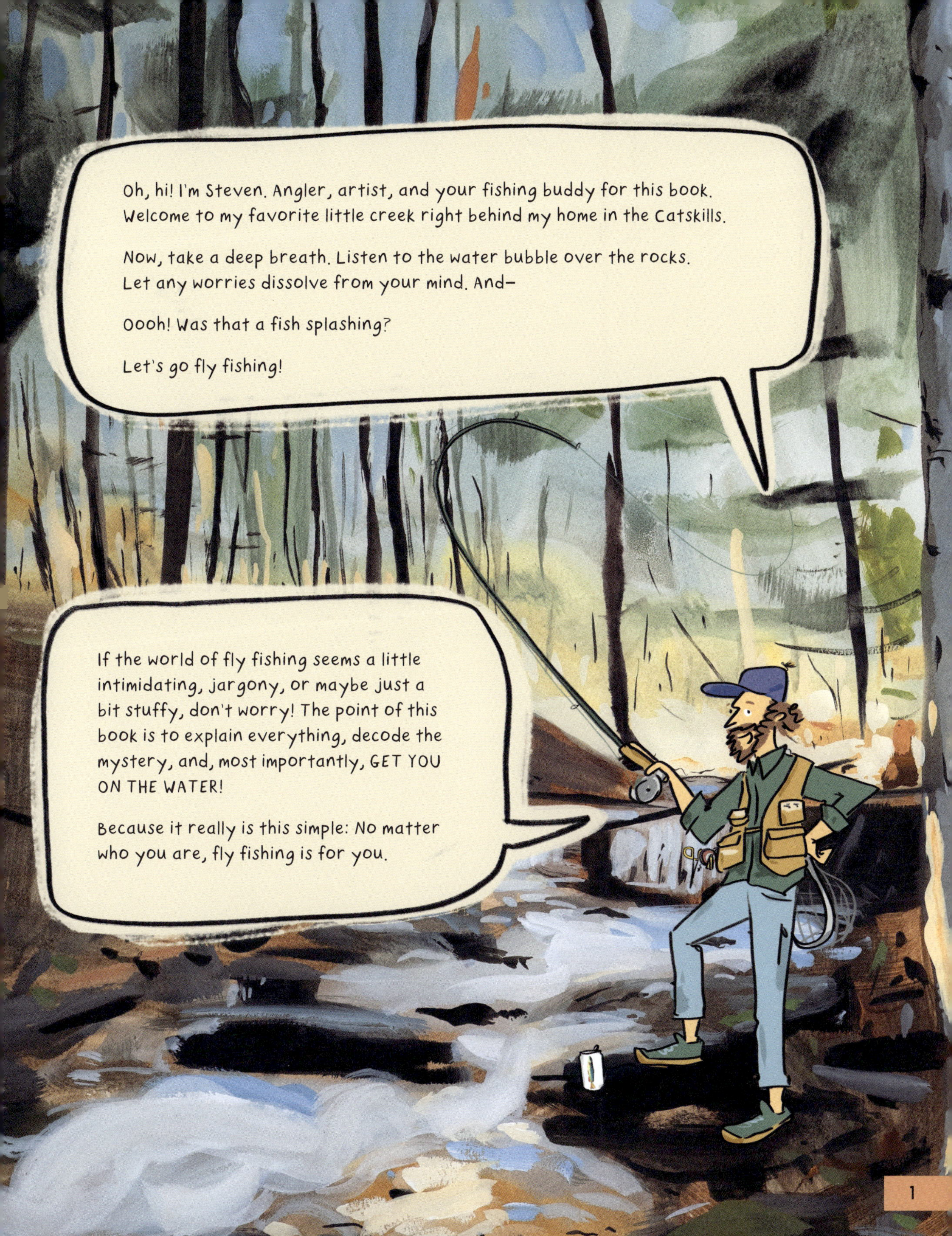
Oh, hi! I'm Steven. Angler, artist, and your fishing buddy for this book. Welcome to my favorite little creek right behind my home in the Catskills.
Now, take a deep breath. Listen to the water bubble over the rocks. Let any worries dissolve from your mind. And–
Oooh! Was that a fish splashing?
Let's go fly fishing!
If the world of fly fishing seems a little intimidating, jargony, or maybe just a bit stuffy, don't worry! The point of this book is to explain everything, decode the mystery, and, most importantly, GET YOU ON THE WATER!
Because it really is this simple: No matter who you are, fly fishing is for you.

To Jon Scieszka.
This is either all your fault or thanks to you!

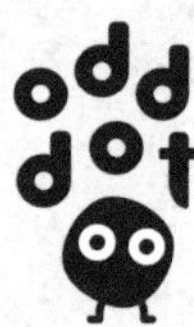

Joyful Books for Curious Minds

An imprint of Macmillan Publishing Group, LLC
Odd Dot® is a registered trademark of Macmillan Publishing Group, LLC.
120 Broadway, New York, NY 10271
OddDot.com
EU representative: Macmillan Publishers Ireland Ltd, 1st Floor,
The Liffey Trust Centre, 117–126 Sheriff Street Upper, Dublin 1, DO1 YC43

EDITOR Deirdre Langeland
DESIGNER Jen Keenan
PRODUCTION EDITOR Kathy Wielgosz
MANAGING EDITOR Jennifer Healey
PRODUCTION MANAGER Jocelyn O'Dowd

Library of Congress Cataloging-in-Publication Data is available.

ISBN 978-1-250-36438-8

First edition, 2026

Printed in China by RR Donnelley Asia Printing Solutions Ltd., Dongguan City, Guangdong Province

1 3 5 7 9 10 8 6 4 2

THE FLY FISHING BOOK

AN ARTFUL GUIDE TO ANGLING

STEVEN WEINBERG

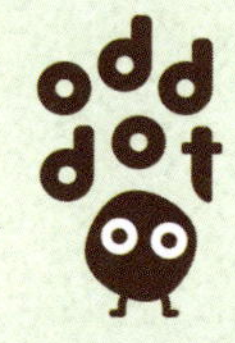

NEW YORK

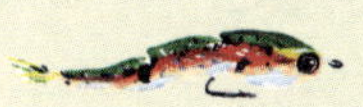

CONTENTS

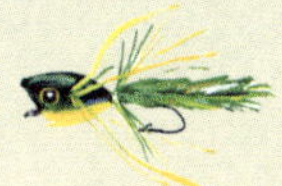

PART ONE: CAST

PART TWO: CATCH

PART THREE: RELEASE

Fly Fishing Is an Art, Not a Science.

(AND THAT'S WHY I'M MAKING THIS BOOK.)

MAYBE I'M BIASED HERE because I'm an artist. I paint fish. I paint landscapes. I write and illustrate books too. And while I love professional fishing guides, biologists, and scientists—that's just not me. (Maybe it's not you either.) And that's OK. Because my favorite part of fly fishing is this: There is NO perfect way to go about it. Just like art, the beauty is in trying. And maybe failing. But then trying again.

STEVEN WEINBERG

FAVORITE WATERS: The backyard creek of the small hotel my wife, Casey, and I own and operate, the Spruceton Inn: a Catskills Bed & Bar

FAVORITE FISH: A Catskills Brookie

FAVORITE FLY: A Parachute Madam X (PMX)

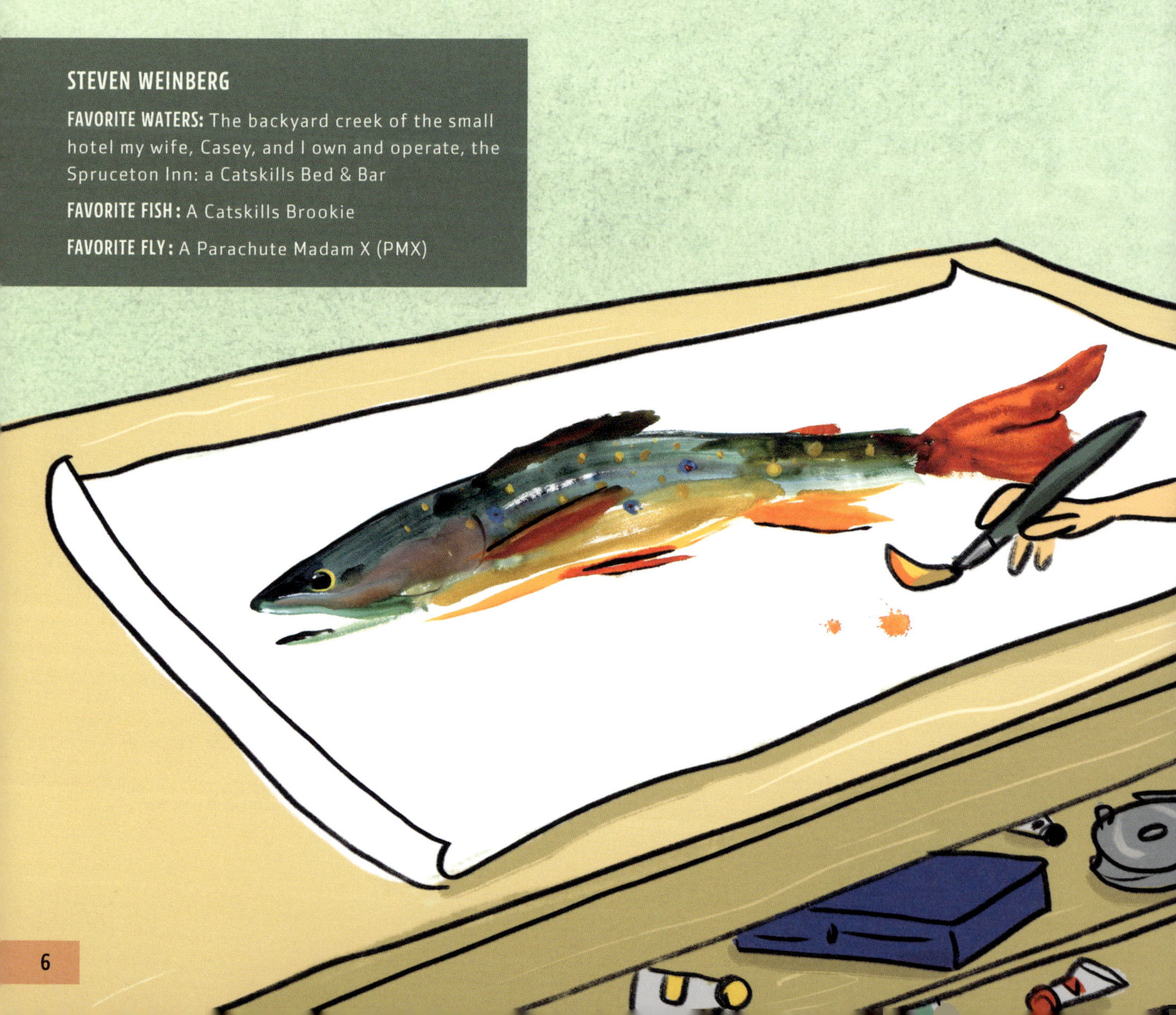

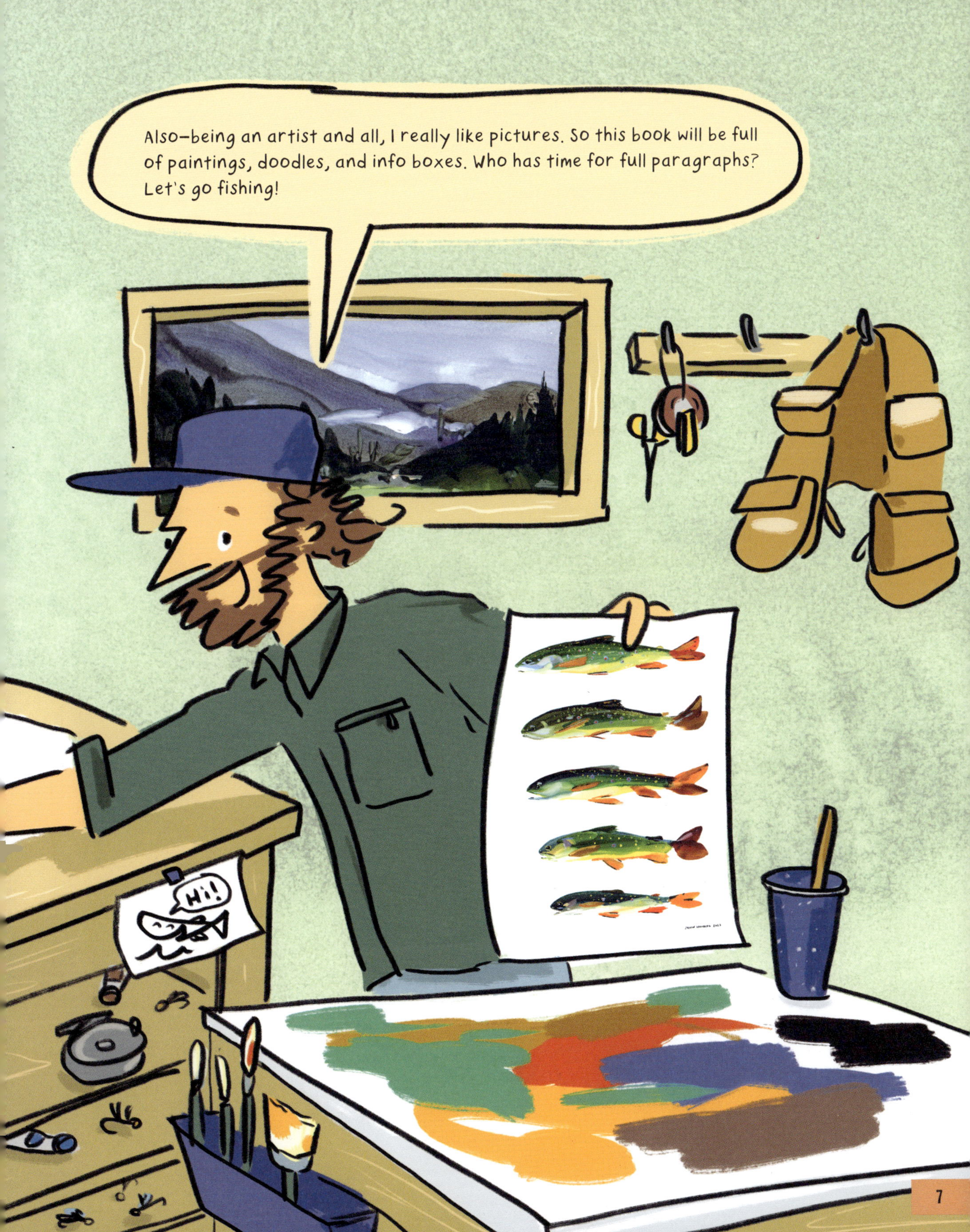
Also—being an artist and all, I really like pictures. So this book will be full of paintings, doodles, and info boxes. Who has time for full paragraphs? Let's go fishing!
Hi!

Ok, Fine. Fly Fishing Is Kind of a Science Too.

(BUT IF I CAN GET IT, SO CAN YOU!)

Imagine if physics and biology had a baby who loved spending time outside! That's basically fly fishing. It rewards you for truly studying nature—the bugs, the weather, the water levels—in a way that isn't matched in other kinds of fishing. Throw in some serious technology, and, well . . .

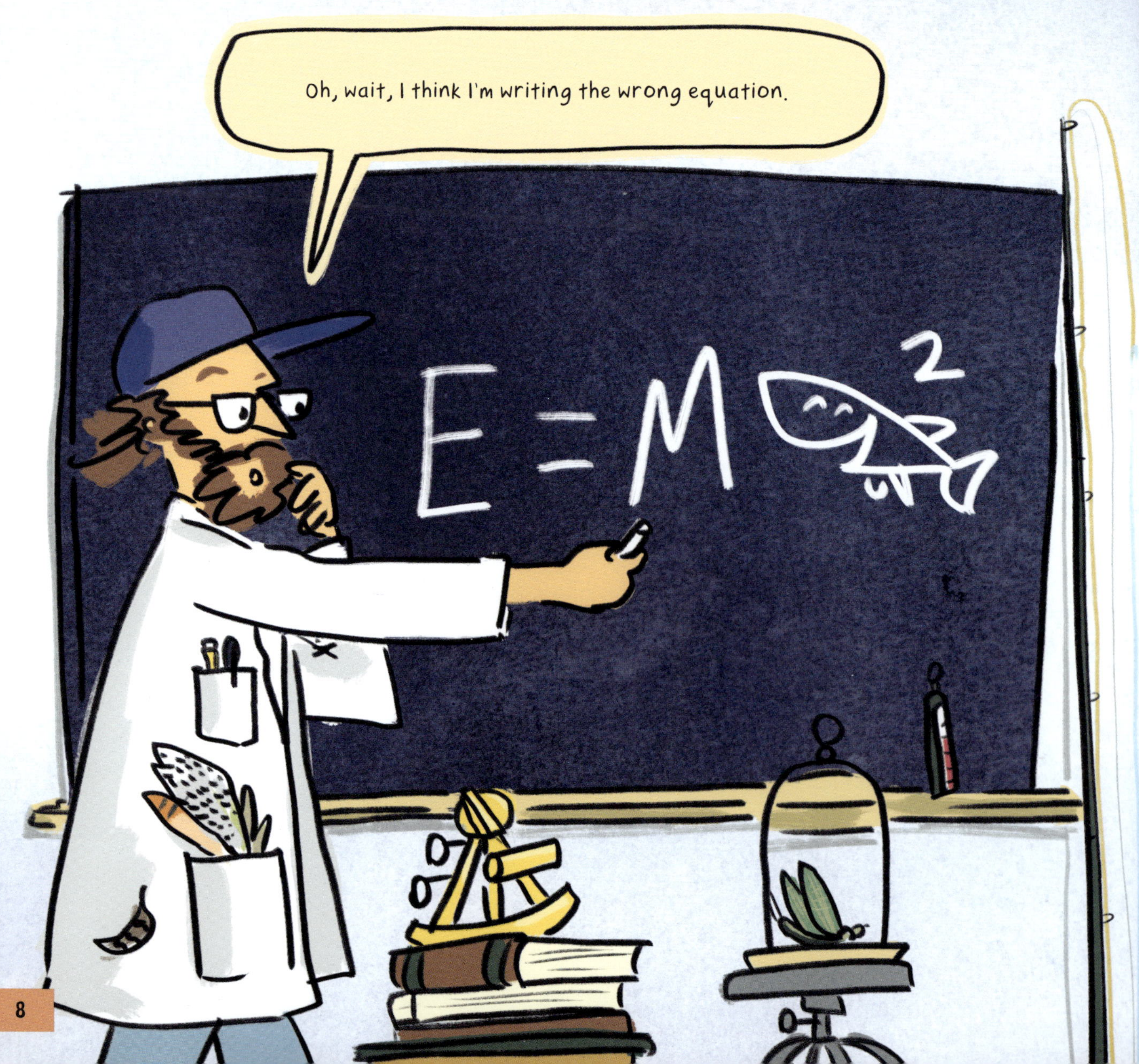

Anyway . . . on the most basic level, two main things make fly fishing different:

#1 You fly fish using flies. Tautology aside, flies are artificial lures that are supposed to look like the critters fish eat. That means NO bait that was (or is still) alive. People use some very creative—dare I say artistic?—materials to make flies:

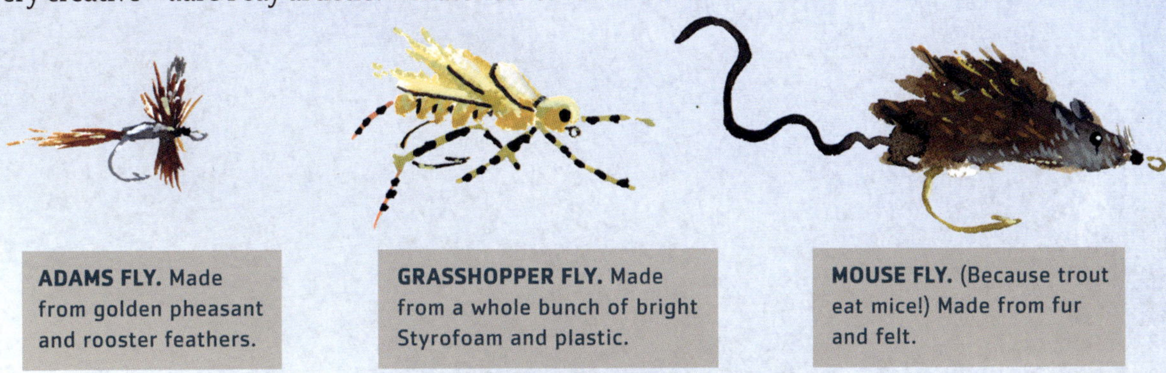

ADAMS FLY. Made from golden pheasant and rooster feathers.

GRASSHOPPER FLY. Made from a whole bunch of bright Styrofoam and plastic.

MOUSE FLY. (Because trout eat mice!) Made from fur and felt.

#2 You use a fly reel and special fly line. Fly reels look different from the spinning reels that are used in conventional fishing and usually sit on a different part of the rod. Fly fishing also uses a special line that's heavier than standard fishing line. I'll explain why this is important later!

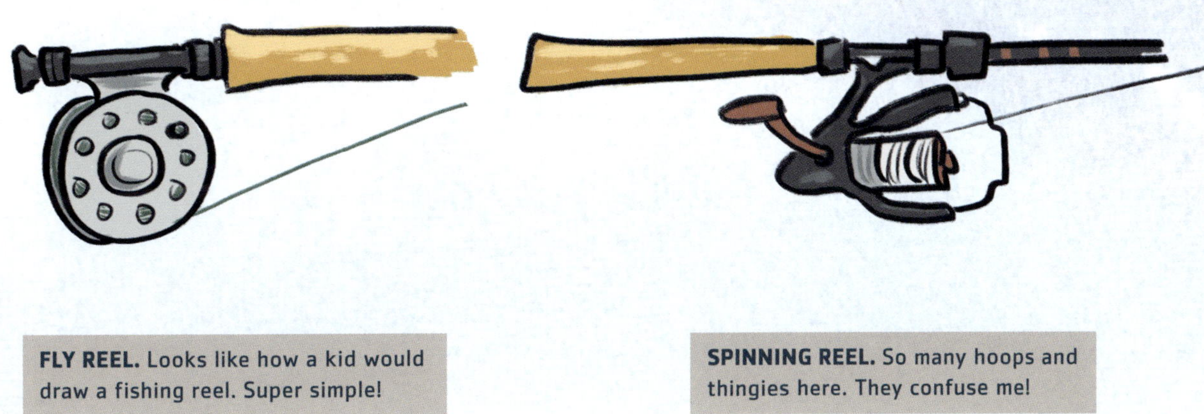

FLY REEL. Looks like how a kid would draw a fishing reel. Super simple!

SPINNING REEL. So many hoops and thingies here. They confuse me!

Fly Fishing Is Full of Experts—

AND SO IS THIS BOOK!

I'm not gonna presume to have all the answers. That's just impossible! And as you'll see, I'll be talking about millennia of knowledge from all over the world. So what to do? Ask for help! Here are some of my friends and idols from the world of fly fishing. They'll be introducing chapters and chiming in from time to time . . . They have a lot of answers, and soon, you will too!

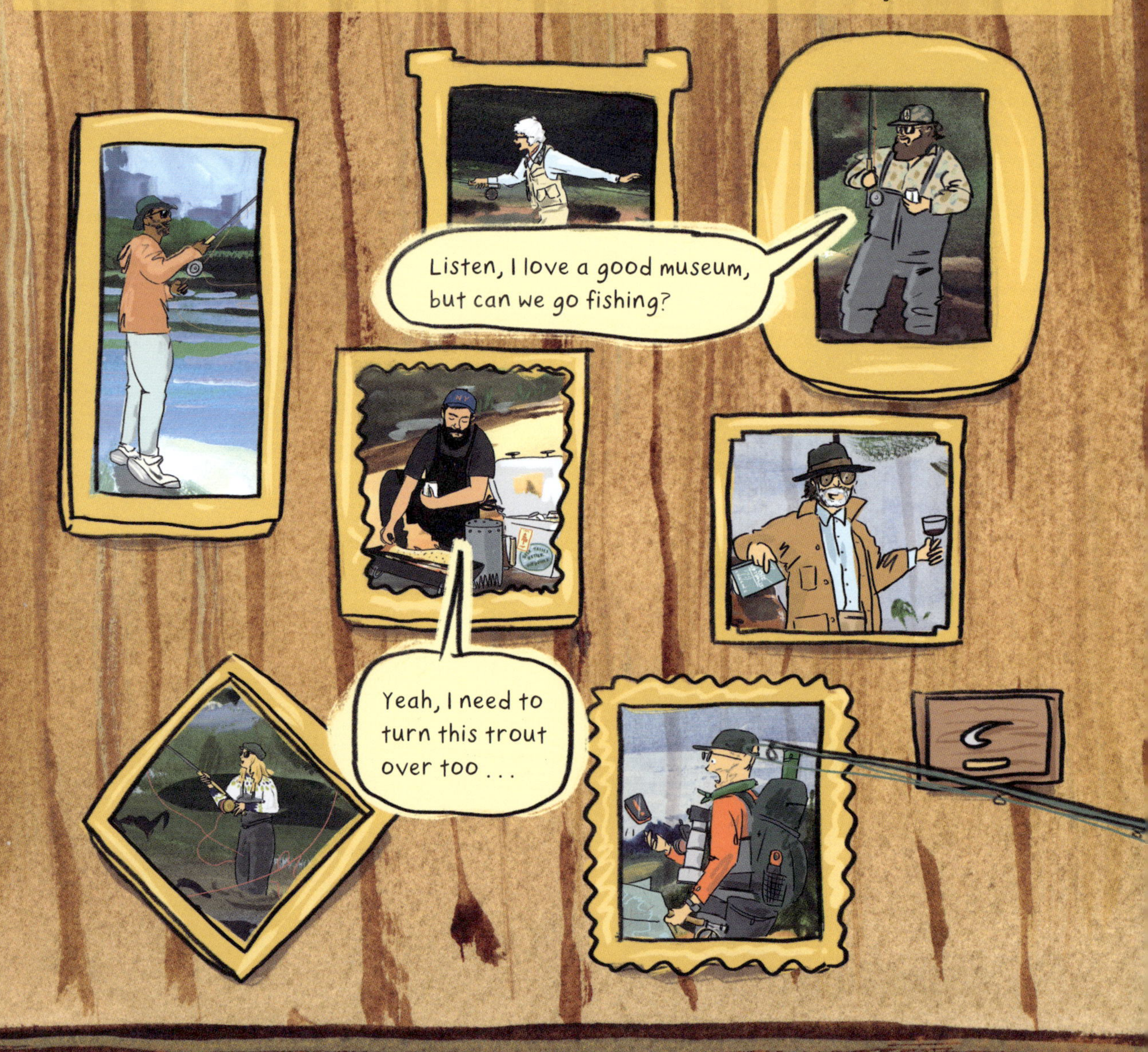

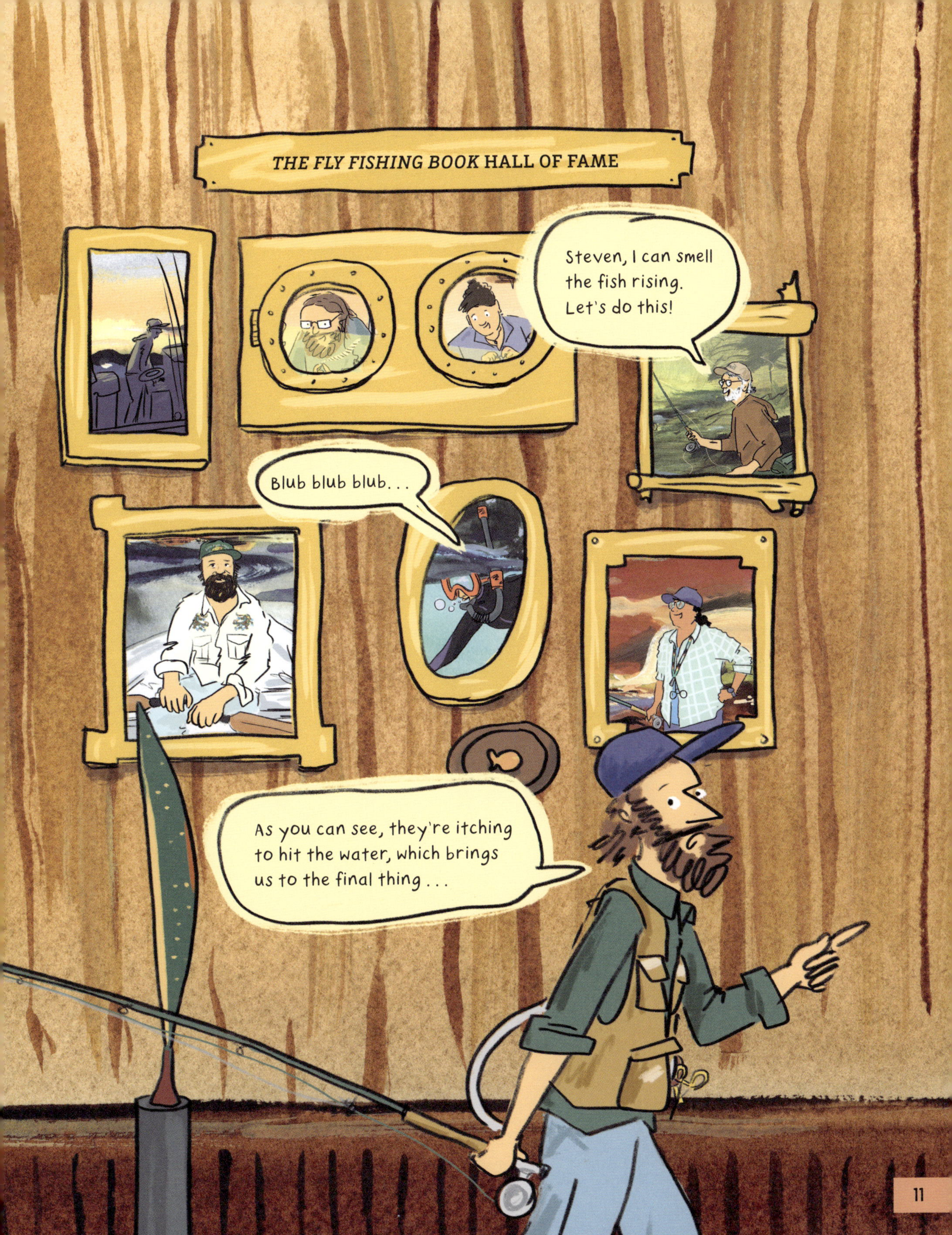
THE FLY FISHING BOOK HALL OF FAME
Steven, I can smell the fish rising. Let's do this!
Blub blub blub...
As you can see, they're itching to hit the water, which brings us to the final thing...

GO FISH!

OK, I know what you're thinking: "I'm too excited to read! I MUST FISH NOW!"

I get it. I learn by doing too! So if you want to hit the water immediately and then pick up where you left off, here are some quick tips:

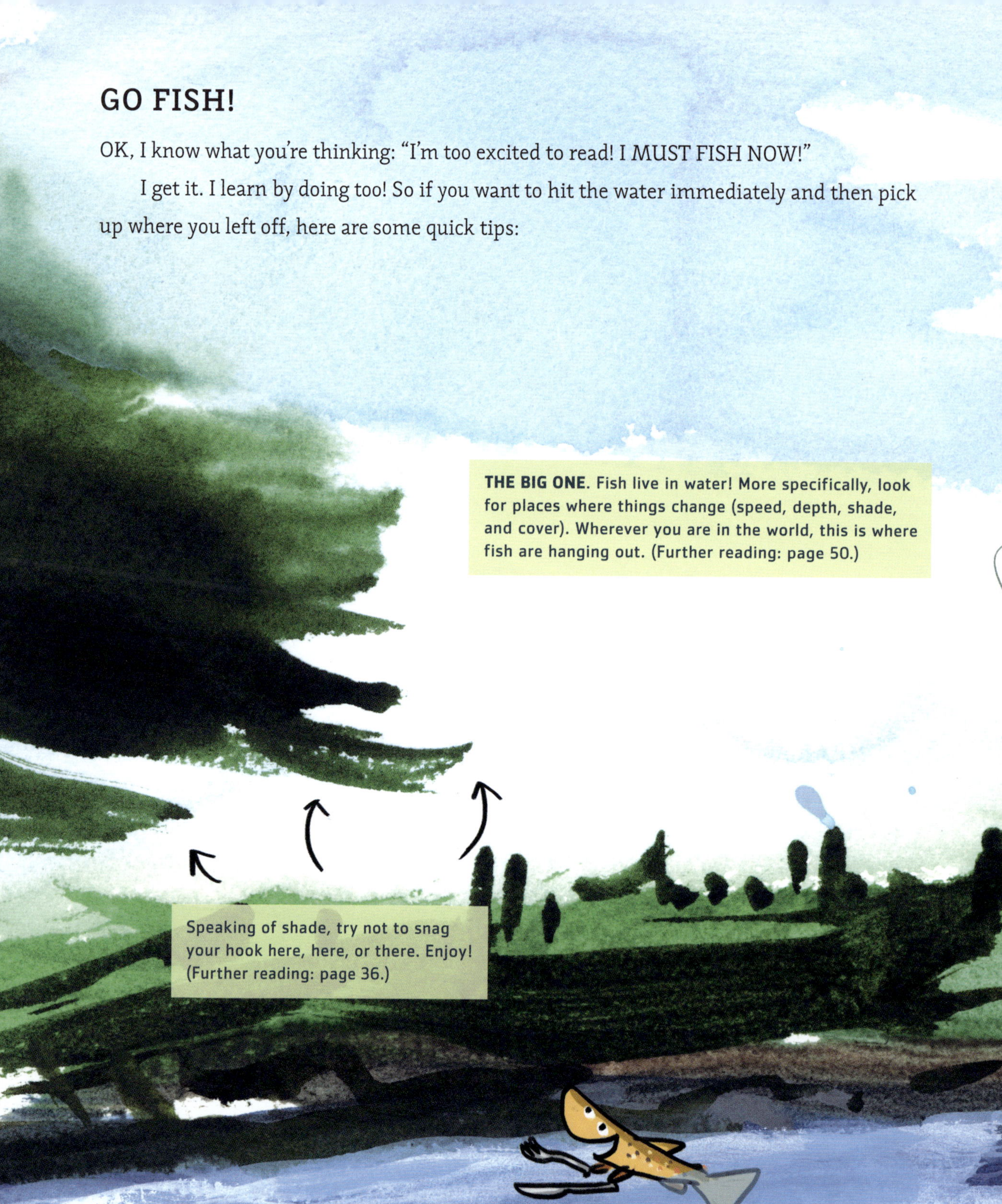

THE BIG ONE. Fish live in water! More specifically, look for places where things change (speed, depth, shade, and cover). Wherever you are in the world, this is where fish are hanging out. (Further reading: page 50.)

Speaking of shade, try not to snag your hook here, here, or there. Enjoy! (Further reading: page 36.)

CASTING. Anglers spend a lifetime perfecting a fly cast, so don't worry if you're sloppy at first. Focus on the momentum of the fishing line, both back and forth. Visualize the fly landing where you want it to land. (Further reading: page 35.)

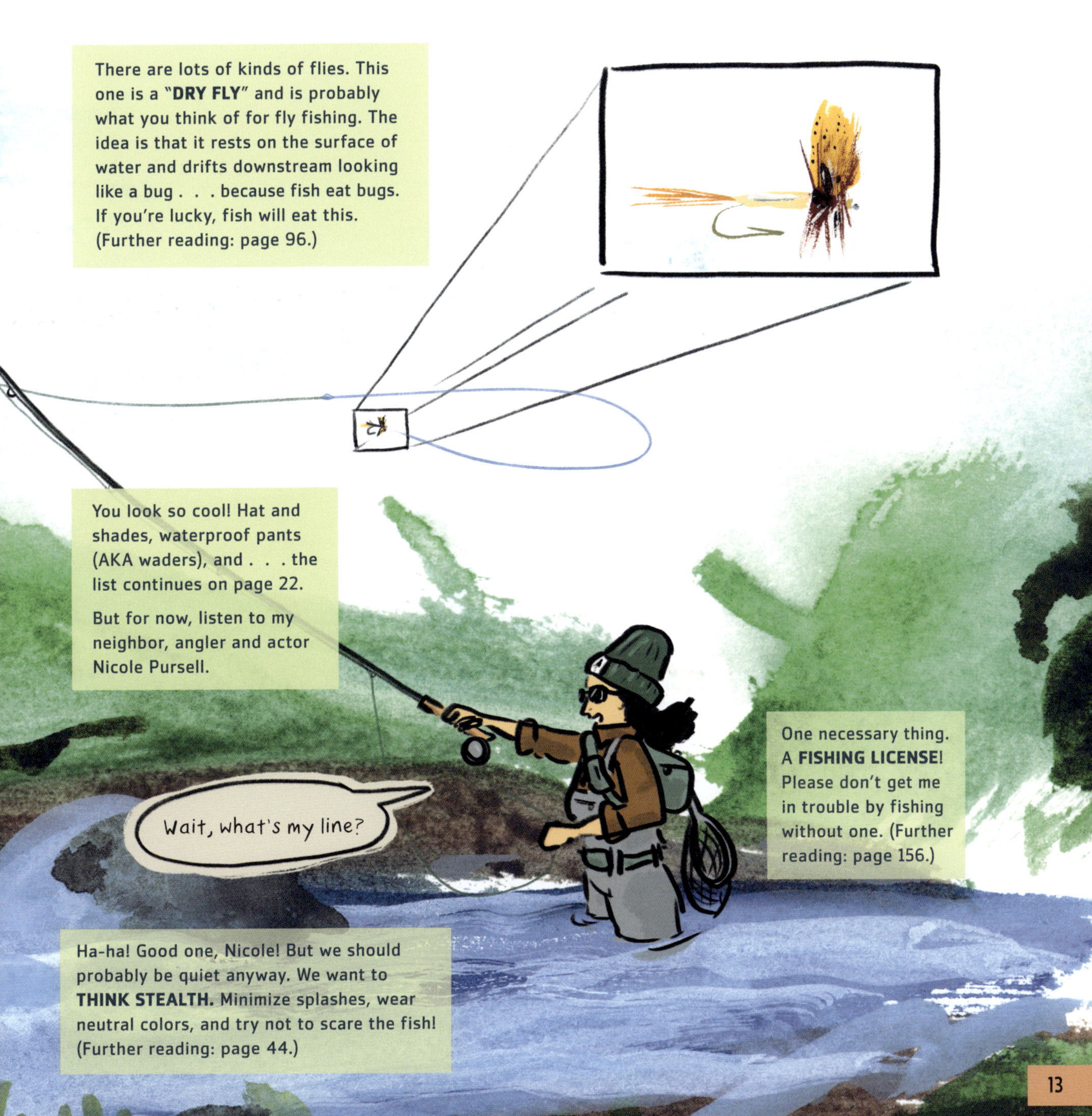

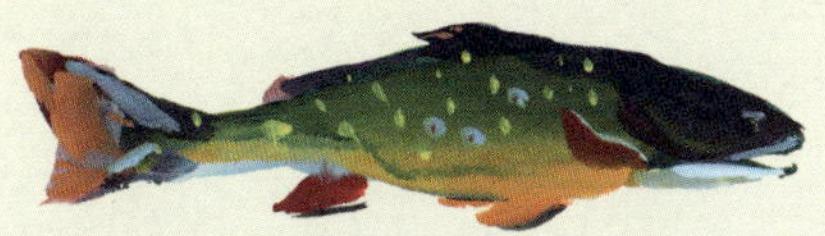

PART ONE: CAST

JUST GET OUT THERE. HERE'S HOW.

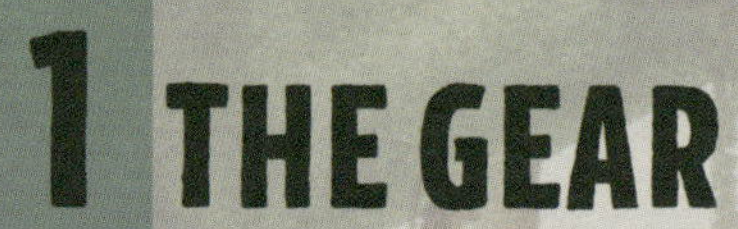

1 THE GEAR

THE THRILL (AND DANGER) OF FLY FISHING is that there are just so many options—in all things, but especially gear. To whittle this down, let's turn to fly fishing author/sartorialist David Coggins.

DAVID COGGINS

FAVORITE WATERS: The spring creeks in Montana's Paradise Valley, the Delaware, the Malleo in Patagonia

FAVORITE FISH: Brown trout and Atlantic salmon

FAVORITE FLY: Parachute Adams

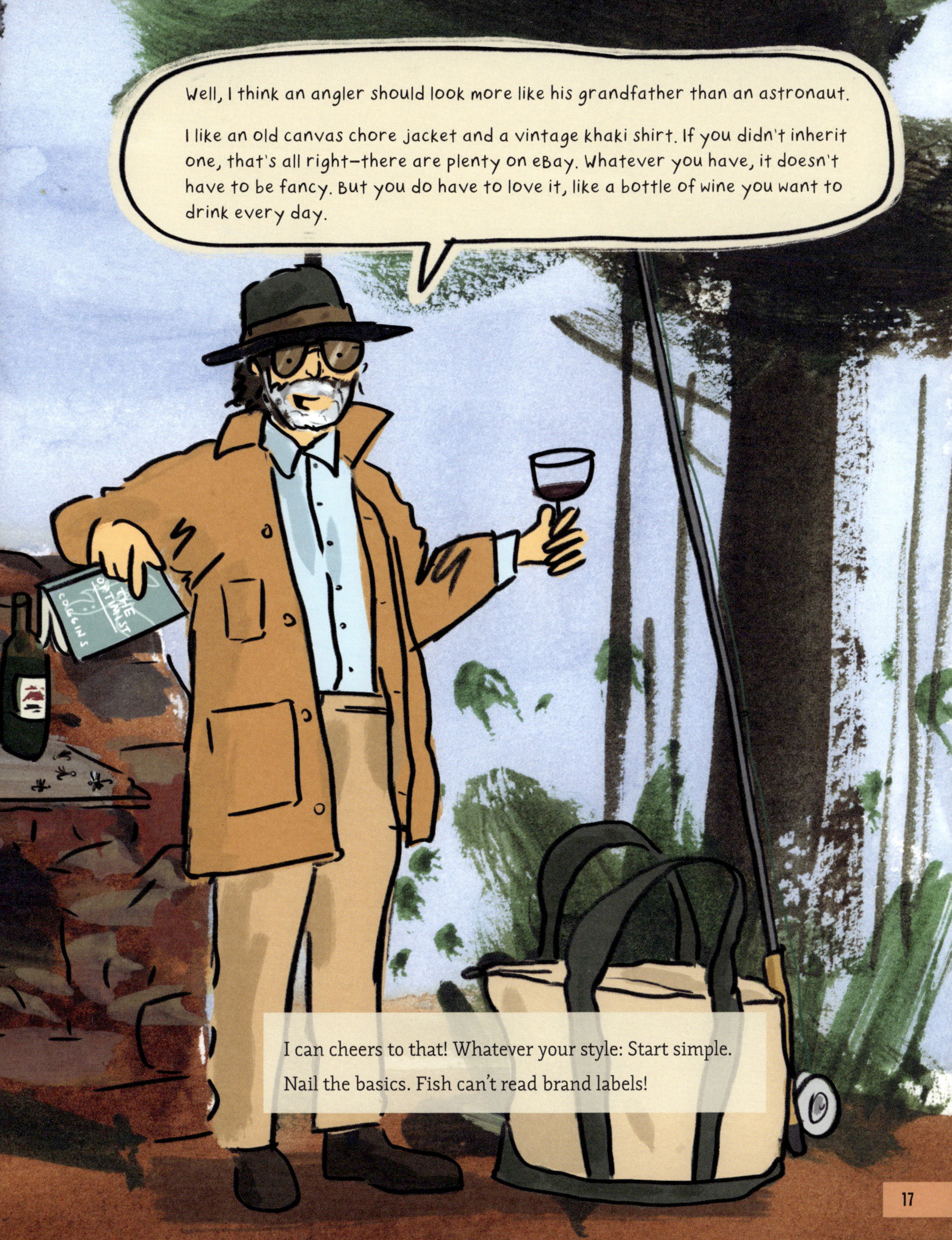
Well, I think an angler should look more like his grandfather than an astronaut.
I like an old canvas chore jacket and a vintage khaki shirt. If you didn't inherit one, that's all right—there are plenty on eBay. Whatever you have, it doesn't have to be fancy. But you do have to love it, like a bottle of wine you want to drink every day.
THE OPTIMIST COGGINS
I can cheers to that! Whatever your style: Start simple. Nail the basics. Fish can't read brand labels!

YOUR ROD AND REEL

Here is your magic wand! It comes in many variations, but the important thing is generally length and strength. Longer rods are often stronger (or stiffer). Shorter rods can be super flexible, like the 7.5-foot one I like to use for fishing brookies in small streams.

Here's how they work:

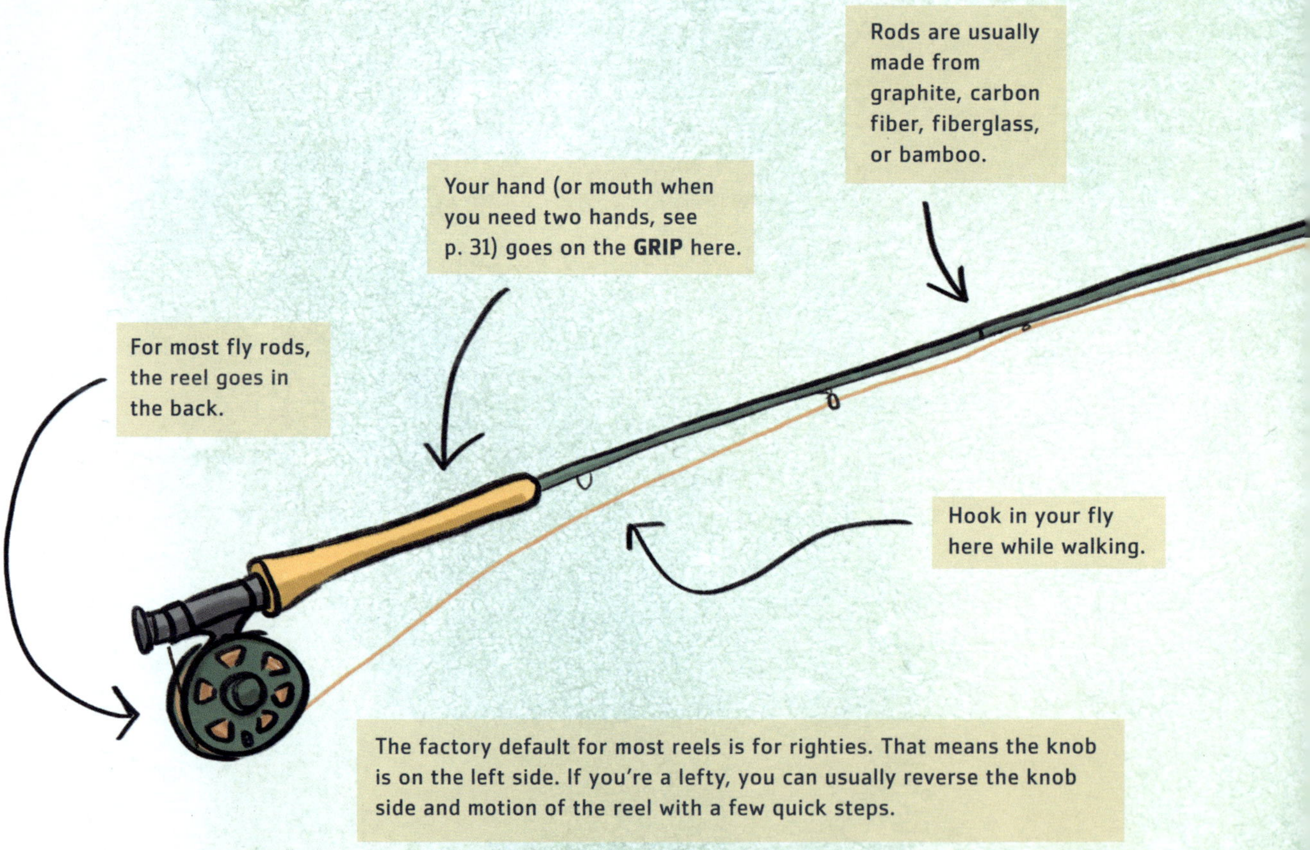

Rods are usually made from graphite, carbon fiber, fiberglass, or bamboo.

Your hand (or mouth when you need two hands, see p. 31) goes on the **GRIP** here.

For most fly rods, the reel goes in the back.

Hook in your fly here while walking.

The factory default for most reels is for righties. That means the knob is on the left side. If you're a lefty, you can usually reverse the knob side and motion of the reel with a few quick steps.

The strength (and flexibility) of rods is measured in their "weight," which you'll often see written as "WT."

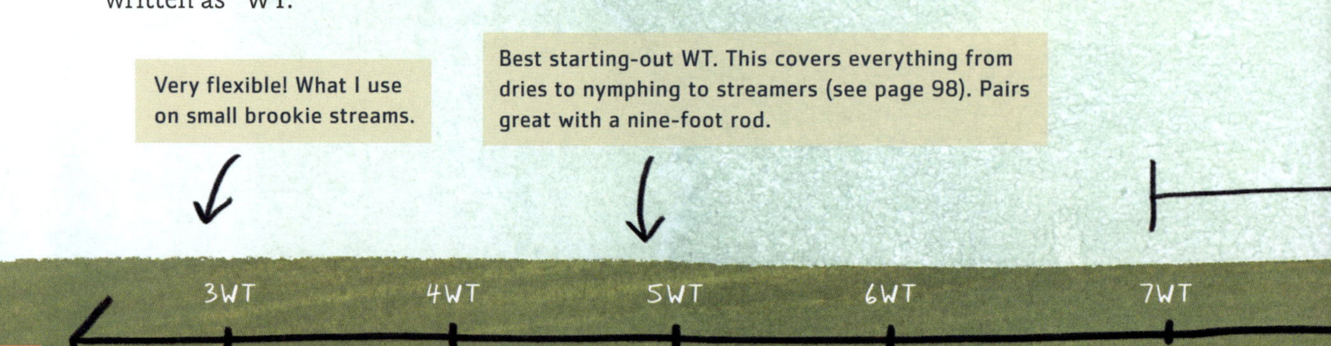

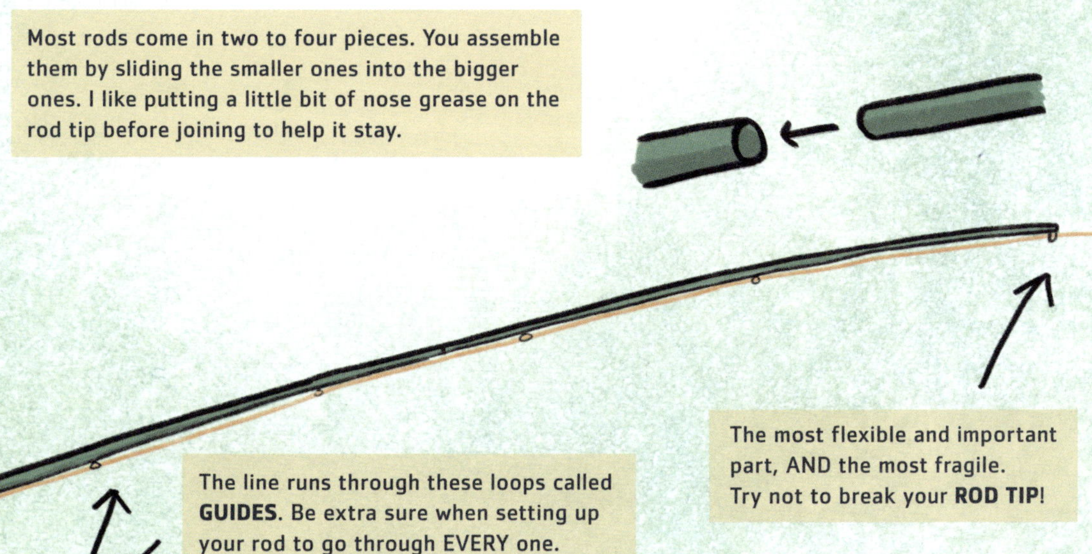

The big things to know about reels are arbor and drag. *Arbor* is a fancy word for the diameter of the wheel the line rests on. For bigger reels where you spend more time fighting fish, the arbor is bigger. *Drag* is the resistance the reel offers when a fish is pulling on the line. So for an eight-inch brook trout, you don't need a lot of arbor or drag. But for an eight-foot tarpon, you need a lot of both!

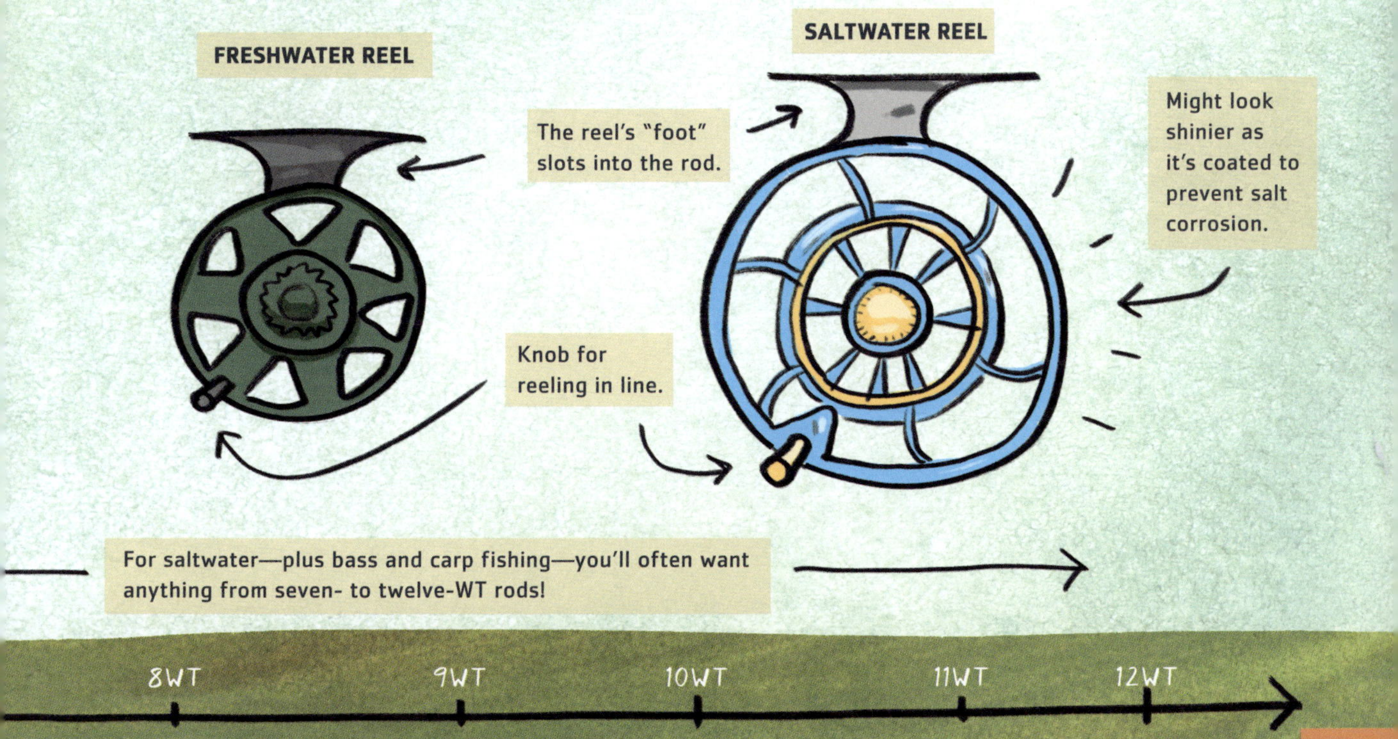

FRESHWATER REEL

SALTWATER REEL

The reel's "foot" slots into the rod.

Might look shinier as it's coated to prevent salt corrosion.

Knob for reeling in line.

For saltwater—plus bass and carp fishing—you'll often want anything from seven- to twelve-WT rods!

8WT 9WT 10WT 11WT 12WT

FLY LINE (AND FLY LINE)

Something new to confuse you: fly line! This term can either refer to all the line you have or to one specific segment. Here it is, all broken down from reel to fly. (The knots that tie this together are in chapter 6.)

It all starts at the reel.

BACKING. The simple nylon thread that's tied directly to the reel. It backs up your normal fly line. You mainly see this when a hooked fish is speeding away across a body of water and the line is whizzing out of your reel. This is a very good feeling. (Also: Hands off a reel spinning at high speeds!)

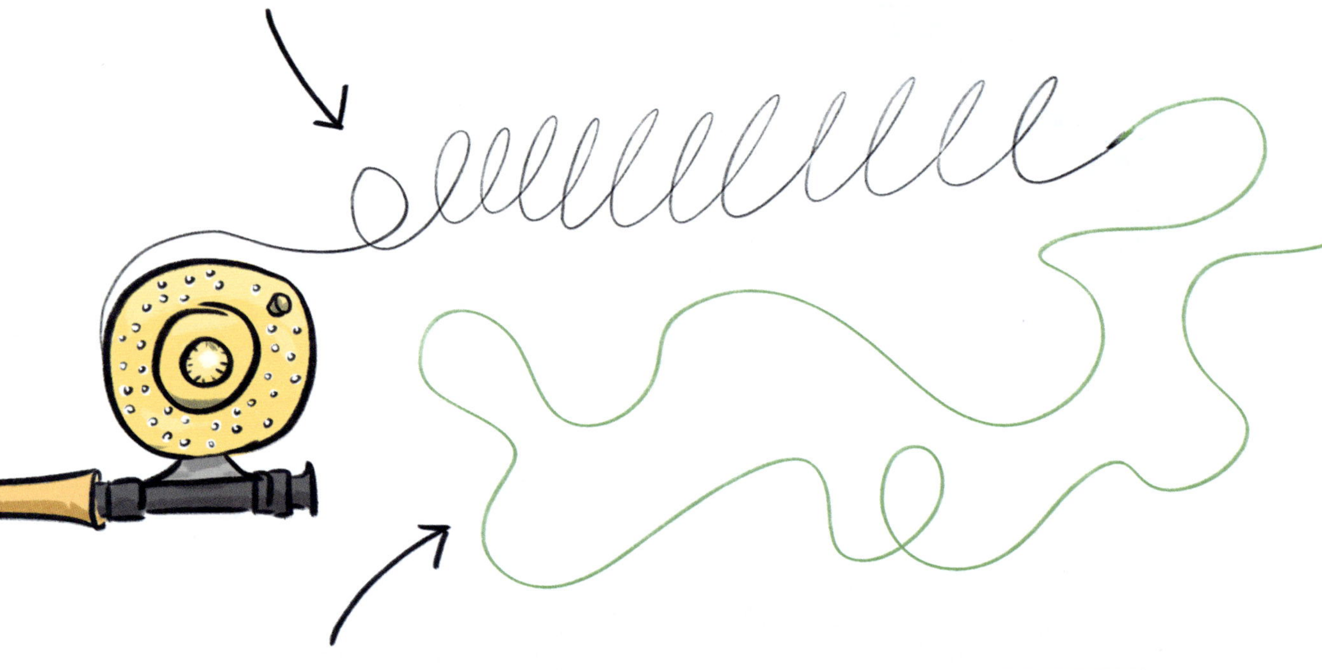

FLY LINE. Unlike traditional fishing line, fly fishing line has some heft. Not a ton, but just enough to bend the rod when you're casting. This is what makes a fly-fishing cast so different from a spinning-reel cast. There is a TON of variety in fly lines. For trout, I like something olive green (so I can see it, but it doesn't stand out too much) and that floats (so the fly can too).

Fly lines get dirty! Every few months, clean your line with dish soap and warm water.

LEADER. You want this line to have less mass and be harder to see. You'll also be knotting and snipping this, NOT the fly line, so it should be more disposable. The goal here is stealth while still being able to hold on to a hooked fish!

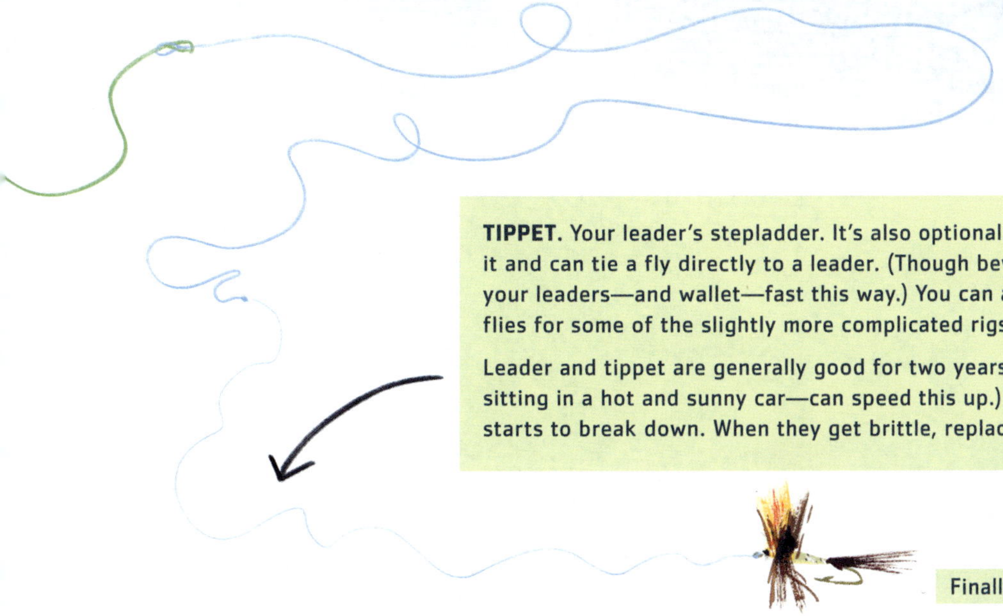

TIPPET. Your leader's stepladder. It's also optional. Sometimes, you don't need it and can tie a fly directly to a leader. (Though beware, you will run down your leaders—and wallet—fast this way.) You can also use a tippet to attach flies for some of the slightly more complicated rigs explained later on.

Leader and tippet are generally good for two years. (UV exposure—think sitting in a hot and sunny car—can speed this up.) After that, the plastic starts to break down. When they get brittle, replace 'em!

Finally, the fly!

Much like rods, leader and tippet are organized by strength. EXCEPT here, the numbers go in the opposite direction.

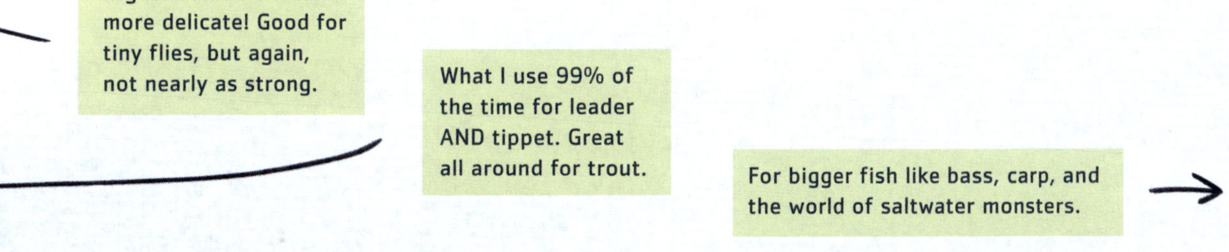

4X

3X

2X

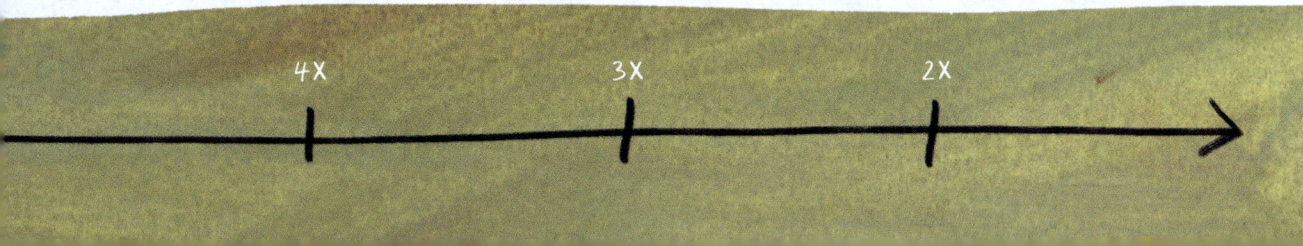

SAFETY THIRD! (LOOKING GOOD, #1.)

Just kidding. Seriously—be safe! But as long as you're keeping that in mind, there are an infinite number of ways to dress for fishing. Here are my two main modes:

This is cold-weather me. Though I can swap my beanie for a baseball hat and drop some layers if I want to keep dry in warmer months.

The right mix of layers, because standing in water can be COLD. Please note: I'm wearing a **DOWN PUFFER** because it is the lightest/warmest option. And, yes, I'll totally catch a fly on it and need to patch it. But that's just life.

WADERS are basically waterproof pants. They come in all shapes and sizes (finally!). The big recent innovation in men's waders is a waterproof zipper fly (for peeing!). Simply amazing. We're living in the future, people!

Old-school waders had a boot at the bottom of the pants. Now, most people use **"STOCKINGFOOT" WADERS**, which end in a neoprene sock. This goes into a separate **WADING BOOT**.

Your **WADING BELT** is your friend! Keep it tight. It will keep a lot of water out should you take a step too deep.

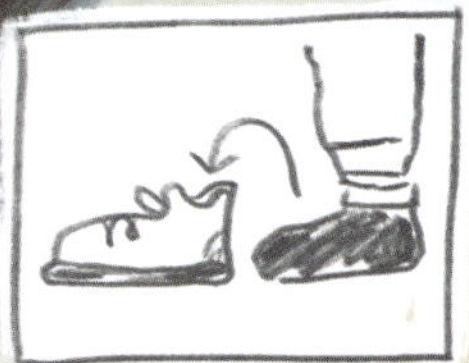

Rocks get slick! Everyone has their favorite gripping option. I like add-on **ALUMINUM DISKS**.

AVOID felt-bottom boots. They're really good at transporting microorganisms between watersheds, plus they're SUPER slippery on dry land!

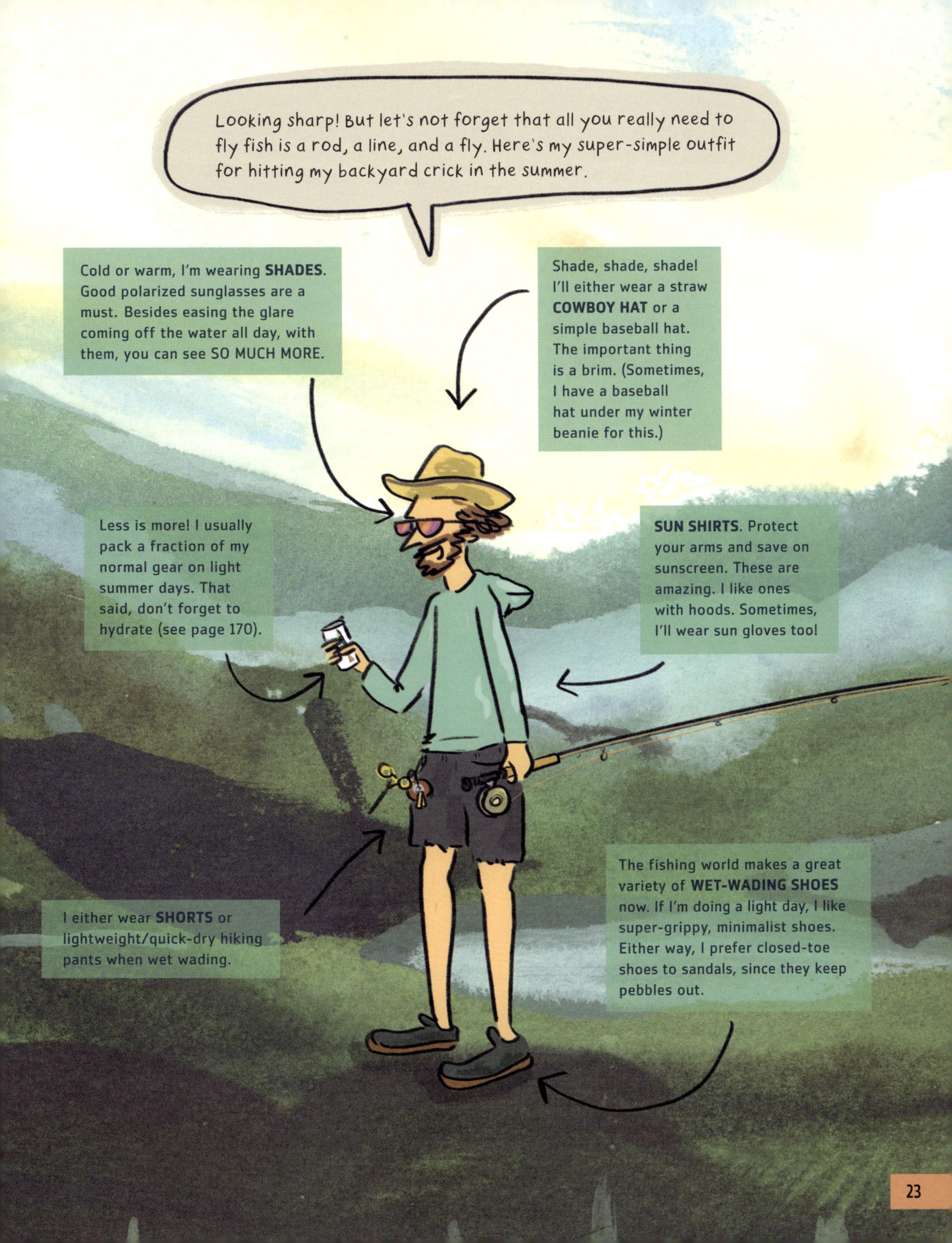

Looking sharp! But let's not forget that all you really need to fly fish is a rod, a line, and a fly. Here's my super-simple outfit for hitting my backyard crick in the summer.

Cold or warm, I'm wearing **SHADES**. Good polarized sunglasses are a must. Besides easing the glare coming off the water all day, with them, you can see SO MUCH MORE.

Shade, shade, shade! I'll either wear a straw **COWBOY HAT** or a simple baseball hat. The important thing is a brim. (Sometimes, I have a baseball hat under my winter beanie for this.)

Less is more! I usually pack a fraction of my normal gear on light summer days. That said, don't forget to hydrate (see page 170).

SUN SHIRTS. Protect your arms and save on sunscreen. These are amazing. I like ones with hoods. Sometimes, I'll wear sun gloves too!

I either wear **SHORTS** or lightweight/quick-dry hiking pants when wet wading.

The fishing world makes a great variety of **WET-WADING SHOES** now. If I'm doing a light day, I like super-grippy, minimalist shoes. Either way, I prefer closed-toe shoes to sandals, since they keep pebbles out.

AND THEN ABOUT ALL THAT GEAR . . .

Gearing up for fly fishing can be either overwhelming (my general view) or the best part (you know who you are, gearheads!). Depending on the trip, I'll bring along some combination of this stuff:

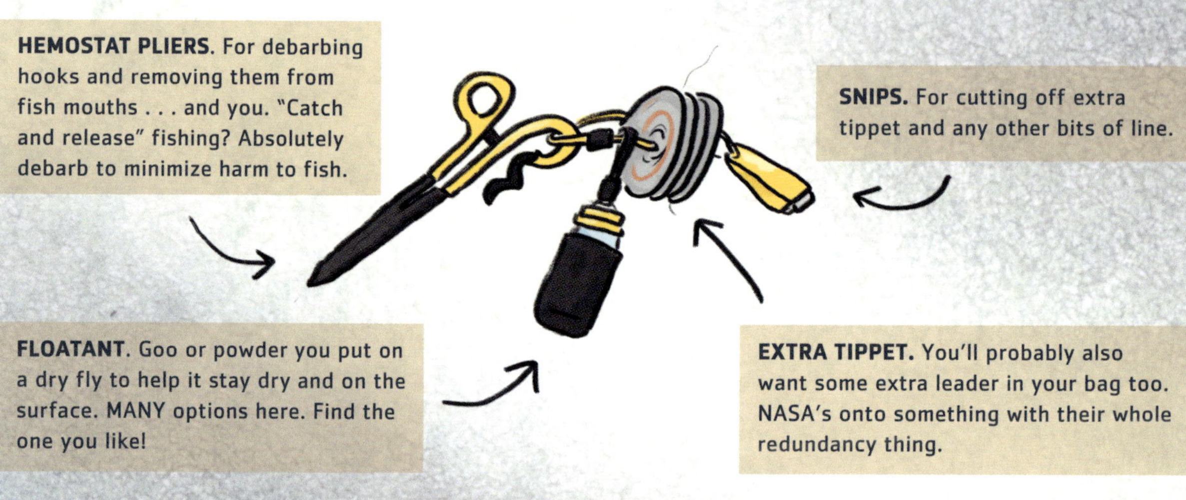

HEMOSTAT PLIERS. For debarbing hooks and removing them from fish mouths . . . and you. "Catch and release" fishing? Absolutely debarb to minimize harm to fish.

SNIPS. For cutting off extra tippet and any other bits of line.

FLOATANT. Goo or powder you put on a dry fly to help it stay dry and on the surface. MANY options here. Find the one you like!

EXTRA TIPPET. You'll probably also want some extra leader in your bag too. NASA's onto something with their whole redundancy thing.

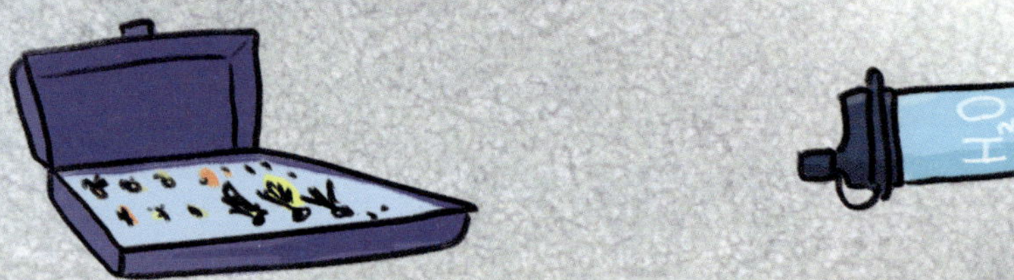

A BOX OF FLIES (or many boxes and random containers). The way you organize your flies WILL immediately reveal your personality.

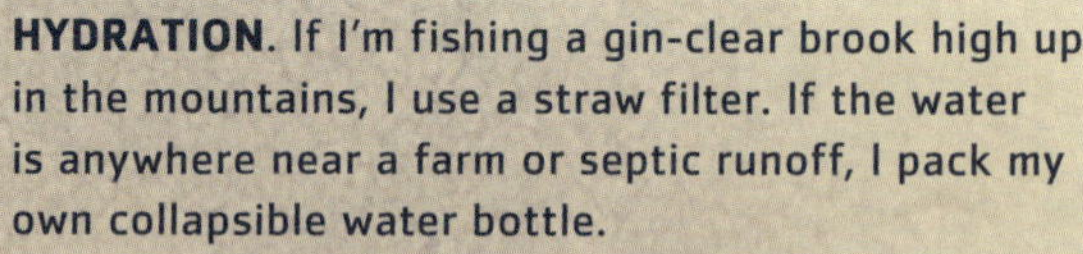

HYDRATION. If I'm fishing a gin-clear brook high up in the mountains, I use a straw filter. If the water is anywhere near a farm or septic runoff, I pack my own collapsible water bottle.

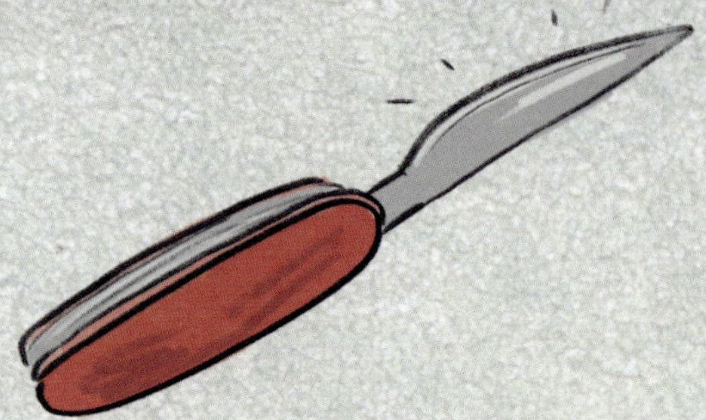

SMALL MULTI-TOOL KNIFE. Your backup pliers and snips. Plus, you can use the knife should you want to gut (and later eat) a fish. (More on page 166.)

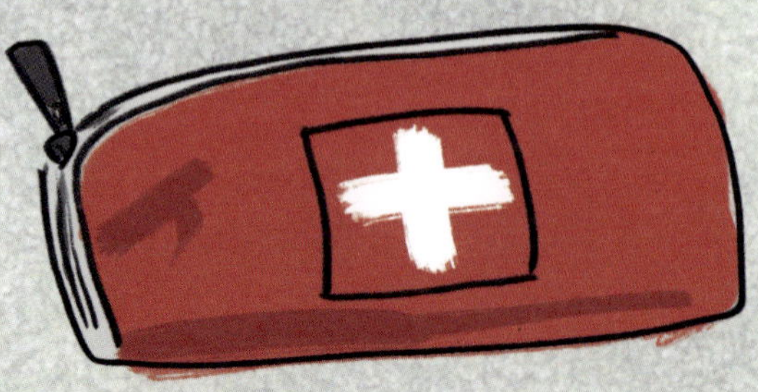

SIMPLE FIRST AID KIT. Mine is basically iodine, tape, gauze, and ibuprofen.

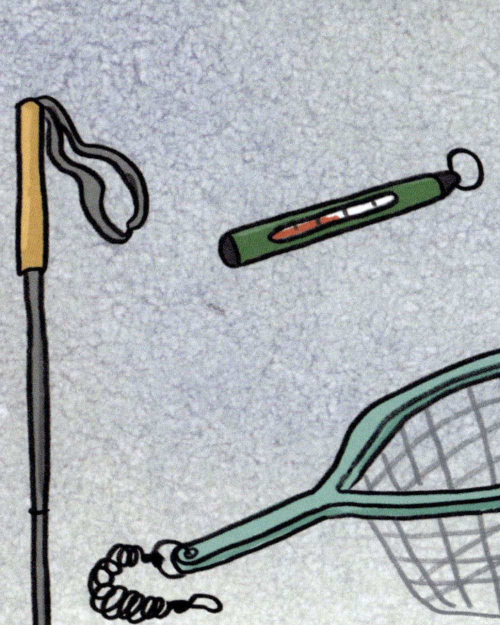

THERMOMETER. It's your responsibility to know when catch-and-release fishing will harm fish. (More on page 128.) For trout, keep it to 45°–65° F (7°–18° C).

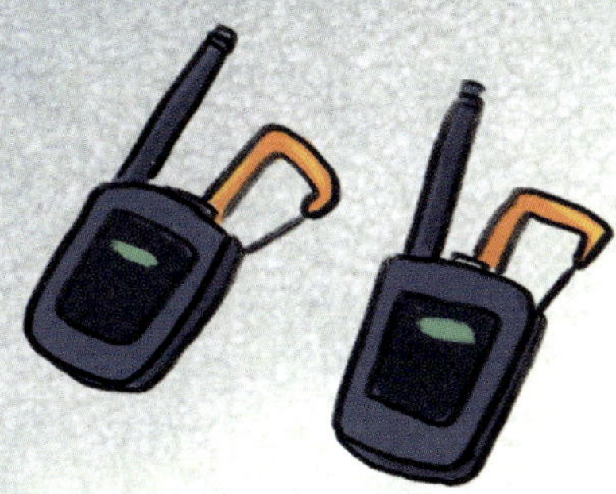

LANDING NET (with a magnetic release). You'll land more fish with a net, and it's better for the fish.

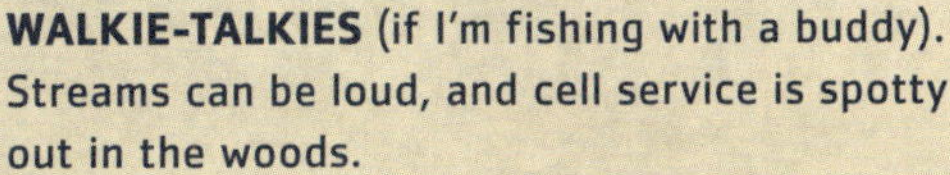

WALKIE-TALKIES (if I'm fishing with a buddy). Streams can be loud, and cell service is spotty out in the woods.

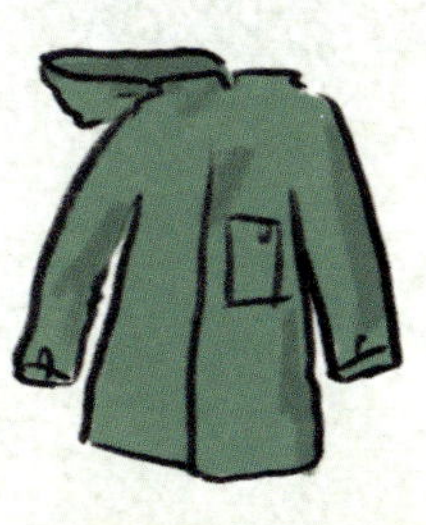

Very packable **RAIN LAYER**.

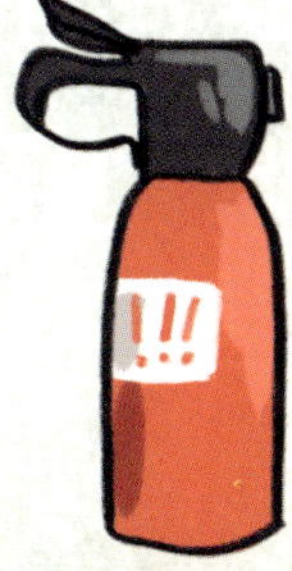

Some kind of **BEAR DETERRENT** (if you're in grizzly country).

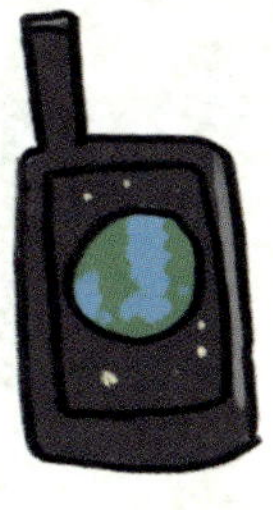

A satellite-equipped **EMERGENCY COMMUNICATION DEVICE** (or app).

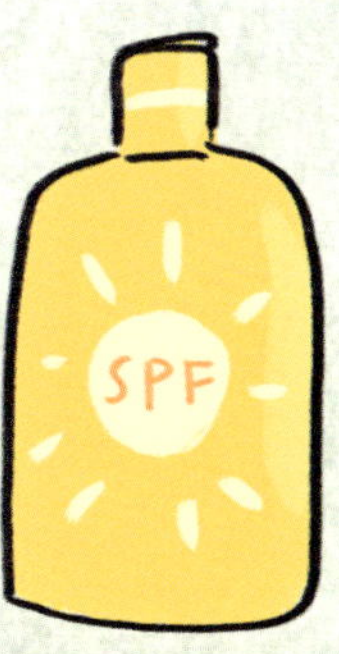

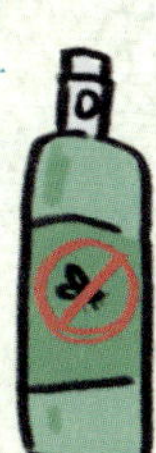

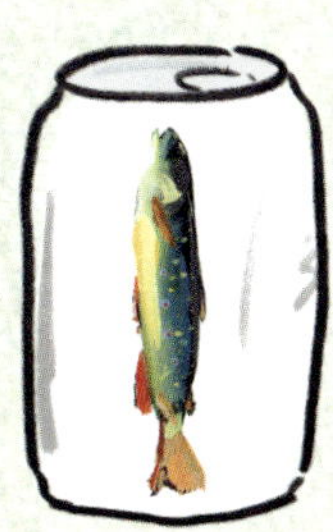

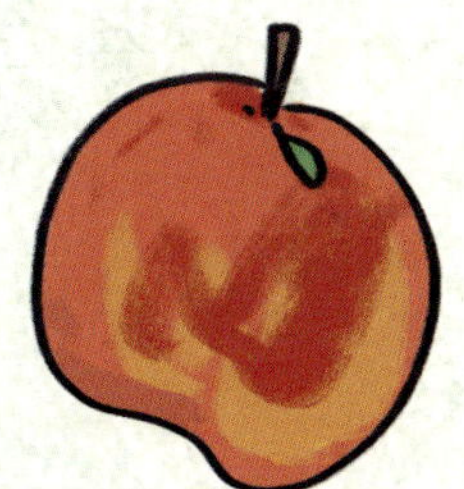

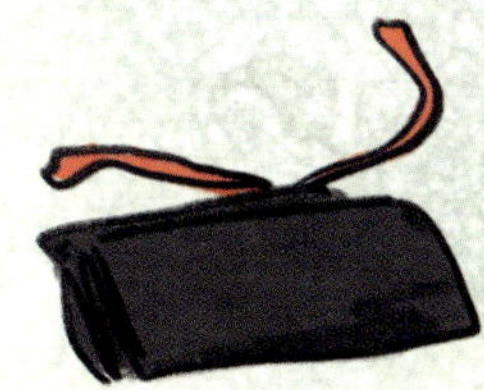

And . . . a collapsible wading staff, sun block, bug spray, cold beer, snacks, garbage bag (to either pack out trash or put a fish in—don't do both!). I mean, I think you've got it from here . . .

You've got your rod and reel and line and outfit and gear—it's a lot! What you need now is some organization! Here are four approaches:

THE TRADITIONALIST

Lee Wulff, famous angler and husband to Joan Wulff (who I'll introduce in the next chapter), is credited with inventing the modern vest by way of a sort of utilitarian fishing/fashion collage. He bought a vest, then a few pairs of Levi's, and sewed the extra jean pockets on the vest. The rest is history.

For a long time, I thought vests were a silly anachronism. But the joke's on me. You don't need to lug around a bag when you're rocking a classic outfit brimming with everything you could possibly need.

Pairs best with a bucket hat covered in flies.

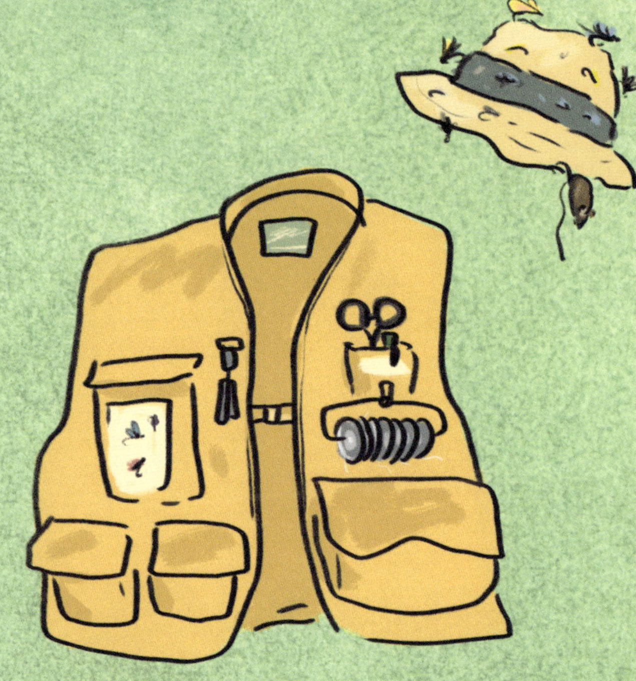

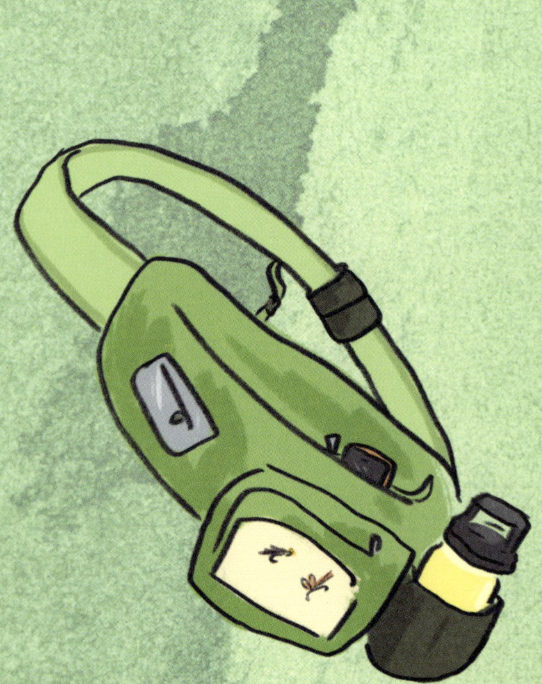

THE MODERN ANGLER

I've spent many years lugging a sling pack over one shoulder. It stays out of your way, but when you need a fly, you can slide it around like a messenger bag.

And yet . . .

The main downside is that, depending on how much gear you have, it can put a lot of weight on one shoulder, which may also be your casting shoulder.

Hmmm . . . what if you could distribute the weight across both shoulders and wear it? Oh, wait. Lee, you really nailed it!

THE MINIMALIST
If your approach to gear is like Hemingway's approach to sentence structure, then this pack is for you.

Wait, wait, wait. I mean . . .

Approach your gear lightly. Like Hemingway. And his words. Here's your pack. Man versus nature.

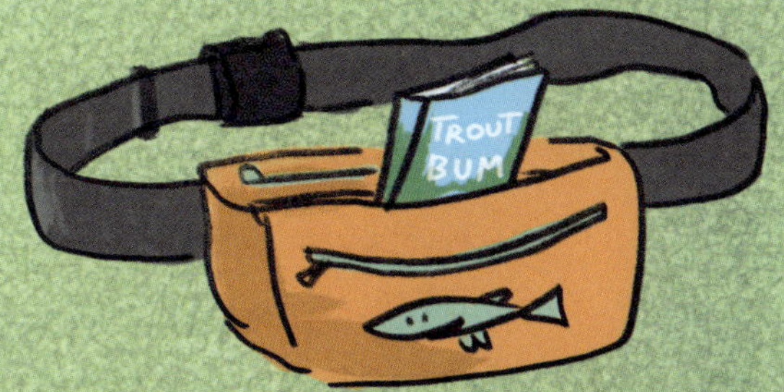

THE PREPARED FRIEND
Jamie, my fishing buddy who I'll introduce in chapter 9, is ready for anything. He carries multiple rods, emergency layers, and, should a bald eagle need to be photographed from four hundred yards, he's got the lens for that too.

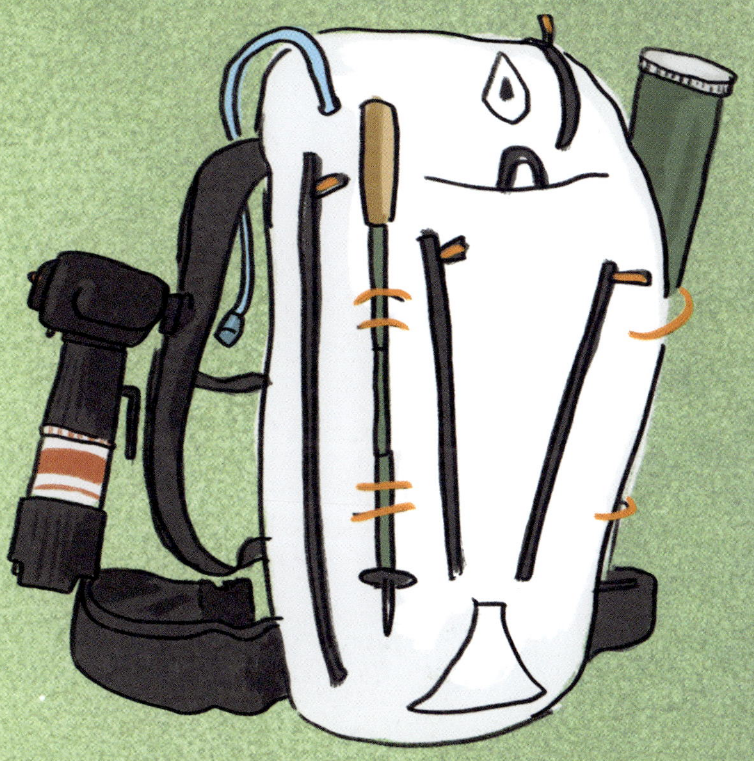

2 HOW TO CAST

COULD YOU IMAGINE asking Keith Richards for a quick sentence or two about how to play the guitar? Or Serena Williams about a good backhand? You'd be laughed away!

Well, such are the dangers of writing a book.

For this chapter on casting, I turned to my neighbor Joan Wulff. She's the co-founder of the Wulff Fly Fishing School, a world-champion fly caster (yes, there are competitions where you only cast), and one of the biggest fly-fishing legends ever. I asked her to distill a lifetime of casting and teaching anglers into a single essential tip. After the requisite "ARE YOU KIDDING ME?" she thought for a moment and laughed.

If you can cast well, you will catch fish. No, make it:
If you cast well, you will ALWAYS catch fish.

JOAN WULFF

FAVORITE WATERS: Beaverkill River, New Brunswick's Restigouche River, Islamorada

FAVORITE FISH: Trout, Atlantic salmon, tarpon

FAVORITE FLY: Royal Wulff, Surface Stone Fly, large streamers

On that note, let's learn to cast. "Learn" in the ongoing sense being key here, because what follows are the tools to set you up. When I chatted with Joan for this book, she was on the verge of a century of living, fishing, and LEARNING.

My tip, then, is this: Know that there's always going to be a way to improve your cast, and it's always worth asking an expert if you can.

Even if they're going to laugh at you.

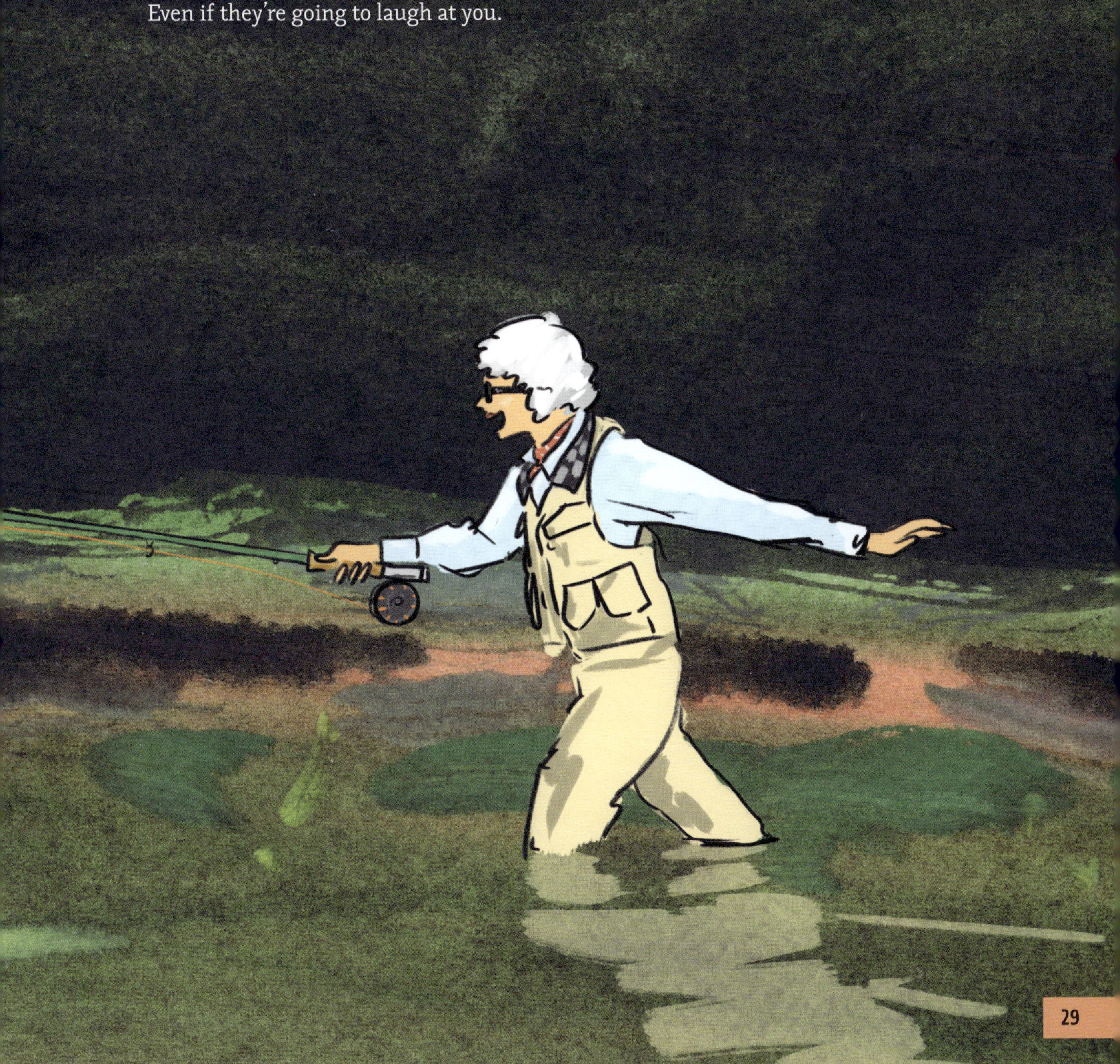

HOLDING YOUR ROD

Before you can cast, you have to know how to hold your rod. The simplest and best way to learn is with your thumb up like this. I find this method allows less room for messing thing up. So for all these diagrams, that's how I'll show it.

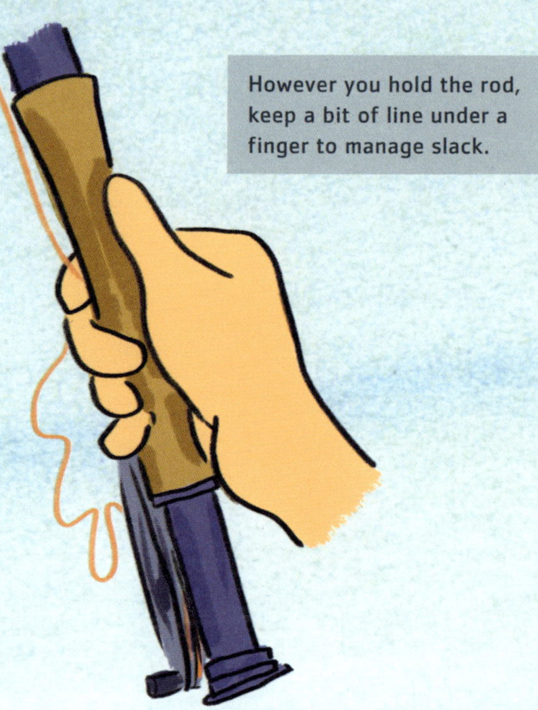

However you hold the rod, keep a bit of line under a finger to manage slack.

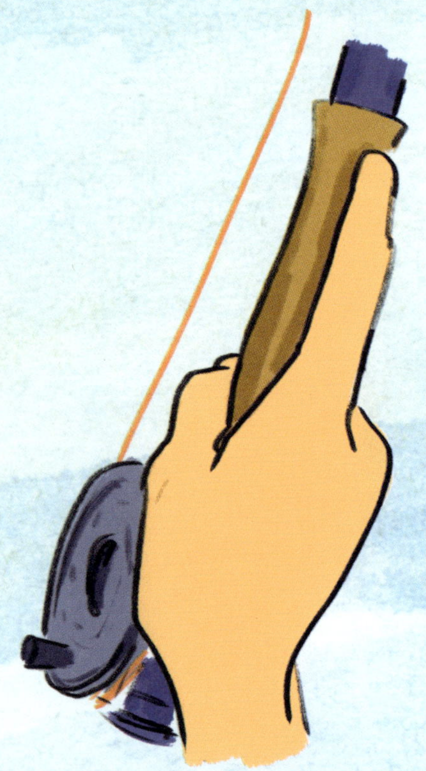

That said, there are many ways to hold a rod. After I learned the basics with my thumb up, I came across the Japanese-style tenkara grip with one's forefinger up. Coming from painting and drawing, I found it more intuitive. (I'm not sure why, but Lee Wulff also fished like this.) As with everything in fly fishing, learn the basics first. Then please reinvent the wheel as much as possible!

And that other hand . . . As a righty, I have the rod set up where my reel knob is on the left side. I use my left hand for a lot of things while I'm fishing . . .

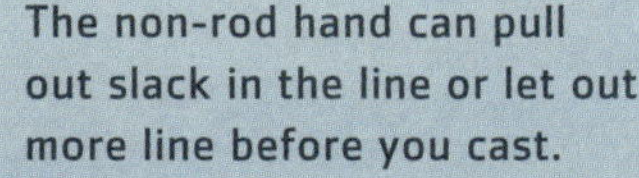

When a fish is on (and you have the line tight), your other hand works the reel.

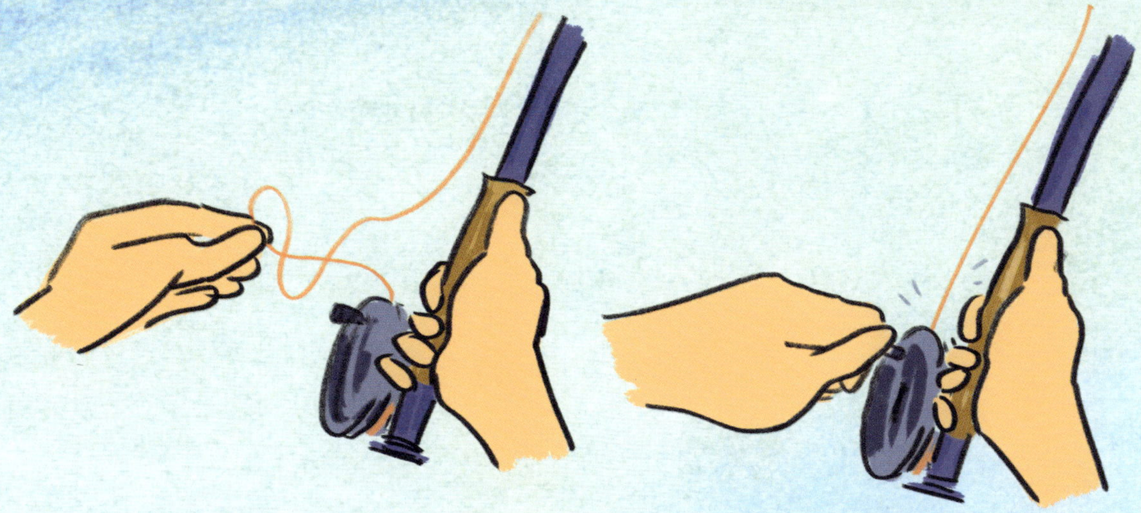

Don't forget about your "third hand," AKA your mouth! Dental and hygiene concerns aside, I use my mouth when I need both hands to do something—like when I'm helping my line out of a snag.

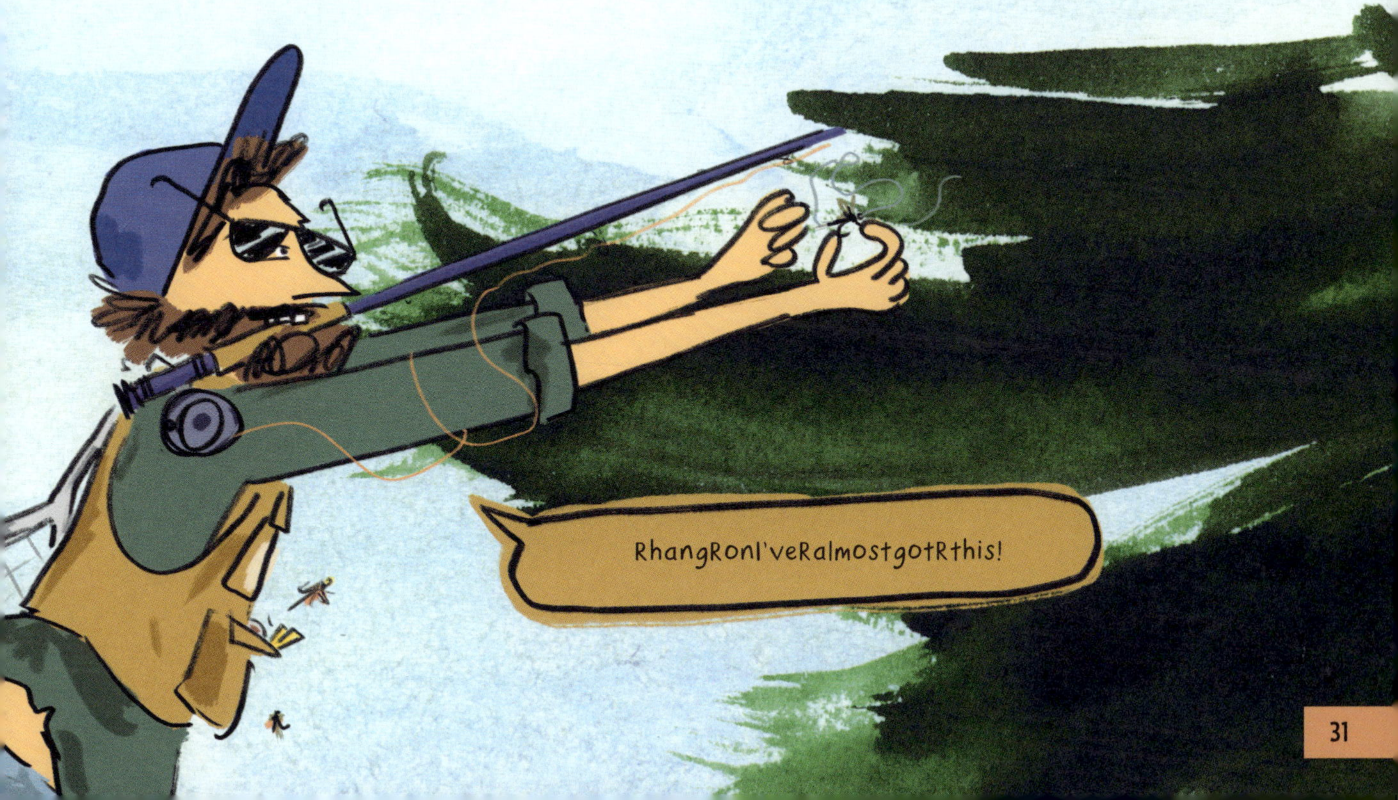

RhangRonI'veRalmostgotRthis!

MEET YOUR NEW BEST FRIEND, THE OVERHEAD CAST

I can't stress enough: This is an introduction! The best way to learn how to cast is to practice and practice and practice some more. I also recommend watching videos (Orvis makes amazing ones) and asking friends and/or guides to demonstrate. But here's how I introduce new people to the idea of casting.

First**:** Get a big field and lay your line out flat in front of you. (NO NEED FOR A FLY AT THIS POINT.)

Have the rod up at this angle. If you're a clock, the rod should be somewhere approaching one o'clock.

Next, pretty quickly and evenly, pull your arm back until it's just past your head. Try not to move your wrist at all. If done right, the line will follow and settle right behind you. Let it hit the ground! You are just trying to get the idea of how the line moves. This is back casting.

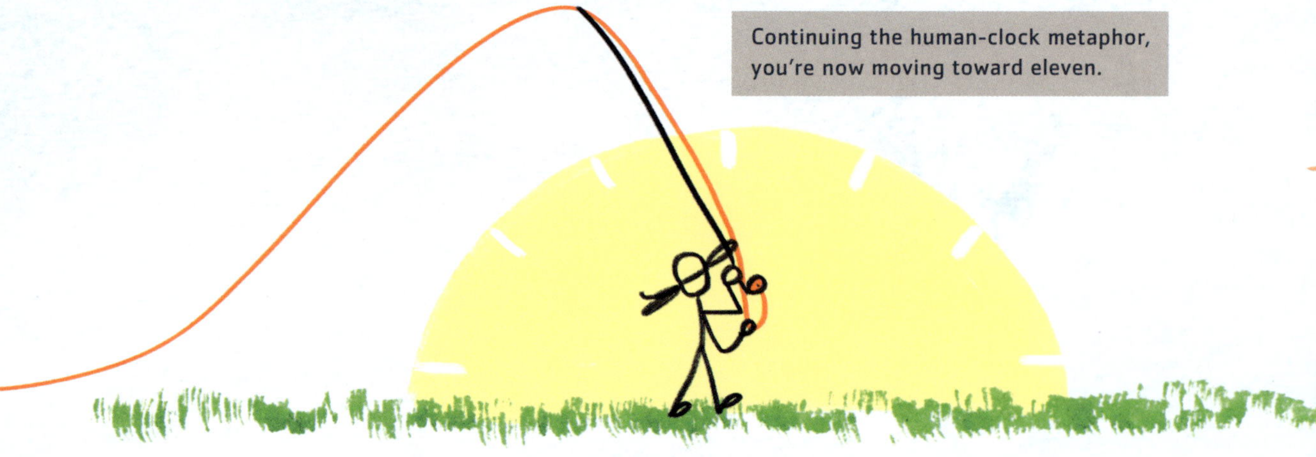

From there, basically do the reverse. Move your arm swiftly and return the rod to where it started. This is all about hitting the right balance. That takes time and practice, so . . .

Repeat this A LOT. Get the feel of how the line moves!

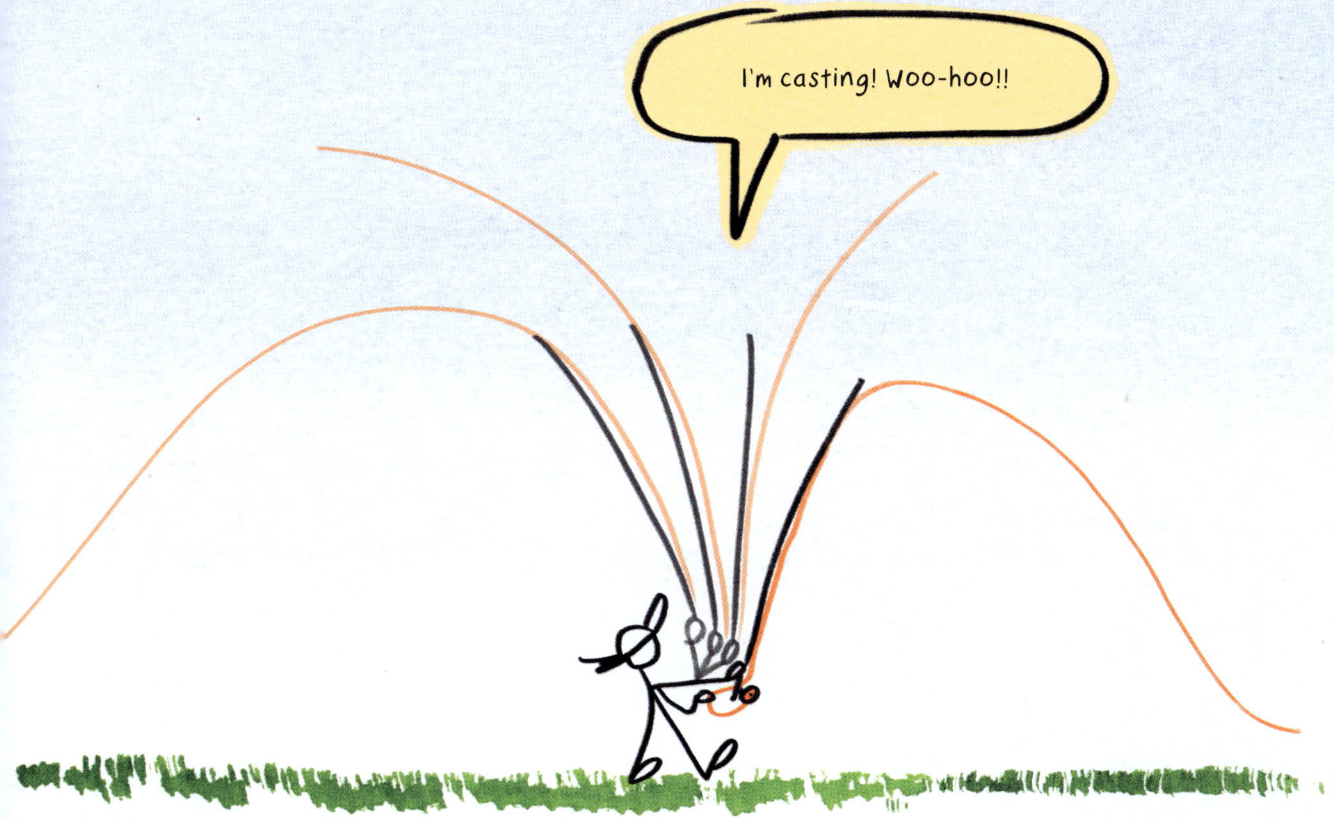

I'm casting! Woo-hoo!!

Once this begins to make some sense, attach a bit of bright yarn to the end of your line. It weighs next to nothing, there's no hook to stab an eager student, and it lets you see where a fly would go!

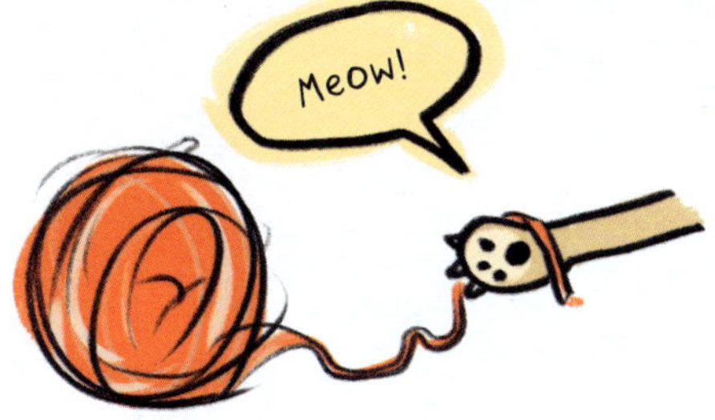

NOW LET'S REALLY CAST!

The big idea here—and a very cool part of fly fishing—is that, when you do that back cast, you want to stop just before the line hits the ground behind you. This REVERSES the momentum of the line. When it all works, it's pretty magical.

To do this, you stop the back cast at just the right moment:

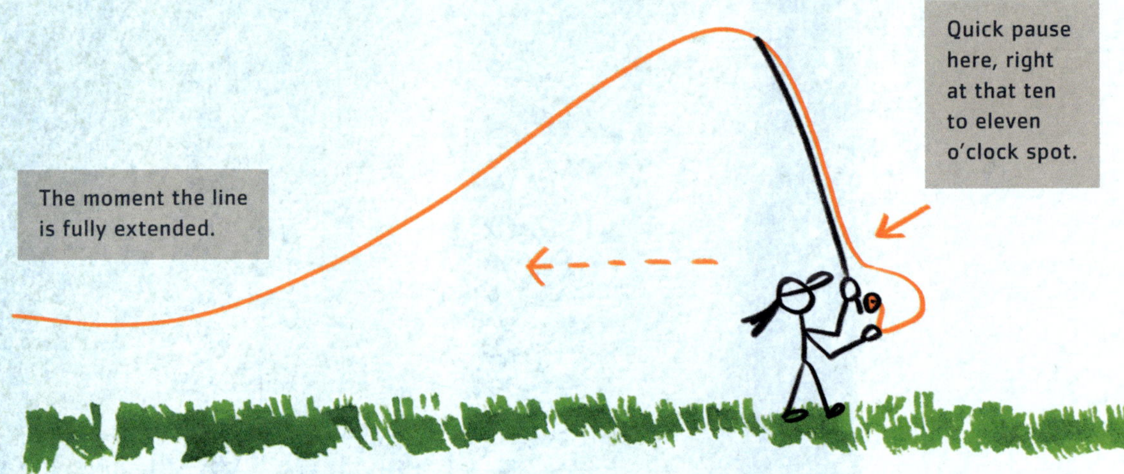

Then you flick your arm. Return the rod top forward to that one o'clock spot. The line and fly should follow. And remember: ONLY MOVE YOUR ARM. At this early stage, you want to minimize variables. There's plenty of time to get fancy later.

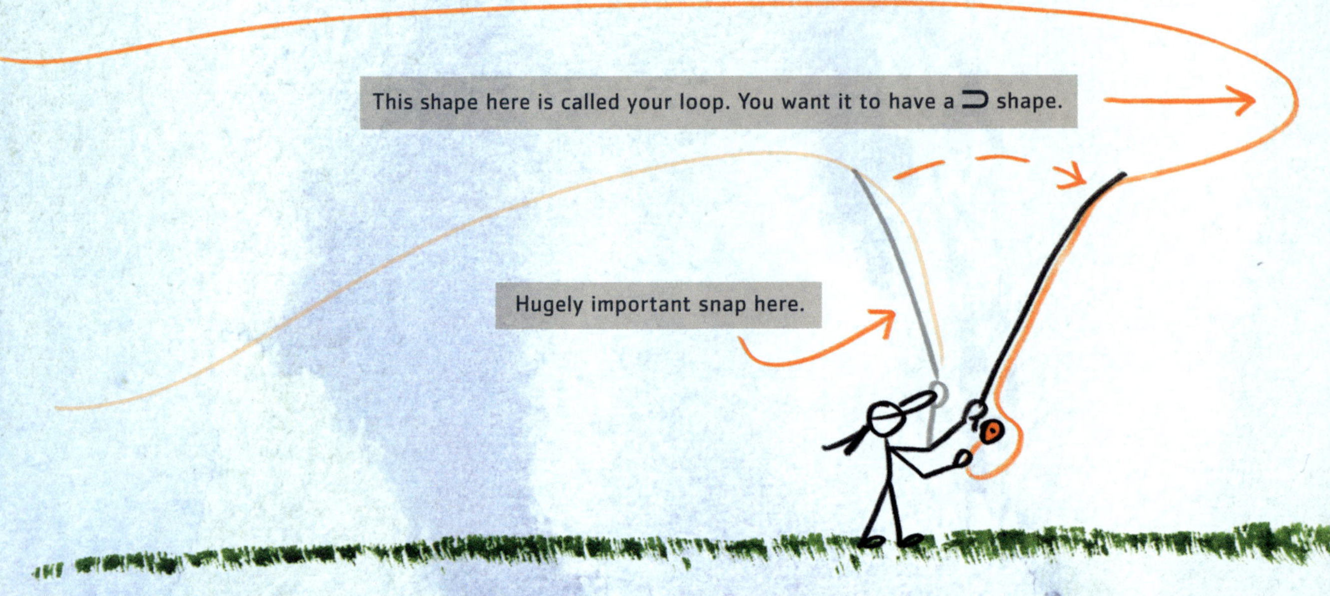

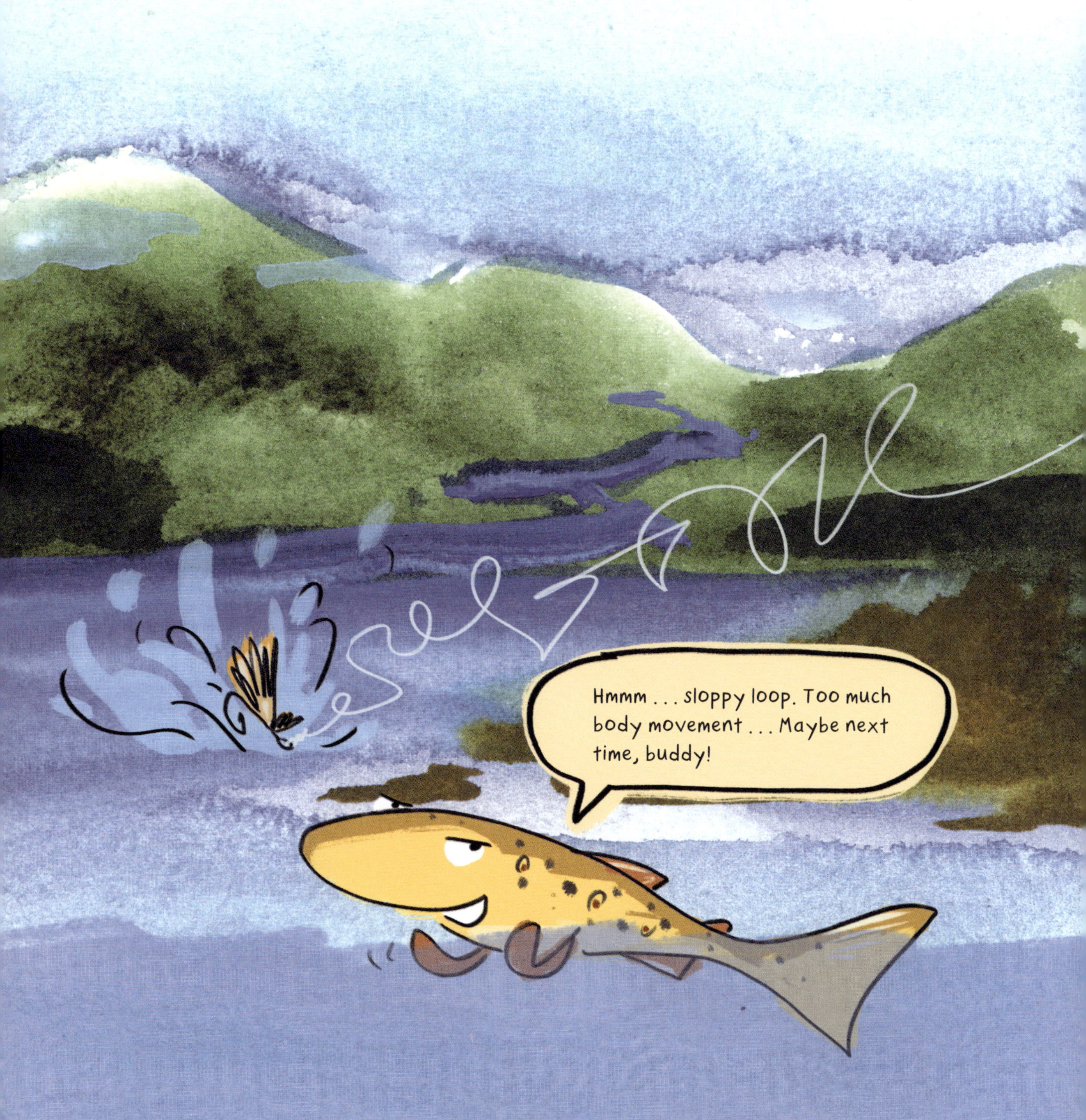

The whole idea is to gently place the fly where a trout will A) think it's a bug and not a weird splashy tangle of fly line and feathers, and B) want to eat it.

As you may have noticed, fly fishing is basically an effort at making something simple a billion times more complex. In other words, there are A LOT more ways to cast.

THE ROLL CAST AND . . .

Both of these casts are used out of necessity. Because sometimes, branches, fences, and who-knows-what are behind you and you can't back cast. If this is the case (and it often is when you're fishing in small brooks or lakeside), you need to work on a roll cast.

It's the same basic idea as the overhead cast. Start with the line resting on the water in front of you . . .

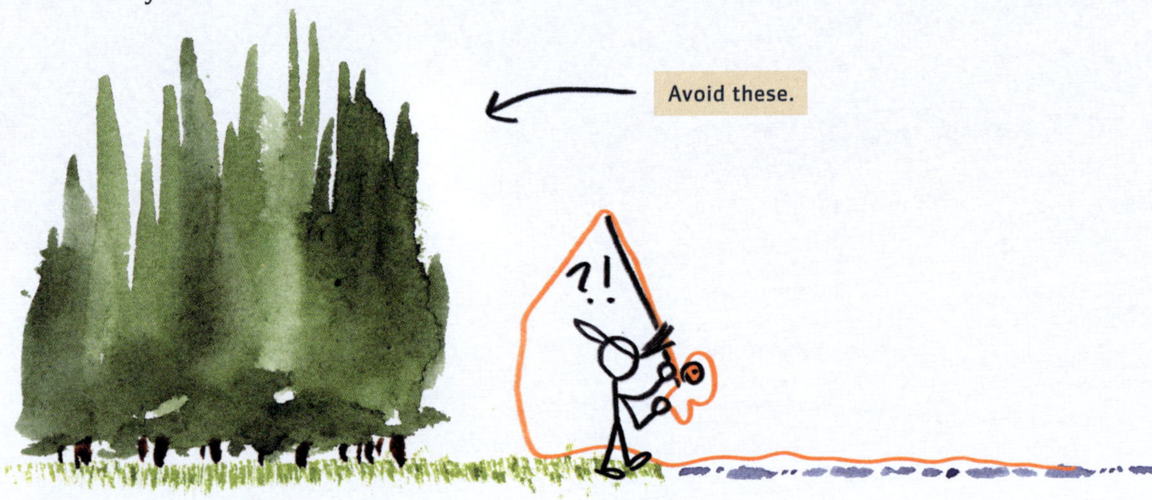

You do a bit of a harder snap of your arm to make up for the whole no-back-cast thing. Again, this is tricky! There is no substitute for trial and error, videos, and in-person instruction!

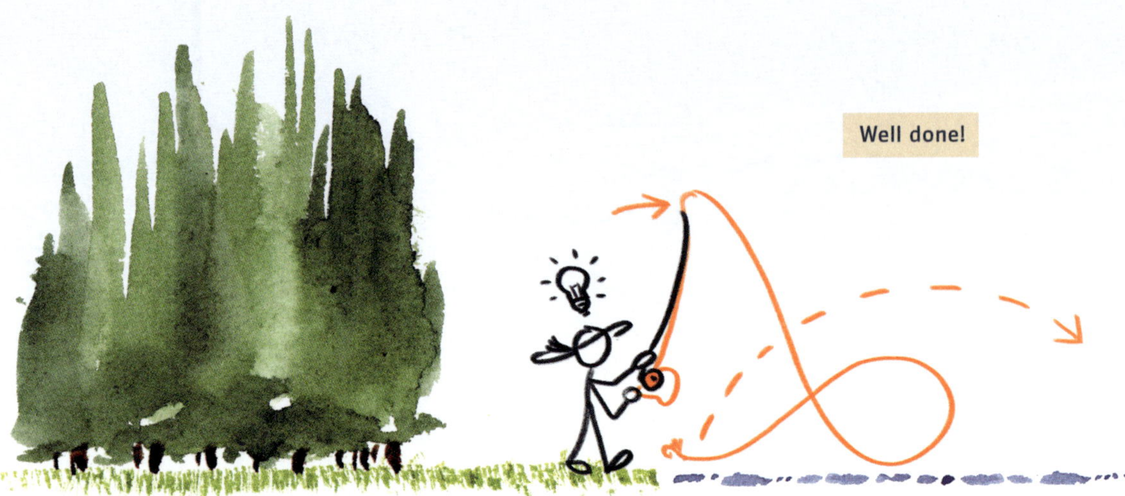

. . . THE BACKHAND

Remember how the overhead cast is basically a full cast backward and a full cast forward? Embrace that for the backhand: Rotate your body, and lead with your casting shoulder. Then essentially end on the back cast.

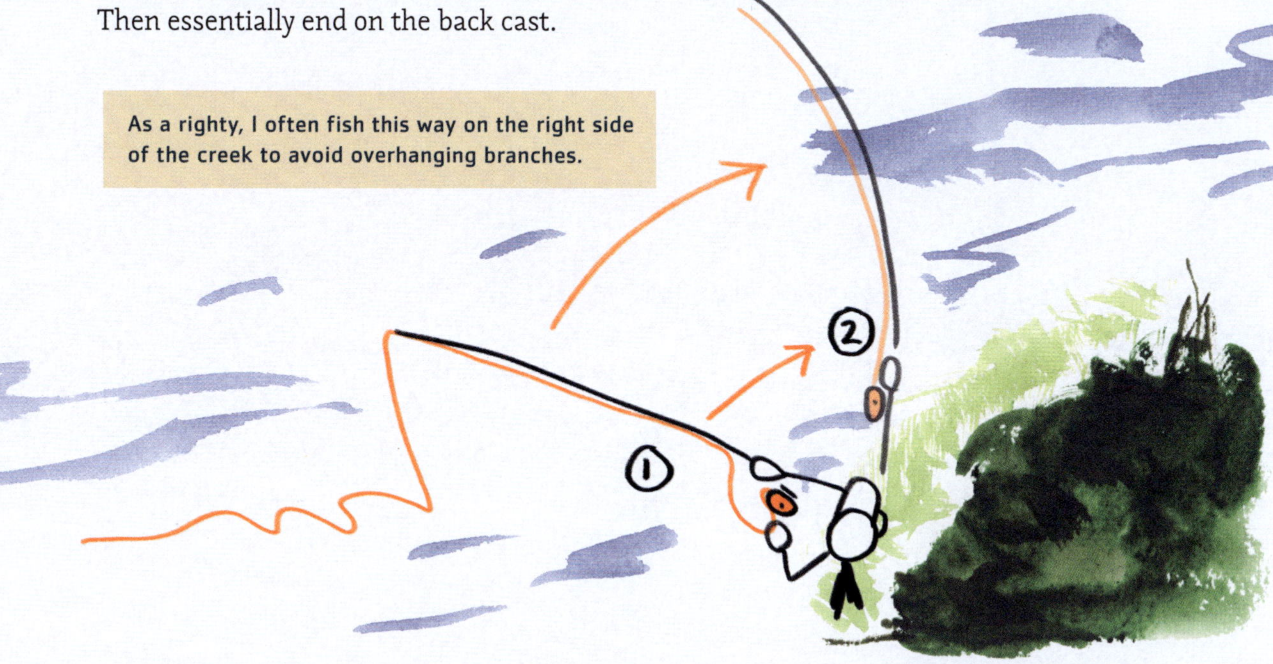

The backhand is VERY helpful if you're on a boat and don't want to cast over someone.

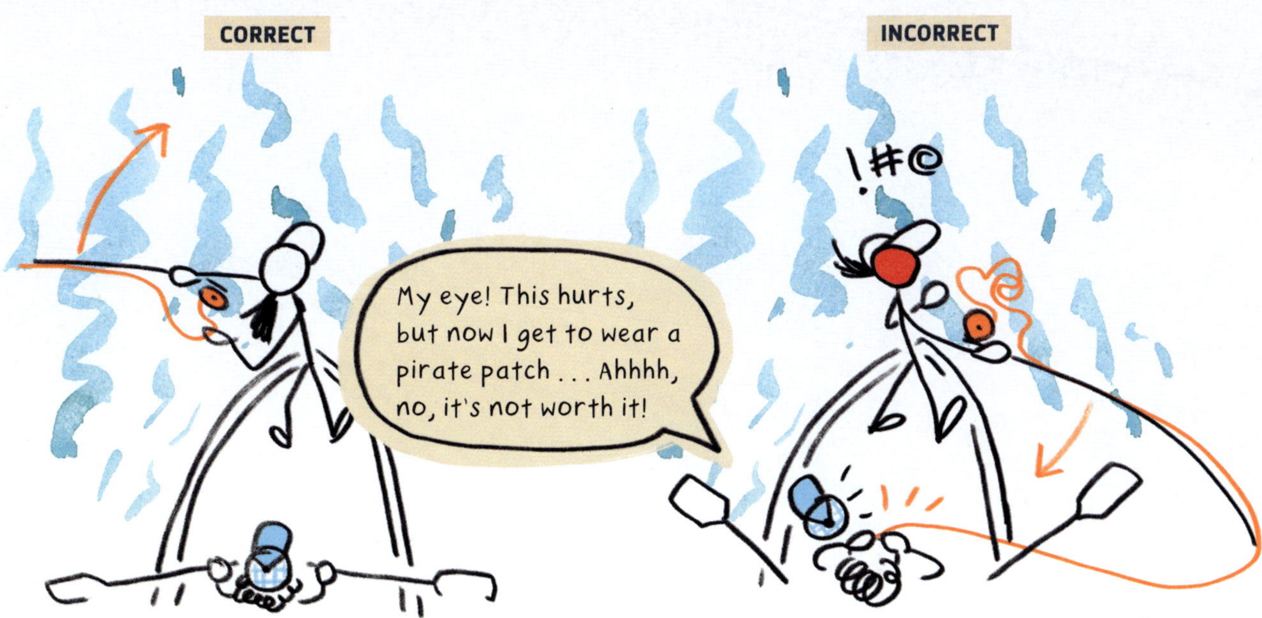

THE DOUBLE HAUL

The unreliable narrator of fly-fishing casts. Pull with your non-casting hand away from where the line is going at just the right moment. Done right, this superpowers the tip strength of the rod and sends your line flying. Done wrong . . . well, it's like a story that loses its way . . .

> No, Steven, I've got this one!
>
> The double haul is the zen koan of casting. It cannot be described. It must be done. Wise teachers like Joan Wulff describe it as a small tug (haul) on the line just before the back cast, and another tug just before the forward cast. These two hauls bend the rod more deeply, and so increase the power/speed/distance of your line. Watch videos. And practice. And practice. And practice some more. Until you feel it.

Jon Scieszka, famous for writing children's books with fractured storytelling. (Can you tell?) He's also my father-in-law and taught me most everything I know about the double haul.

SIDEARM

Turn an overhead cast on its side! That's all it is. For whatever reason, I most often find myself casting neither a side cast nor overhead but somewhere in between. Maybe that's how my shoulder turns. Who knows? Experiment. Ask questions. You WILL find your perfect cast!

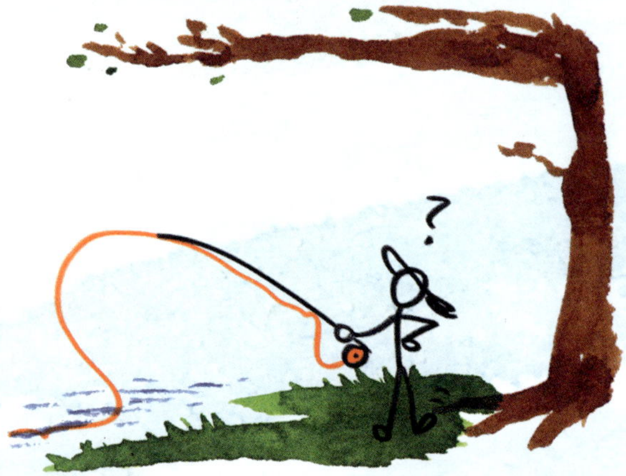

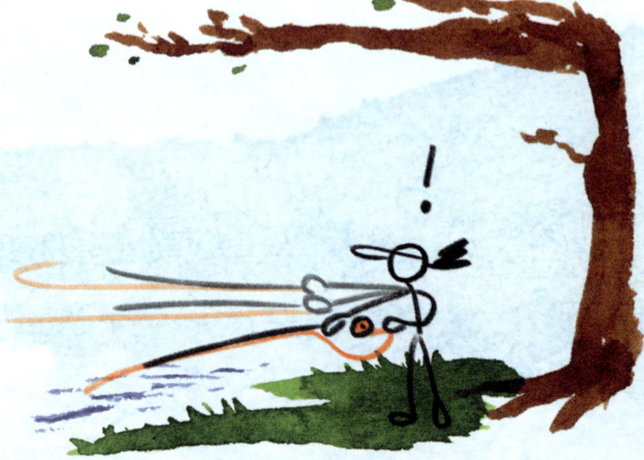

THE FALSE CAST

Avoid too much of this! Remember the movie version of *A River Runs Through It*? Brad Pitt's character's "shadow casting" is basically him "false casting" again and again. It looks very cool in a movie and makes sense for the story, but in real life, it will just spook the fish.

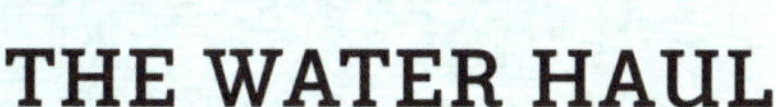

THE WATER HAUL

No, this is not referring to how you load up a watercolor brush to paint a fish—though for me, it sometimes is.

Generally speaking, this means letting the water do your back cast for you. Let your line drift back in the current as far as you'd normally back cast. Cast up from there!

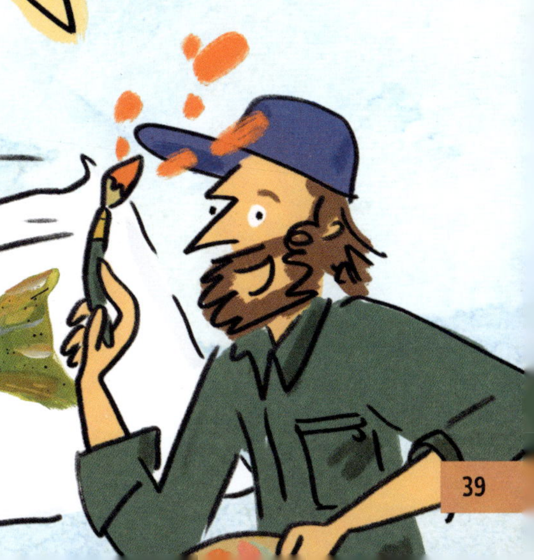

TENKARA!

Overwhelmed yet? Then I recommend simplifying things a bit and trying tenkara. This is a Japanese style of fly fishing where there's no reel—just a rod with a fixed line. You attach a bit of tippet to the line, then a fly. That's it!

While tenkara is very much a Japanese style, it's also representative of how folks may have fly fished in ancient Rome, medieval Europe, and many other places long ago.

I personally love tenkara. Patagonia founder (and tenkara evangelizer) Yvon Chouinard does too!

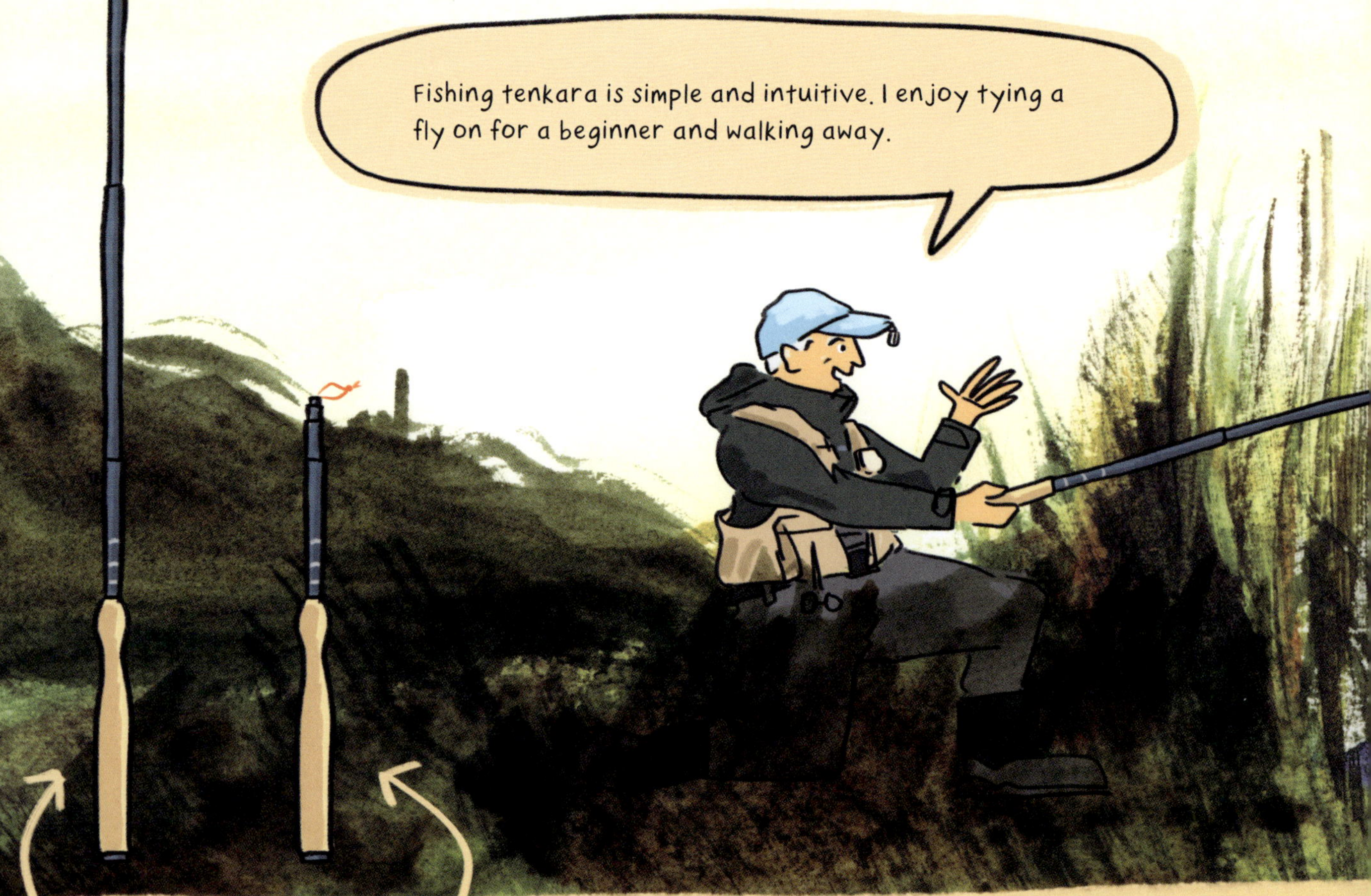

Tenkara rods were historically made from bamboo pieces that could telescope down into each other. Today, they're made of materials like carbon fiber. (They still telescope, though!)

For more about tenkara fishing, I highly recommend Tenkara USA founder Daniel Galhardo's book, *Tenkara*, and Chouinard's book, *Simple Fly Fishing*.

Tenkara flies are called **KEBARI**. Traditionally, they're less about mimicking one bug in particular than they are about looking generically bug-like.

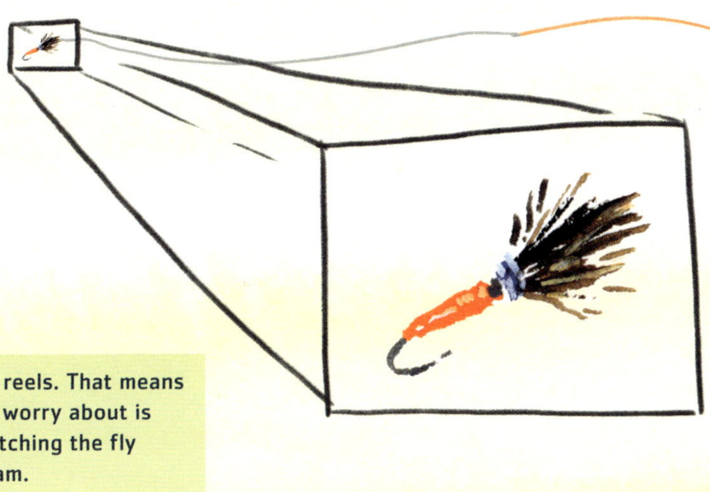

Remember: NO reels. That means all you have to worry about is casting and watching the fly drift downstream.

No reel also means you have to get a bit closer to the fish, which reinforces one of the biggest parts of fly fishing: stealth. Chouinard sometimes wears knee pads to help kneeling.

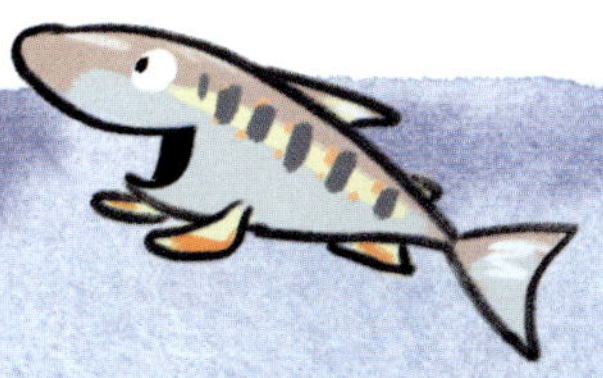

Tenkara anglers in Japan often fish for trout species like the yamame or "cherry trout." That said, you can catch pretty much anything with this outfit!

All of this makes for a rod that's super easy to transport—a good thing, since traditional ones are often more than ten feet long!

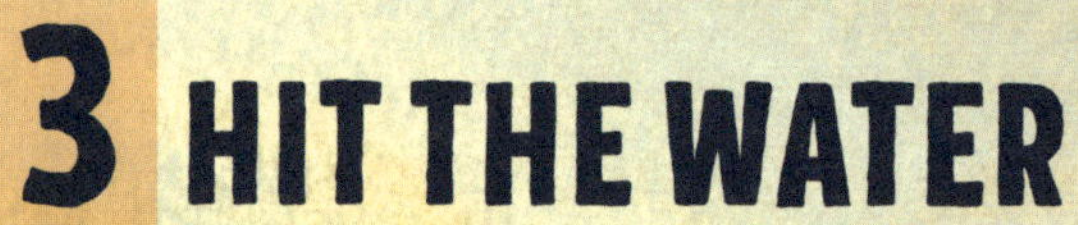

3 HIT THE WATER

DON'T WORRY, we'll get to bug life cycles and rod anatomy later in the book. For now, let's just fish.

In an effort to hook you—ha! Sorry, I had to—here's Oliver White, manager and head guide of Jimmy Kimmel's South Fork Lodge on the Snake River in Idaho. Oliver has fished from the Bahamas to Bhutan, is sponsored by brands like Yeti, and is one of the few anglers you might know because you saw him on a billboard.

But don't let any of that intimidate you. The important thing is that he knows how to fish, he loves to fish, and he's a great teacher too. Remember: The whole idea here is to trick fish. And fish don't email. They don't have school pickup. They don't do taxes. They just have being a fish. They're pretty good at it!

OLIVER WHITE

FAVORITE WATERS: South Fork of the Snake, flats fishing anywhere

FAVORITE FISH: Permit and big brown trout

FAVORITE FLY: Bear Back Rider, Strong Arm Merkin

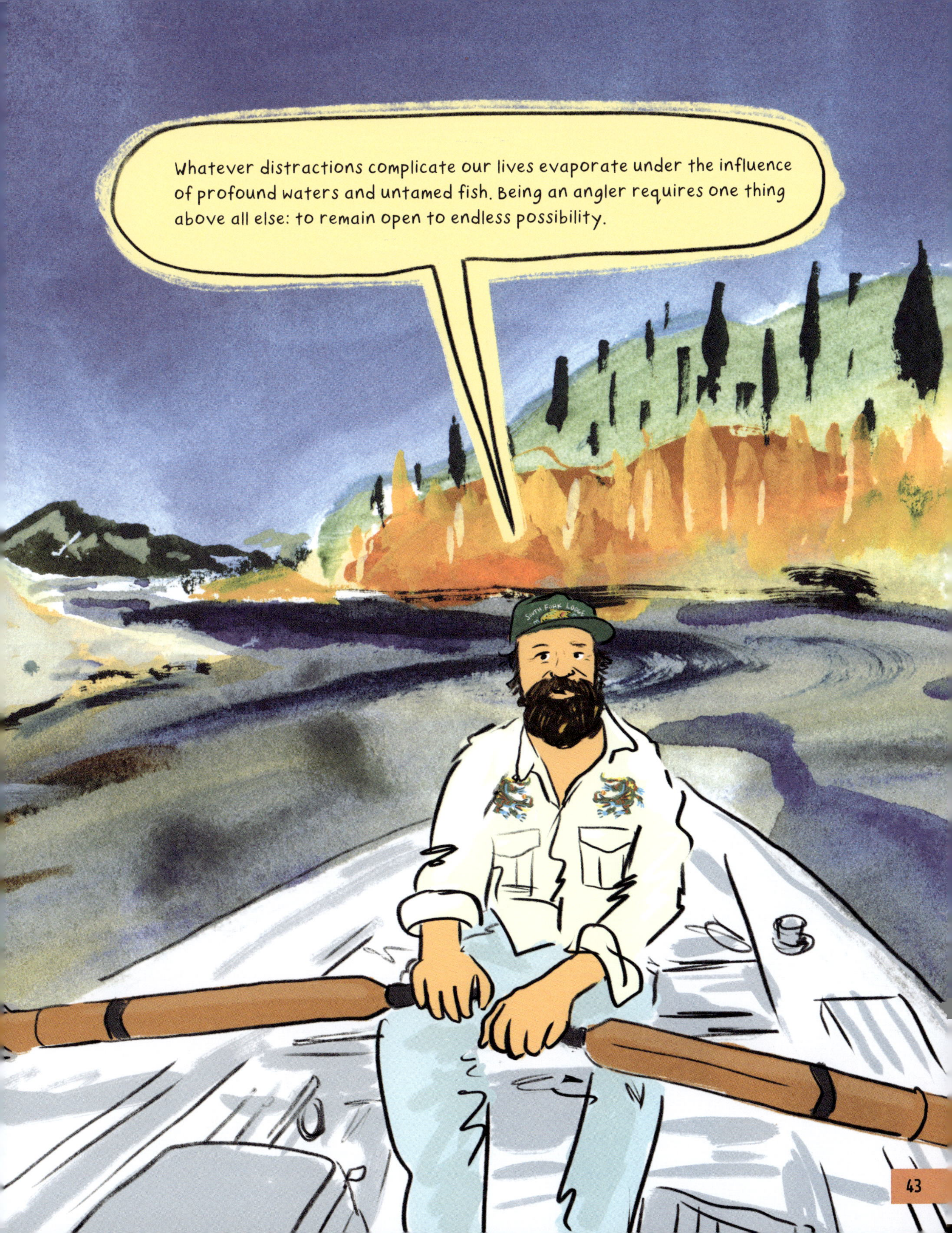
Whatever distractions complicate our lives evaporate under the influence of profound waters and untamed fish. Being an angler requires one thing above all else: to remain open to endless possibility.

For new anglers, I like to reduce variables. We go small. Let's start at my little creek in the Catskills. It requires all the same skills you'd use on a big river like the Snake, but it's much more manageable.

Now, let's see if we can sneak up on some fish . . .

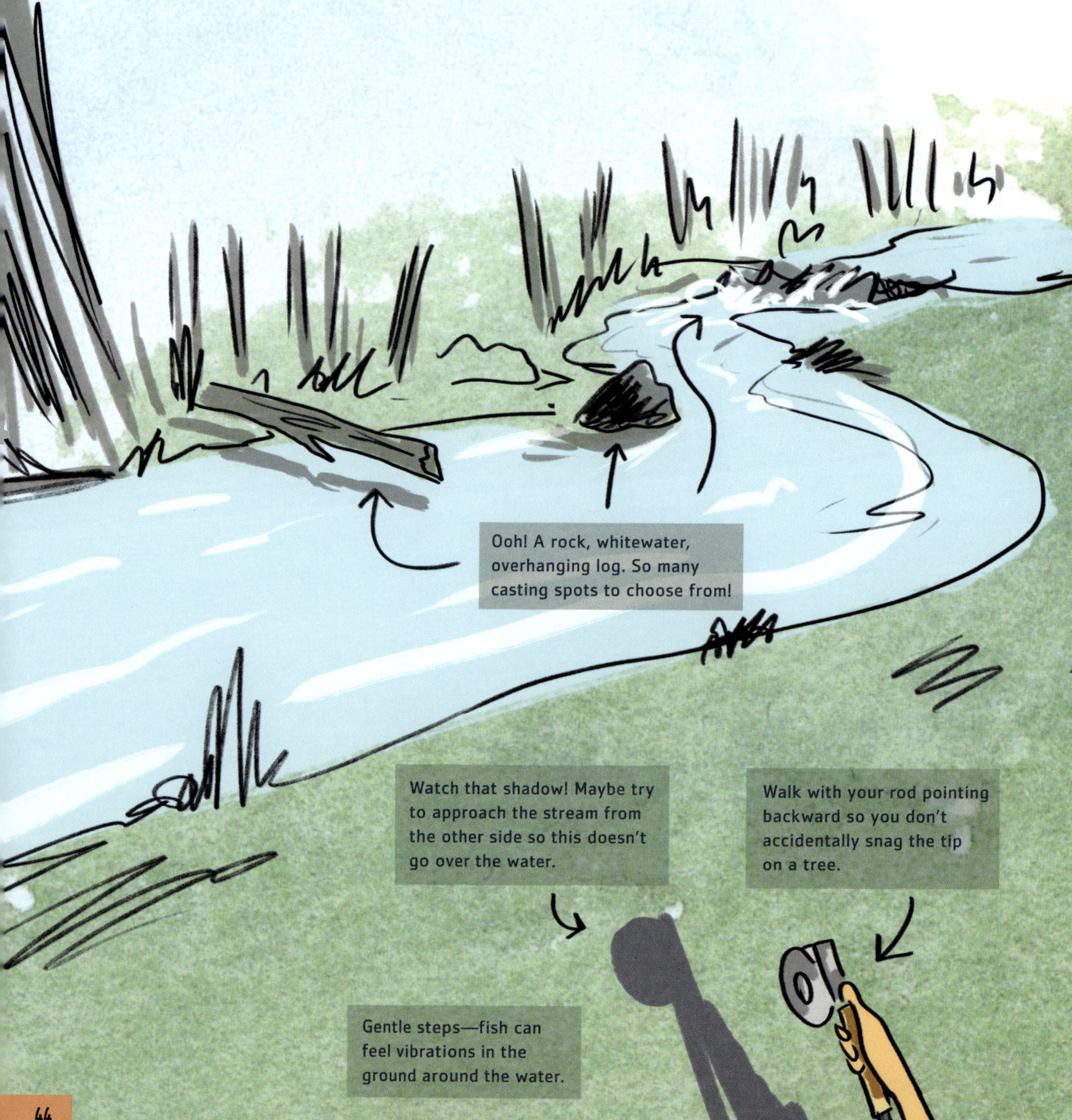

Next, find a spot that looks fishy. What's "fishy"? Usually any place where there's a change in the current. So, rock to no rock, branch to no branch, shallow to deep. Any kind of cover helps too!

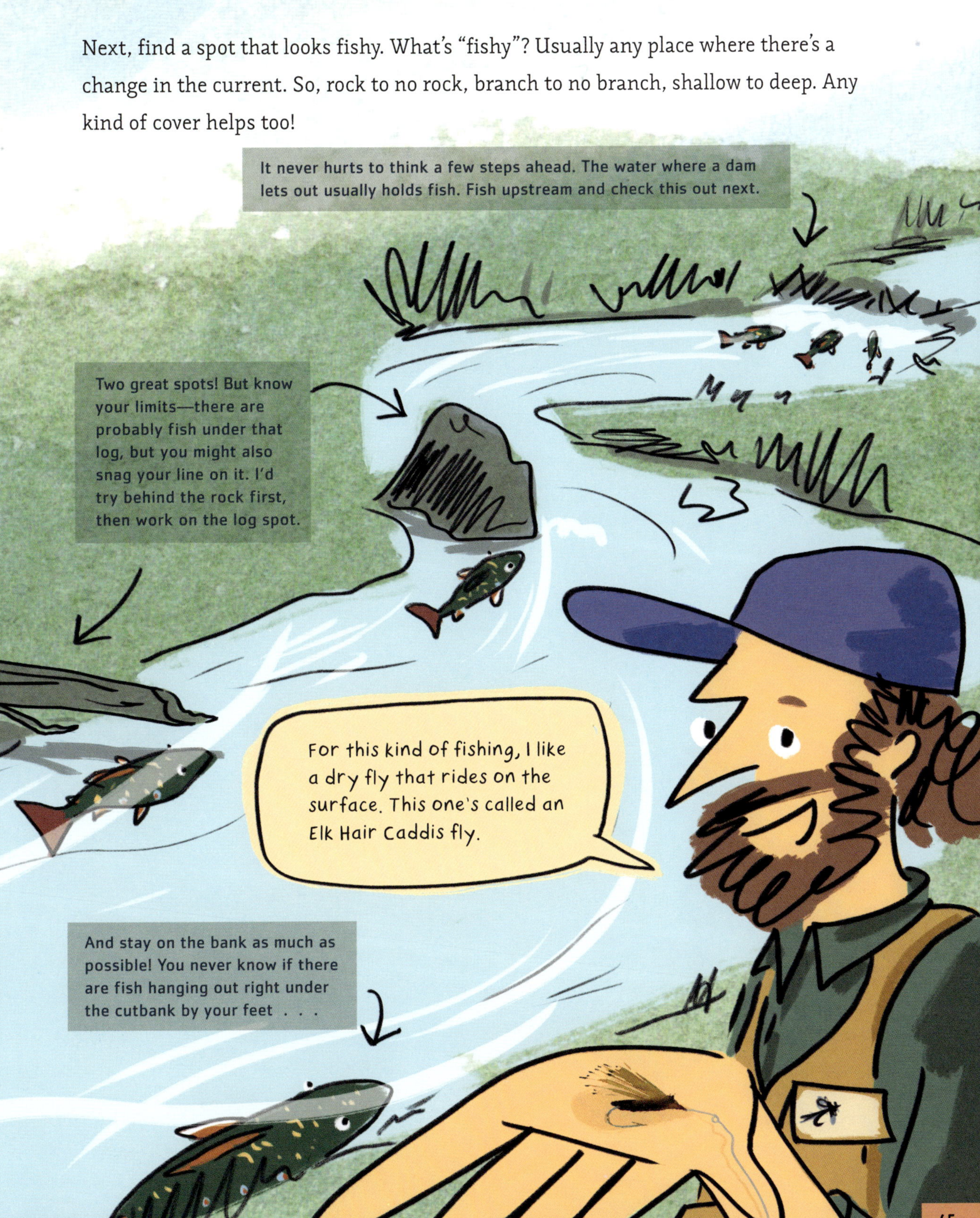

You've approached. You've scouted. Now cast! (Well, maybe take a second to make sure you're not about to cast into a tree branch right over your head.)

The important thing is to get your fly right where you think the fish wants to eat a bug. Generally speaking, this means casting upstream from the fish and letting the fly drift down naturally.

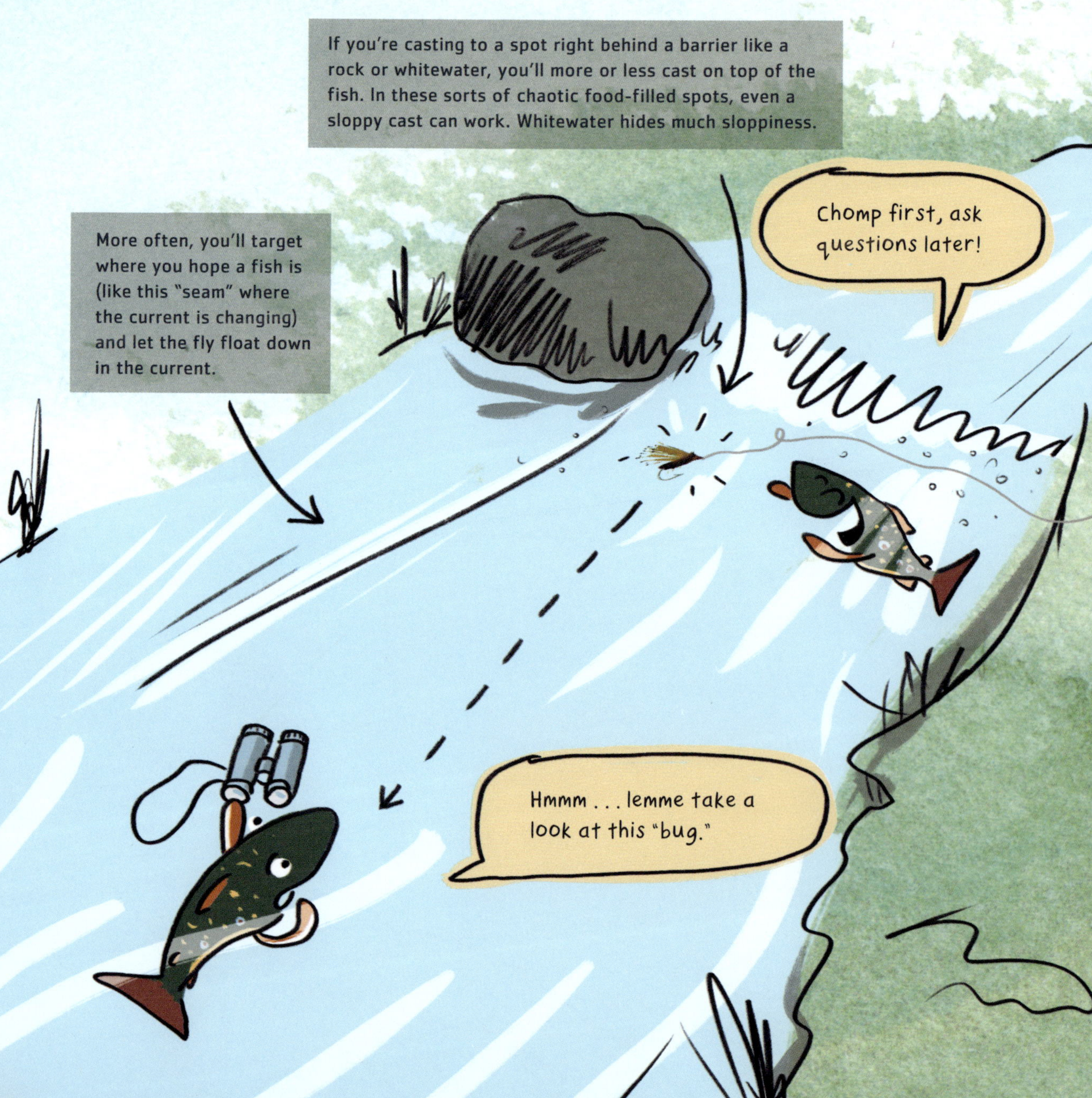

On water big and small, you will obsess over the fly "drifting" on or through the water naturally. If part of the fishing line is caught in faster current, the fly will be dragged. This will not look like food to a trout.

The solution is called "mending." This is an art and takes time to master, but the general idea is to gently flop the rod and line in such a way that the line goes behind the fly. This lets the fly drift naturally, like it's a yummy meal.

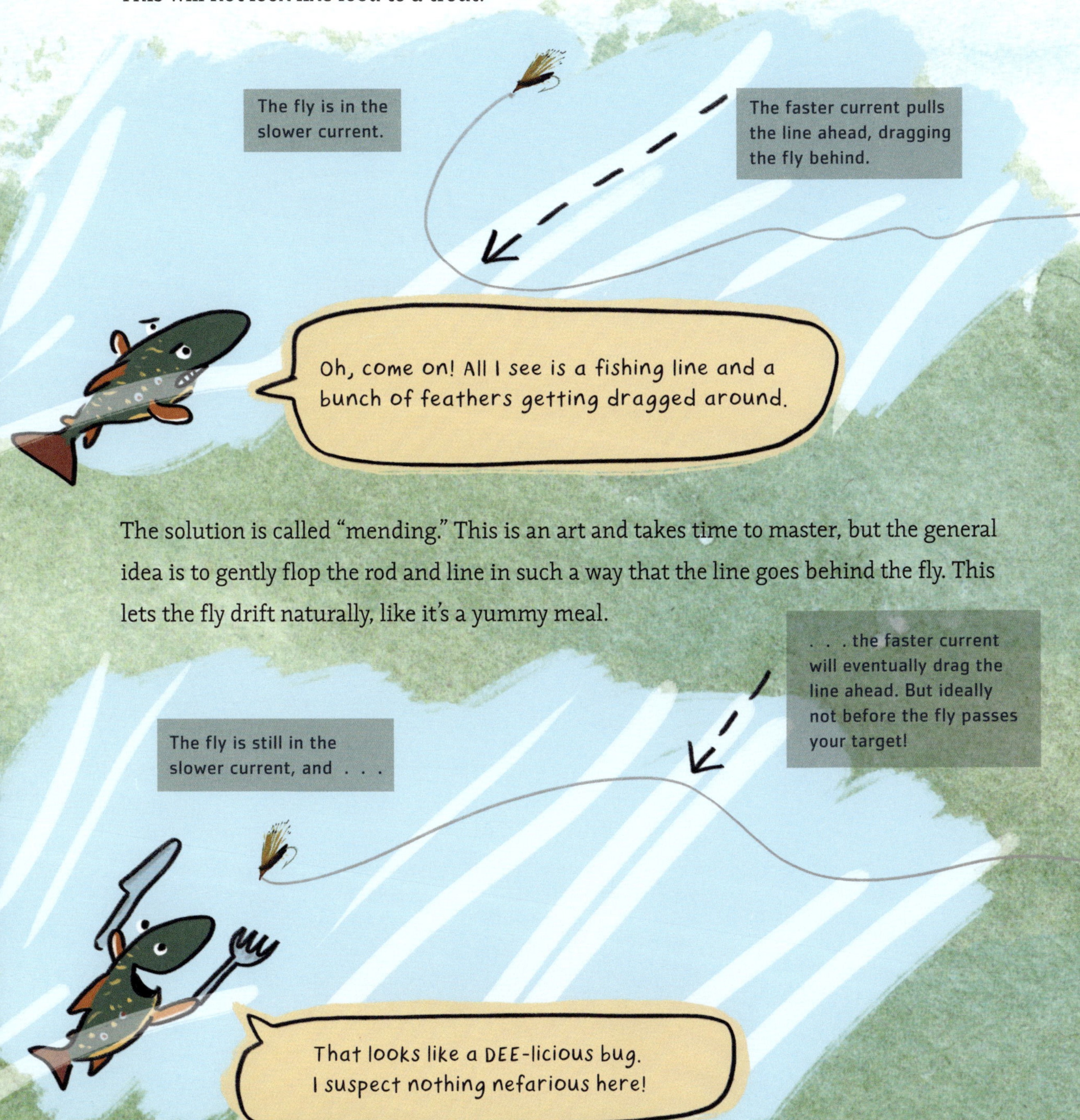

If all goes well, you'll hook a fish!

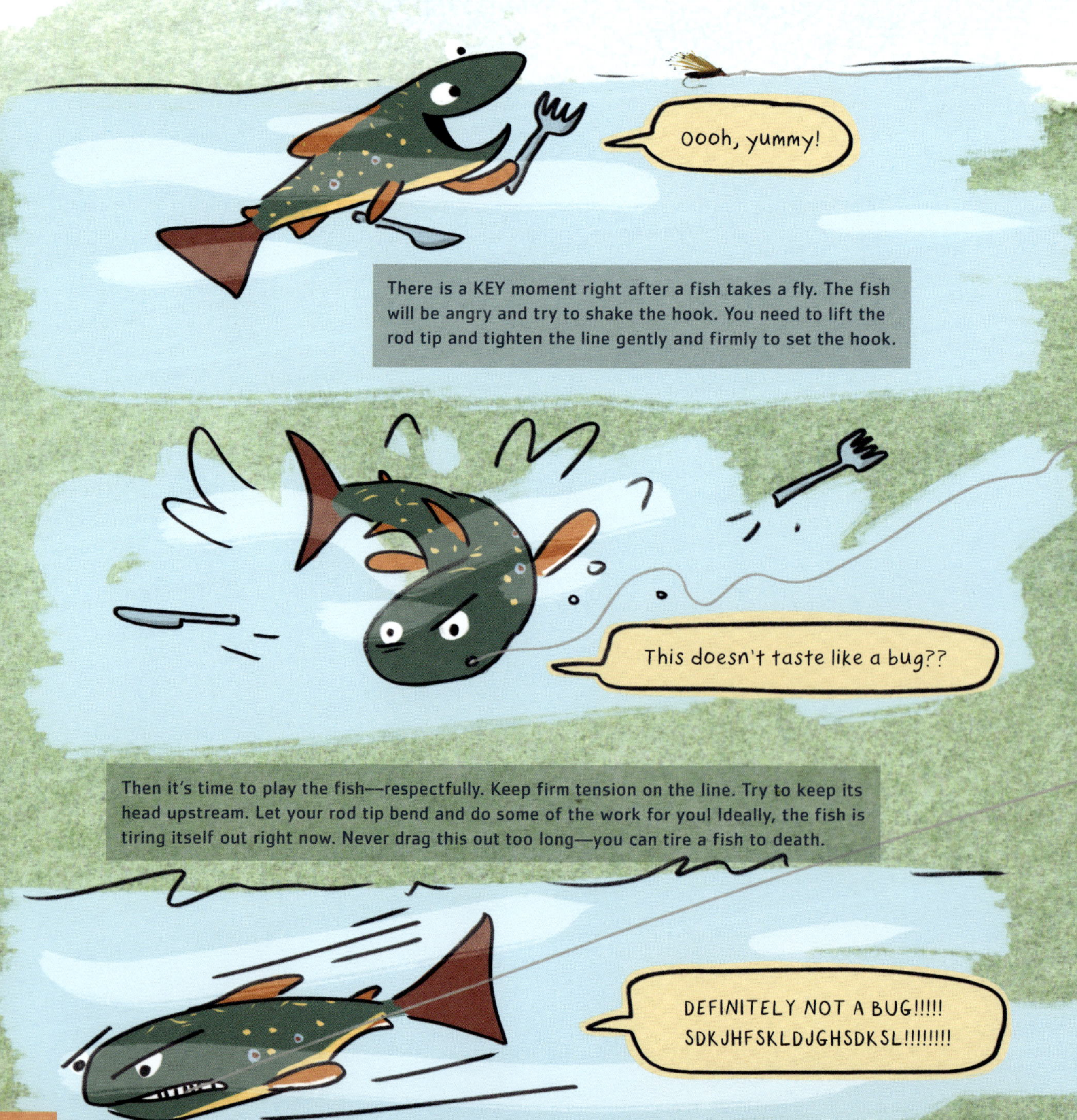

Time to catch and release. (Or not release! For more on responsible eating, see page 164.) And PLEASE, at this stage, HANDLE MINIMALLY and RELEASE GENTLY!

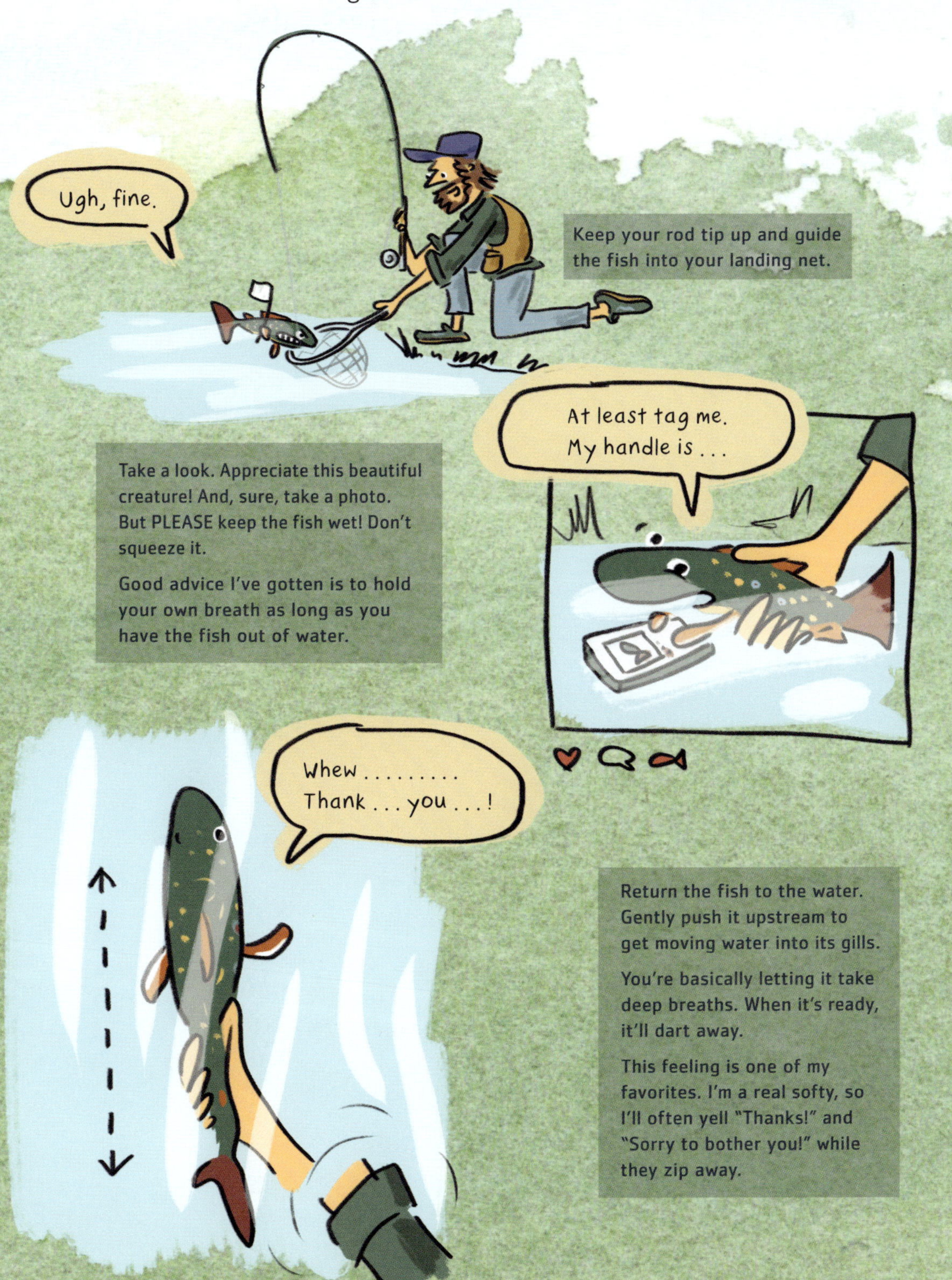

Wherever you cast, remember that fish are ALL OVER THE PLACE—but mainly in some key spots. (Of course, in real life, trout are incredibly well camouflaged. Don't expect to peer into a creek and have it look like this diagram.) Here's where to look:

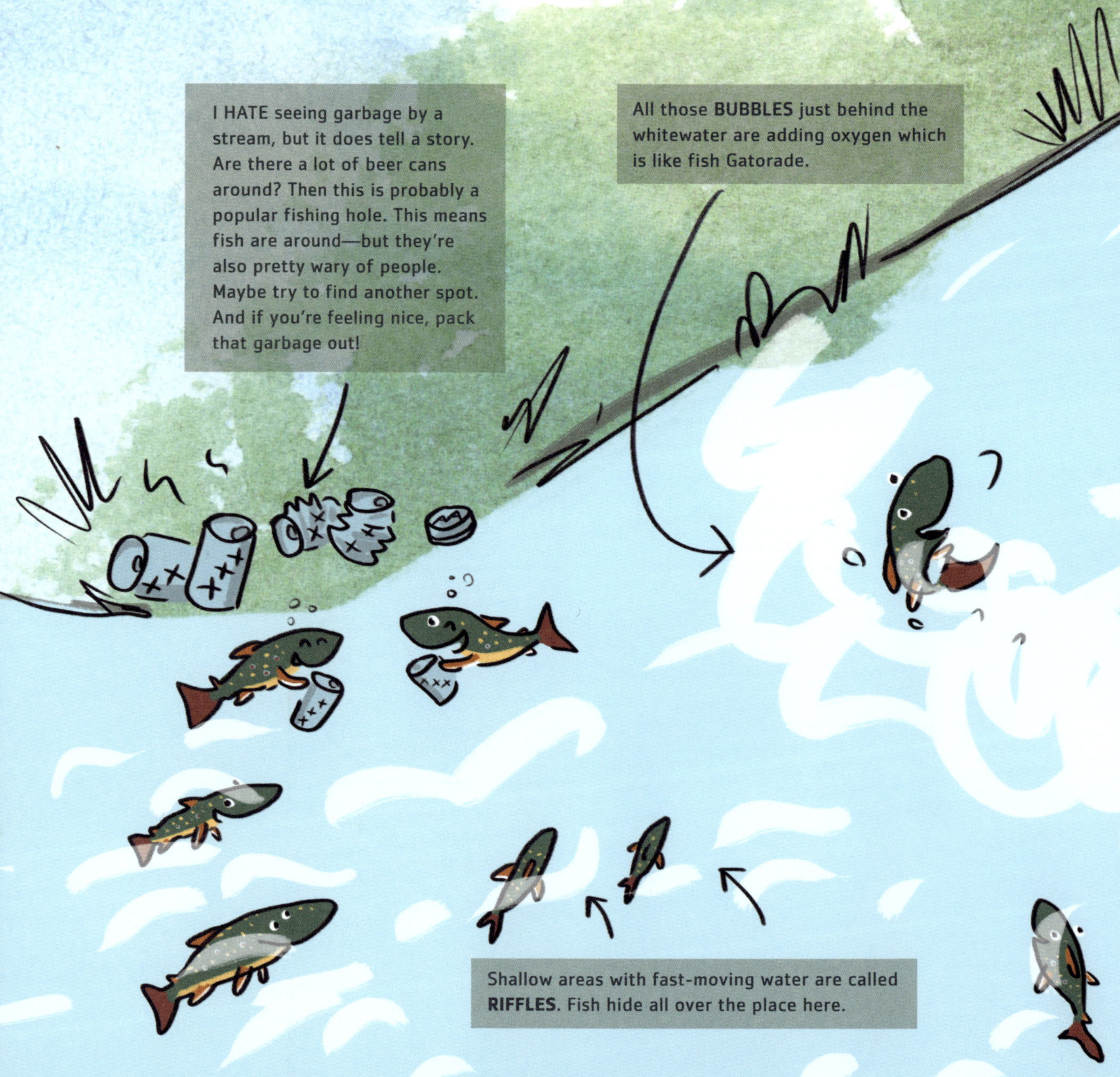

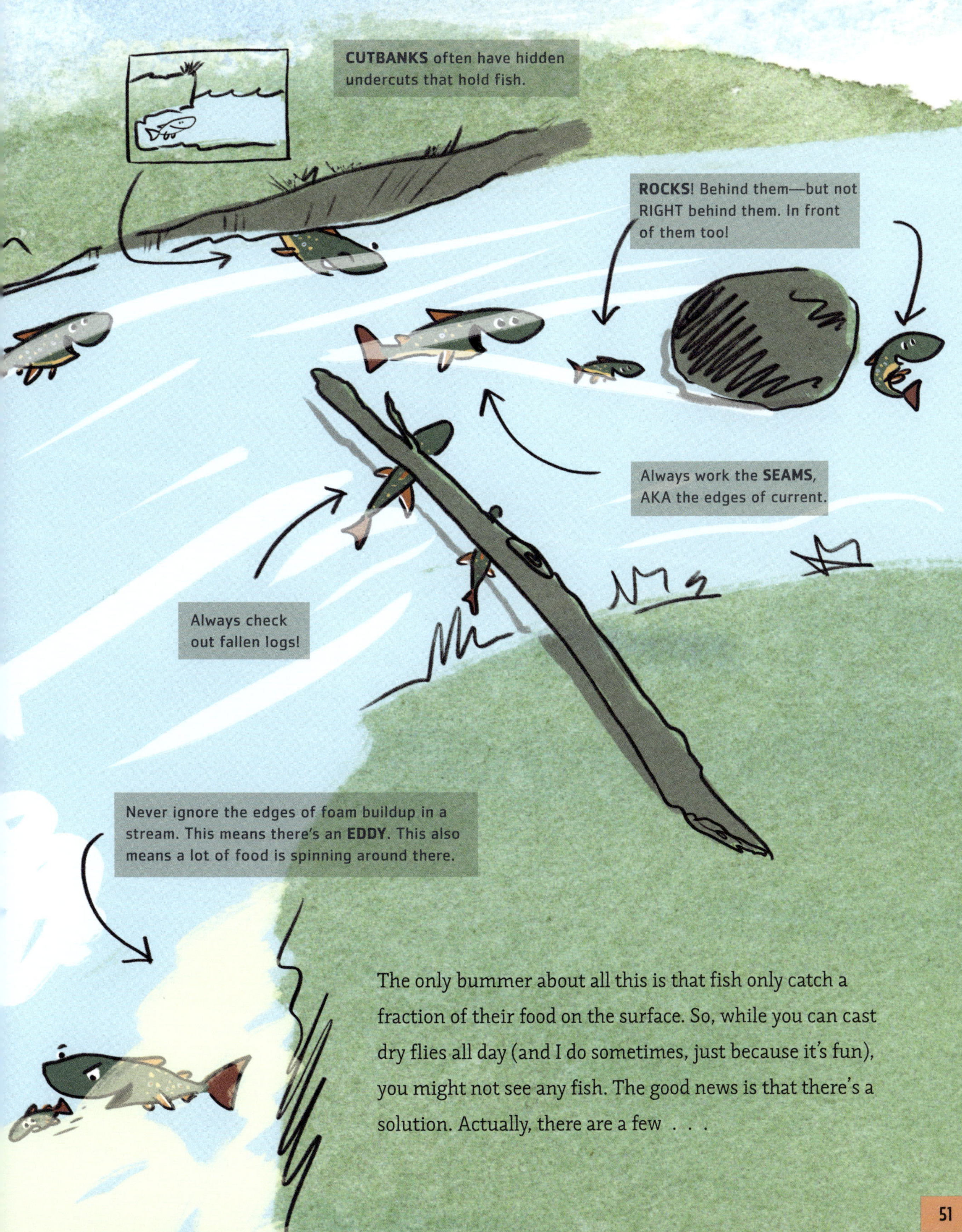

The only bummer about all this is that fish only catch a fraction of their food on the surface. So, while you can cast dry flies all day (and I do sometimes, just because it's fun), you might not see any fish. The good news is that there's a solution. Actually, there are a few . . .

NYMPHS!

Eat me! I'm a nymph.

Nymphs are a broad category of flies. They're made to look like bugs that live IN the water—the bugs that will one day grow up (and go through a whole metamorphosis, which you can read about on page 138) to sit on the water surface like a dry fly. For now, just know they're food down deep!

Nymphs, like their grown-up counterparts, come in many shapes and sizes.

You know who loves nymphs? BIG FISH! They are experts at conserving energy, so you need to bring food to them . . .

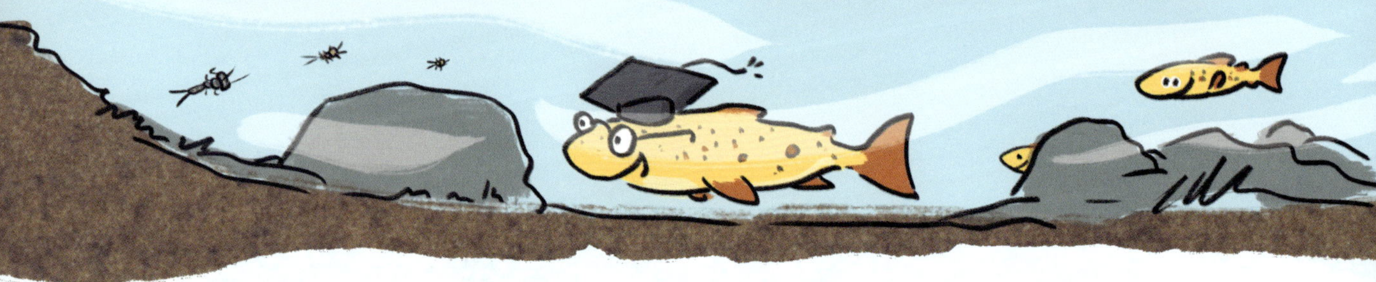

You mainly cast nymphs similarly to dry flies. You want to aim for that same natural drift—you just also want to give the nymph time to sink. (That's what the brass or tungsten "beadhead" on the tip of the fly is for.)

One downside to nymphing is it can be . . . well . . . boring. There's just so much happening underwater that you won't see! I recommend embracing the uncertainty. Let yourself get into a nymphing trance while you watch for the teeniest twitches in the line.

I'm just gonna stay home tonight and order in. You know, nymph and chill!

Want to go even deeper into the boring-yet-trancelike world of nymphing? You can! It's called Euro nymphing, and however well it works (hint: REALLY WELL), it feels like someone removed all the art from fly fishing. So, apologies. It's just not for me. I'll let my pal, guide, and Euro-expert Landon Brasseur explain . . .

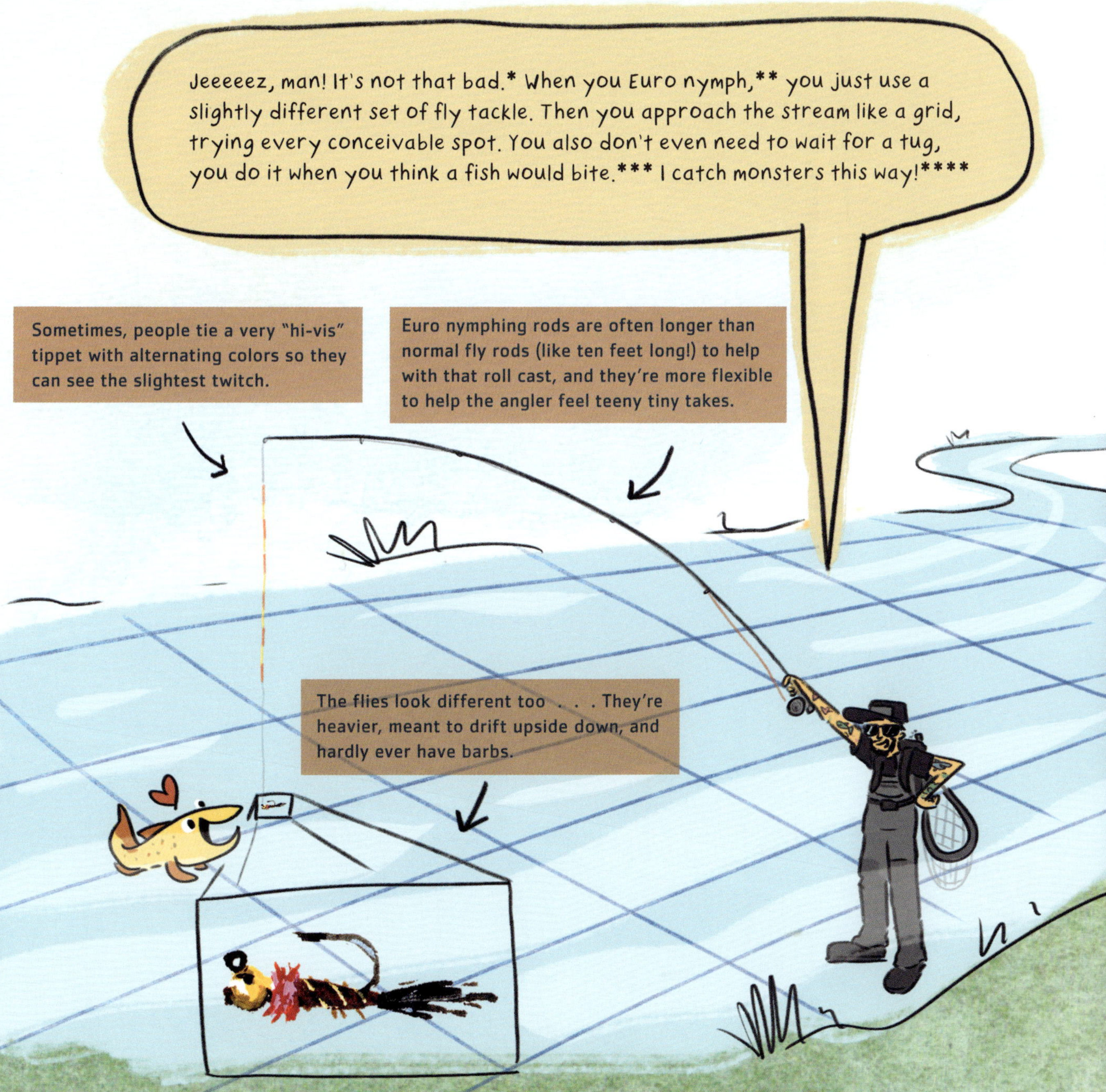

*Fine, it's obviously not my personal favorite. **It was developed for fly-fishing competitions in Europe, hence the name. (It's also called "Czech nymphing.") ***An admittedly good plan, since fish tend to investigate food-looking things with their mouths before biting. ****He really does! OK, fine, Landon. (And every other Euro nympher.) I'm sorry! We're one big happy fly-fishing family.

STREAMERS!

You've tried the surface—you've tried below. Still nothing? Then let's throw in the kitchen sink of flies: streamers. Streamers are meant to look like small baitfish and move like them too!

I may look like a mutant fish-crayfish-ball of yarn, but I am a streamer.

You want to replicate something big and scared, so don't worry about a splash when casting a streamer. The whole idea is ATTENTION.

As the streamer drifts in the current, "strip" in the line with your non-rod holding hand. The idea here is to mimic the movement of something in the water to draw predators.

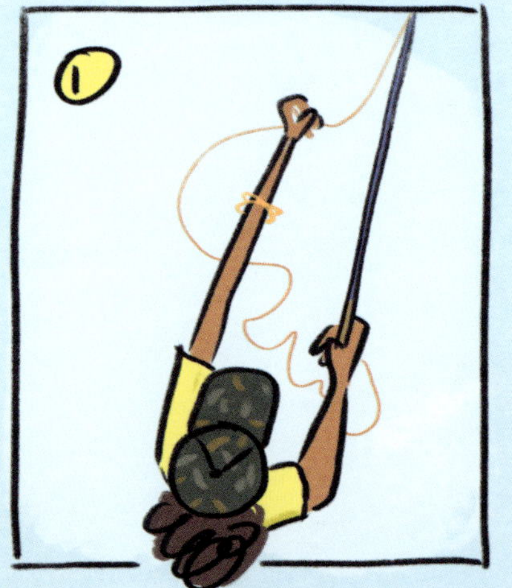

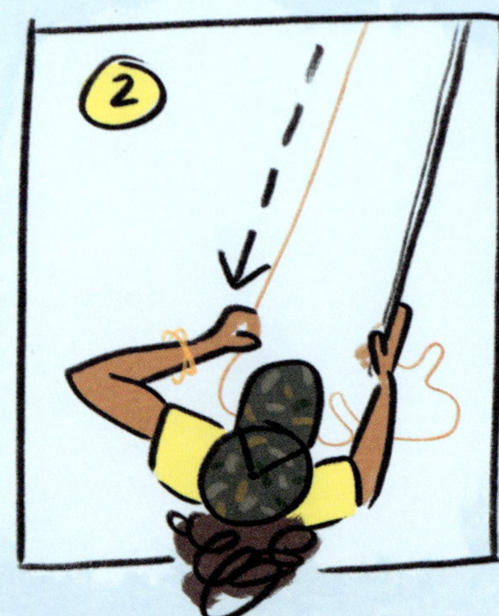

You can also fish what's called a "wet fly" similarly to a streamer. You use that same swing, but usually little or no stripping. These are some of the earliest designs for fly fishing, but they aren't used as much these days.

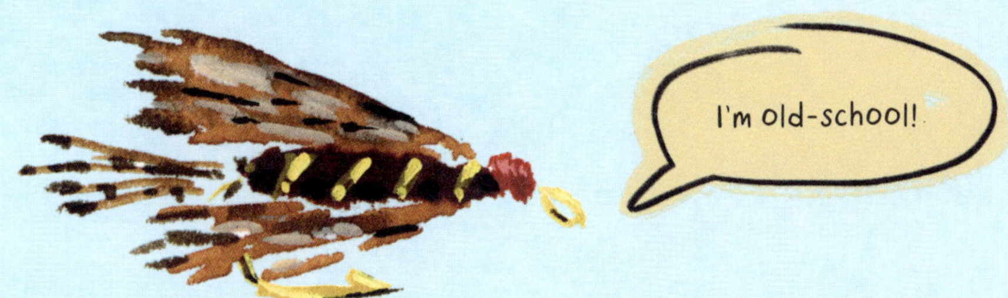

But let's imagine we've fished my little creek with dry flies, nymphs (Euro and otherwise), and even streamers—plus a few geriatric wet flies.

There's still one last category of fly fishing you can try—even if it feels straight-up medieval . . .

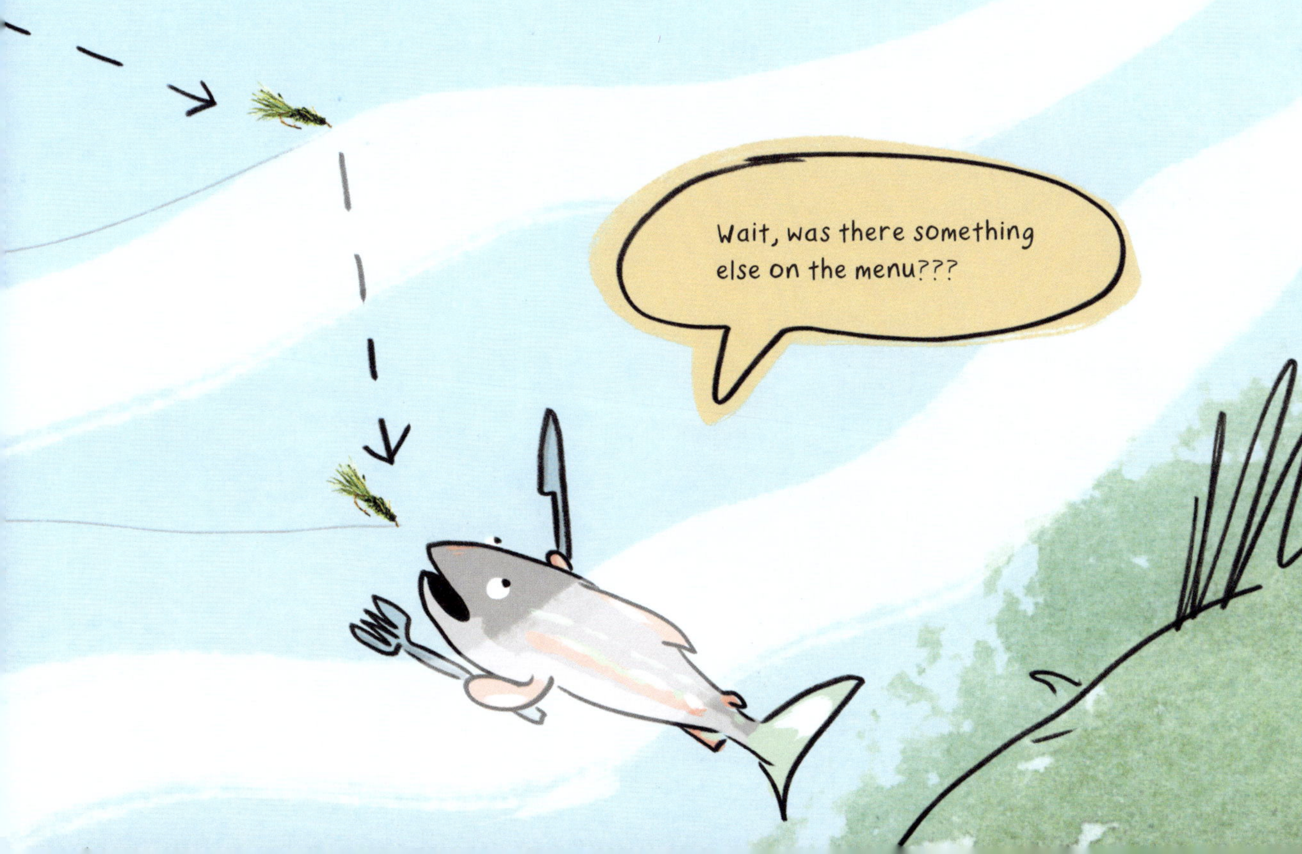

Wait, was there something else on the menu???

BWHAHAHAHA!
WELCOME TO THE DARK ART OF MOUSING!

The biggest fish are nocturnal. They also eat the biggest food, like mice that fall into the water at night. Oops!

You'll need:

Mouse flies . . . which I guess should be called mouse mice?

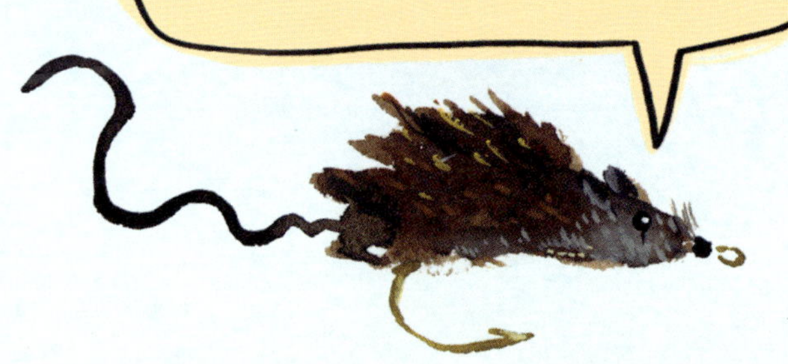

A short leader (about 5 feet long). You want something very strong because nocturnal fish are BIG. And because it's night, you don't need the subtlety that longer leaders and tippet give you.

REALLY good knowledge of your surroundings. Fish where you know the rocks and path well so you barely need a light. Watch the moon phase too. You want dark! Less moon is better.

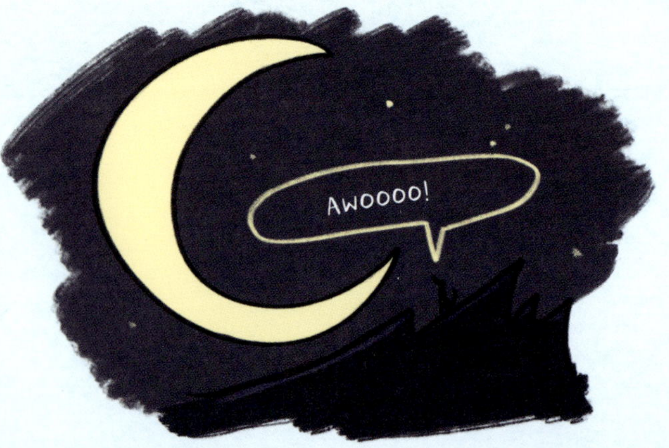

A headlamp, ideally with a dim red-light setting. If possible, avoid using any light until you're reeling in your monster fish!

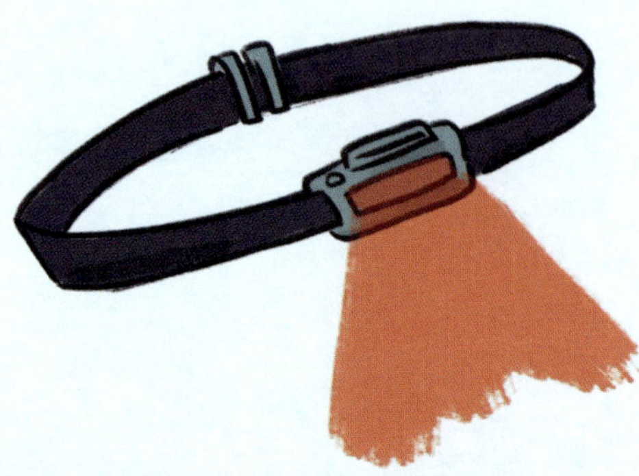

Most mousing is pretty much just like streamer fishing but on the surface. You don't need a subtle cast at night. You'll want a big splash and then to strip in a lot. The idea is to replicate the wake and pace of a panicked mouse trying to escape imminent fish death.

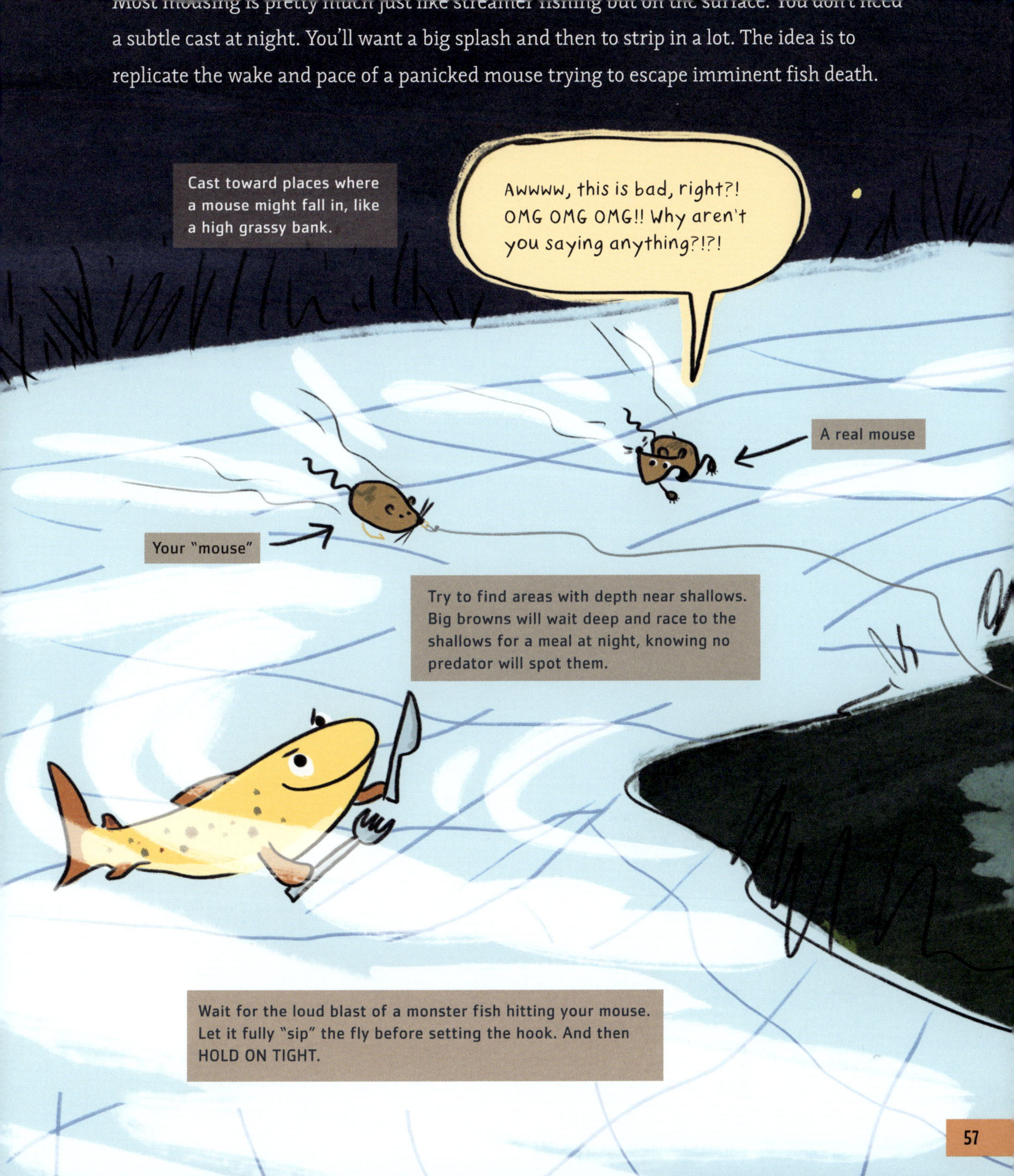

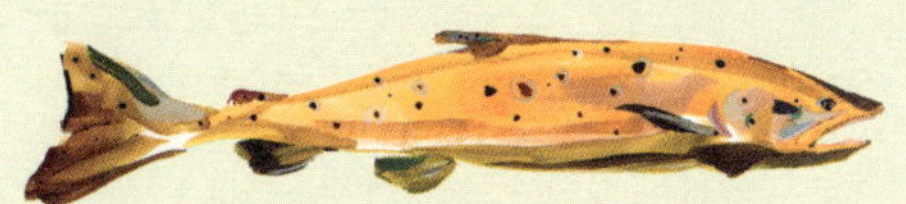

PART TWO: CATCH

THE NUTS AND BOLTS (AND FINS AND KNOTS) OF FLY FISHING.

4 MEET YOUR FISH

THAT'S THE WHOLE POINT of this, right? Meeting some fish? The following chapter is nearly all the fish you could—and hopefully will—meet on the water.

And truly—it's a lot of kinds of fish!

Take it from Tom Rosenbauer, the host of the *Orvis Fly Fishing Podcast*, star of innumerable how-to-fish videos, and, of course, the author of the *Orvis Fly-Fishing Guide*—the be-all and end-all textbook of fly fishing. (My copy is well-worn from continual reference over the years!)

It's not *all* about trout in fly fishing. Find a place close to home and fish for bass or panfish. You'll be able to get more practice, and the more you get in the water, the better you'll get. And you will have fun! You can even catch fish on a fly in the desert, in places like Scottsdale, Arizona.

TOM ROSENBAUER

FAVORITE WATERS: Small streams of Vermont, Henry's Fork and South Fork of the Snake, the Madison, any river in Chile I have ever fished, Cape Cod, the Bahamas, Cuba

FAVORITE FISH: Really, whatever I am fishing for at the time

FAVORITE FLY: I'm a fly tier, so I like to experiment with different flies and don't really have a favorite

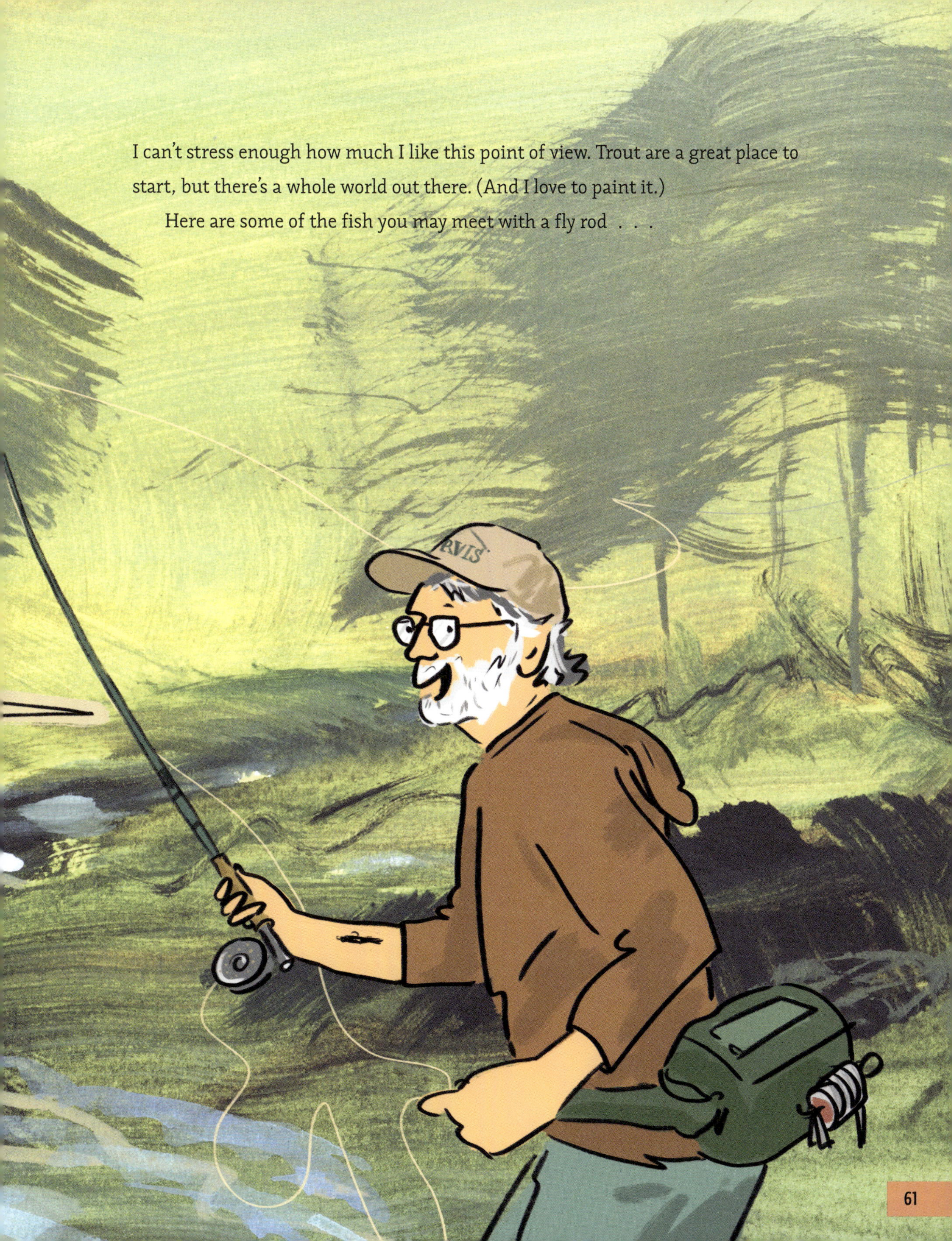

I can't stress enough how much I like this point of view. Trout are a great place to start, but there's a whole world out there. (And I love to paint it.)

Here are some of the fish you may meet with a fly rod . . .

BROOK TROUT

AKA Brookies, Squaretails

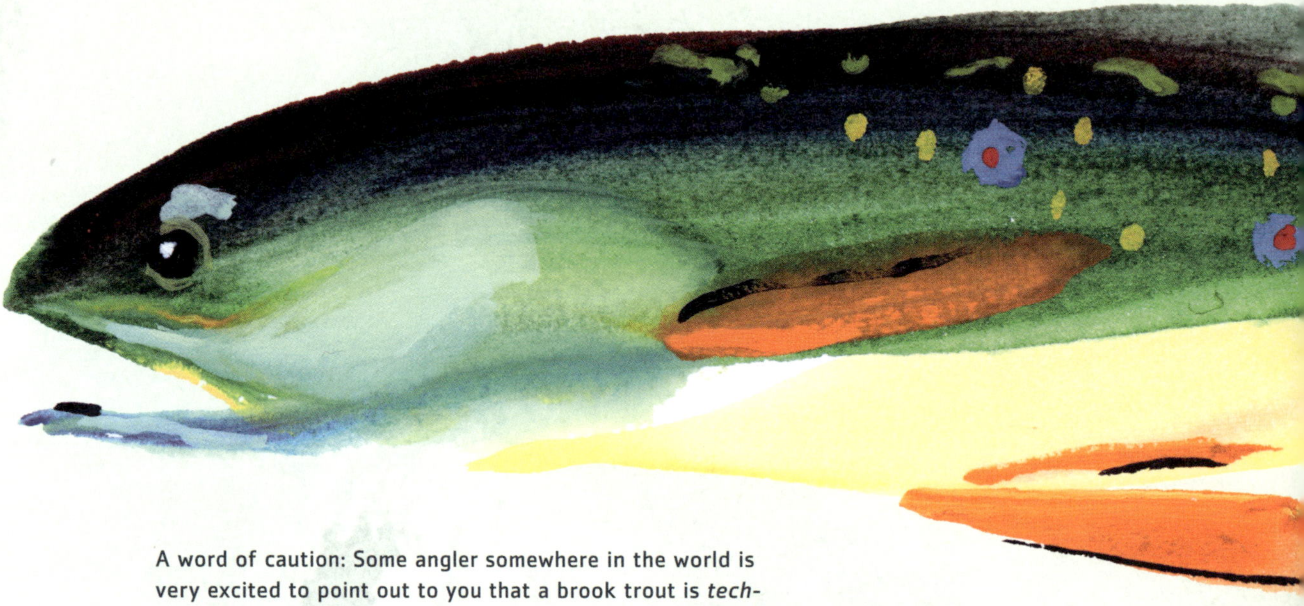

A word of caution: Some angler somewhere in the world is very excited to point out to you that a brook trout is *technically* a char, not a trout. Does this matter? Not really. Will we call brookies trout in this book anyway? Absolutely. That said, the char family is vast and stunning.

Here are two other fish from the char family:

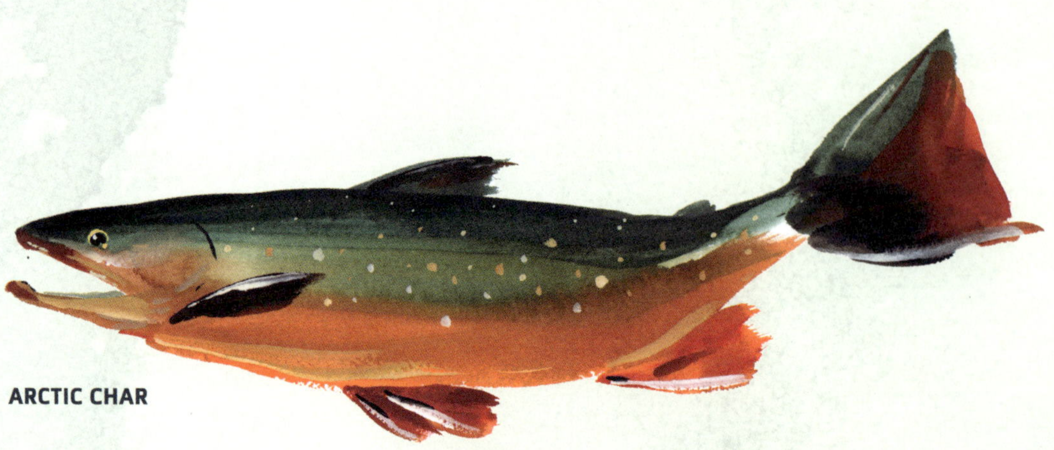

ARCTIC CHAR

My favorite. To fish, to paint, to just watch holding water in a mountain pool. Besides looking stunning—they seem straight out of a coral reef! Ounce for ounce, brookies are simply ferocious. I've seen a four-inch fish go after a three-inch fly. I've seen ones so stuffed with food, their bellies jut out like an emerging second head. I've watched them try to impossibly jump my local twenty-foot waterfall.

They're forgiving too. Did a brookie miss your fly? Try again! It will.

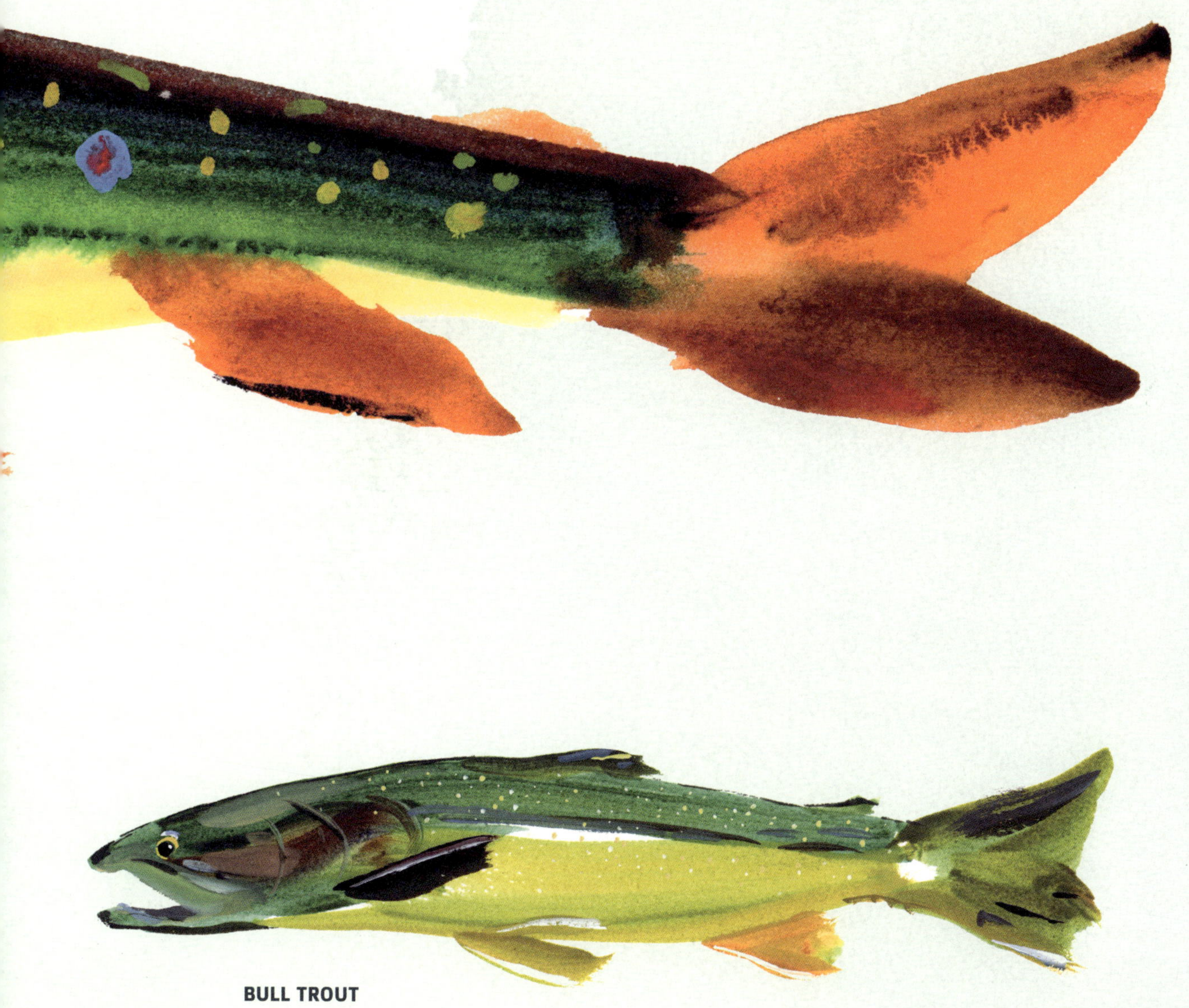

BULL TROUT

BROWN TROUT

AKA Browns, Brownies

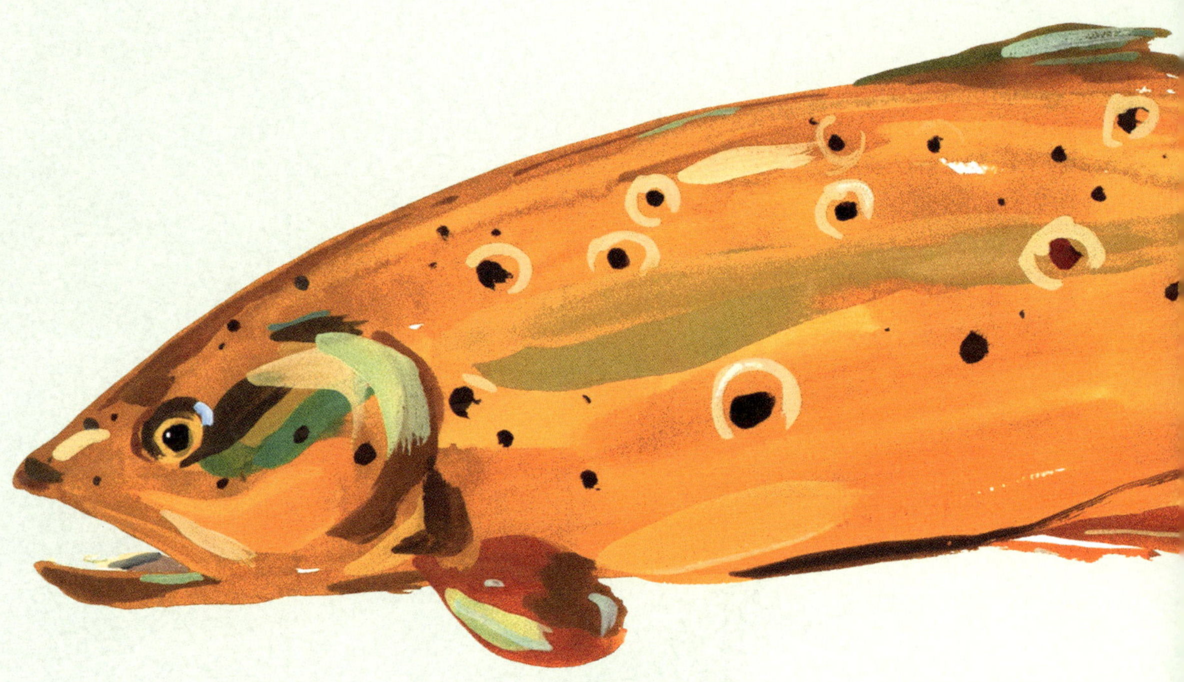

When a brown trout meets a brook trout, they usually eat it. But the other way around, love can be in the air. Very rarely, brook trout will fertilize brown trout eggs, creating a whole other kind of fish: the tiger trout.

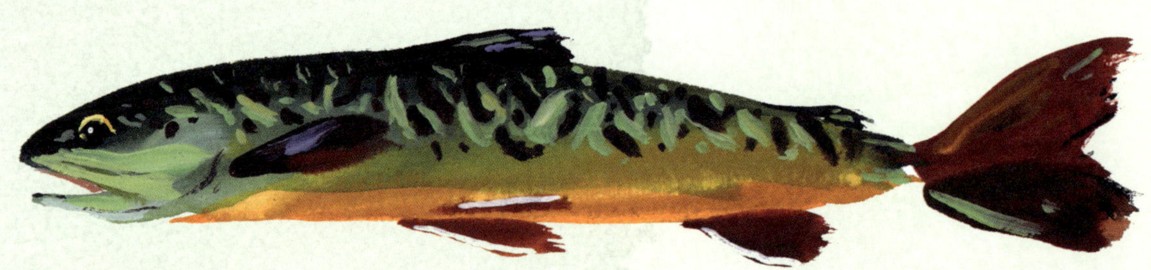

Brookies may be my favorite, but for most fly fishers, it's browns. Modern fly fishing has more or less evolved as a way to trick brown trout into taking a fly. Why? They're smart! They're stealthy. They put up a good fight too. Stocked hatchery browns are beige in every sense of the word. But a healthy wild brown will have a buttery yellow color. And fine, I'll admit it. They make for a worthy adversary. They're fun to paint too.

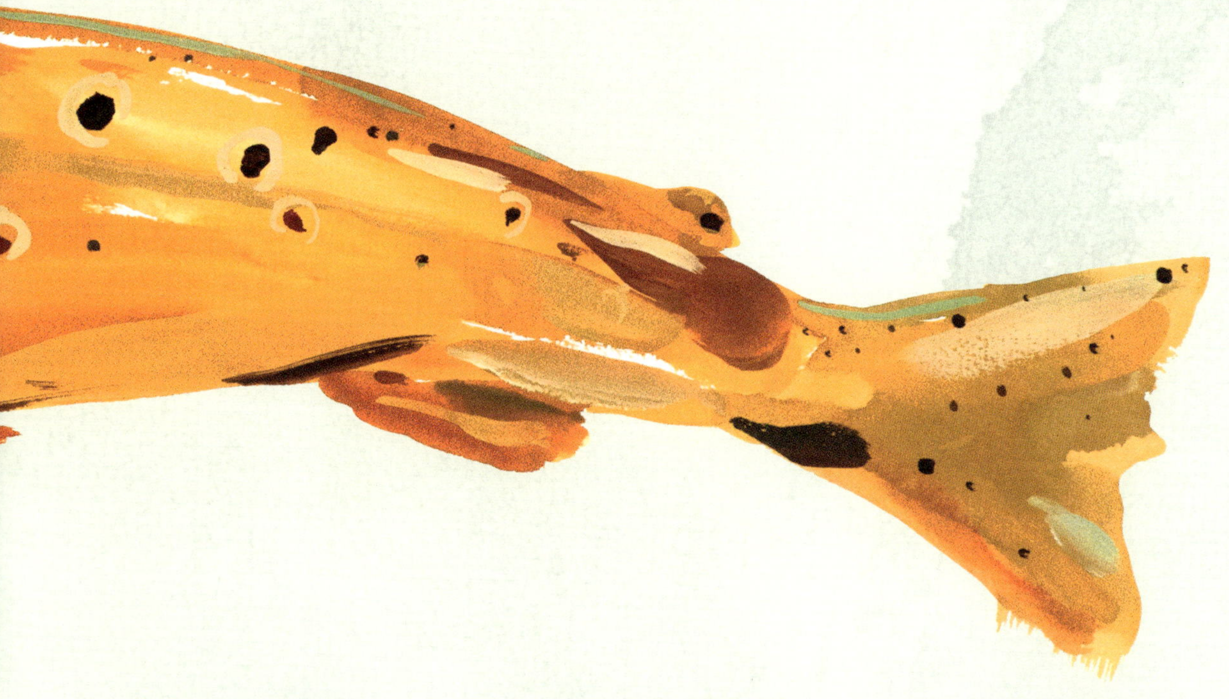

Brown trout in Europe go by many names—my favorite is in Germany where they're called "backforelle" . . . which translates to brook trout. Confused yet? This is a brown from Southern Europe, sometimes called **MEDITERRANEAN TROUT**. They're generally smaller and require some very subtle casting.

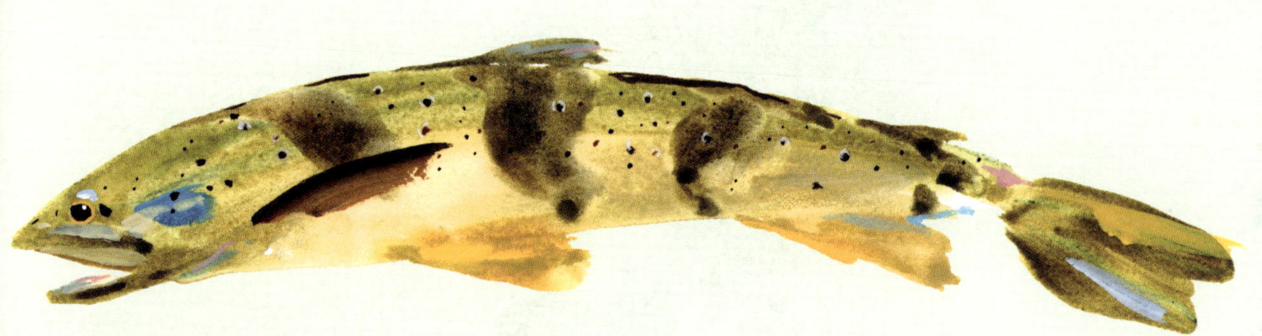

RAINBOW TROUT

AKA Bows

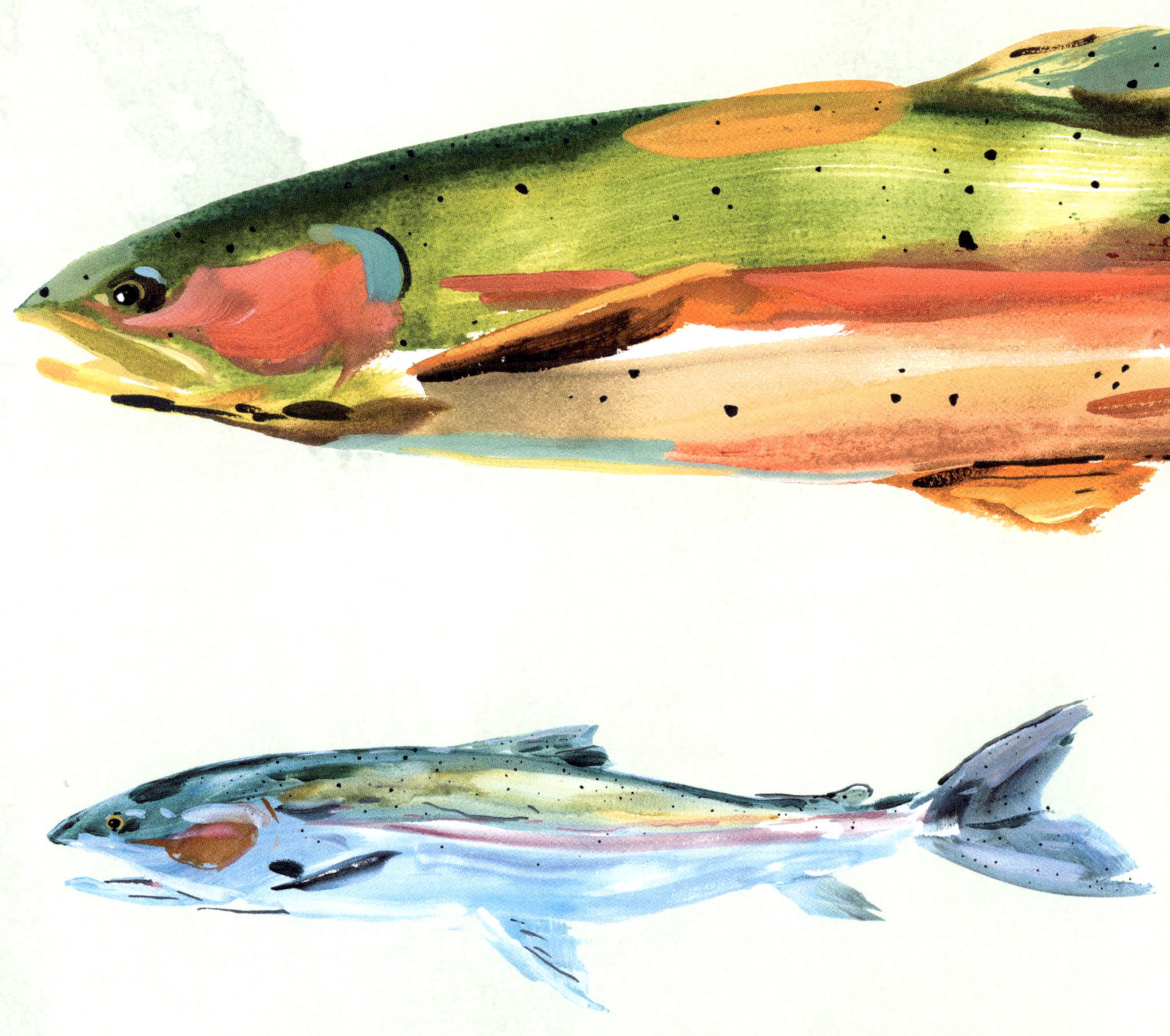

"Anadromous" fish spend some of their life in the ocean and some in freshwater, where they come to spawn. All the trout I've introduced so far can act like this or live exclusively in freshwater. When rainbows run back and forth from the ocean to freshwater, they transform into something massive called a **STEELHEAD**.

Meet the acrobats of the trout world. More than any other fish, bows will leap out of the water as soon as they're hooked. It all makes for a very dramatic netting experience and even more dramatic when you take a closer look. (They're called rainbow trout for a reason.) Partially because of their high energy, bows generally like faster moving water with higher oxygen levels. So never overlook riffles and rapids when rainbows are in a stream!

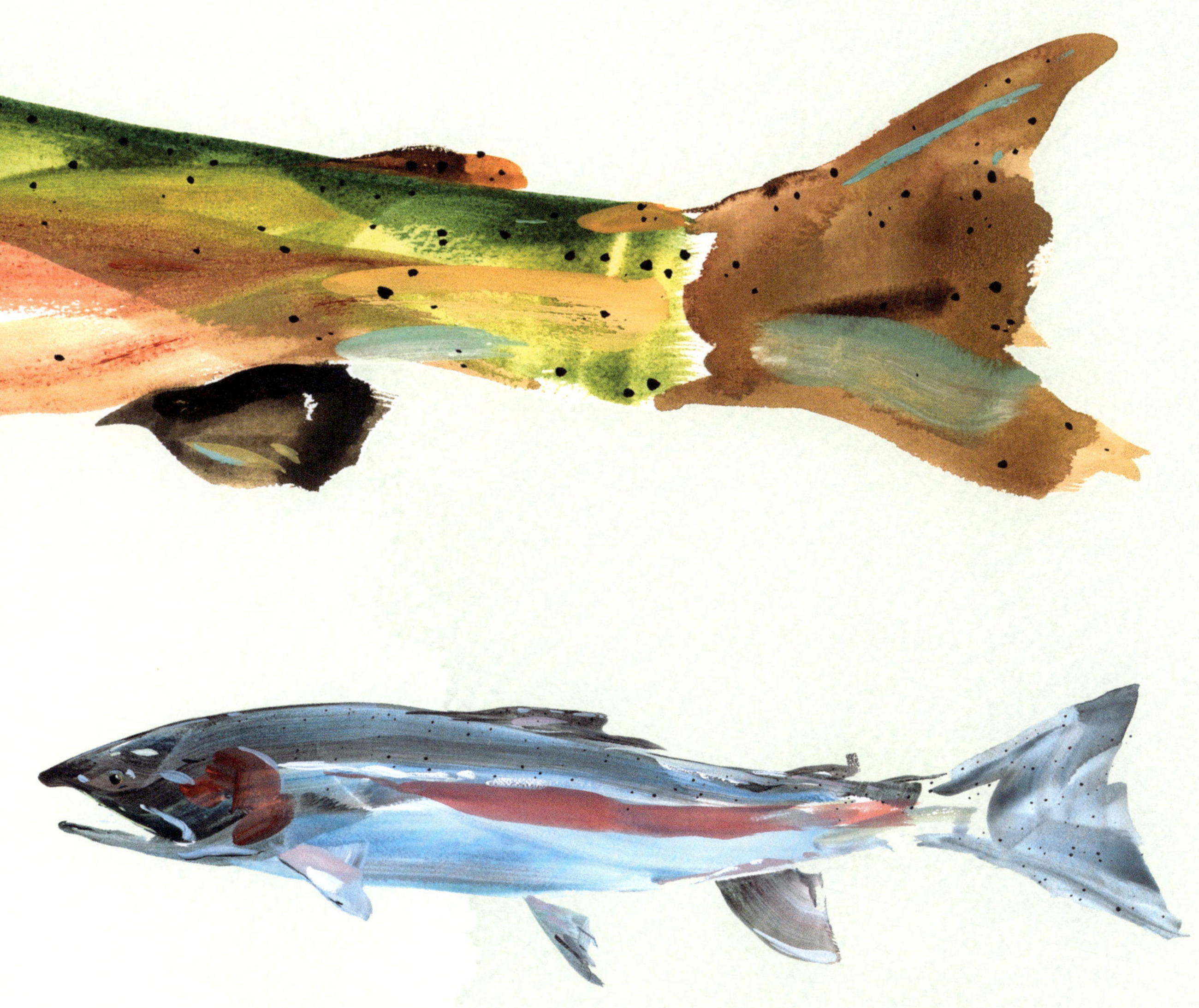

People argue a lot in the fishing world—especially about steelhead. This is a **GREAT LAKES STEELHEAD**, which runs from Lake Erie to the Pulaski River. Because it never reaches a saltwater ocean, some purists don't call it a steelhead. But it's the same basic idea. It's also similarly ENORMOUS!

CUTTHROAT TROUT

AKA Cutties

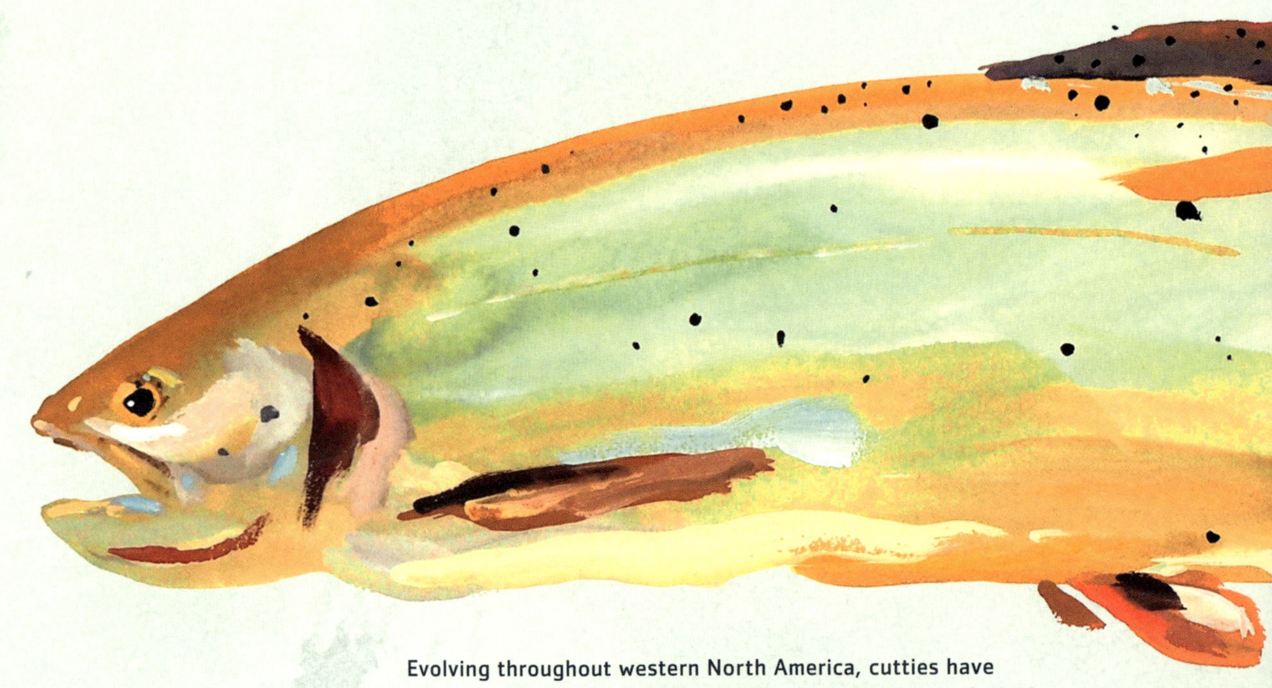

Evolving throughout western North America, cutties have specialized into plenty of distinct subspecies—many of which are either threatened or endangered. Here are a few of them:

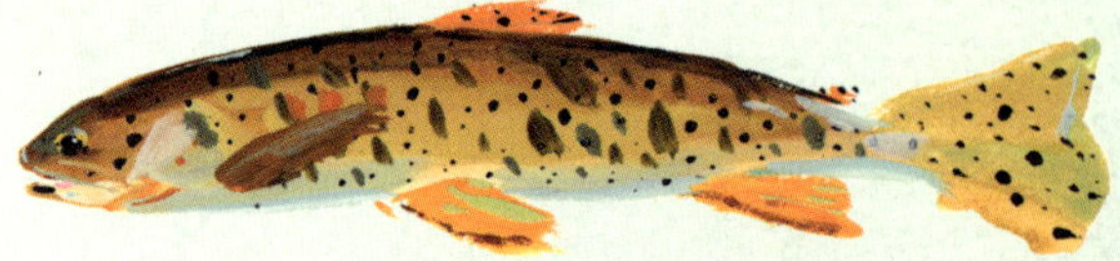

GREENBACK

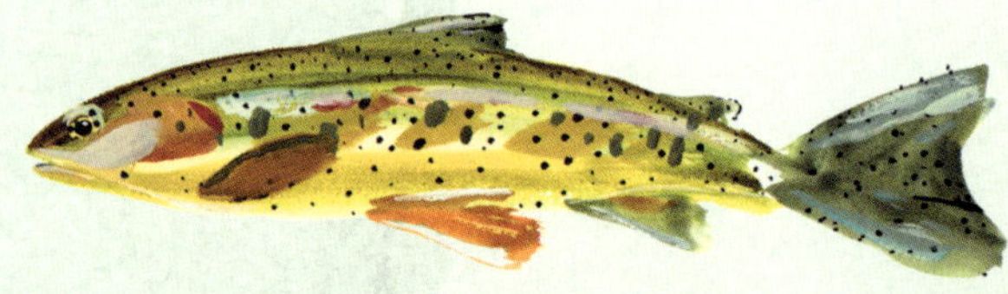

GILA

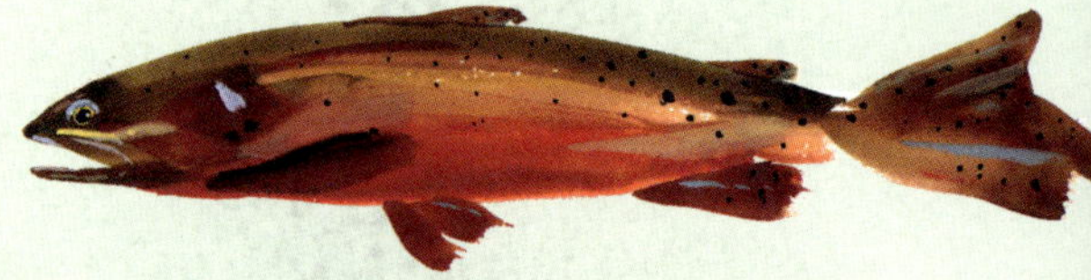

COLORADO RIVER

I like to think of these as the brookies of the West. They're a native trout population west of the Rocky Mountains, not too picky when it comes to flies, and are currently fighting for their lives while being crowded out by browns, rainbows (which are their cousins), and even transplanted brookies. None of this is why they're called "cutthroat," though. For that, look to the red mark they naturally have under their jaw.

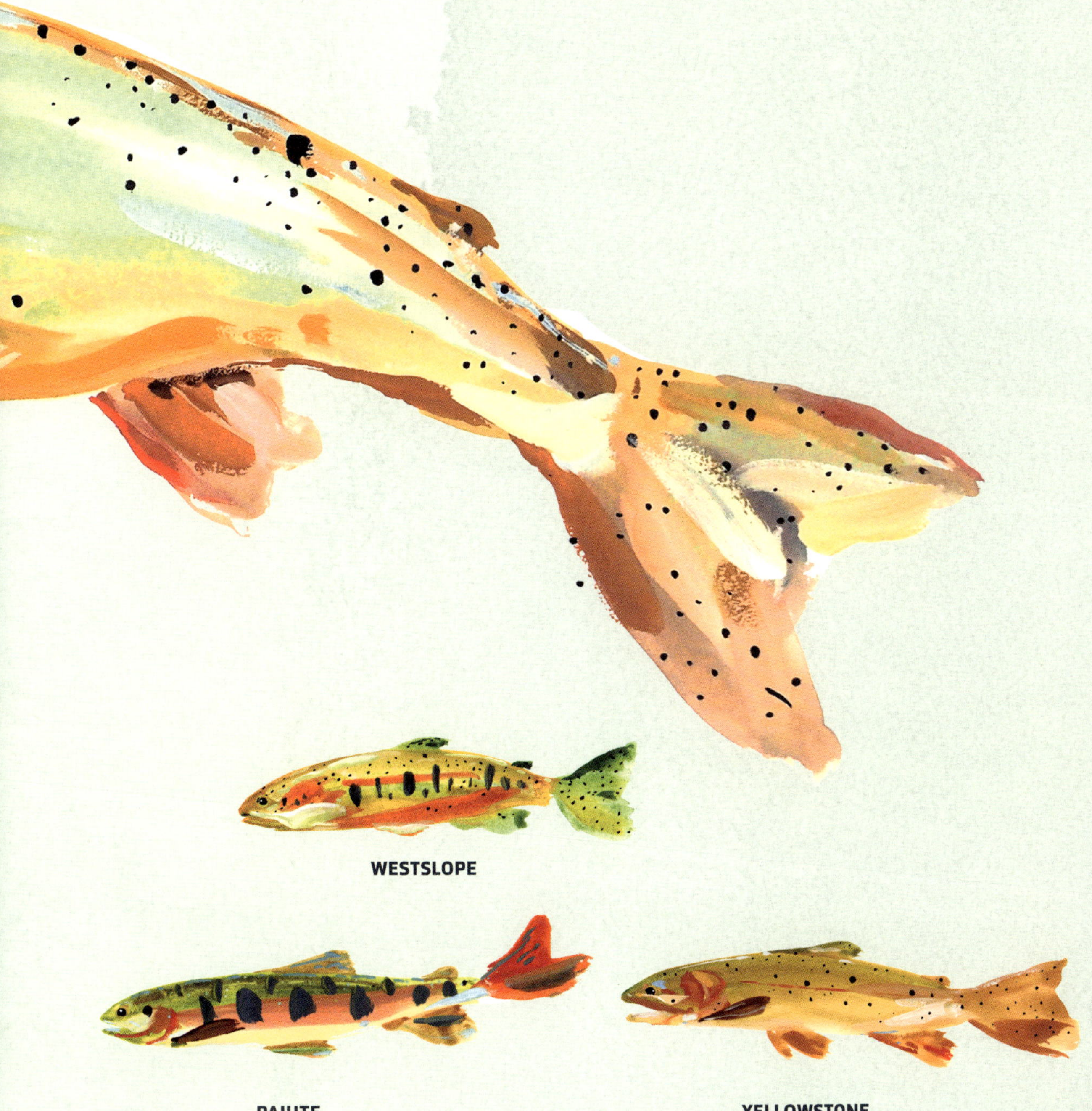

Now let's head toward the coast and meet . . .

ATLANTIC SALMON

AKA the King of Fish!

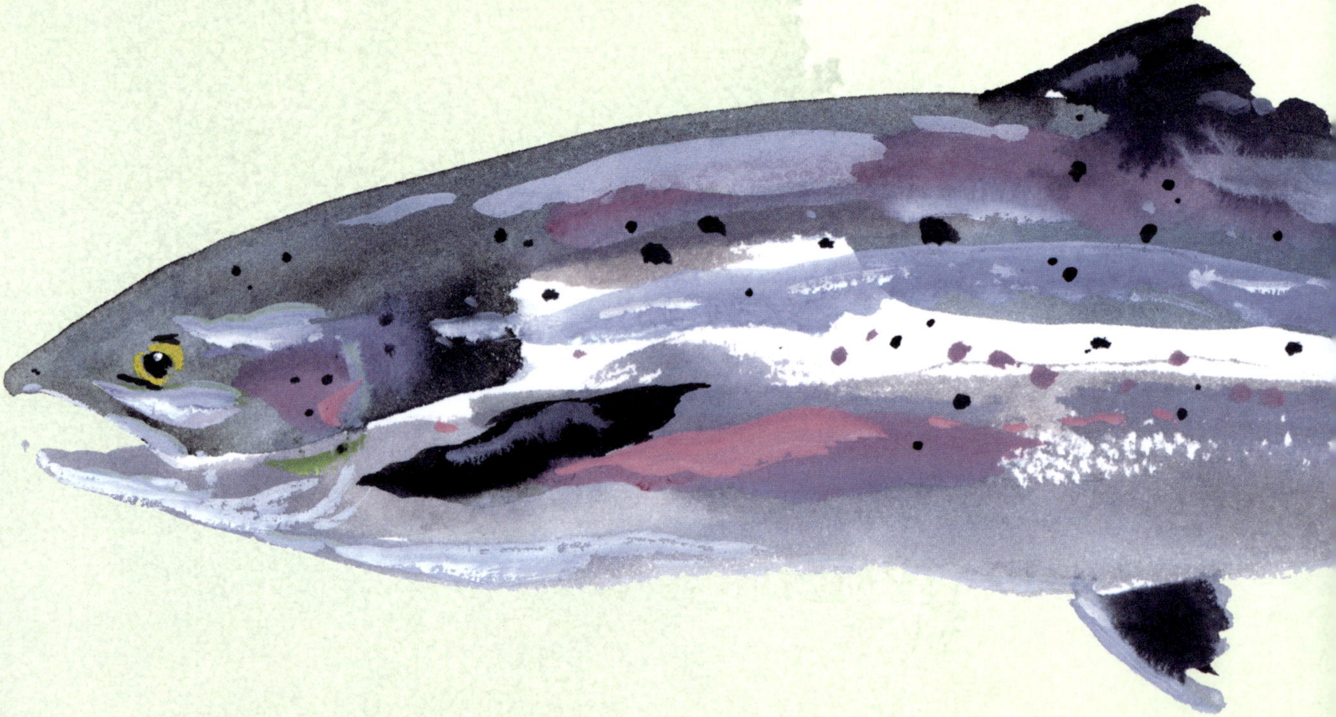

Lox more salmon! **LANDLOCKED SALMON** are nearly identical to their ocean relatives. But, thanks to behavioral changes and/or post-Ice Age geography, they live in freshwater. Young landlocked salmon are often confused for browns. The key differences are the forked tail and the slightly different jawline.

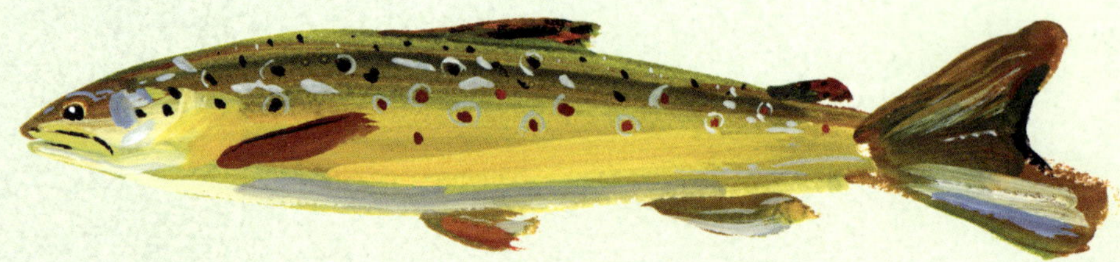

You many have noticed a lot of these species exist on a bit of a spectrum. From cutties to rainbows to brookies making babies with browns, hard edges aren't always easy to find. (Welcome to genetics!) Salmon are a great example of this. Atlantic salmon and brown trout are related fish that have evolved to live differently in the ocean and freshwater. So while (most) browns live exclusively in freshwater, salmon live the majority of their lives in the ocean and return to freshwater to spawn. This is when you fly fish for them, and, considering that they're mainly looking to "get some" versus have a bite, it's not easy.

Still, this is exactly what keeps anglers coming back for more!

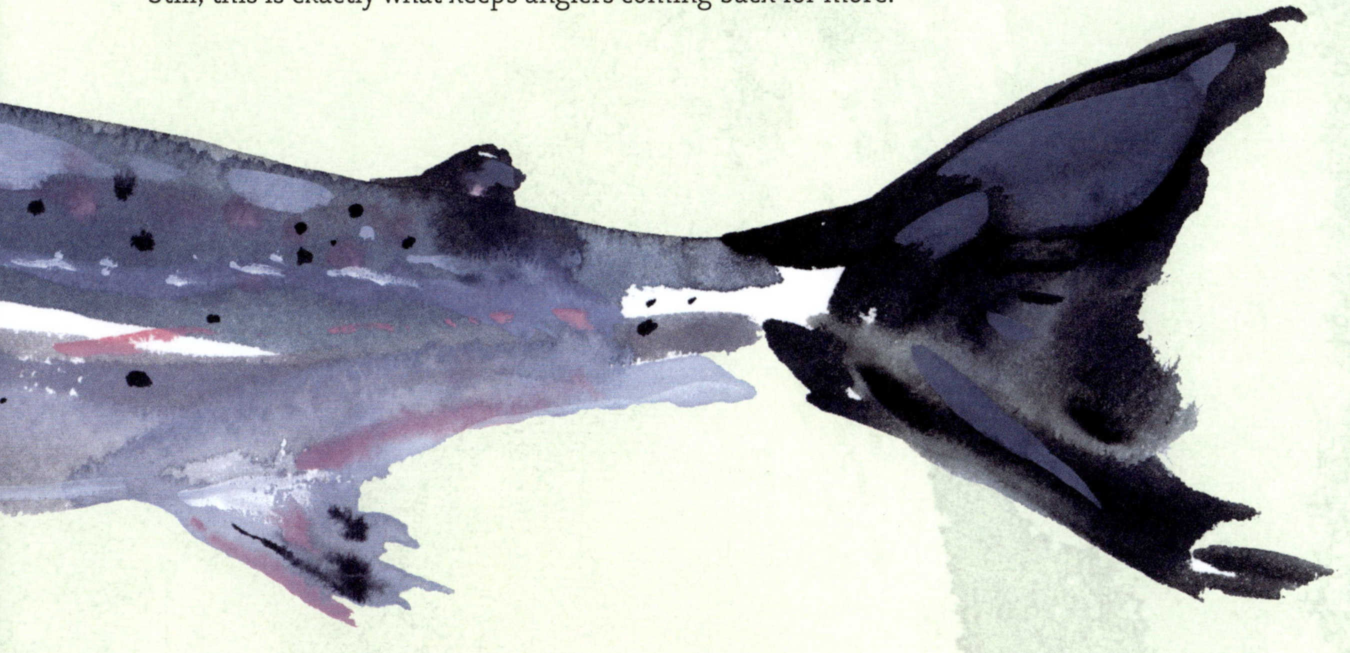

So how do you convince a salmon looking for love to eat? Historically, the idea was to put the most ridiculous combination of exotic feathers together. (For the British, this meant plundering* the world's birds.) Next, attach a hook. Finally, put it in front of the fish and hope it's so moved, it takes a bite.

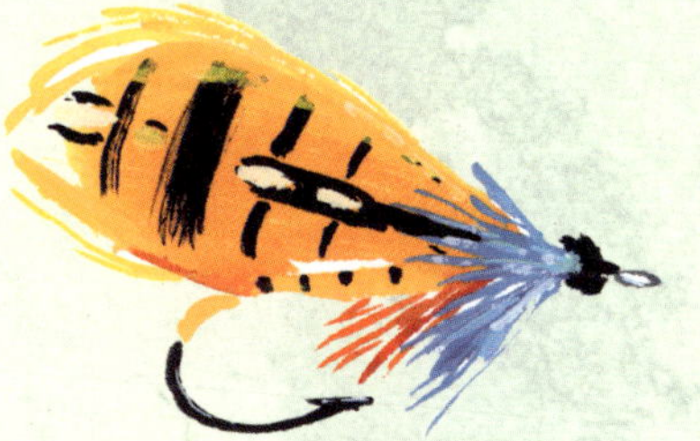

DURHAM RANGER

*For more about this plundering, old and new, I highly recommend *The Feather Thief* by Kirk Wallace Johnson.

PACIFIC SALMON

In the north Pacific, there's a similar Atlantic salmon/brown trout dynamic, but this time, it's with rainbows and cutthroats. Their oceangoing relatives make up the wide (and colorful!) family of Pacific salmon. Here are the main groups:

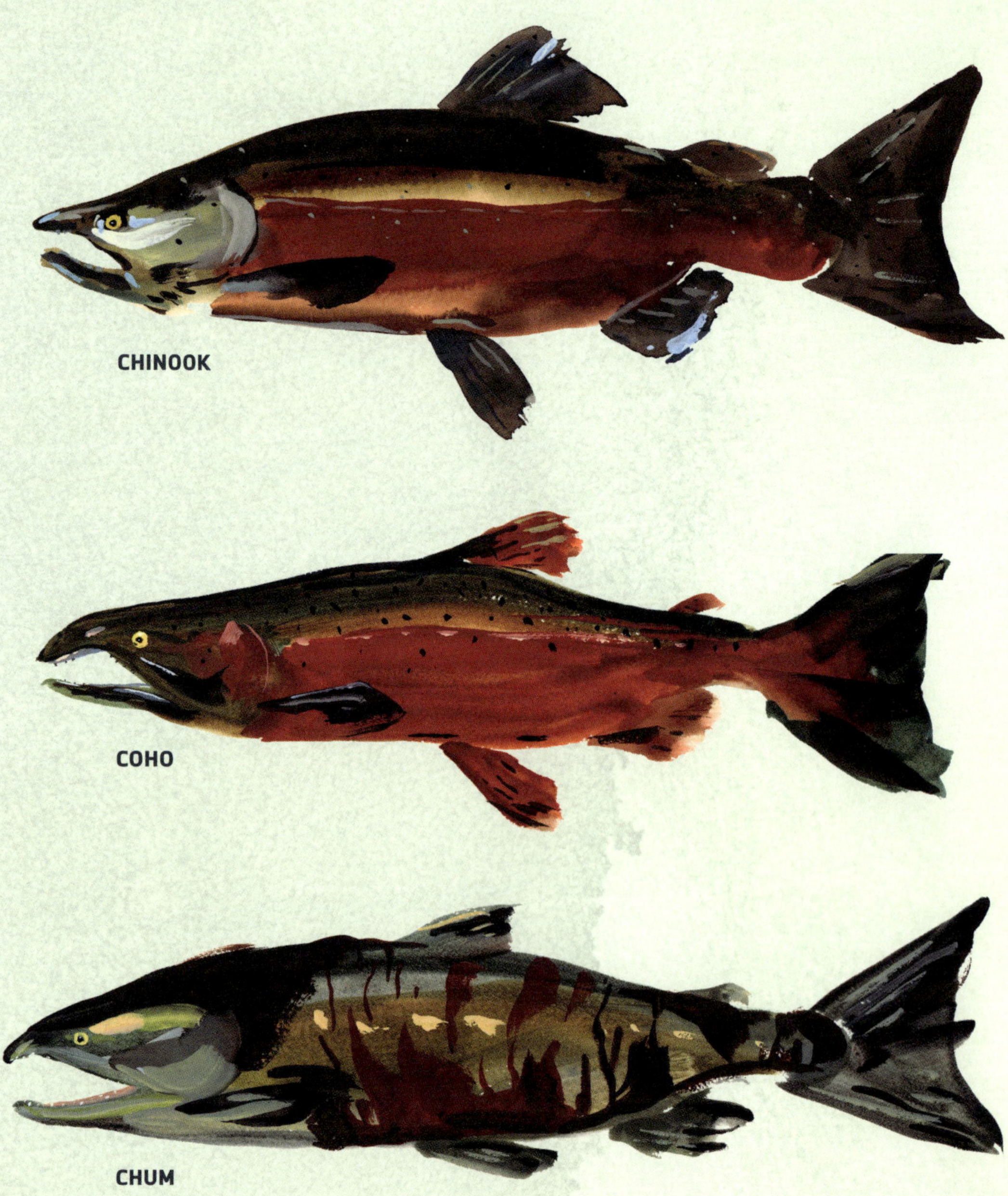

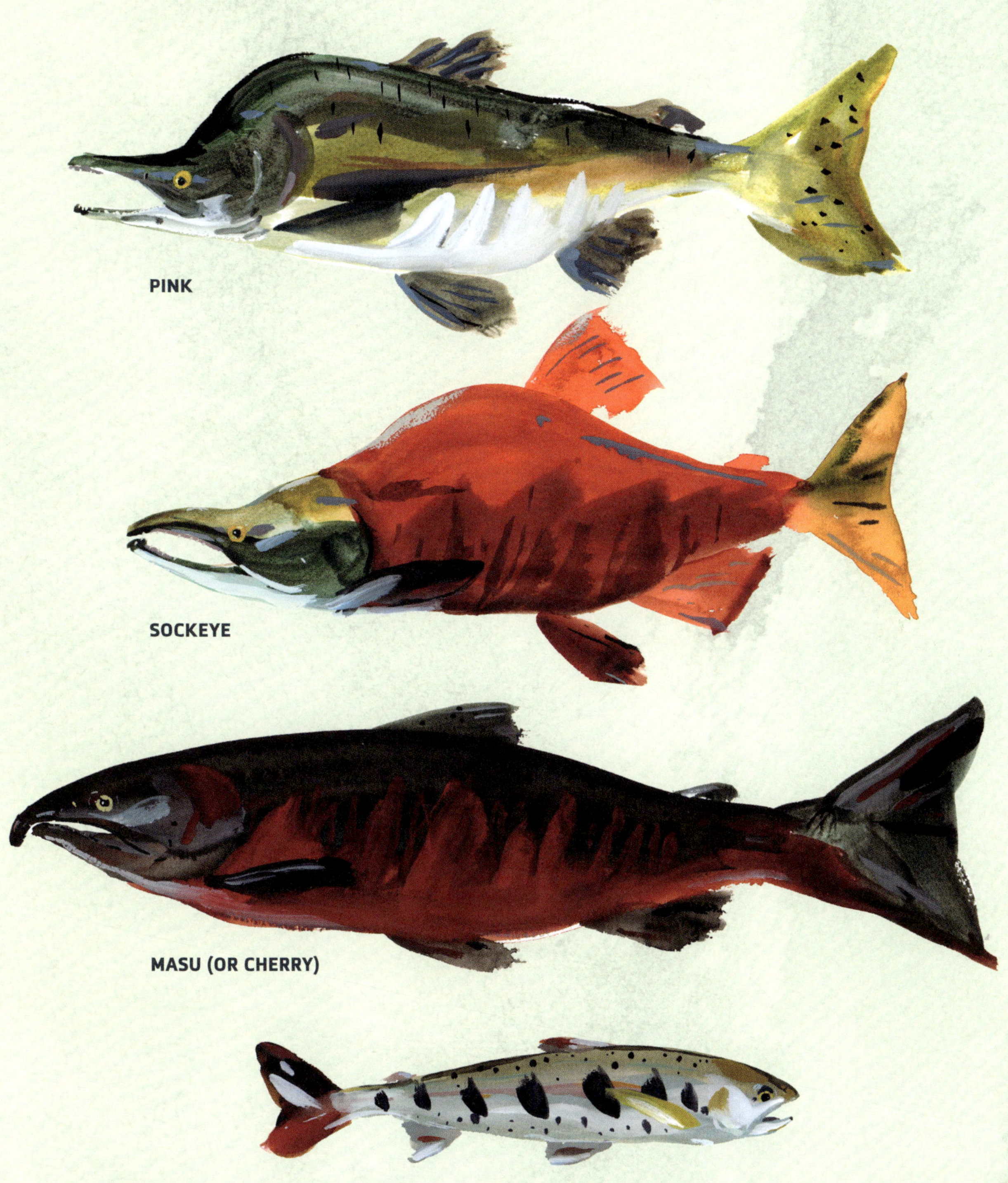

MASU SALMON are found in the waters around Northeast Asia. Their freshwater relatives, **YAMAME TROUT** (from page 41), are famous in Japan where people often fly fish for them tenkara-style.

Brook, brown, rainbow, and cutthroat trout (plus salmon) are probably the most famous in terms of fly fishing, but as the rest of this chapter will show you, THERE ARE A LOT OF FISH IN THE SEAS/LAKES/RIVERS/PRETTY MUCH ANYTHING WET. Here are some of trout's long-lost cousins:

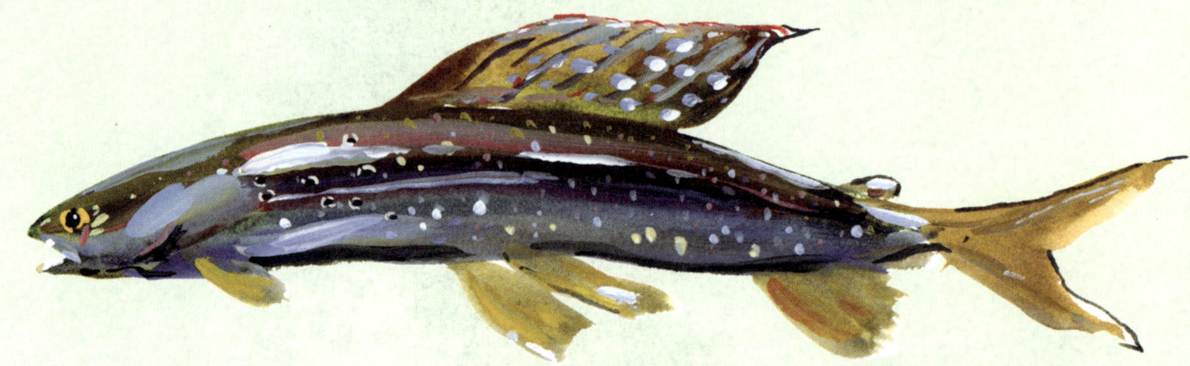

THE COLDEST: ARCTIC GRAYLING. Come for the outrageous dorsal fin, stay for hungry bites.

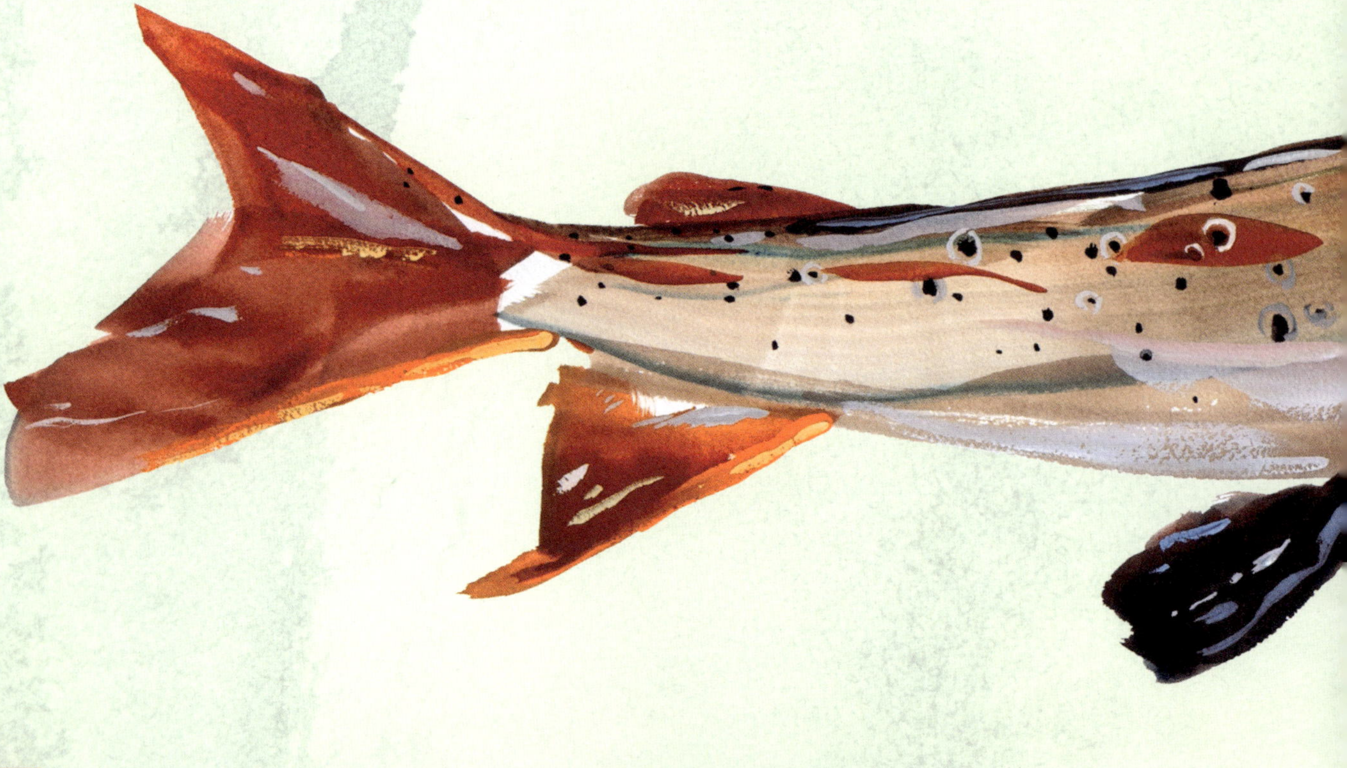

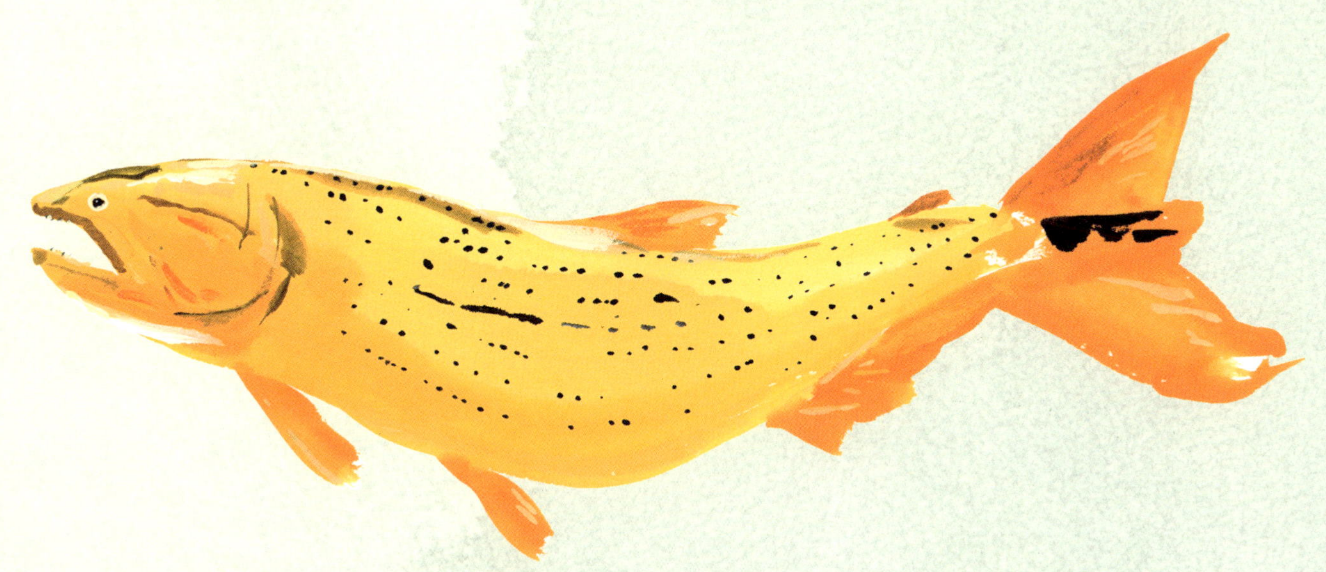

THE FANCIEST: GOLDEN DORADO. They're not trout or char, but they are golden—and POWERFUL! These are native to South America and have teeth so sharp you need to fish with a special wire tippet.

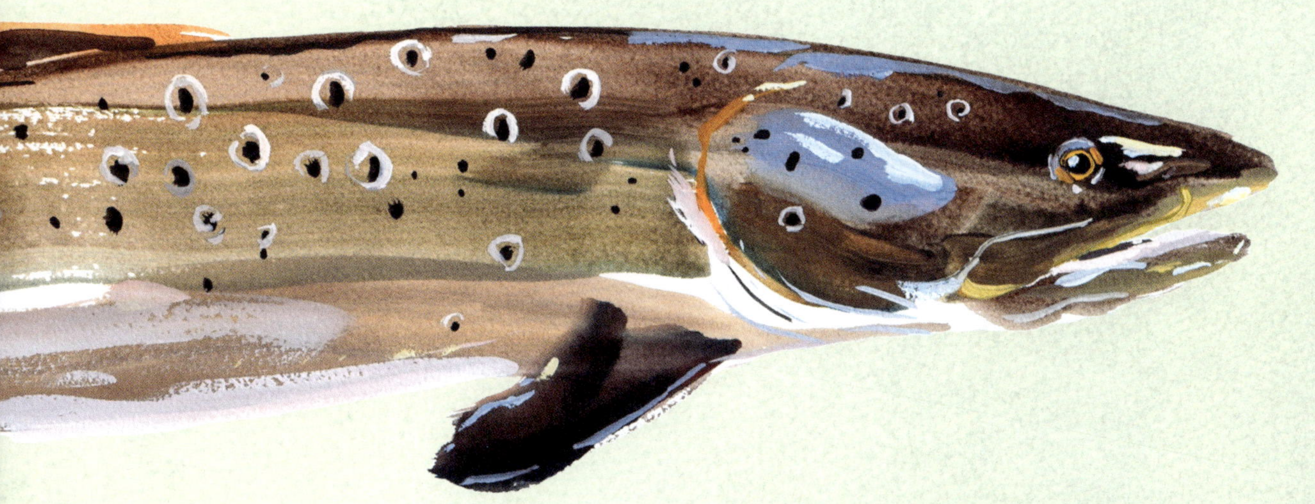

THE BIGGEST: SIBERIAN TAIMEN. For most people, this is a fish found only via several long connecting flights to somewhere like Mongolia. Is it worth it? Depends on whether you like hooking something as tall as you! (That said, their nearly-as-large cousins, called "huchen," can also be found in Europe.)

TROUT AND CHAR NEIGHBORS . . .

And, look, just because you're fishing for trout doesn't mean you'll always catch one. These fish share the water with trout. They generally live lower in the water column and feed on smaller bugs. They're also, well . . . not known for their looks.

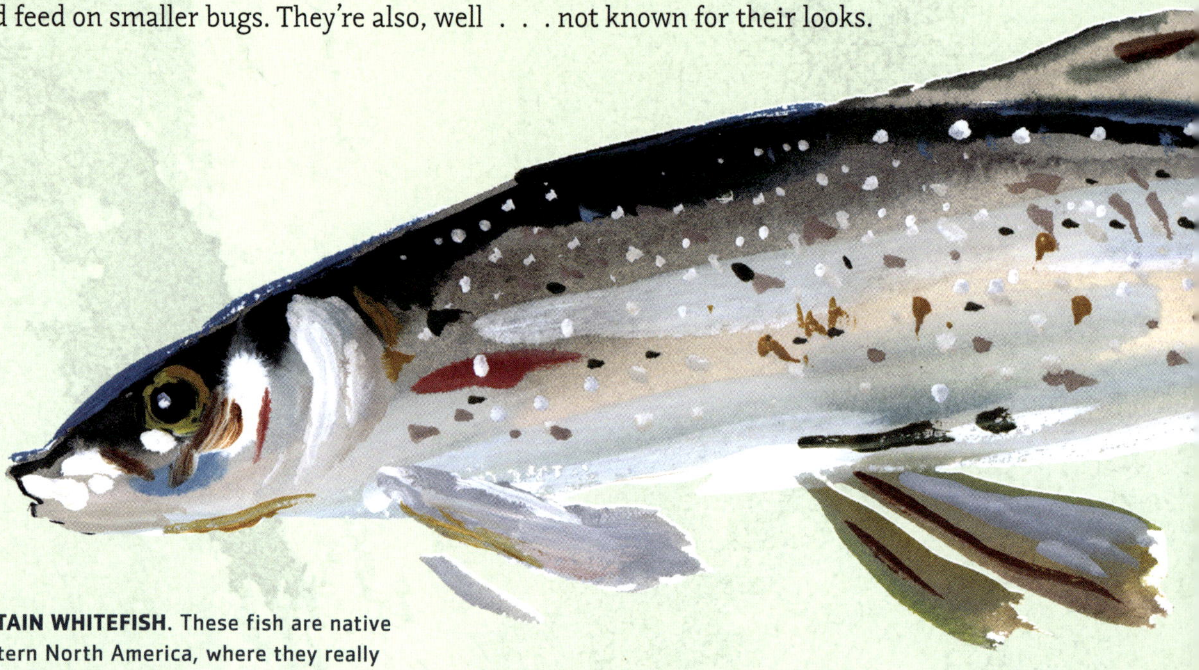

MOUNTAIN WHITEFISH. These fish are native to western North America, where they really get a bad rap. They even put up a good fight sometimes! And as someone who especially loves smoked whitefish (often made from their cousins "lake whitefish") on a bagel, I have to appreciate seeing these in the wild.

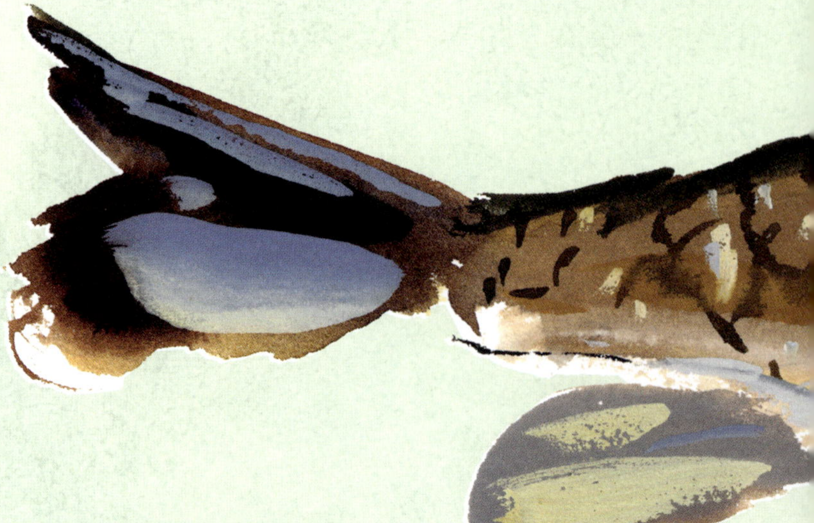

. . . YOU MIGHT MEET BY ACCIDENT.

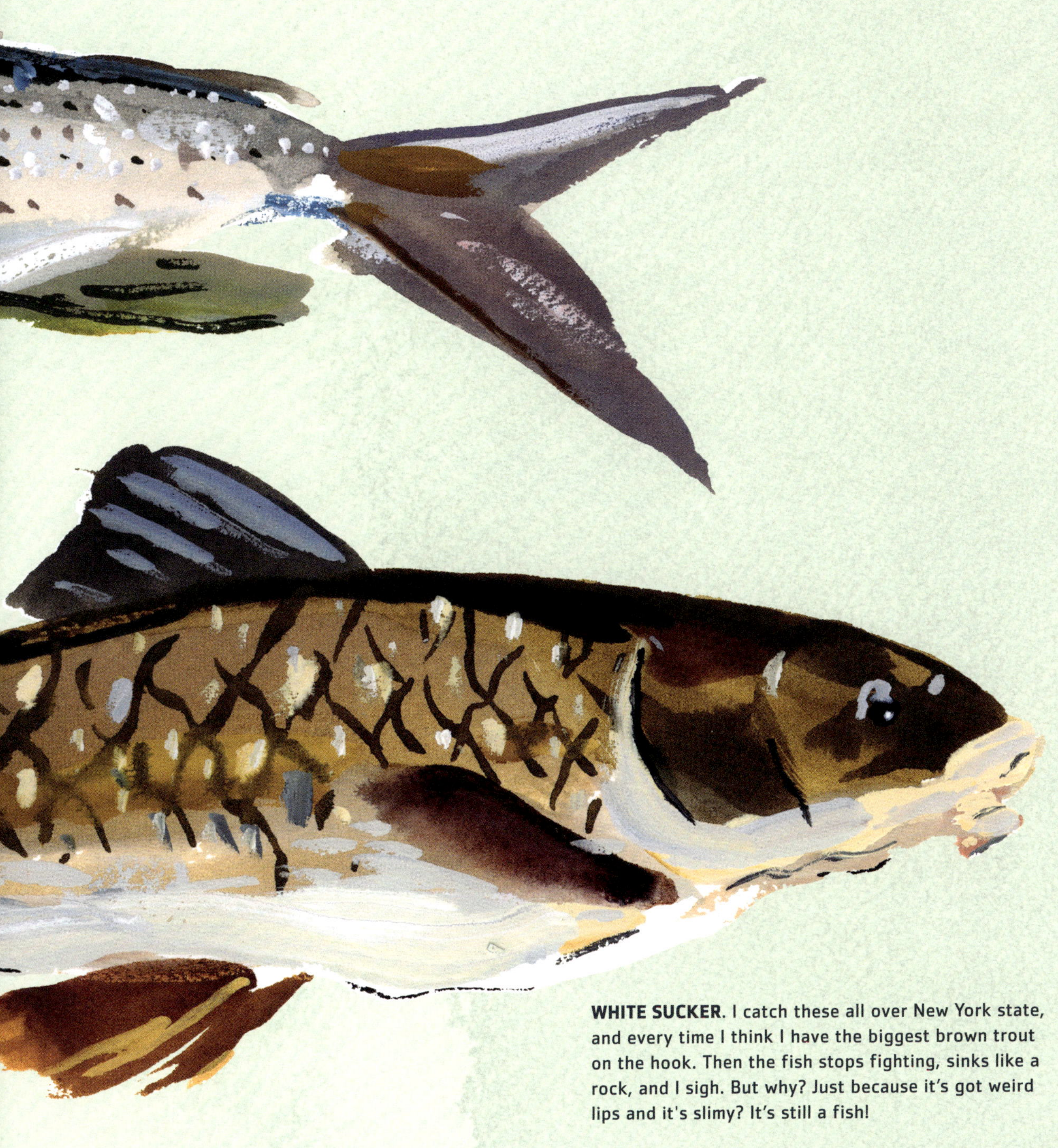

WHITE SUCKER. I catch these all over New York state, and every time I think I have the biggest brown trout on the hook. Then the fish stops fighting, sinks like a rock, and I sigh. But why? Just because it's got weird lips and it's slimy? It's still a fish!

CARP! (IT'S COMPLICATED.)

I'm haunted by many elements of Peter Heller's dystopian novel *The Dog Stars*. But I'm probably most scarred by the angler-protagonist coming to terms with fly fishing for carp—instead of trout—in his warmed-up future. That said, while carp are an increasingly troublesome invasive species who do everything from gobble up plankton to endanger boaters, leave it to Heller to make fishing for them sound somehow romantic. And fun! I've come to terms with fishing for carp and now love it. Give it a go!

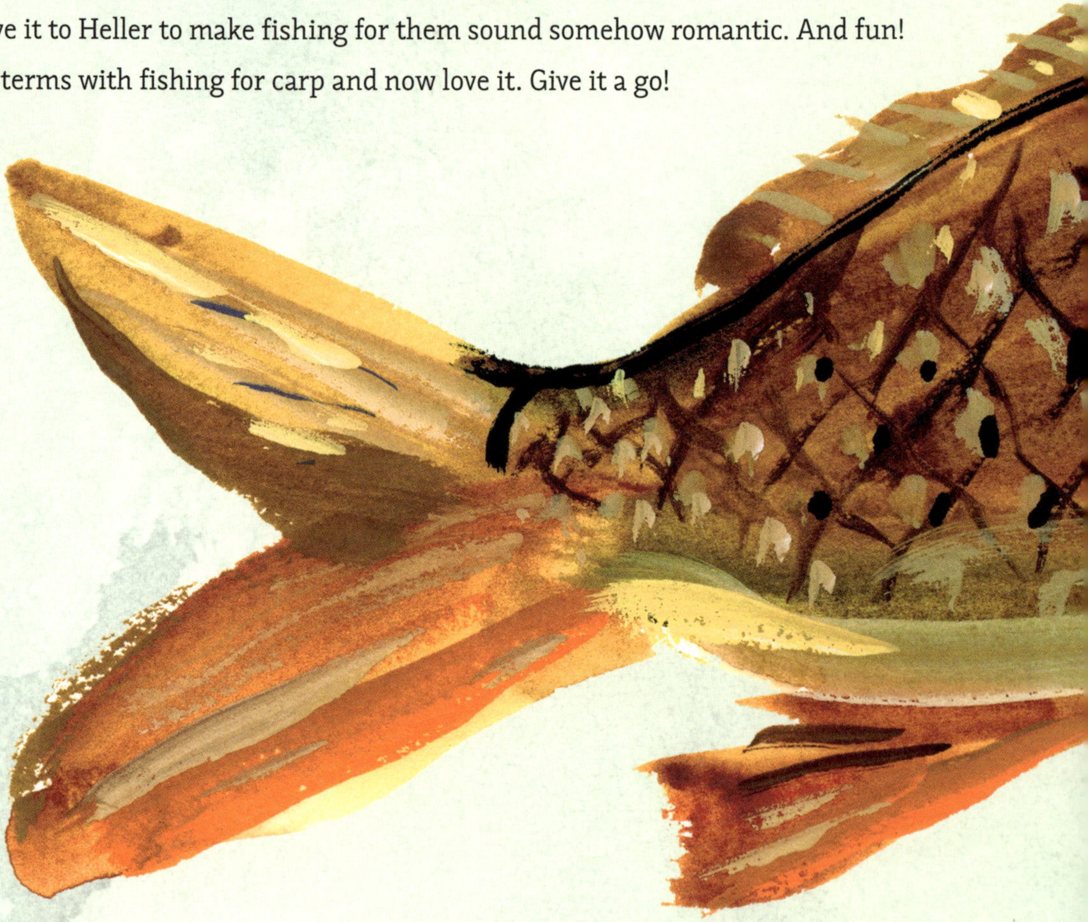

Not to scare the carp out of you, but these other species are causing a lot of trouble in North American waterways . . .

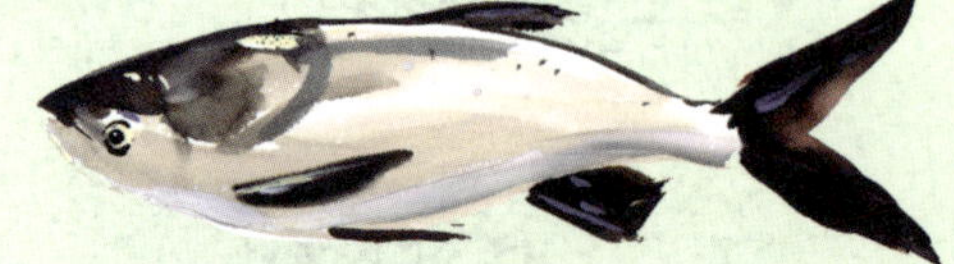

SILVER CARP. Infamous for jumping out of the water and injuring boaters.

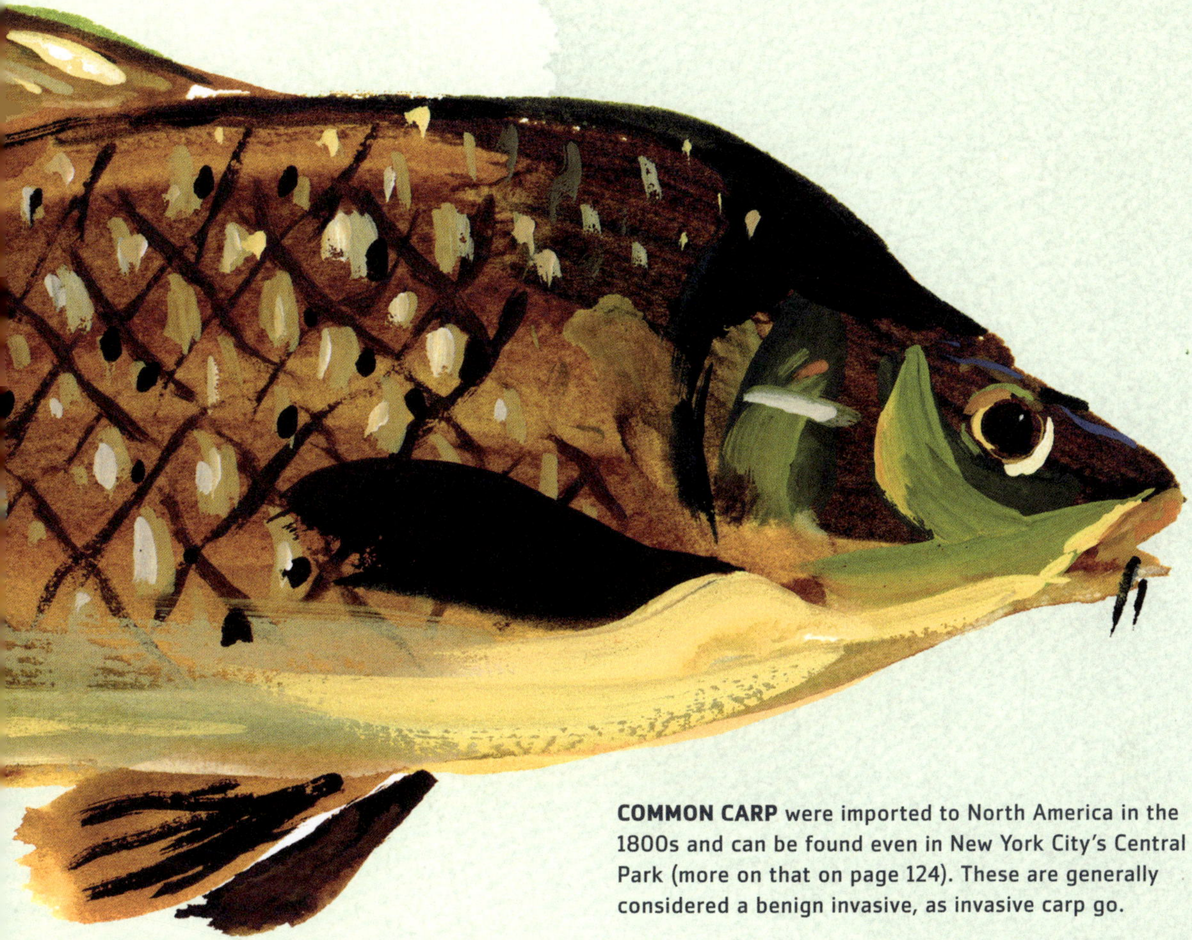

COMMON CARP were imported to North America in the 1800s and can be found even in New York City's Central Park (more on that on page 124). These are generally considered a benign invasive, as invasive carp go.

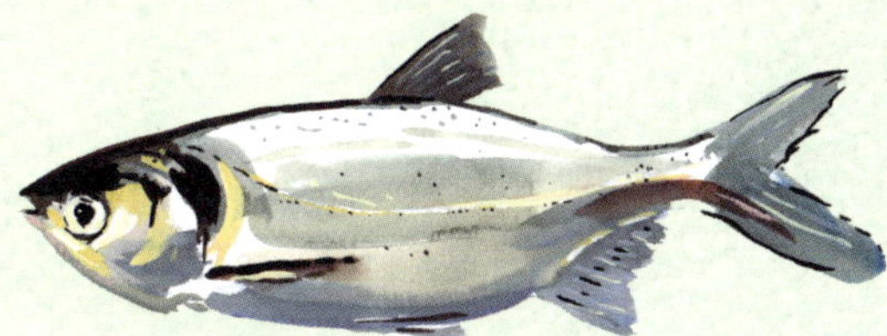

BIGHEAD CARP. Infamous for that creepy low-set eyeball on a big head.

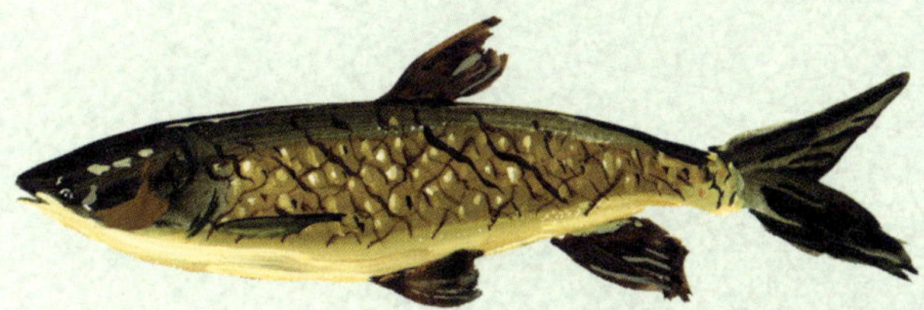

GRASS CARP. Just plain old infamous.

BASS. THE FUTURE?

What other fish am I simultaneously haunted and intrigued by? Bass! Smallmouth bass have been creeping up my home stream for decades and threaten to gobble up our trout population in the Catskills. This is not good!

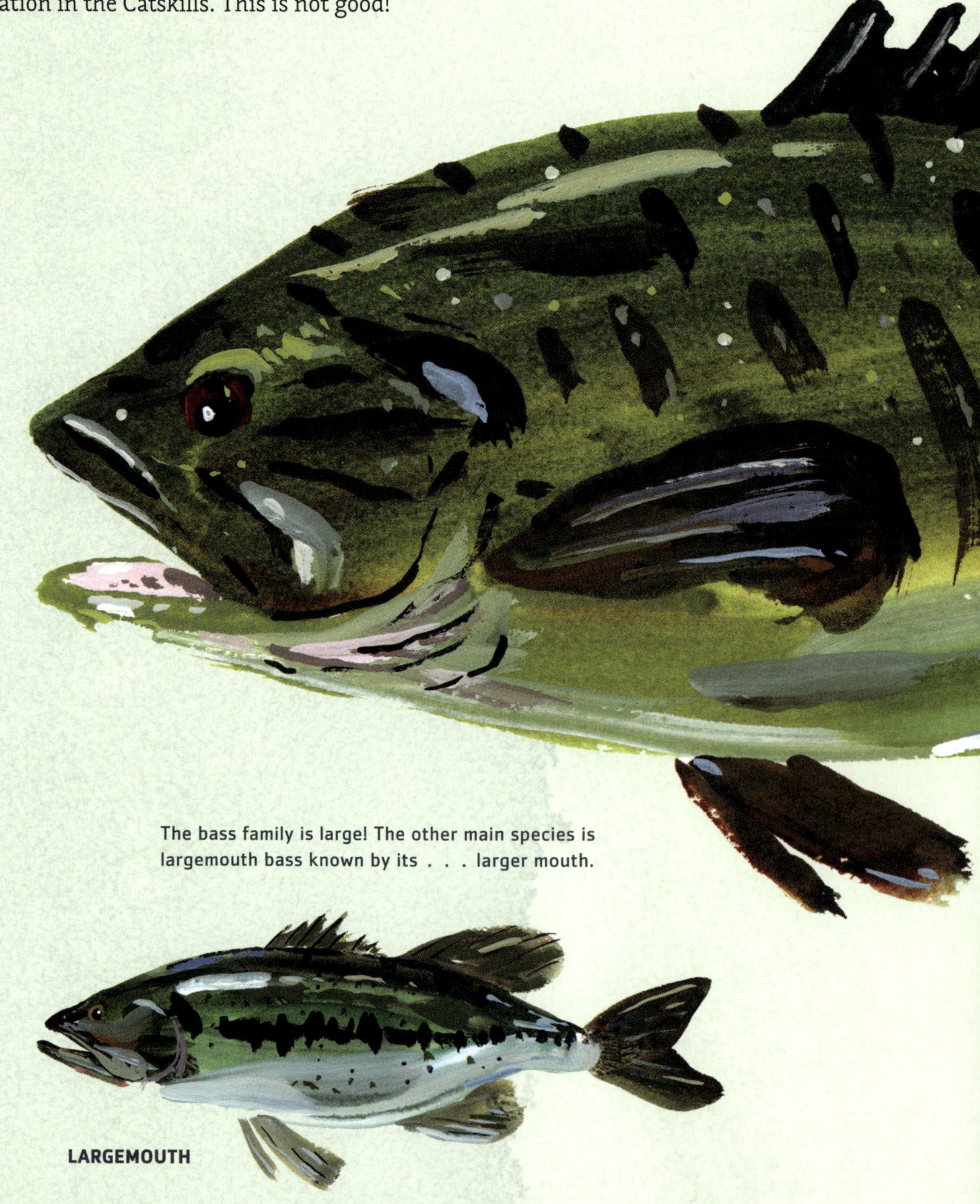

The bass family is large! The other main species is largemouth bass known by its . . . larger mouth.

Still, if you asked ALL anglers in the USA—as in, not just the fly fishers—to pick their favorite fish, it'd likely be bass. Why? They're fun to catch, kinda everywhere, and, like carp, important to think about targeting when it's warmer.

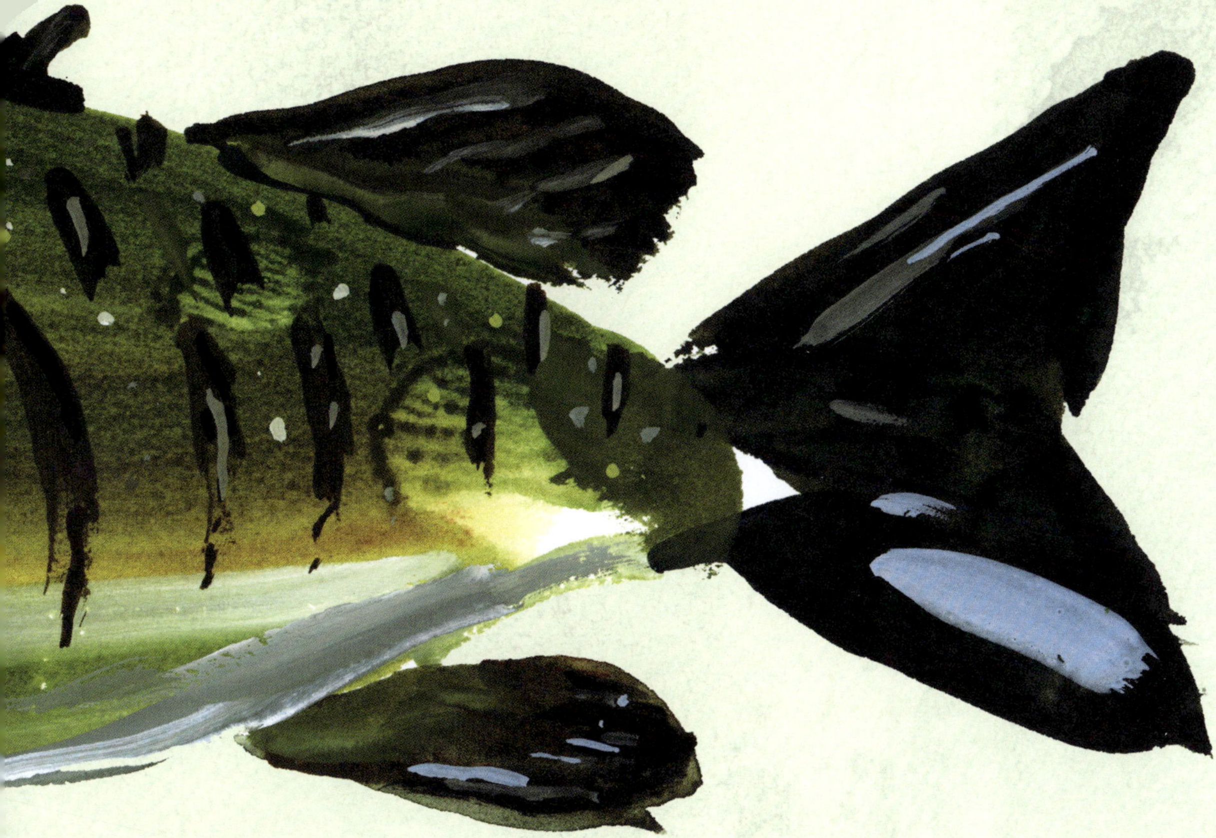

Guadalupe are a smaller subspecies you can find only in Texas. I recommend fishing for them after a morning of delicious breakfast tacos.

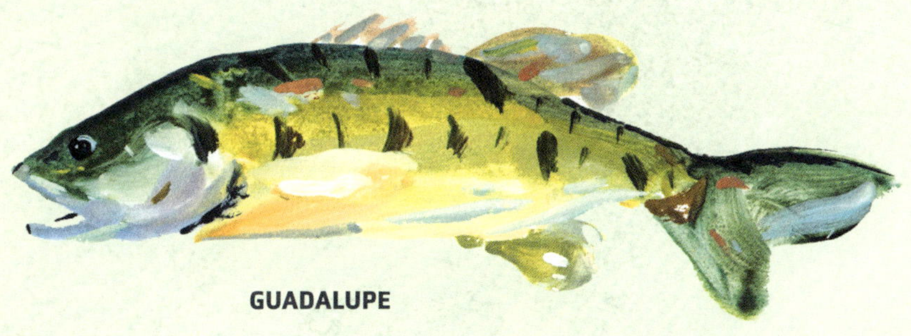

GUADALUPE

THE FISH OF TEN THOUSAND CASTS

Every muskie angler I know has the same thing in common: They are obsessed. This can express itself in driving long distances for incredibly low-odds fishing opportunities, talking about muskies at length whenever possible, or maybe doing something like casting ten thousand times for the same fish. (Hence the moniker.)

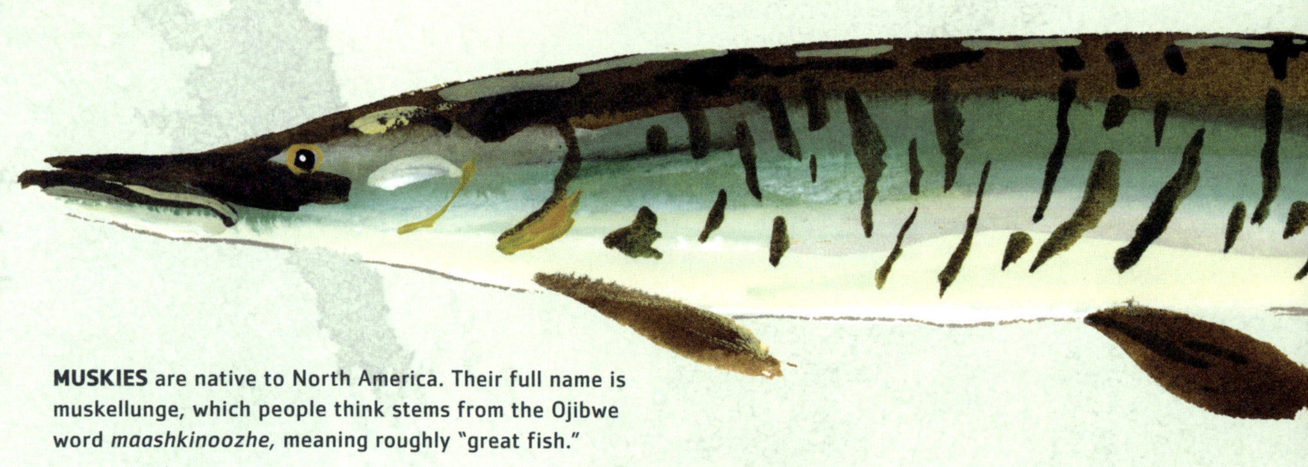

MUSKIES are native to North America. Their full name is muskellunge, which people think stems from the Ojibwe word *maashkinoozhe,* meaning roughly "great fish."

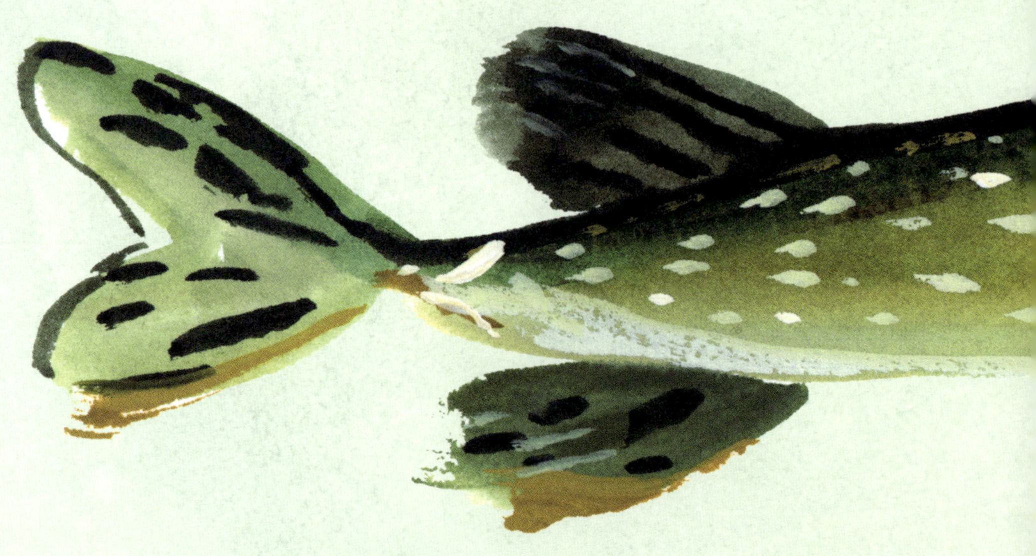

At a glance, people often confuse pike for muskies, which, as a non-obsessed muskie/pike appreciator, I totally get. Genetically, they're very related. They also live in a lot of the same places. They eat a lot of the same food too! The key difference? Pike tend to eat more, and more often. So maybe expect slightly less than ten thousand casts per fish. Still, don't expect anything easy.

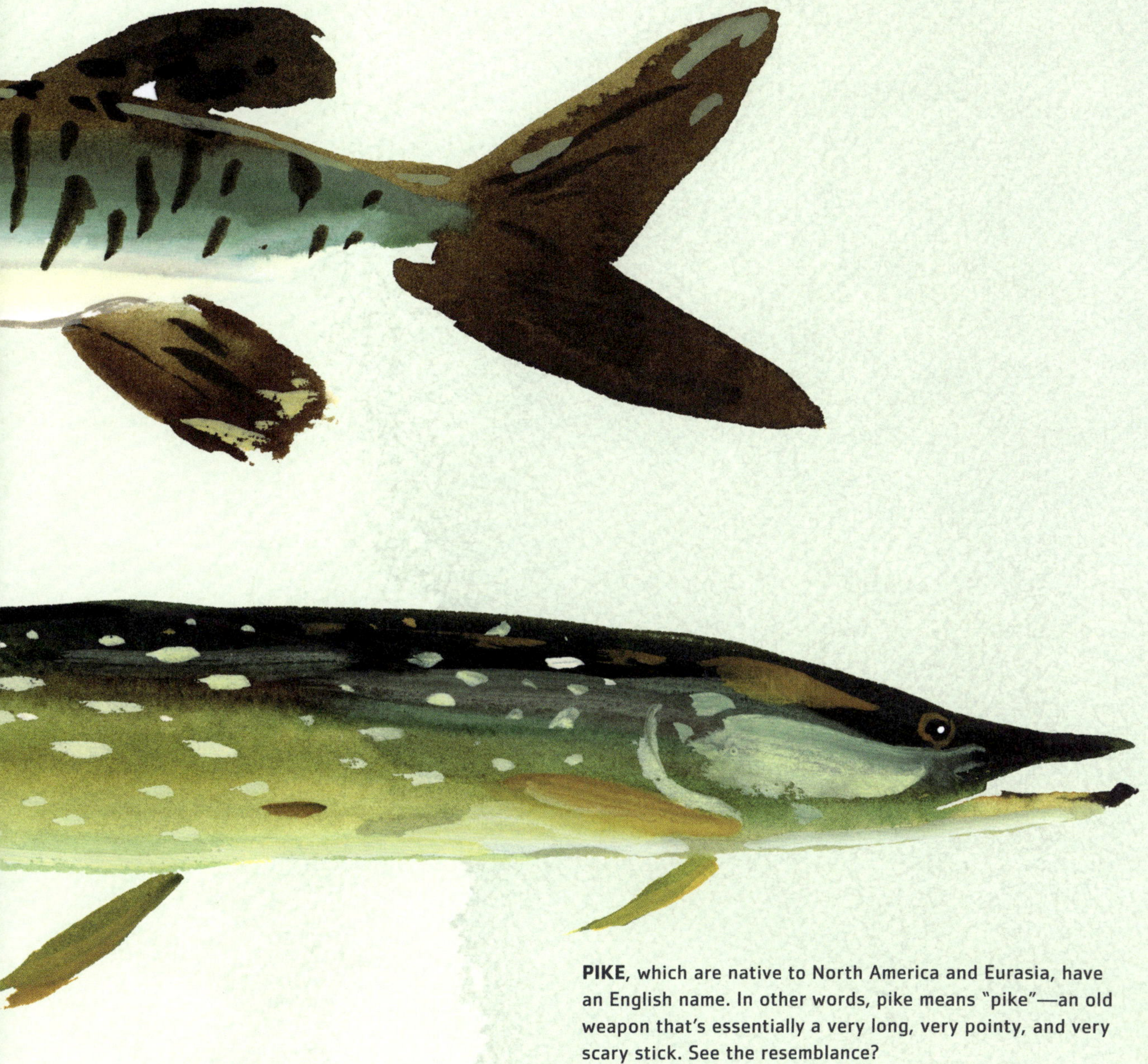

PIKE, which are native to North America and Eurasia, have an English name. In other words, pike means "pike"—an old weapon that's essentially a very long, very pointy, and very scary stick. See the resemblance?

SALTWATER GRAND SLAM

You may have noticed that this book's more about the journey than the destination. In other words, if you only think a good day of fishing is catching a ton, then you're gonna be disappointed. That said, it IS fun to catch fish. These are the three most famous fish for fly fishing in warmer saltwater locales. If you catch them all in one day, it's often called a "grand slam." You don't earn four runs or get a parade, but if you're lucky, maybe your fishing buddy will buy you a beer.

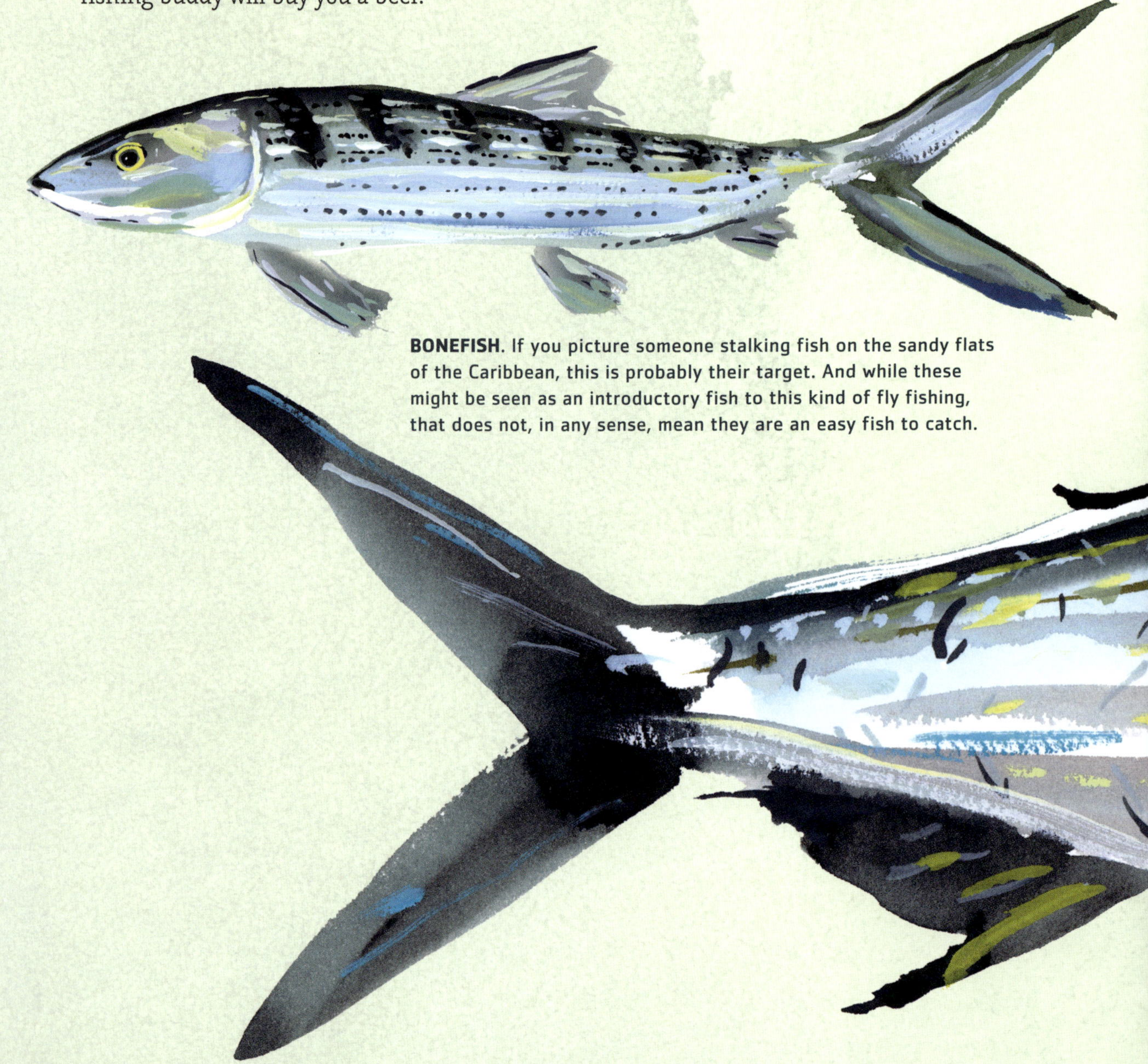

BONEFISH. If you picture someone stalking fish on the sandy flats of the Caribbean, this is probably their target. And while these might be seen as an introductory fish to this kind of fly fishing, that does not, in any sense, mean they are an easy fish to catch.

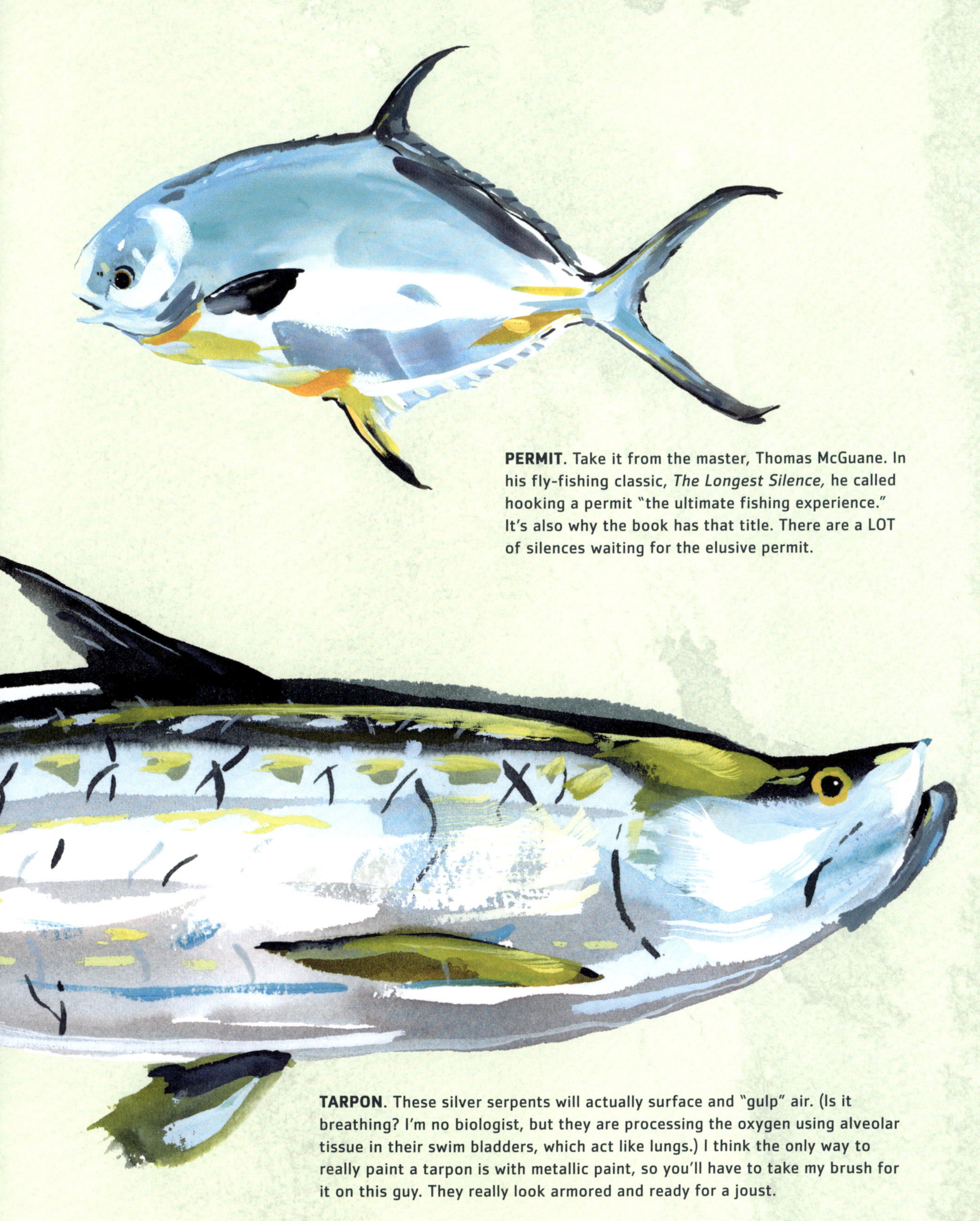

PERMIT. Take it from the master, Thomas McGuane. In his fly-fishing classic, *The Longest Silence,* he called hooking a permit "the ultimate fishing experience." It's also why the book has that title. There are a LOT of silences waiting for the elusive permit.

TARPON. These silver serpents will actually surface and "gulp" air. (Is it breathing? I'm no biologist, but they are processing the oxygen using alveolar tissue in their swim bladders, which act like lungs.) I think the only way to really paint a tarpon is with metallic paint, so you'll have to take my brush for it on this guy. They really look armored and ready for a joust.

EVEN MORE FISH IN THE SEA. . .

Is it a fish? Does it eat things? Then you can fly fish for it. Here's a few more saltwater favorites.

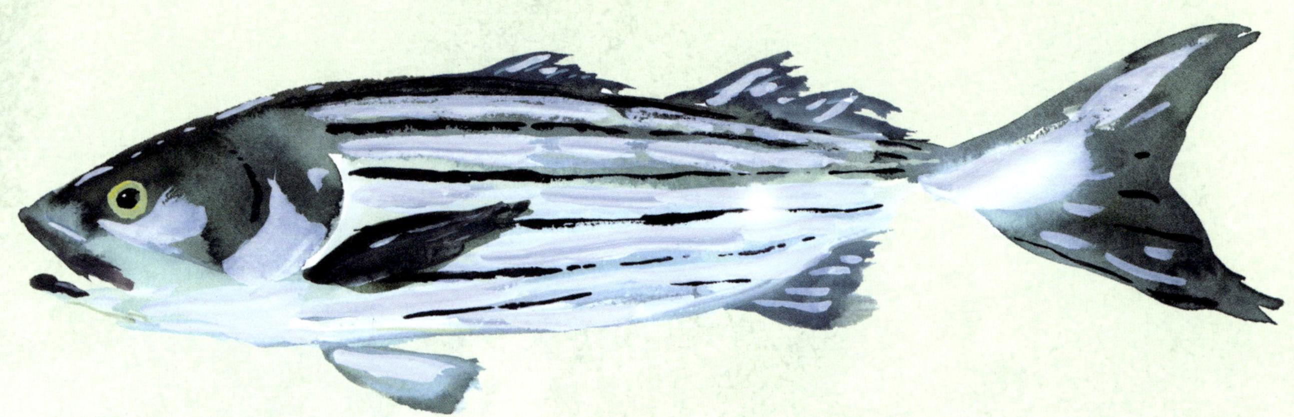

STRIPED BASS, AKA stripers, AKA strippers if you've ever texted about them and not checked autocorrect. Also AKA rockfish to me and anyone else who grew up in Maryland. Many anglers (I think rightfully) consider these the ultimate saltwater gamefish.

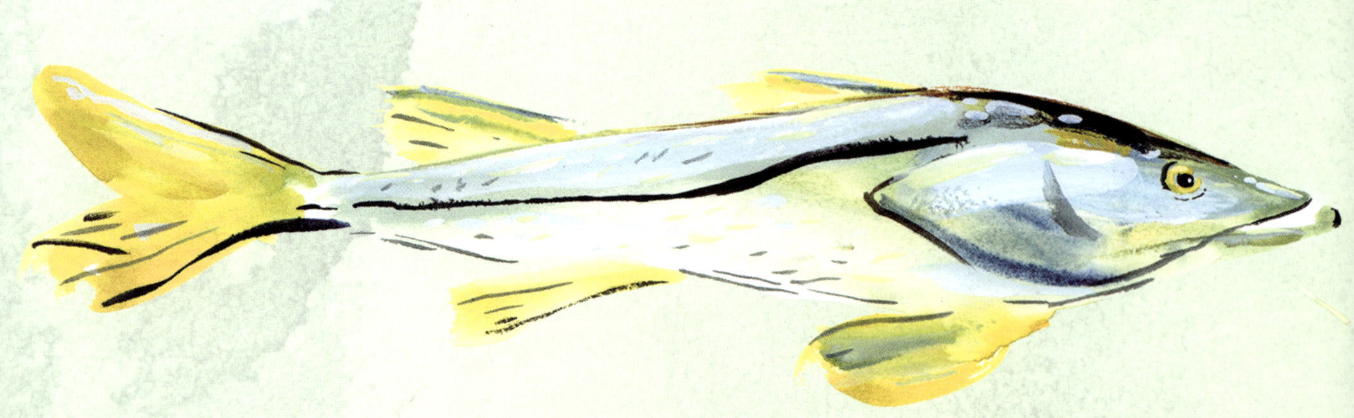

SNOOK. It's hard to beat the thrilling feeling of seeing one of these pop out of mangrove roots and chase your fly.

Oh, the places you'll go fishing! As you can see, there are more than one fish or two fish, there's . . .

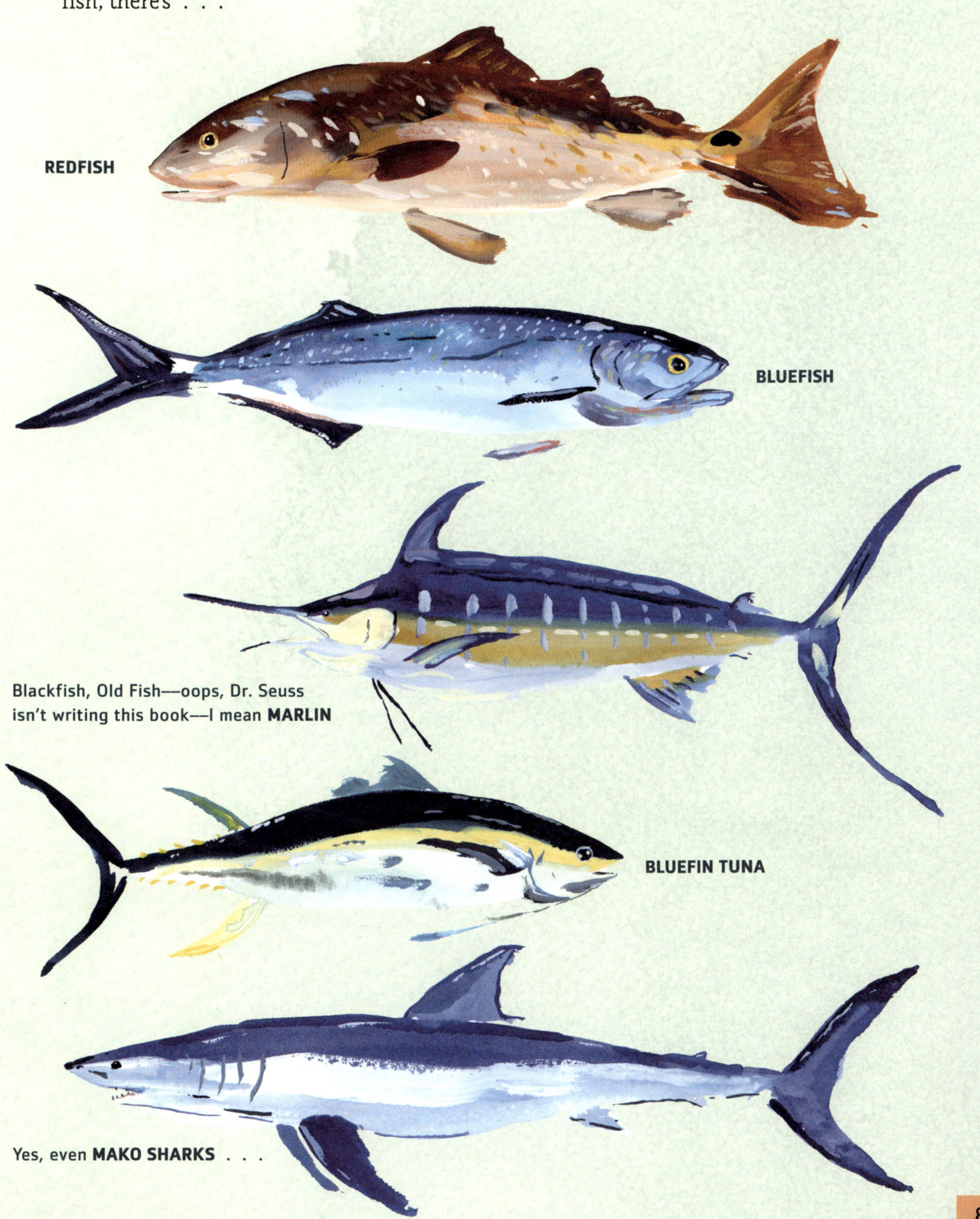

OK, fine, so if it's a fish,
you can catch it on the fly. (Get it?)

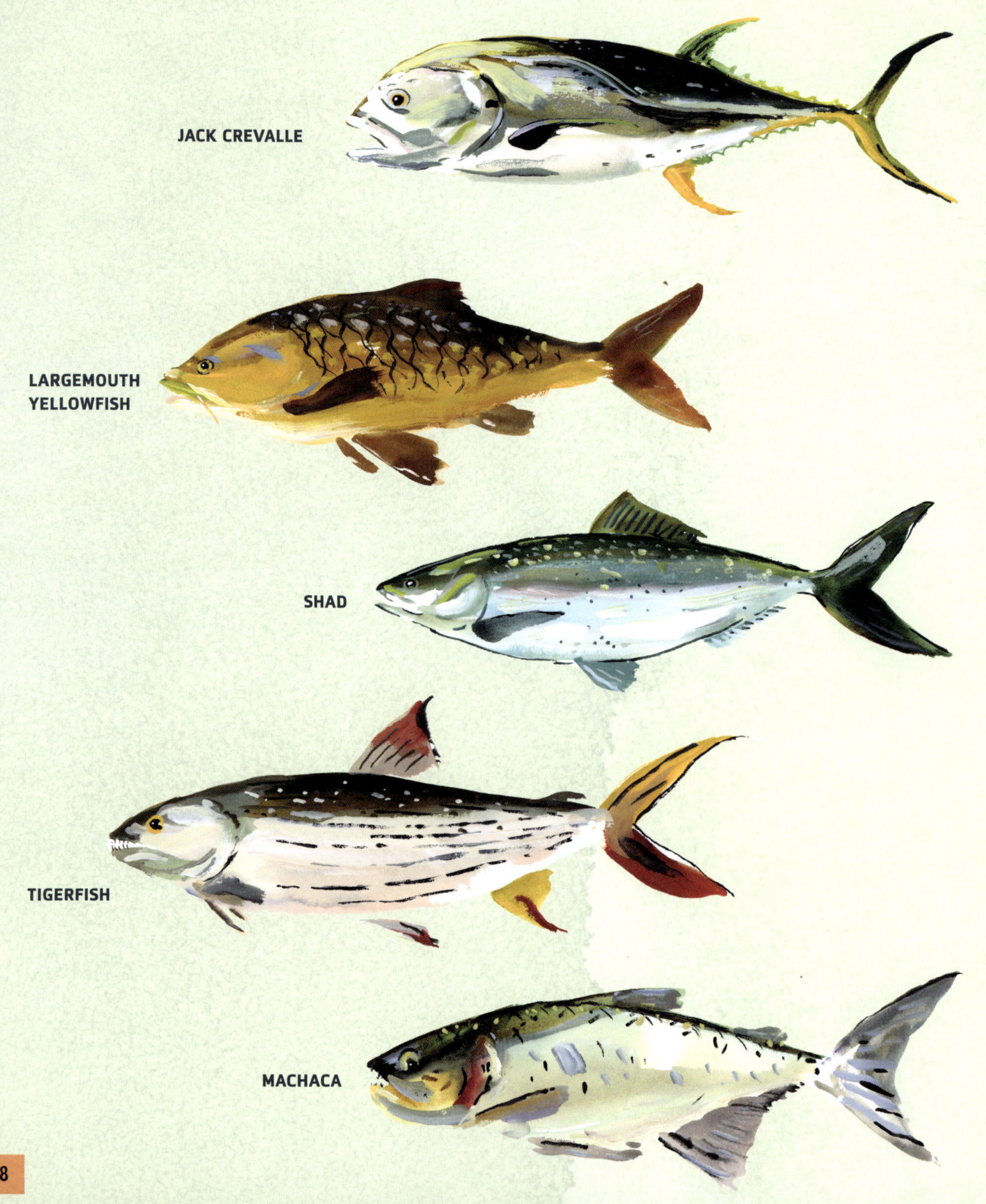

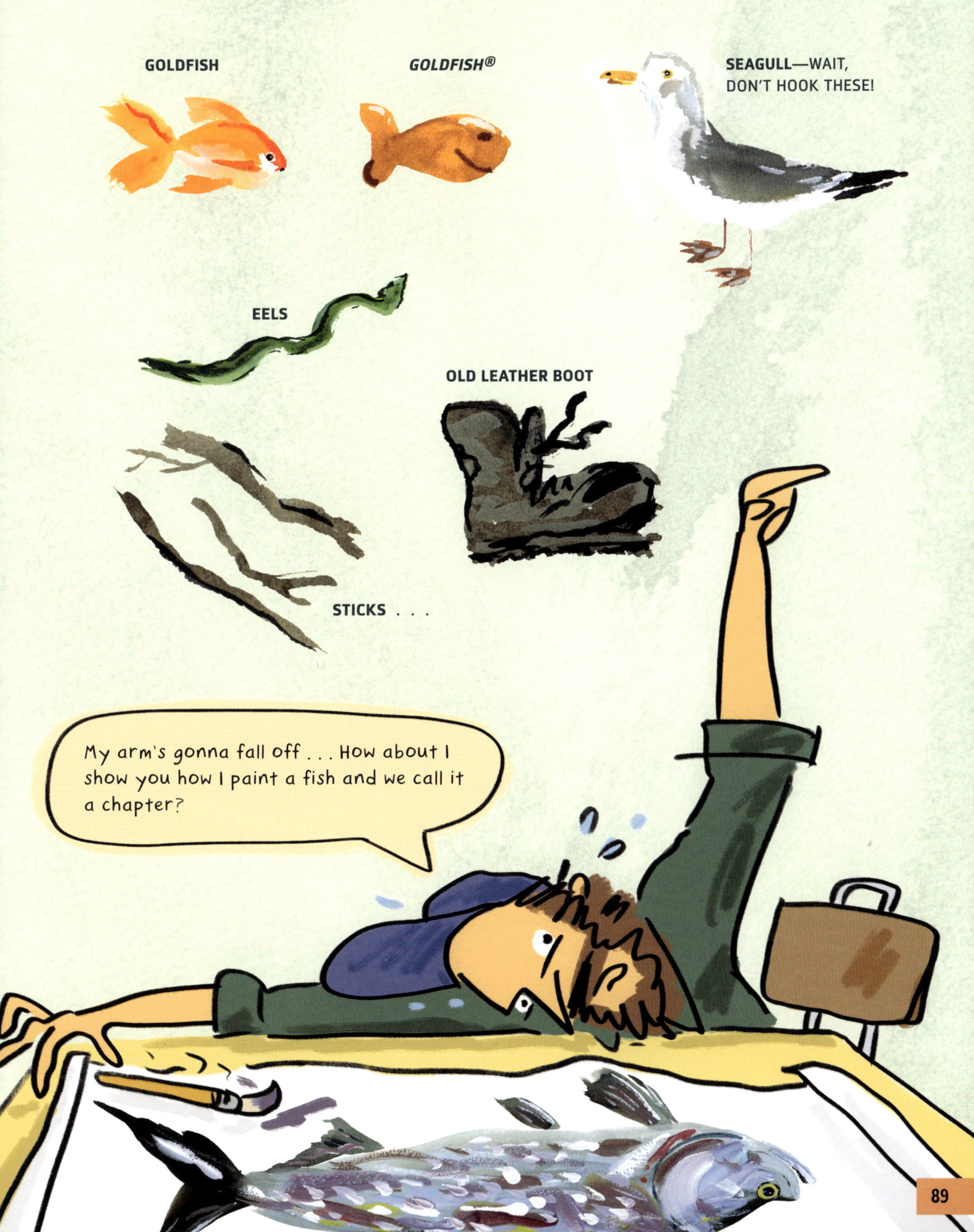
GOLDFISH
GOLDFISH®
SEAGULL—WAIT, DON'T HOOK THESE!
EELS
OLD LEATHER BOOT
STICKS . . .
My arm's gonna fall off . . . How about I show you how I paint a fish and we call it a chapter?

Of course, I've found the best way to truly get to know a fish is to paint it. Which is what I do A LOT! Here's how I paint a brook trout in eight easy-ish steps.

1. The first brushstroke is like a first cast. You don't want to rush it, but you have to nail it.

2. The body can be more loose. Just remember: Most fish have a darker top and a lighter bottom.

3. Don't forget about the trout's jaw! Just imagine it inhaling your Elk Hair Caddis.

4. Fins! You've got the big one in the back, a few on the bottom . . . Let the flick of your brush do the work here.

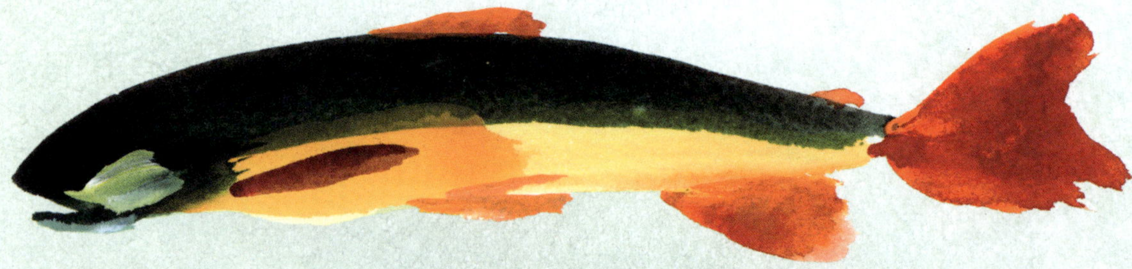

5. Dots. From browns to bows to cutties to brookies, they've all got dots. I find this step very meditative.

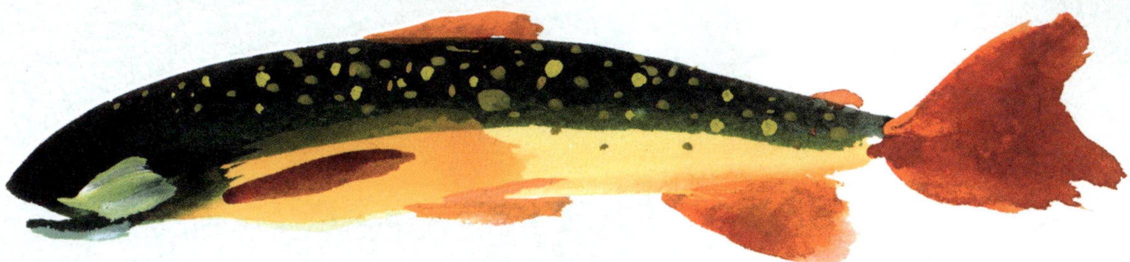

6. For the eye, less is more. Think about the thin yellow ring. Don't overdo any highlights!

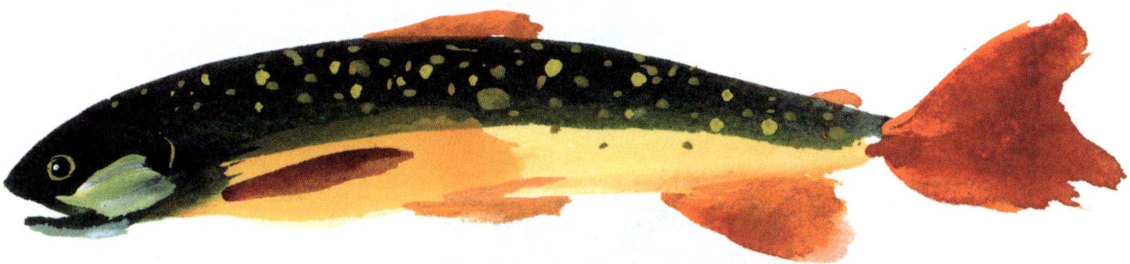

7. Even more dots: Besides the yellow ones, brookies happen to have pure cadmium red dots surrounded by a light blue halo.

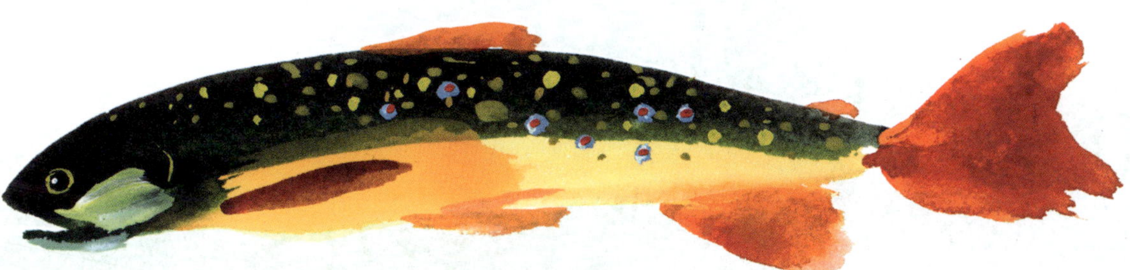

8. And . . . while the paint on this one dries . . .

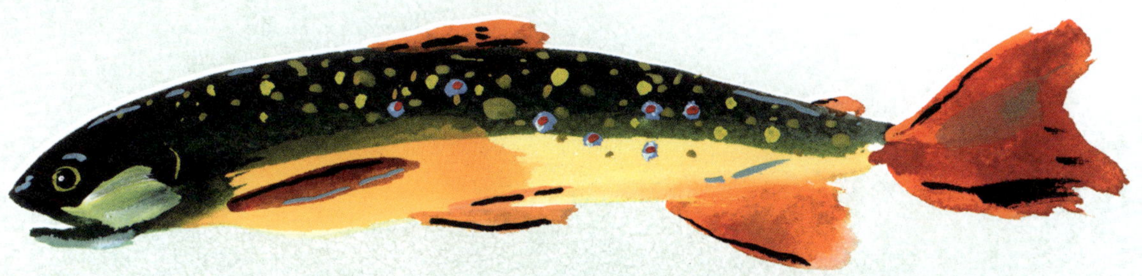

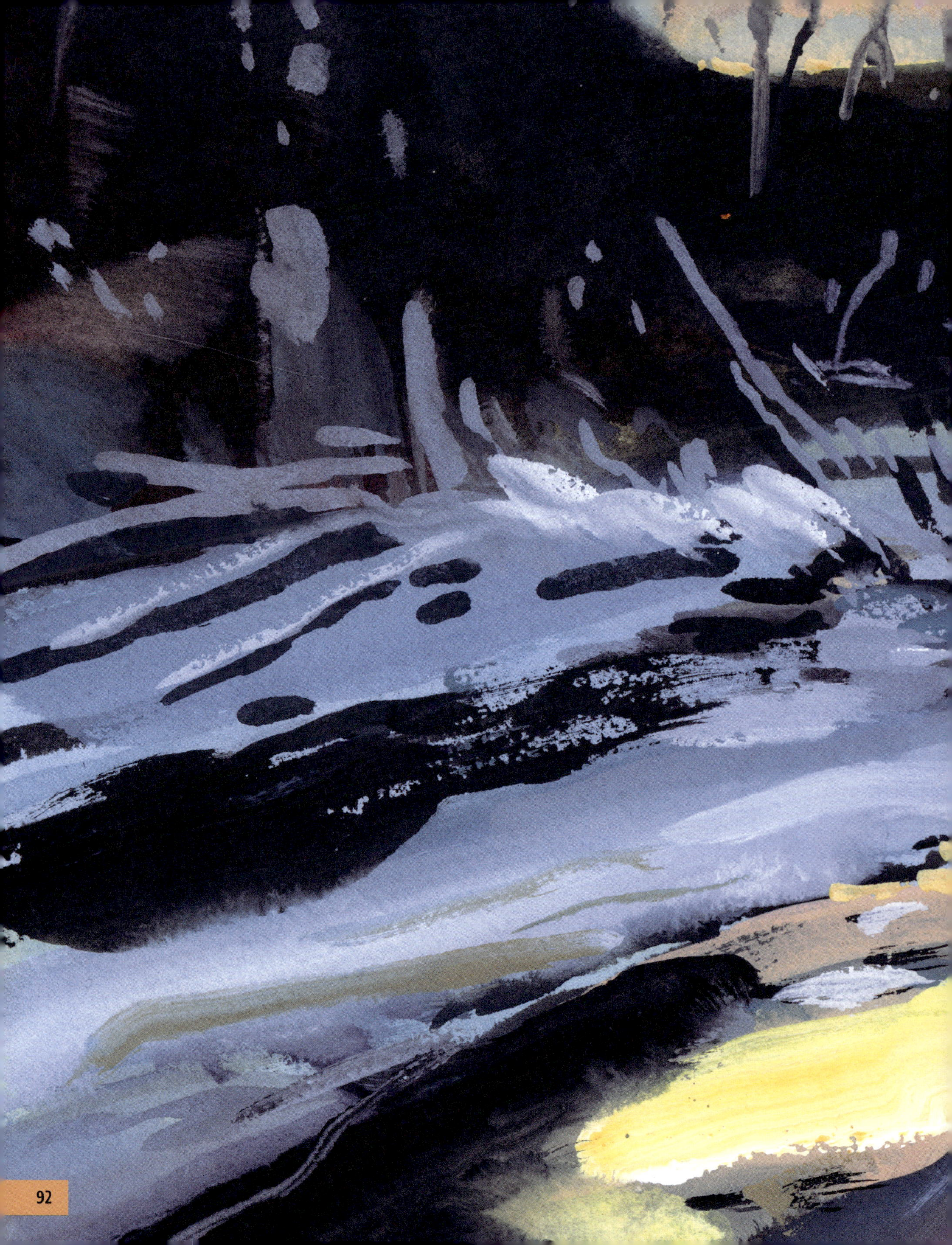

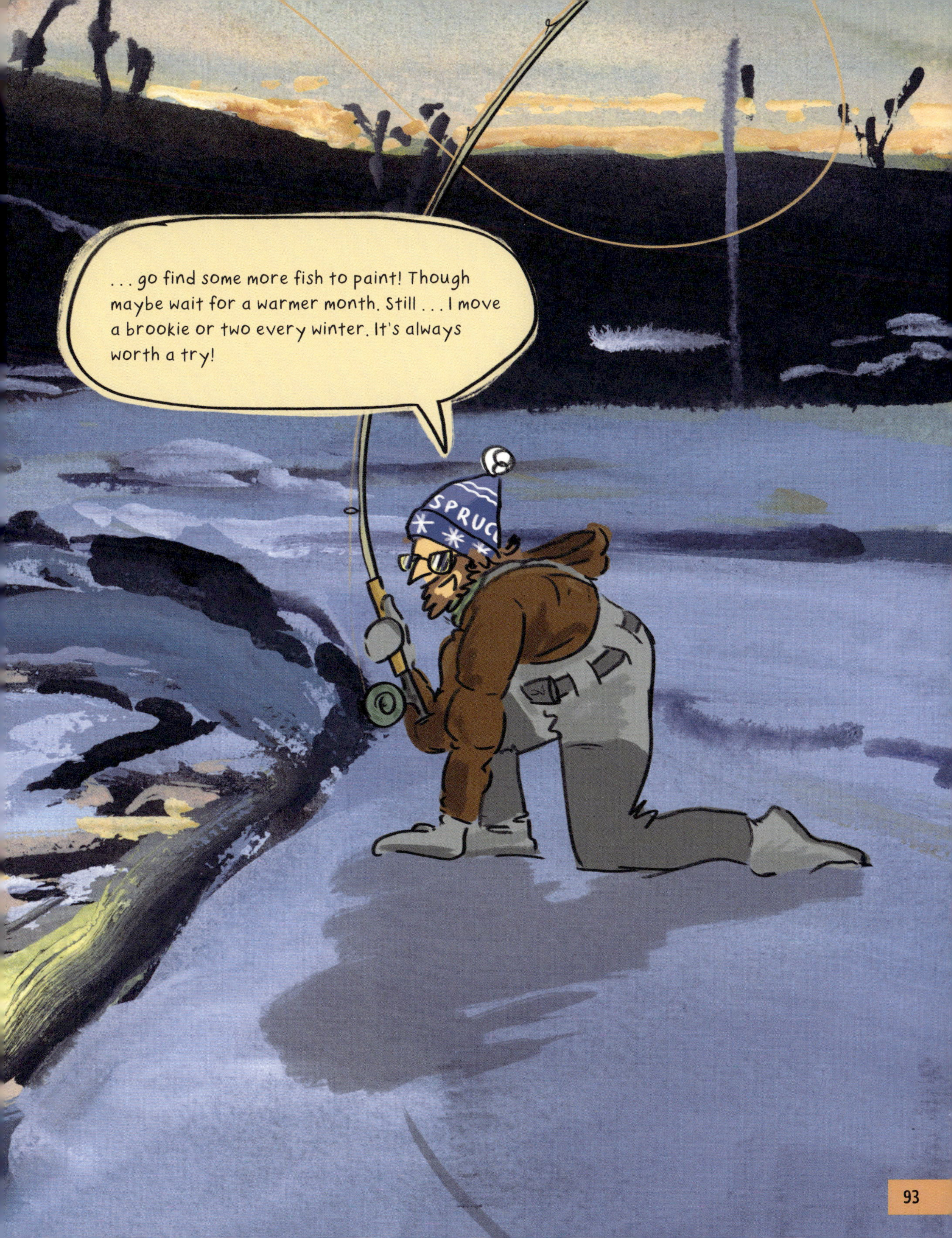
. . . go find some more fish to paint! Though maybe wait for a warmer month. Still . . . I move a brookie or two every winter. It's always worth a try!
SPRUC

5 FLIES

WHAT'S A GOOD DAY? One where you pop into your local fly shop! For me, that's Dette Flies. Since 1928—and through four generations!—they've been tying flies and helping anglers find fish. Which is important, because flies are probably THE MOST intimidating part of fly fishing. You have to learn the names, you have to know which ones to use, then you have to constantly second-guess yourself. Did you choose the right fly? Did you buy enough flies?

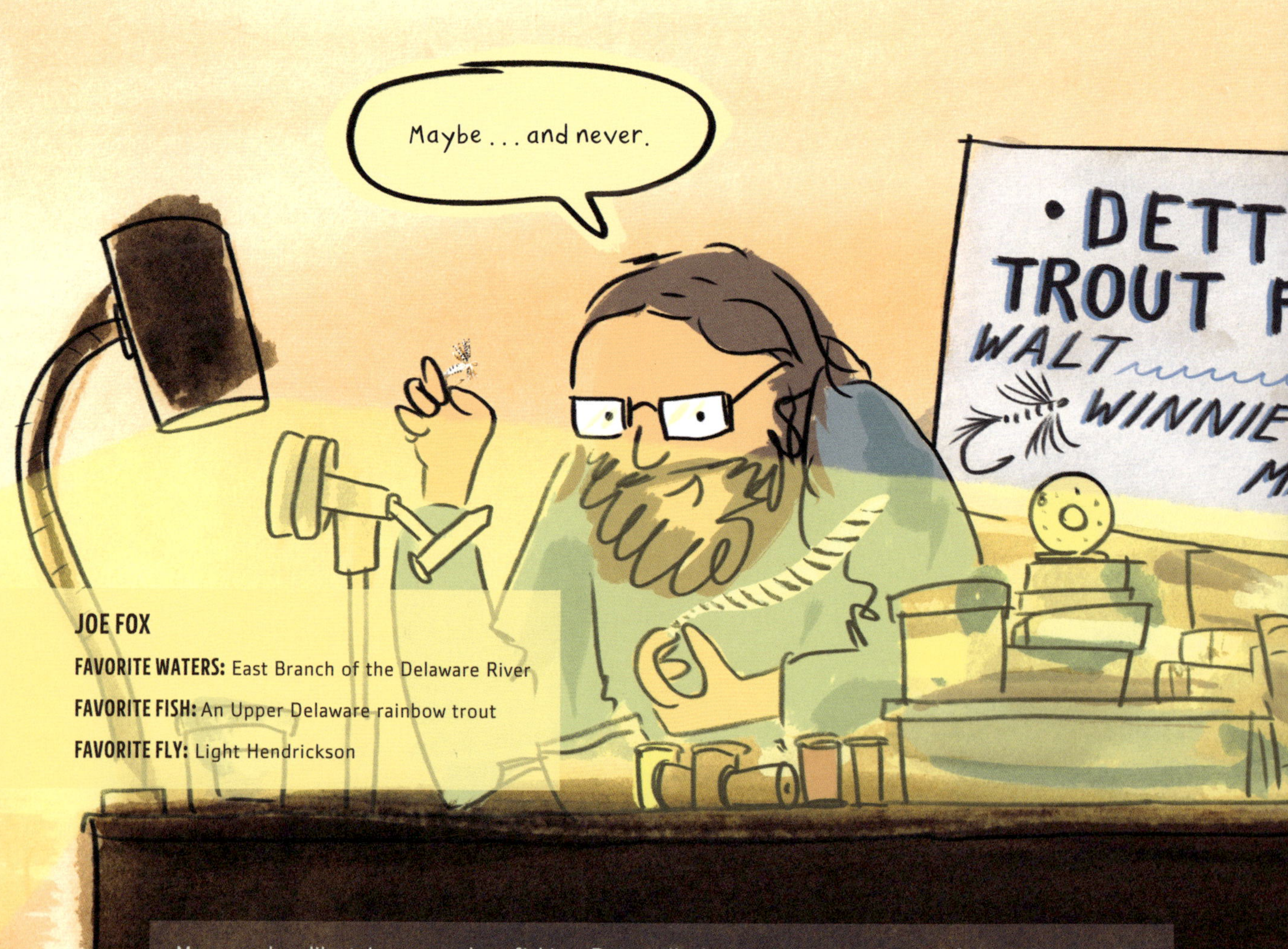

JOE FOX

FAVORITE WATERS: East Branch of the Delaware River

FAVORITE FISH: An Upper Delaware rainbow trout

FAVORITE FLY: Light Hendrickson

Many anglers like tying as much as fishing. Personally, between the time I spend fishing and painting fish, I'm honestly afraid to add in one more fishing-related hobby. Still, it's hard to beat a hand-tied fly by someone you know. (I love trading art for flies.) I swear the fish like them more too!

Here's Joe Fox (great-grandson of Winnie and Walt Dette, who started the shop) and his wife, Kelly Buchta. They own the shop, help tie flies, and, most importantly, have the best approach to this complicated subject:

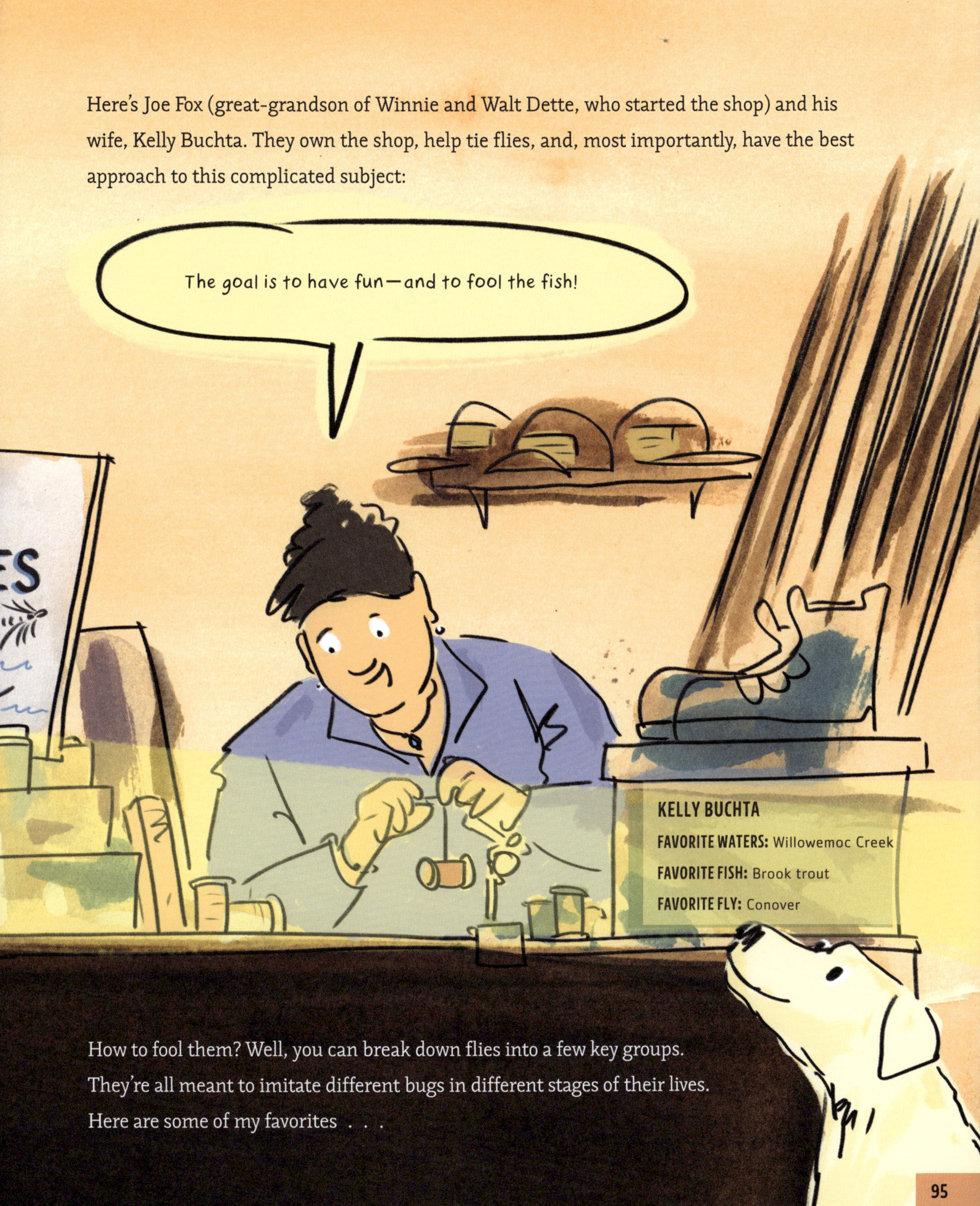

KELLY BUCHTA

FAVORITE WATERS: Willowemoc Creek

FAVORITE FISH: Brook trout

FAVORITE FLY: Conover

How to fool them? Well, you can break down flies into a few key groups. They're all meant to imitate different bugs in different stages of their lives. Here are some of my favorites . . .

DRY FLIES

When you think of fly fishing, you are probably thinking of dry flies, AKA dries. These imitate bugs that live on the surface of the water for a specific—and highly vulnerable—part of their life cycle. Here are some of my favorites:

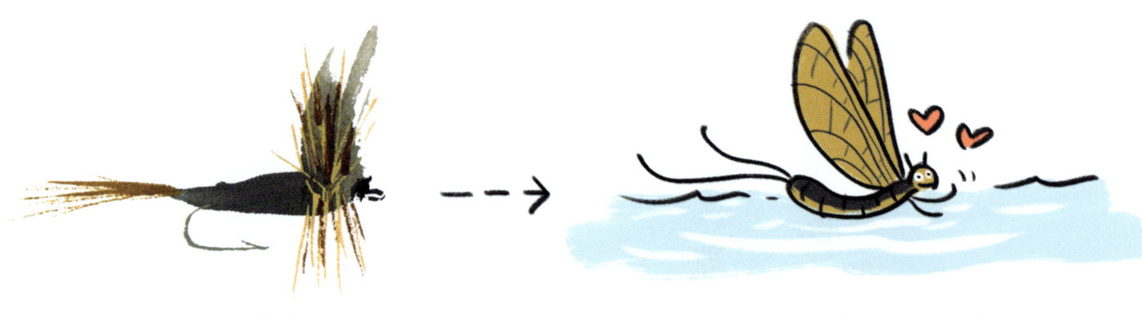

ADAMS

This imitates a mayfly on the surface of the water. Note how the feathers kind of match the wings and tail of the bug.

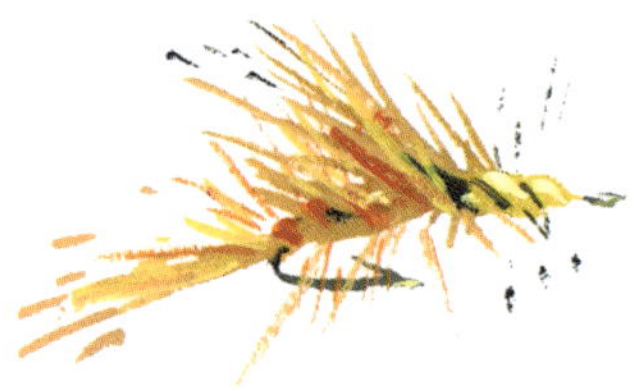

STIMULATOR. This is a generalist meant to, well, stimulate. Some flies are named after the bugs they mimic. Some describe the materials used. Some where they're from. All others generally are just meant to sound cool and get you excited to use them.

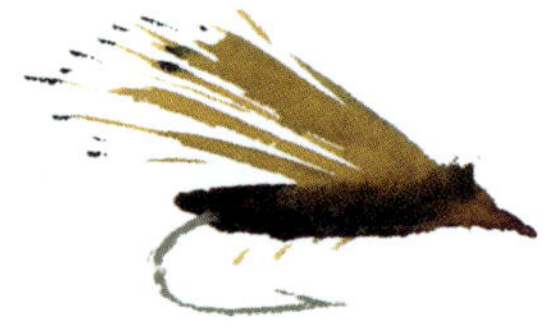

ELK HAIR CADDIS. Looks like a caddis bug. Made with some elk hair. It's a classic for a reason.

BLUE-WINGED OLIVE, AKA BWOs or *baetis* (shorthand from their genus). These are a *very* common bug, so it's always good to have a few of these on hand.

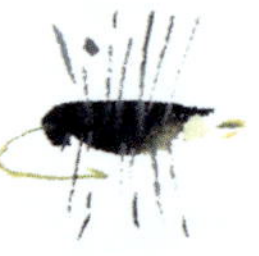

MIDGE. Resembles a small bug, or a collection of smaller bugs conveniently grouped for a trout's meal.

TERRESTRIALS

These are fished like dry flies on the surface but are meant to look like other bugs that live near the stream. They are EXCEPTIONALLY fun to fish with in the summer and also quite easy to use, as they're often big and float well.

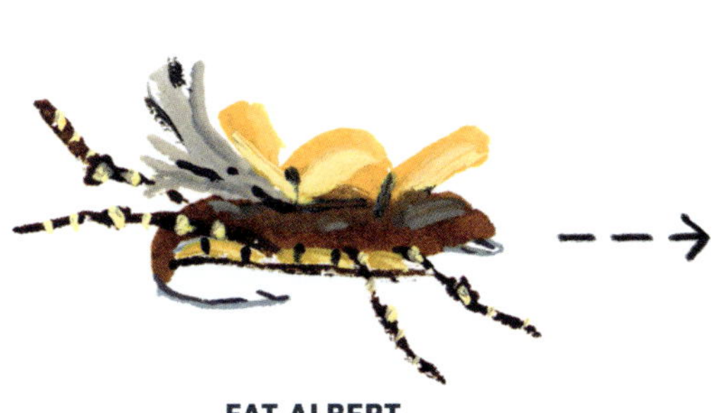

FAT ALBERT

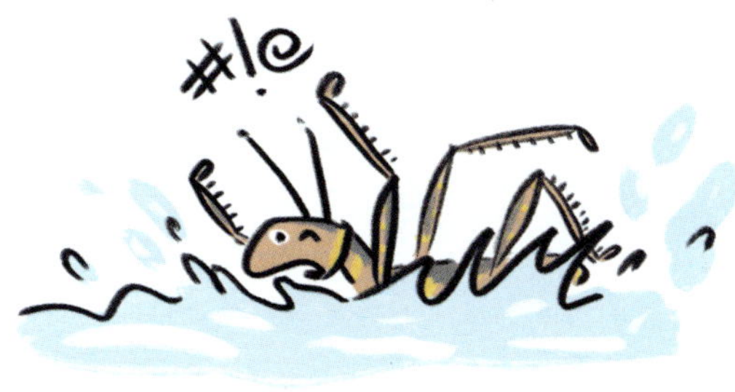

Imitates an unfortunate, grasshopper-ish bug that jumped into the creek—whoops!

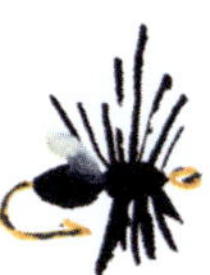

ANT. Looks like a regular old ant who unfortunately fell off a log or a blade of grass. Excellent in small brookie water.

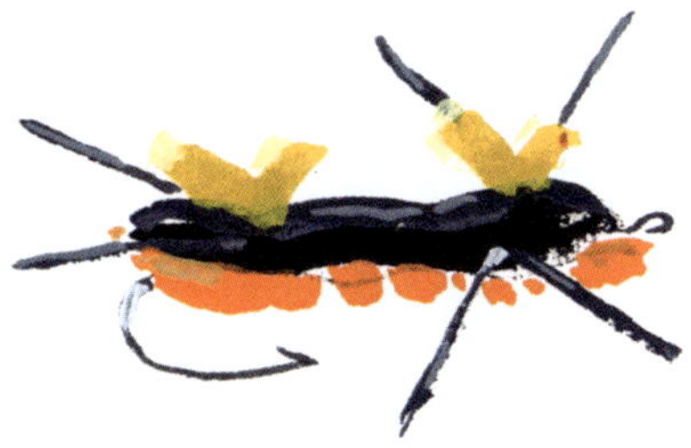

CHERNOBYL ANT. Imitates a giant mutant ant that *shouldn't* exist, hence the name. But it's big enough that fish can't help but investigate.

PARACHUTE MADAM X (PMX). The "parachute" refers to the tuft of white hair on top. This helps it float and also helps you SEE it. I love parachute flies.

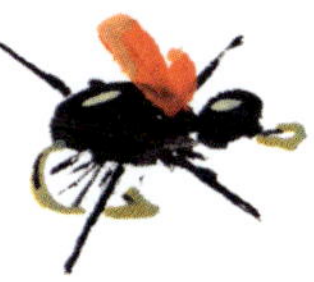

BEETLE. A Beatles fan? Think of your favorite of the four while fishing this beetle look-alike. I enjoy casting while whispering "peace and love."

NYMPHS

Fish catch most of their food underwater versus dramatically and carelessly on the surface. I know, what gives?! Well, at least we have nymphs. These imitate the mayflies and caddis that fish find so delicious in their underwater forms.

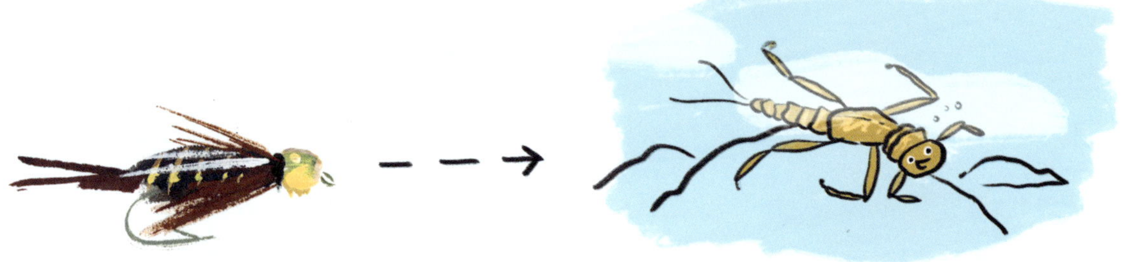

BEADHEAD PRINCE NYMPH

Imitates pretty much any nymph-stage bug in the water. Note the "beadhead" in the name. This means just what it sounds like. There are other versions with no beads (to help it sink) on the head.

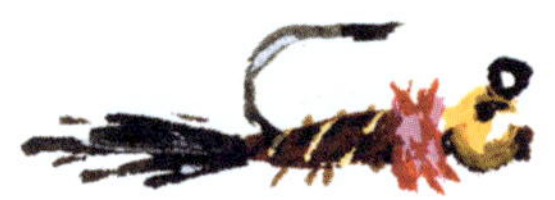

FRENCHIE. The name refers to its euro-nymphing roots.

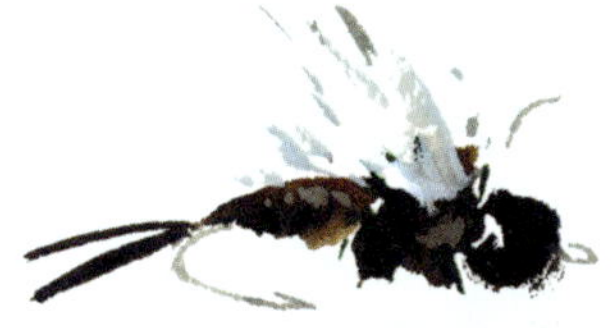

NEW AMERICAN. Developed by a neighbor of mine in the Catskills, Todd Spire, this fly is loved dearly by the rainbow trout of his home stream, the Esopus.

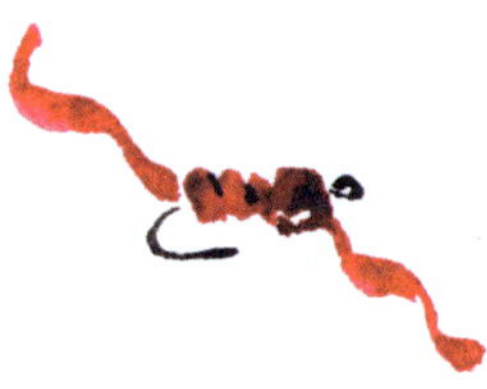

SQUIRMY WORMY. Part nymph, part worm. It just works. Just ask Eeland Stribling, my favorite (OK, the only, but still!) stand-up comedian and fishing guide.

If I'm not fishing dry flies, I'm putting the worm on. If I can't get the fish on the worm, I'm going home.

STREAMERS

Underwater puppetry! Remember, these are mimicking things actively trying to swim away from big fish.

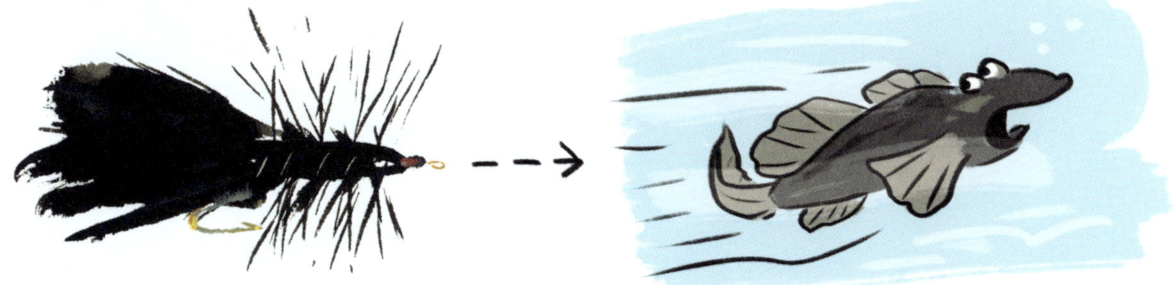

WOOLLY BUGGER

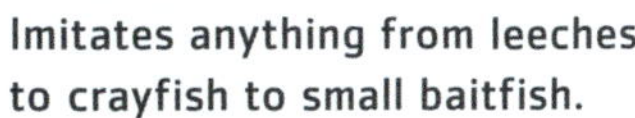

Imitates anything from leeches to crayfish to small baitfish.

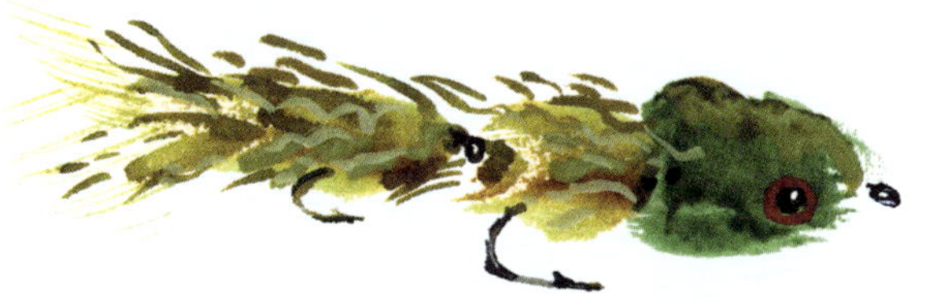

ARTICULATED STREAMER. Articulated means it has more than one part (and often multiple hooks) that allow it to move more like a fish.

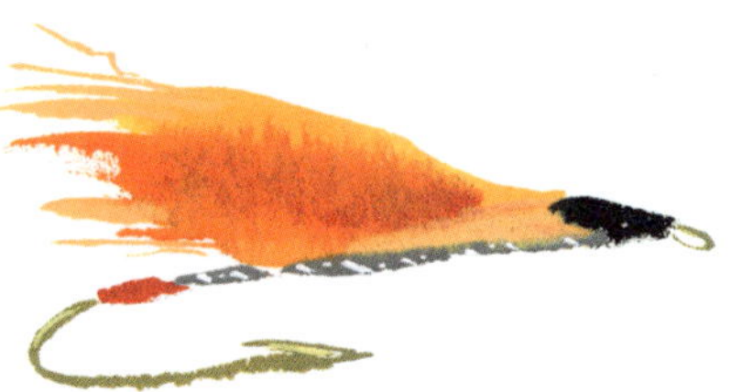

MICKEY FINN. Just like "stimulator," this name is meant to sound cool and fishy. That said, when it was named in 1936, a Mickey Finn was slang for a laced drink. Says a lot about what was cool in the '30s . . .

WET FLIES

Wet flies imitate bugs at various stages of their life cycle while they're in the water. You fish them kinda like streamers, swung through the water.

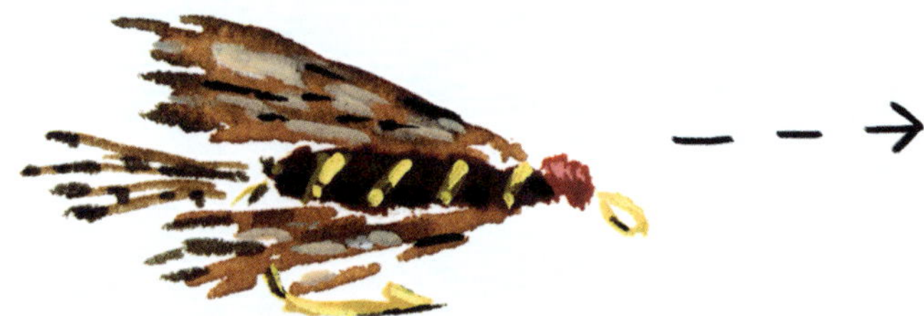

MARCH BROWN WET FLY

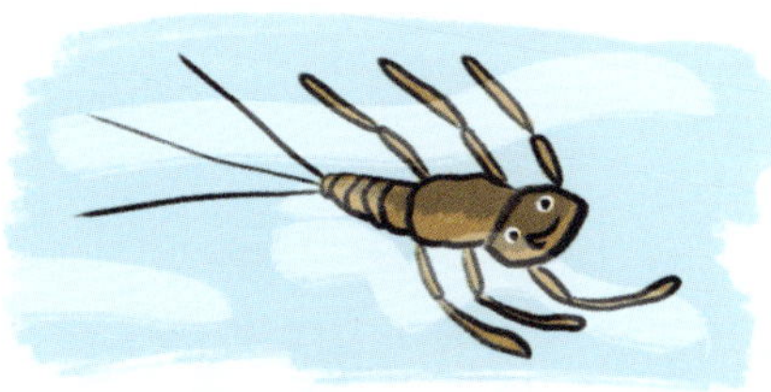

Imitates the March brown bug while it's swimming through the water.

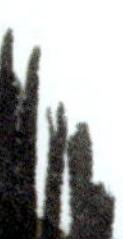

BASS FLIES

To wildly generalize, bass like to chase stuff—like fish and frogs—above and below the surface.

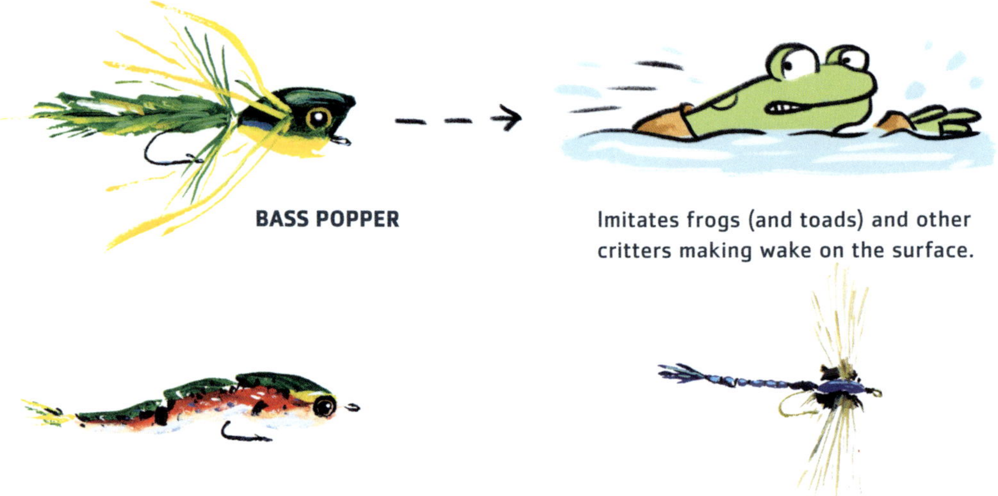

BASS POPPER

Imitates frogs (and toads) and other critters making wake on the surface.

GAME CHANGER. Another "game-changing" generalist.

GIBSON'S DRAGONFLY. Fish these slower than a popper. Think twitches and pauses.

CARP FLIES

Carp have those funny-shaped mouths and usually feed down low, so upside-down flies that rest on the bottom are traditionally used. But . . . carp also live in urban waterways, so don't be surprised if someone is fishing what looks like a hunk of bread sitting on the surface. Either way, always remember carp have an excellent sense of smell, so avoid floatant!

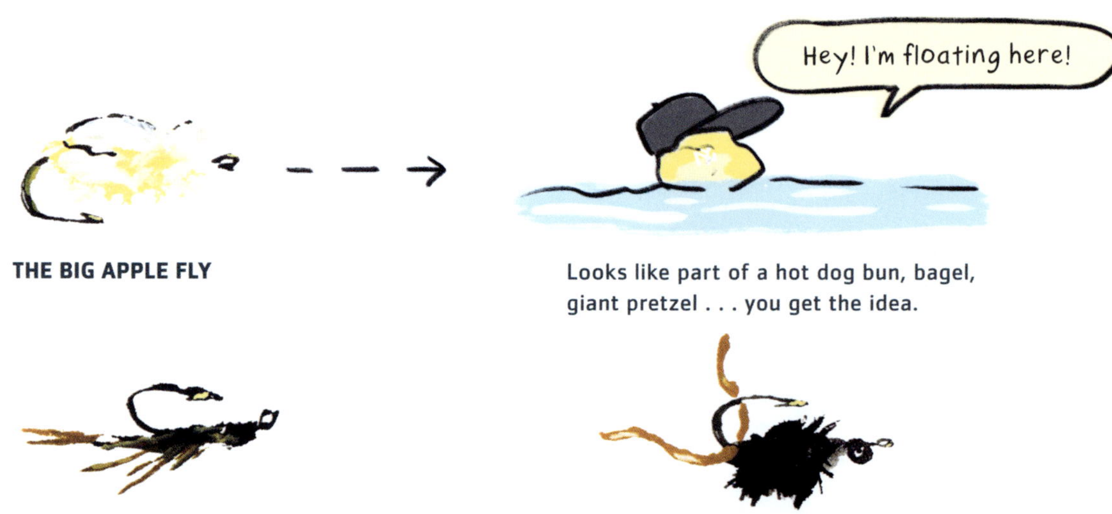

THE BIG APPLE FLY

Looks like part of a hot dog bun, bagel, giant pretzel . . . you get the idea.

DAMSELFLY NYMPH. Imitates the young state of a damselfly, a close relative of dragonflies.

CARP WORM. Carp have excellent eyesight, so any fly with bits that can flutter in the water, like that wormy part, are often great.

SALTWATER FLIES

Like bass, most of the saltwater species you would target feed on smaller bait creatures, like fish, shrimp, or crabs. Similar to a streamer fly, you'll want to strip in these flies to give them a sense of movement. You'll also want to hold on tight to your rod while stripping—many saltwater fish are VERY BIG compared to their freshwater neighbors.

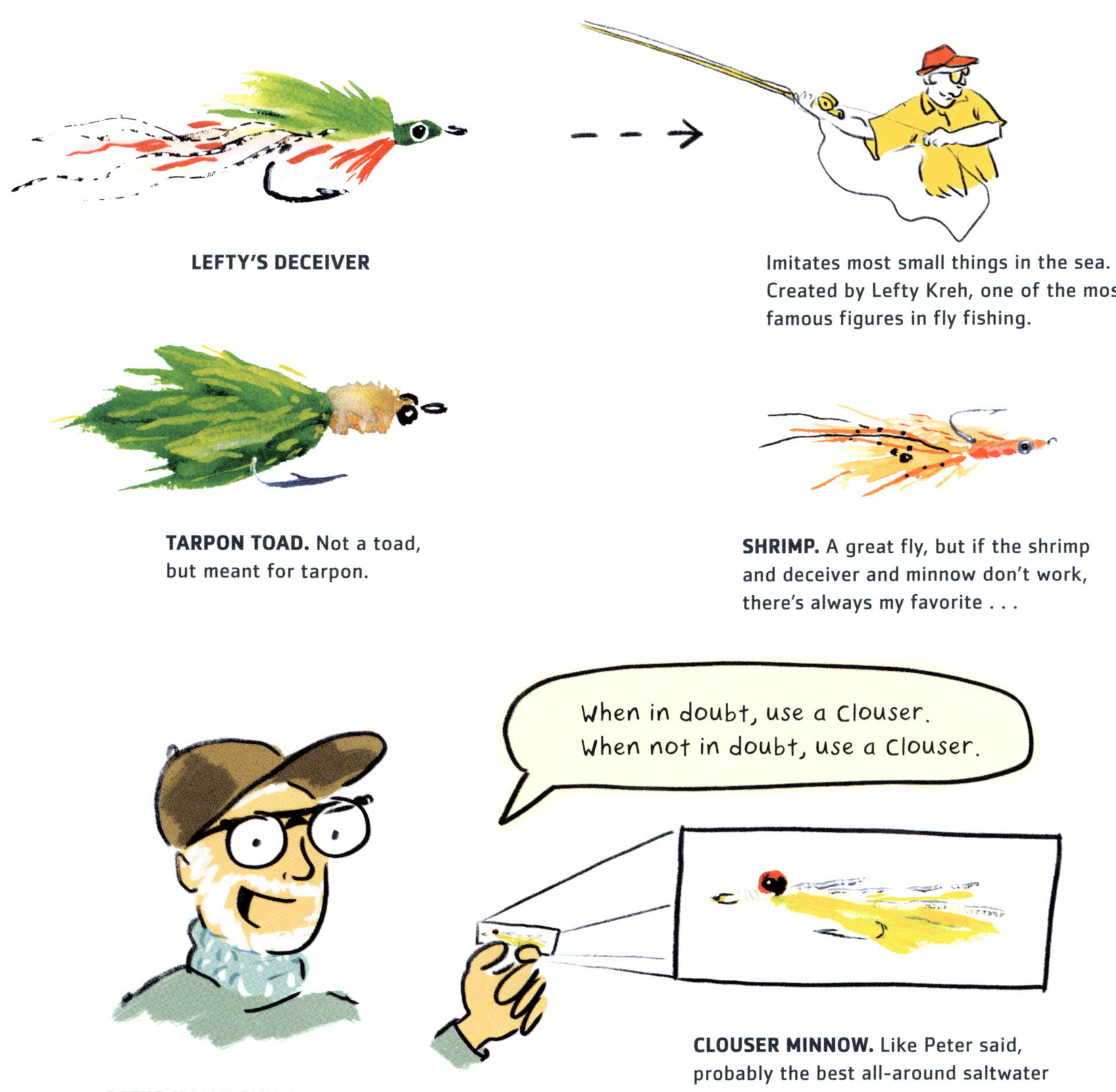

LEFTY'S DECEIVER

Imitates most small things in the sea. Created by Lefty Kreh, one of the most famous figures in fly fishing.

TARPON TOAD. Not a toad, but meant for tarpon.

SHRIMP. A great fly, but if the shrimp and deceiver and minnow don't work, there's always my favorite . . .

PETER KAMINSKY. Not a saltwater fly but someone who's written brilliantly about them and all kinds of fishing.

CLOUSER MINNOW. Like Peter said, probably the best all-around saltwater fly. Always worth a try!

MIX AND MATCH!

Sometimes (often!), two hooks are better than one. One of my favorite ways to fish is using a variation on what's called a "hopper dropper" or "dry dropper." The idea here is to cover as much of the water column as possible.

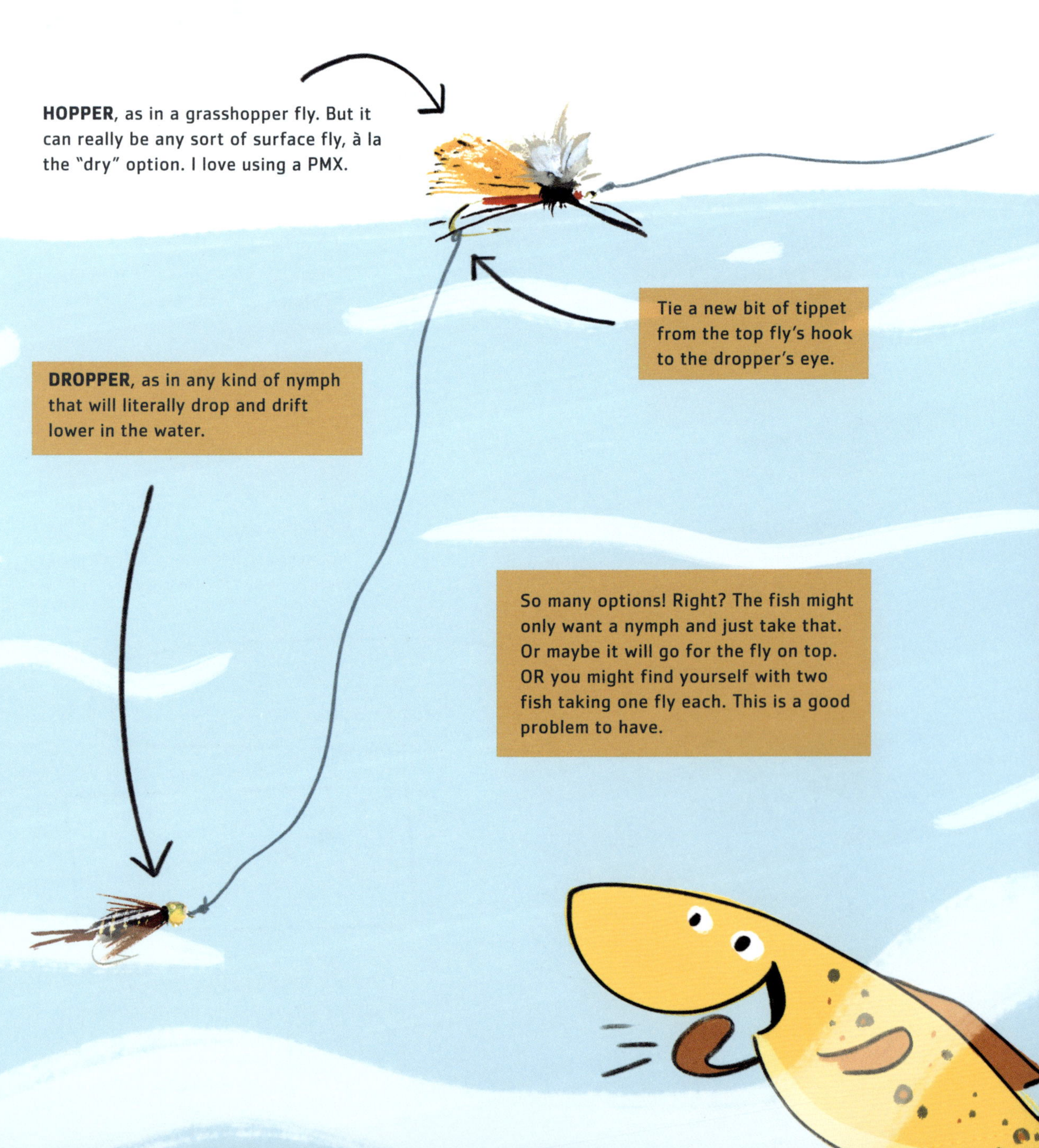

See how this combines the visual connection of dry fly fishing and the depth of nymphing? I love it and I fish this way the bulk of the time. When I see the fly on top twitch—and really, it can be a tiny twitch—I set the hook!

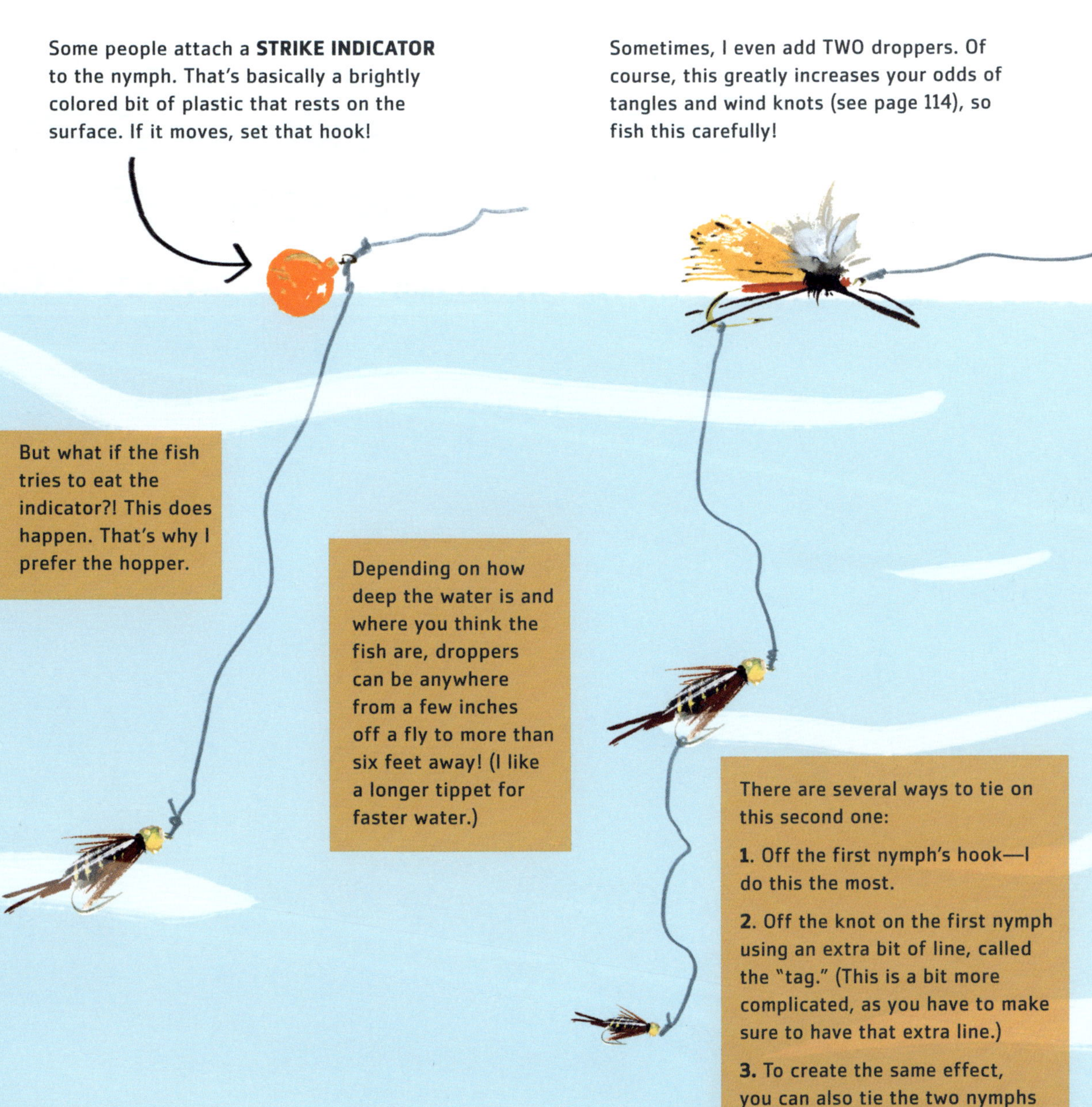

Traditional trout flies (and many others) are often variations on the same bug, just at a different moment in the bug's life.*

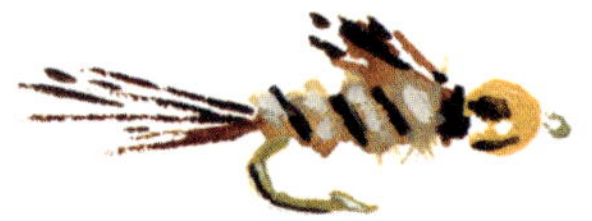

MARCH BROWN NYMPH

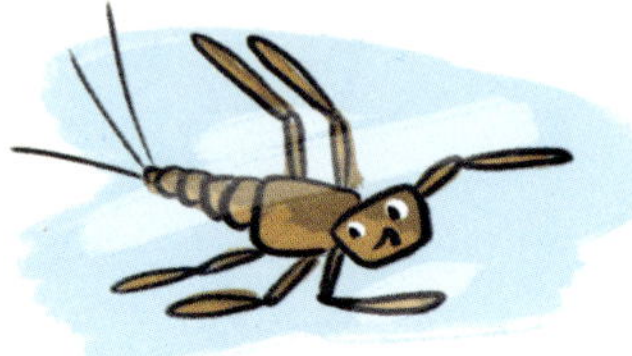

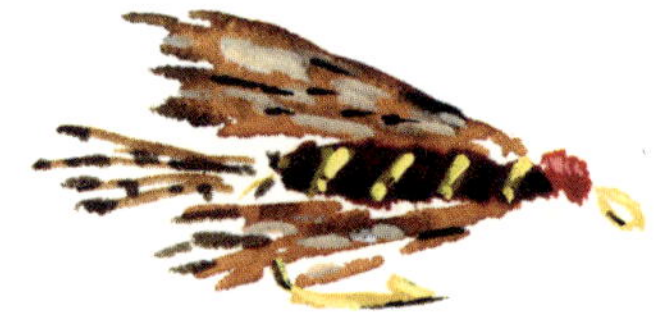

MARCH BROWN WET FLY

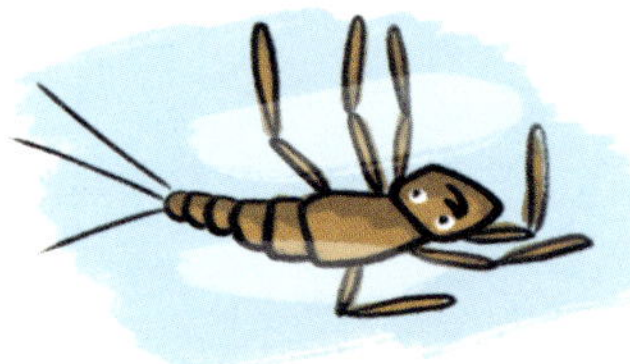

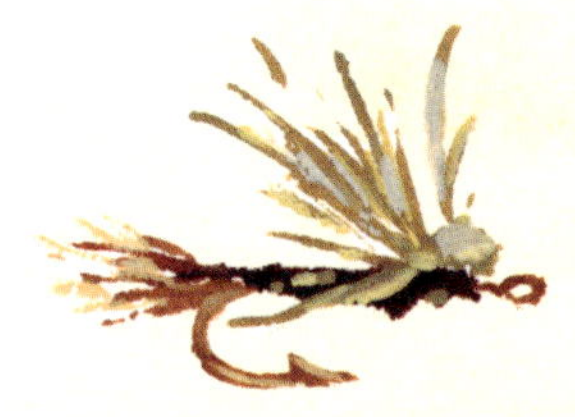

MARCH BROWN EMERGER.
"Emerger" is basically a fancy word for teenager. It's the awkward yet necessary stage when a nymph spreads its wings. Aren't you glad you didn't have aquatic predators when you were in middle school?!

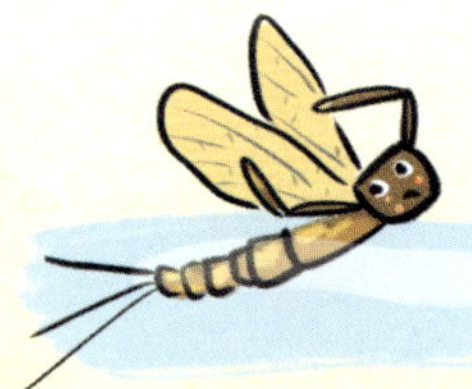

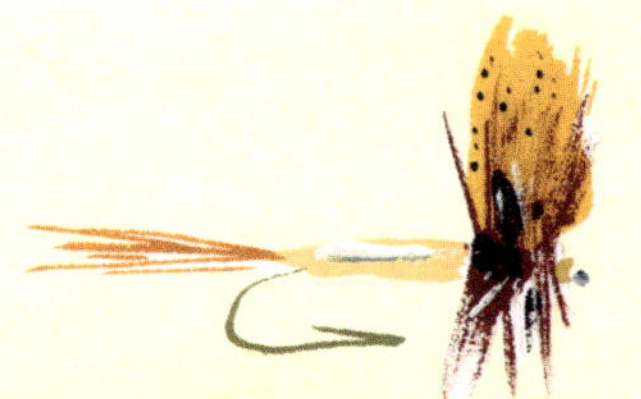

MARCH BROWN DRY FLY

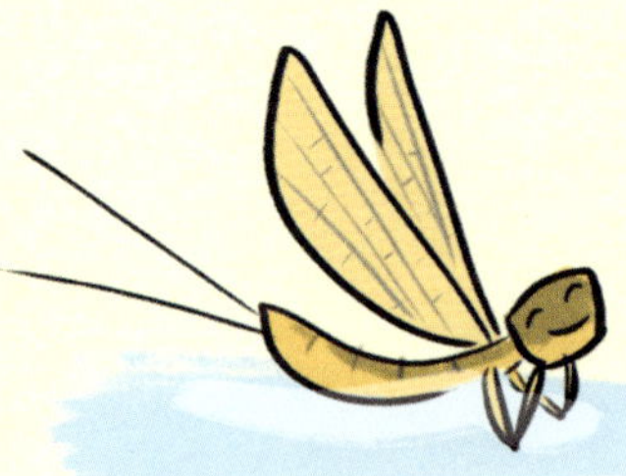

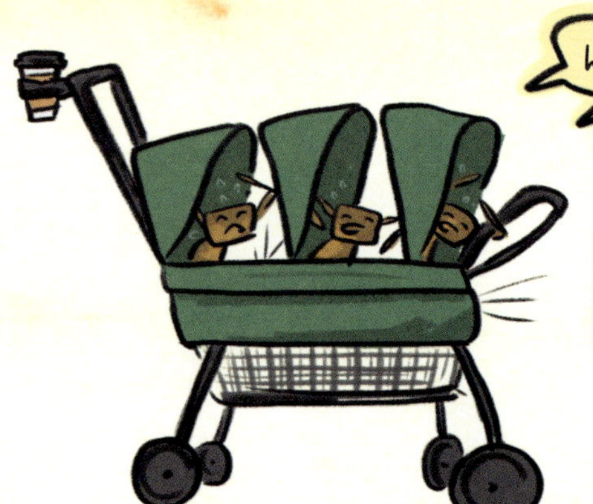

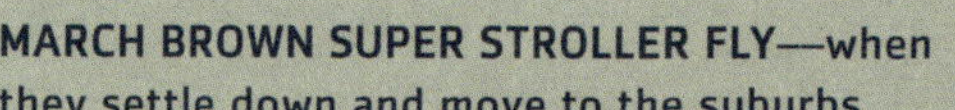

MARCH BROWN SUPER STROLLER FLY—when they settle down and move to the suburbs . . .

*For a full life cycle diagram, see page 138.

Flies also come in a HUGE variety of sizes and are always listed in a SUPER-counterintuitive manner where bigger numbers mean smaller hooks. Here is a hook chart, drawn pretty much to scale so you never have to hurt your head doing backward math . . .

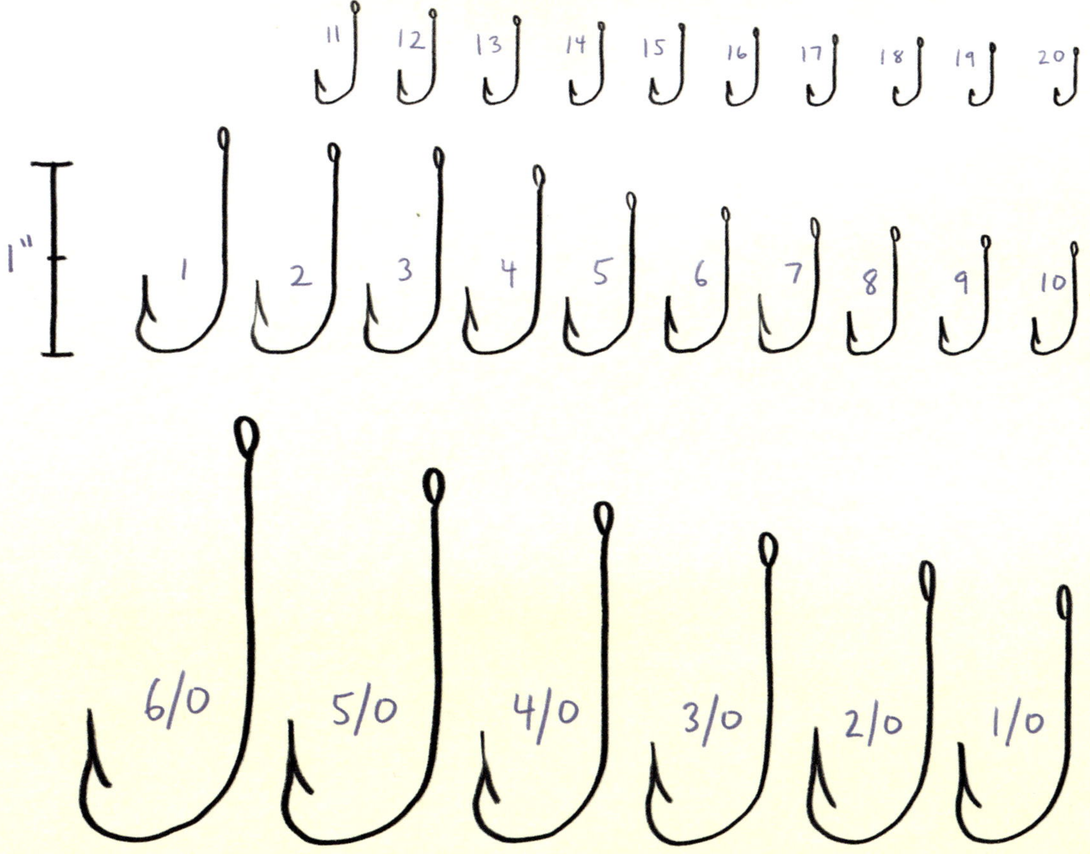

Speaking of hooks, I always debarb. Constant pressure on a fish will keep a hook in place just fine. As far as I'm concerned, the barb is just a good way to tear out a fish's jaw. Debarb by pinching down the barb with your fishing pliers. (See the gear section on page 24.)

AND HOW DO YOU TIE A FLY? Well . . . as someone who paints flies more than I tie them, I put this question to my neighbor/fly fishing mentor/glimpse into my octogenarian future, Judd Weisberg. He's been a fishing guide for decades. Been tying even longer. If anyone could help me, this is the guy.

"Could you show me how to tie something simple for my book?" I asked.

"Ha, sure," he said, lying. (Though I didn't know it at the time.)

What followed was a delightful morning where NOTHING simple happened. Bowstring wax was sporadically dabbed on string, feathers were twisted and repurposed, and fur was bent perfectly and then shorn down even more perfectly. I mostly watched. And painted.

By the the end, I realized there was only one simple way to tie a fly.

HOW TO TIE ANY FLY IN THREE EASY STEPS:

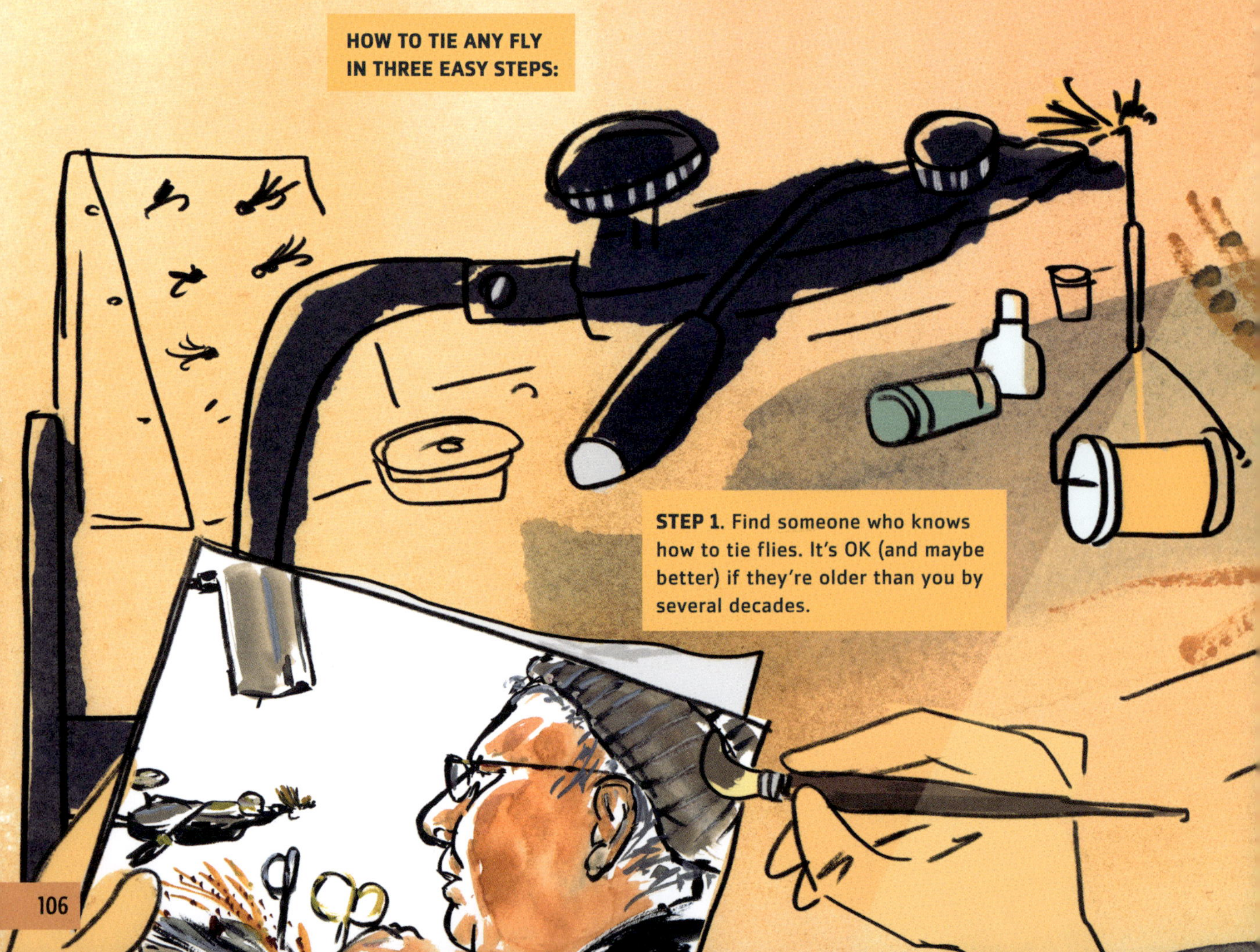

STEP 1. Find someone who knows how to tie flies. It's OK (and maybe better) if they're older than you by several decades.

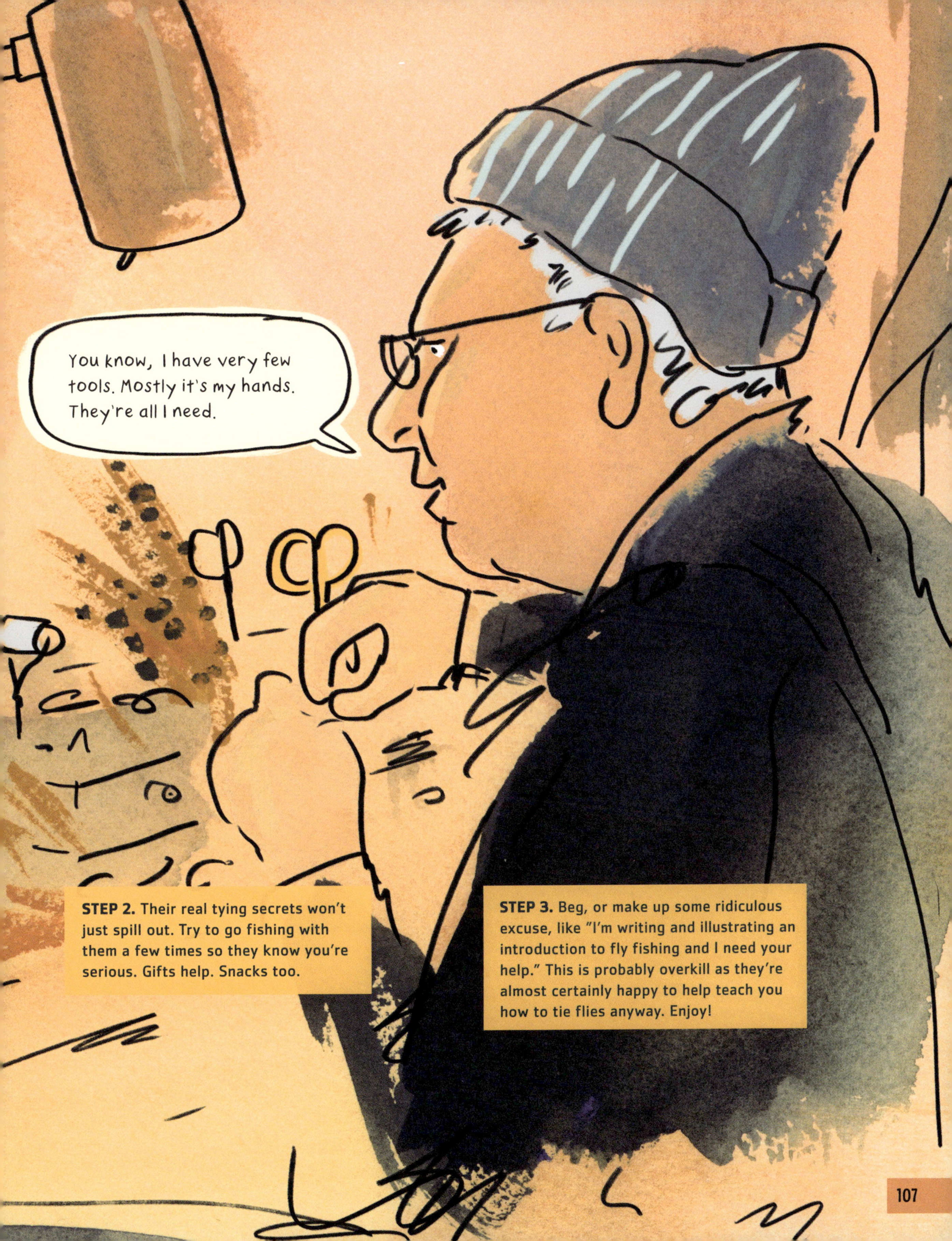
You know, I have very few tools. Mostly it's my hands. They're all I need.
STEP 2. Their real tying secrets won't just spill out. Try to go fishing with them a few times so they know you're serious. Gifts help. Snacks too.
STEP 3. Beg, or make up some ridiculous excuse, like "I'm writing and illustrating an introduction to fly fishing and I need your help." This is probably overkill as they're almost certainly happy to help teach you how to tie flies anyway. Enjoy!

6 KNOTS

THIS IS AWKWARD. I mean, knots are—hard to do, hard to undo, and then SO tangled. So who better to introduce these than Erica Nelson, AKA the Awkward Angler?

Erica is a Diné fly-fishing guide, a podcast host, and an activist helping to start inclusivity programs, like the Angling for All pledge and Brown Folks Fishing, in the angling and wider outdoor world.

She also cracks me up.

When I asked her to pass along some key wisdom about knots, she cackled, thought of a few jokes she decided would be rather inappropriate, and began a fishing-guide-style koan. "Well, you know what they say . . ."

ERICA NELSON

FAVORITE WATERS: I live in the Gunnison Valley with lots of float options (freestone, spring creeks, tailwater, etc.) all within a ten minute to one hour drive.

FAVORITE FISH: Any I can catch!

FAVORITE FLY: The one that catches fish.

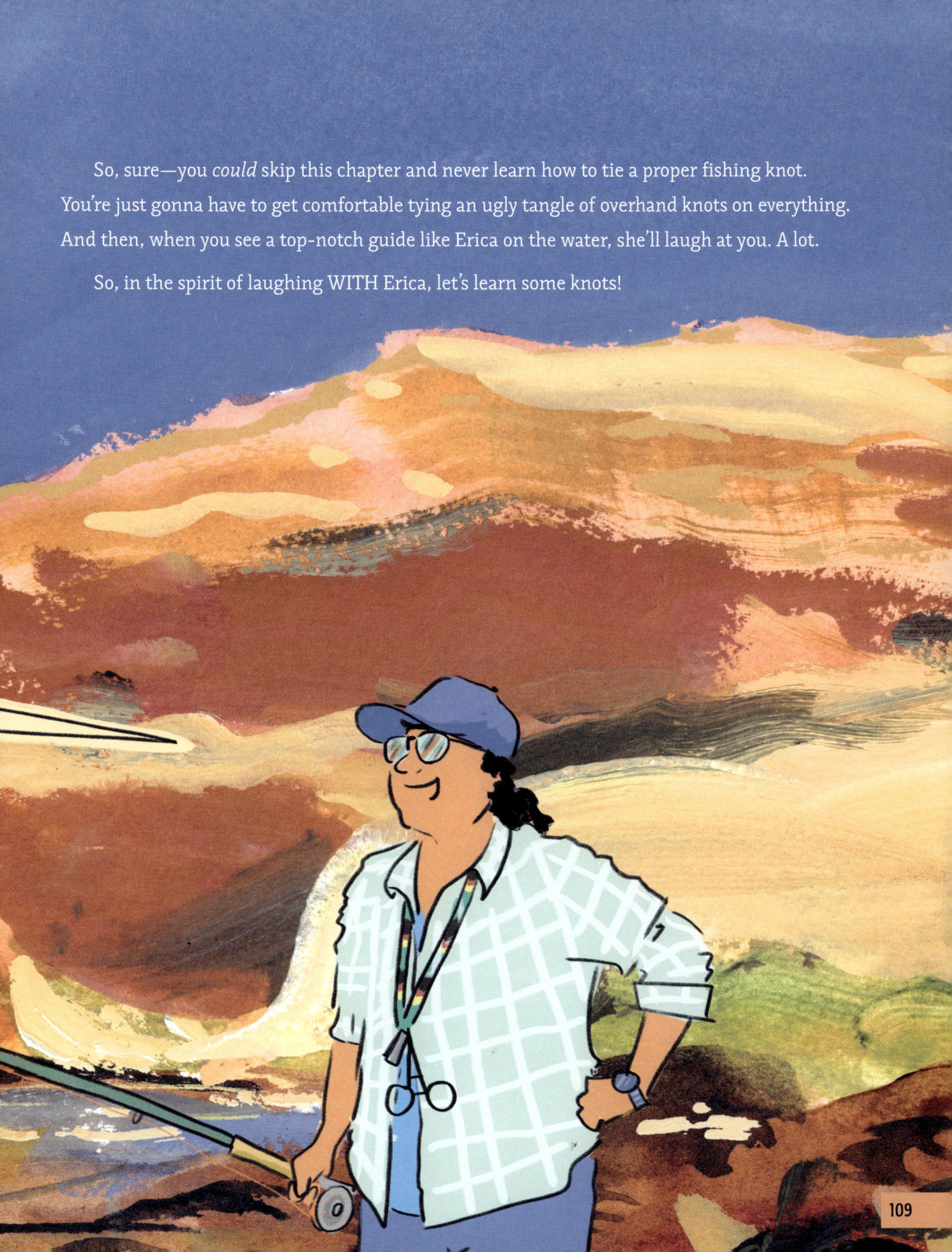

So, sure—you *could* skip this chapter and never learn how to tie a proper fishing knot. You're just gonna have to get comfortable tying an ugly tangle of overhand knots on everything. And then, when you see a top-notch guide like Erica on the water, she'll laugh at you. A lot.

So, in the spirit of laughing WITH Erica, let's learn some knots!

LOOP TO LOOP CONNECTION

Your fly line ends with a loop. Most leaders end with a loop. Thanks to factory-made loops, those knots are covered. But how do you connect those loops? Here goes!

The green loop is your fishing line that connects back to your reel. The blue is your leader.

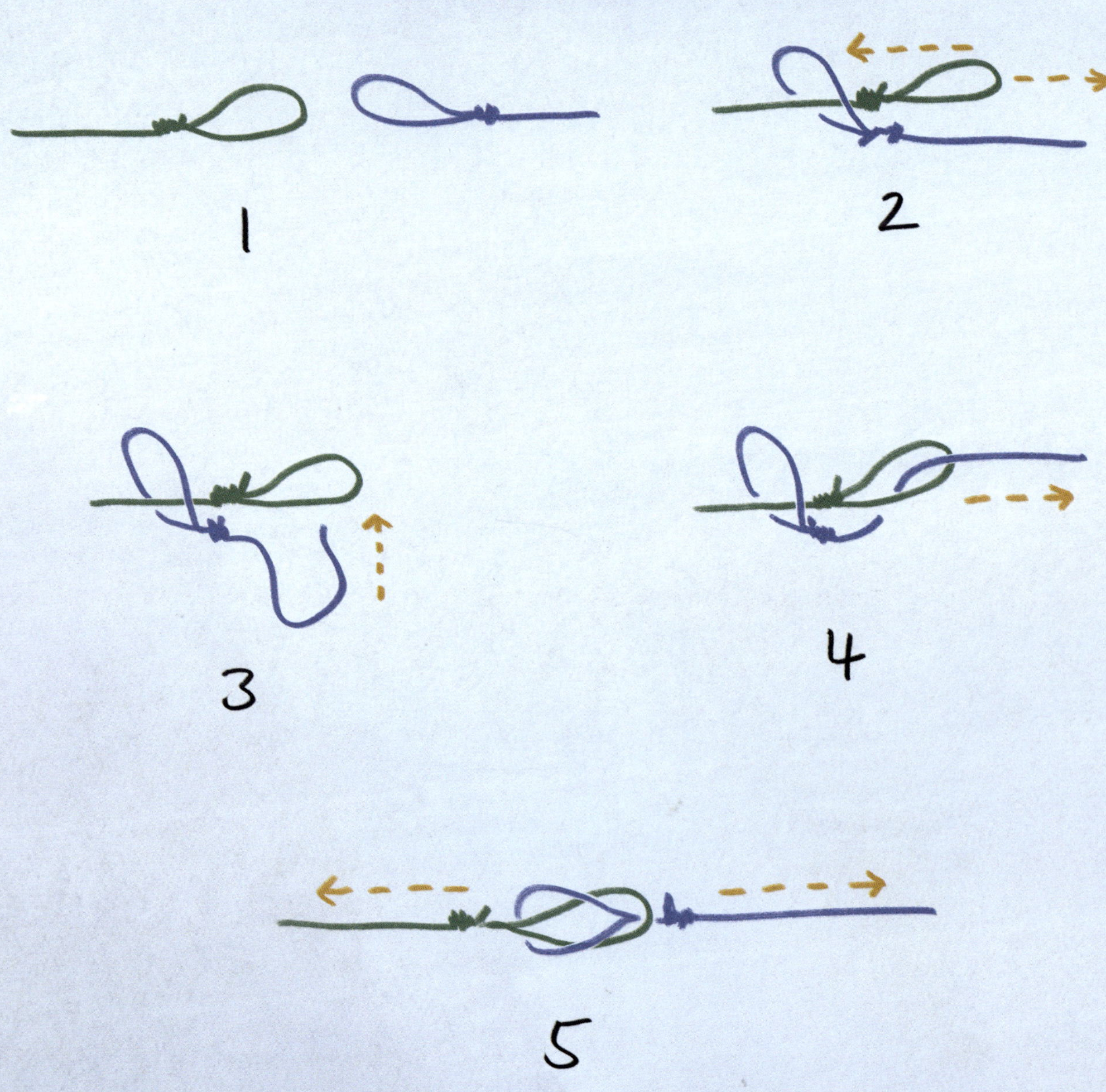

IMPROVED CLINCH KNOT

Your MOST important and MOST common knot. You use this to connect your leader or tippet to the fly. Learn this and learn it well. Because it'll only be your fault when you lose a lunker to a poorly tied knot.

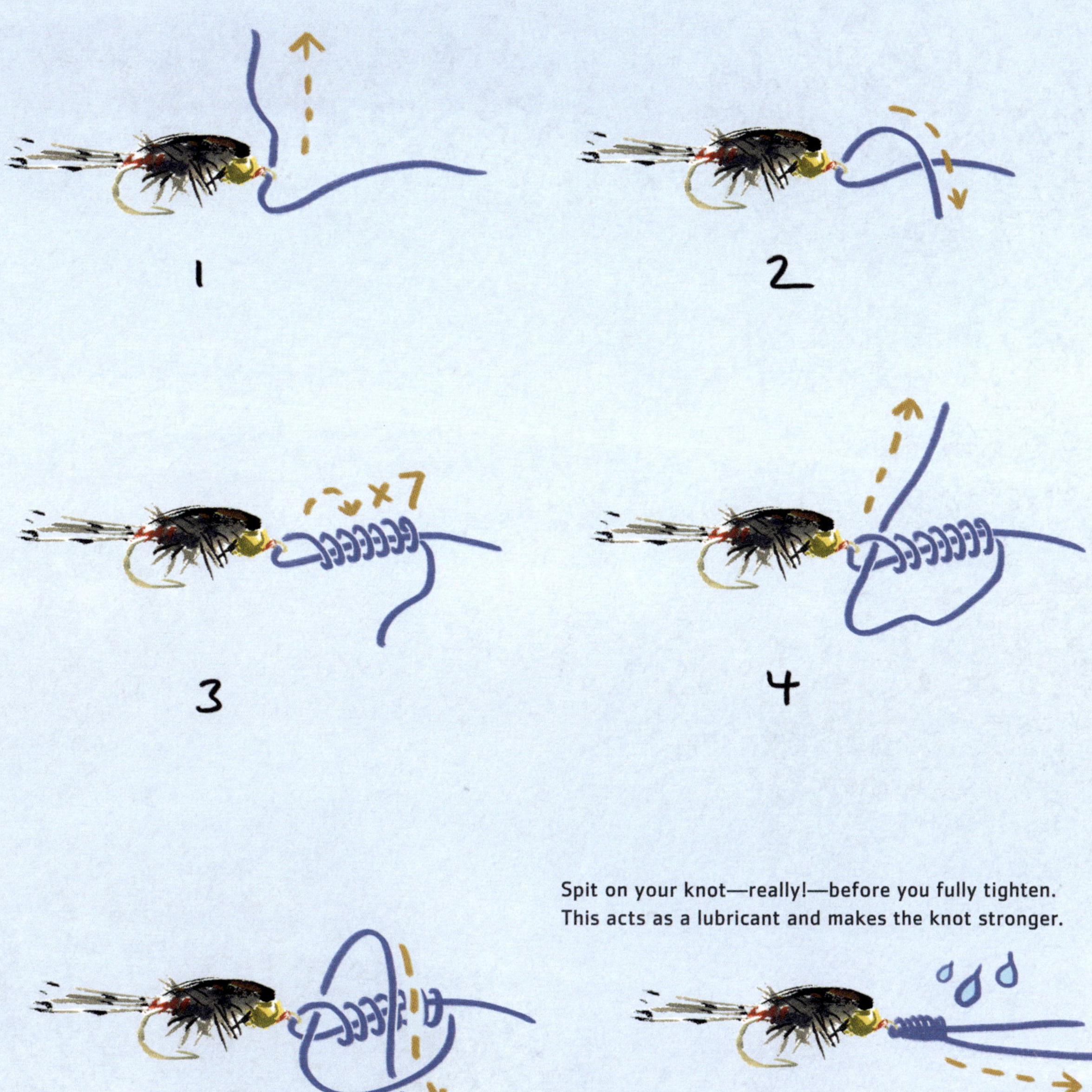

STREAMER KNOT

The improved clinch knot is almost too perfect. It forms a tight, strong connection between line and fly. Sometimes, though, you want a bit of a loop to remain to let something like a streamer "play" a bit more in the water. To do that, we add a regular old overhand knot at the beginning.

First, tie an overhand knot with plenty left over at the end. From here, it's basically an improved clinch knot . . .

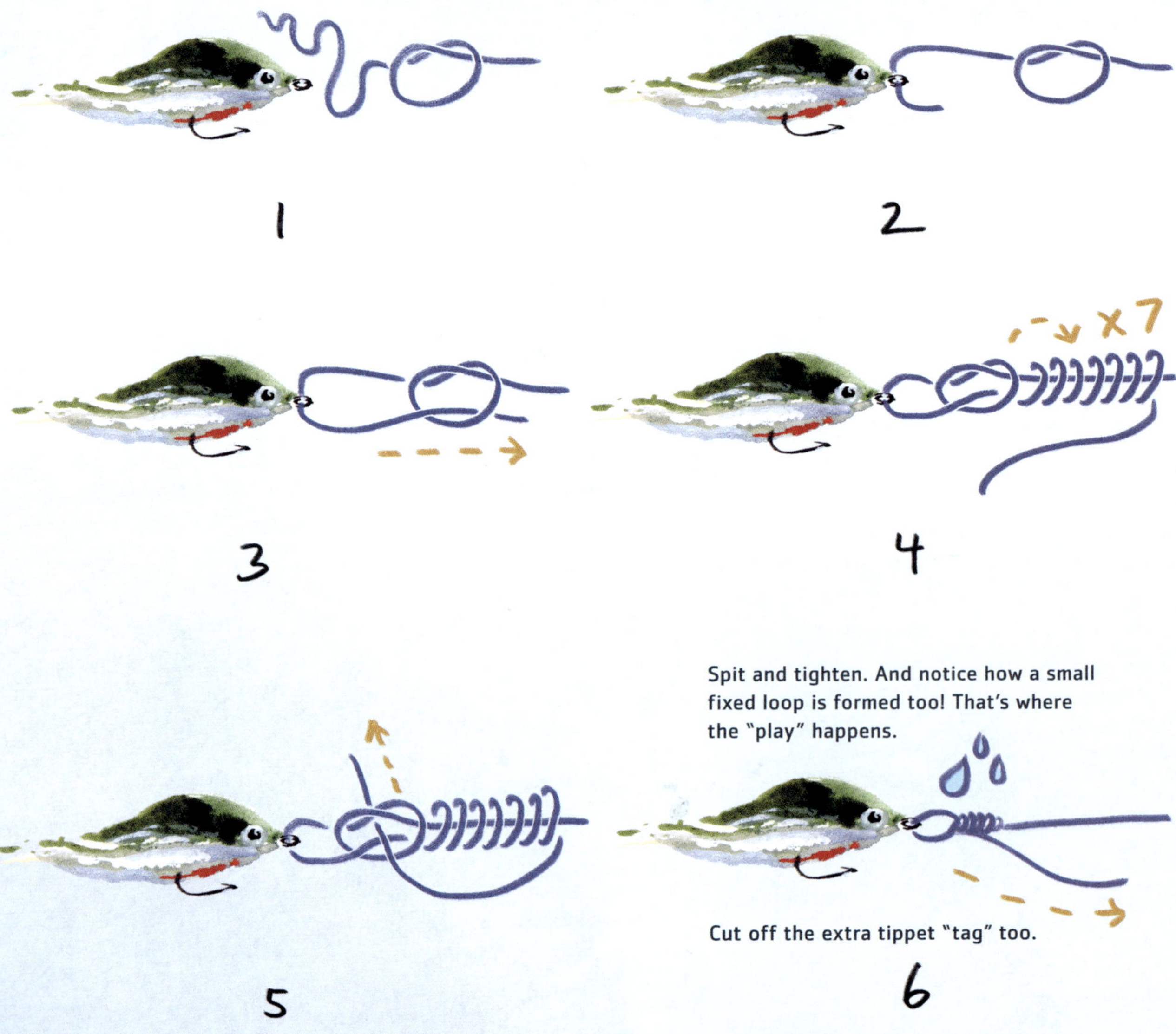

TRIPLE SURGEON'S KNOT

This one looks complicated, but is really just a series of overhand knots. It connects a leader (in blue) to tippet (in red). Or, occasionally, tippet to more tippet. Done well, it only leaves a tiny knot and bump between the two lines. Done poorly, it'll look like a glob of line and might even spook a fish!

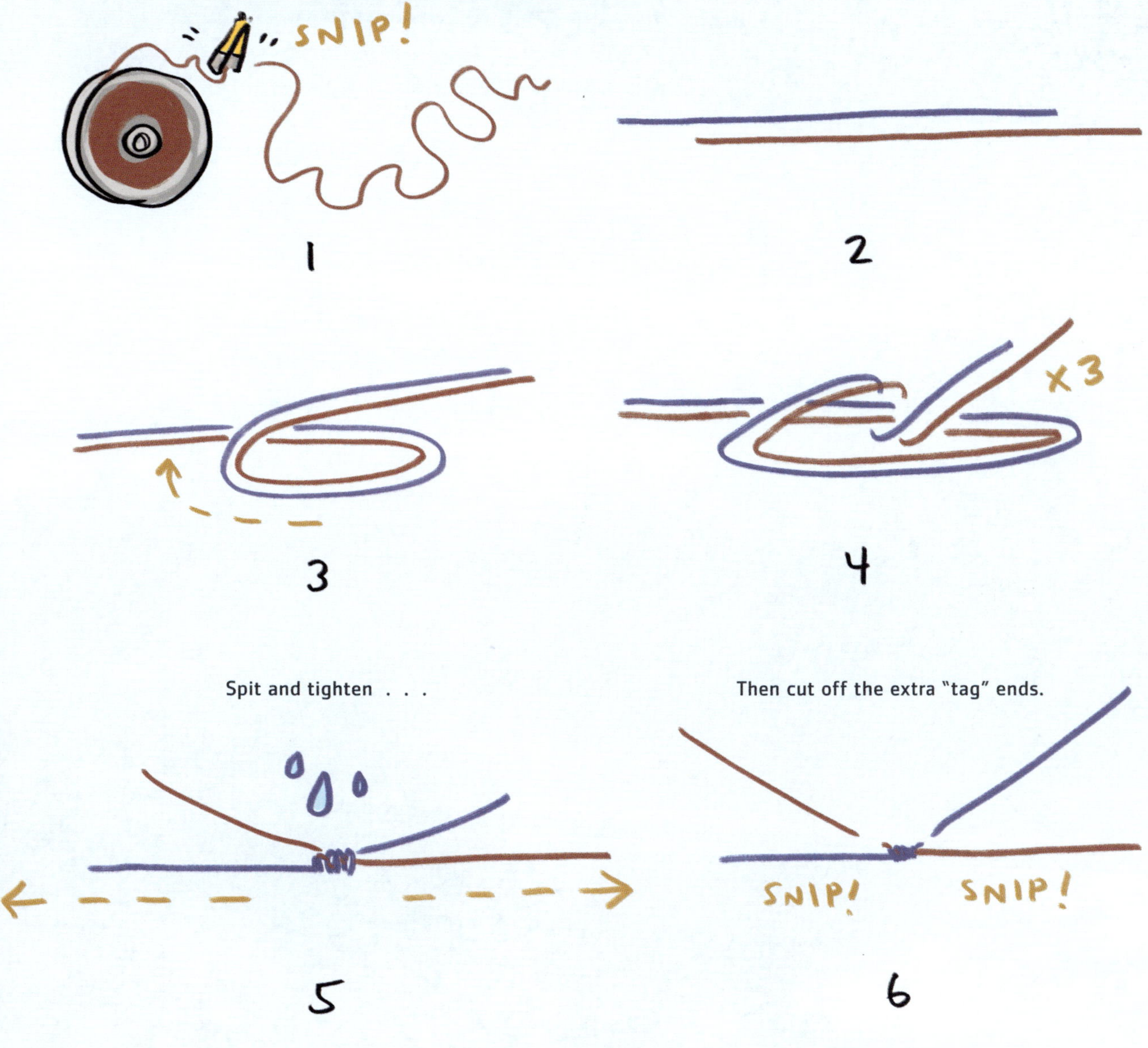

THE DREADED WIND KNOT . . .

It's a windy day. You do a less-than-ideal cast, try to fix it mid-cast, maybe try to fix it again, and then—

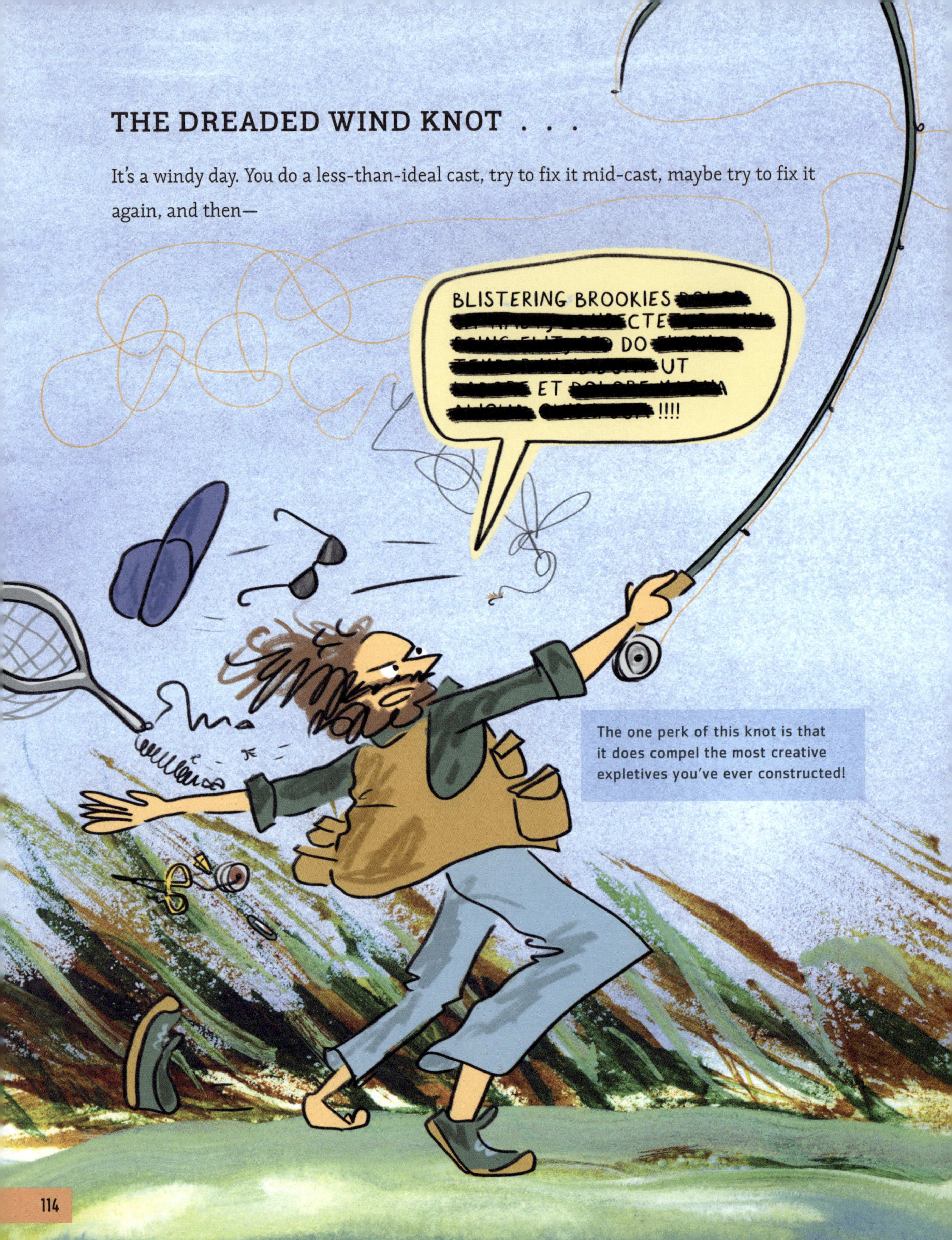

The one perk of this knot is that it does compel the most creative expletives you've ever constructed!

Undoing a wind knot requires a state of deep, deep calm. Ignore the bugs swirling around you. Ignore your friend pointing out the trout rising right in front of you. Just. Focus.

1. Assess the massive tangle in front of you. Try gently pulling it apart. Oh . . . sorry. Is that not working?

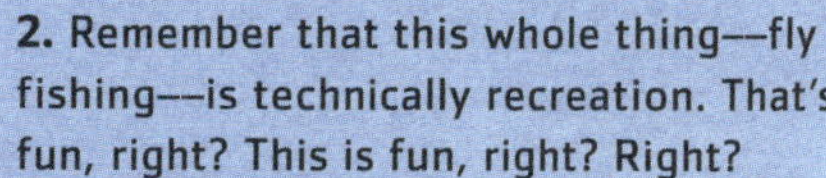

2. Remember that this whole thing—fly fishing—is technically recreation. That's fun, right? This is fun, right? Right?

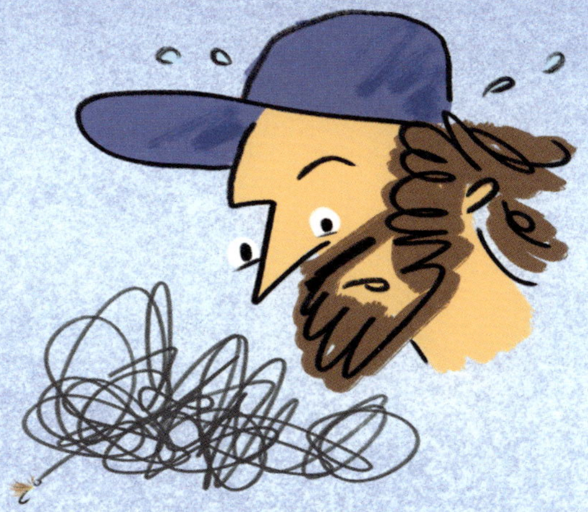

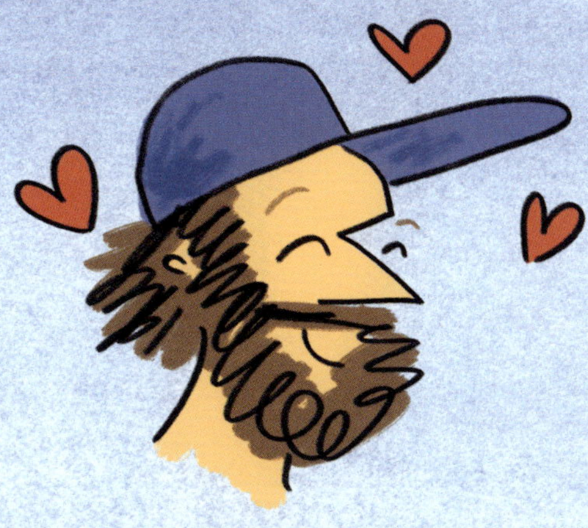

3. GENTLY pull at the line. Maybe use the hook of another fly to loosen it up. There's a chance it will all come undone. After all, what are the odds that you spontaneously invented the world's strongest knot? I mean, how long could this even take? GAHHHHHHHH! I'm missing so many fish right now!

4. Feel totally fine about cutting the damn thing apart and re-rigging your line. Remember: This is recreation. Have fun!

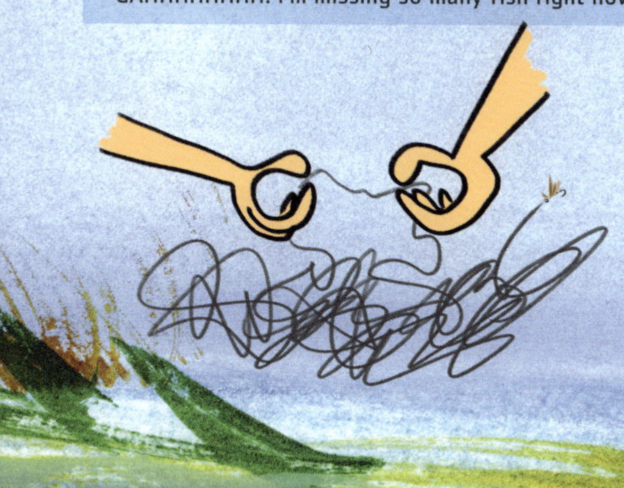

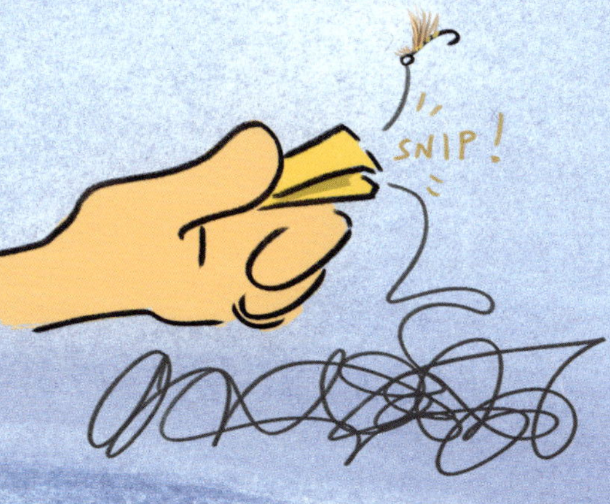

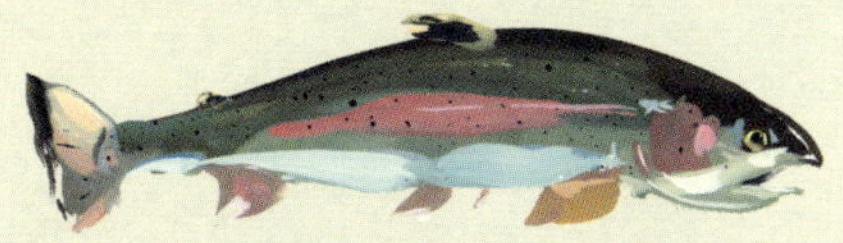

PART THREE: RELEASE

THE DEEPER KNOWLEDGE
YOU'LL NEED TO BE AN EXPERT.

7 KNOW YOUR HISTORY

ONE OF THE BEST PARTS of making this book was researching it. That's how I found myself motoring toward the Atlantic at sunrise with Captain Cody Rubner in Florida.

Cody's my favorite kind of guide: a friend, an expert, and an environmental advocate. When he's not pointing out a snook, he'll be explaining his last trip to Tallahassee or Washington, DC to bug someone in government, or sneaking in a mini-lecture on the history of seagrass versus Big Sugar. He sees the big picture. Or as he puts it . . .

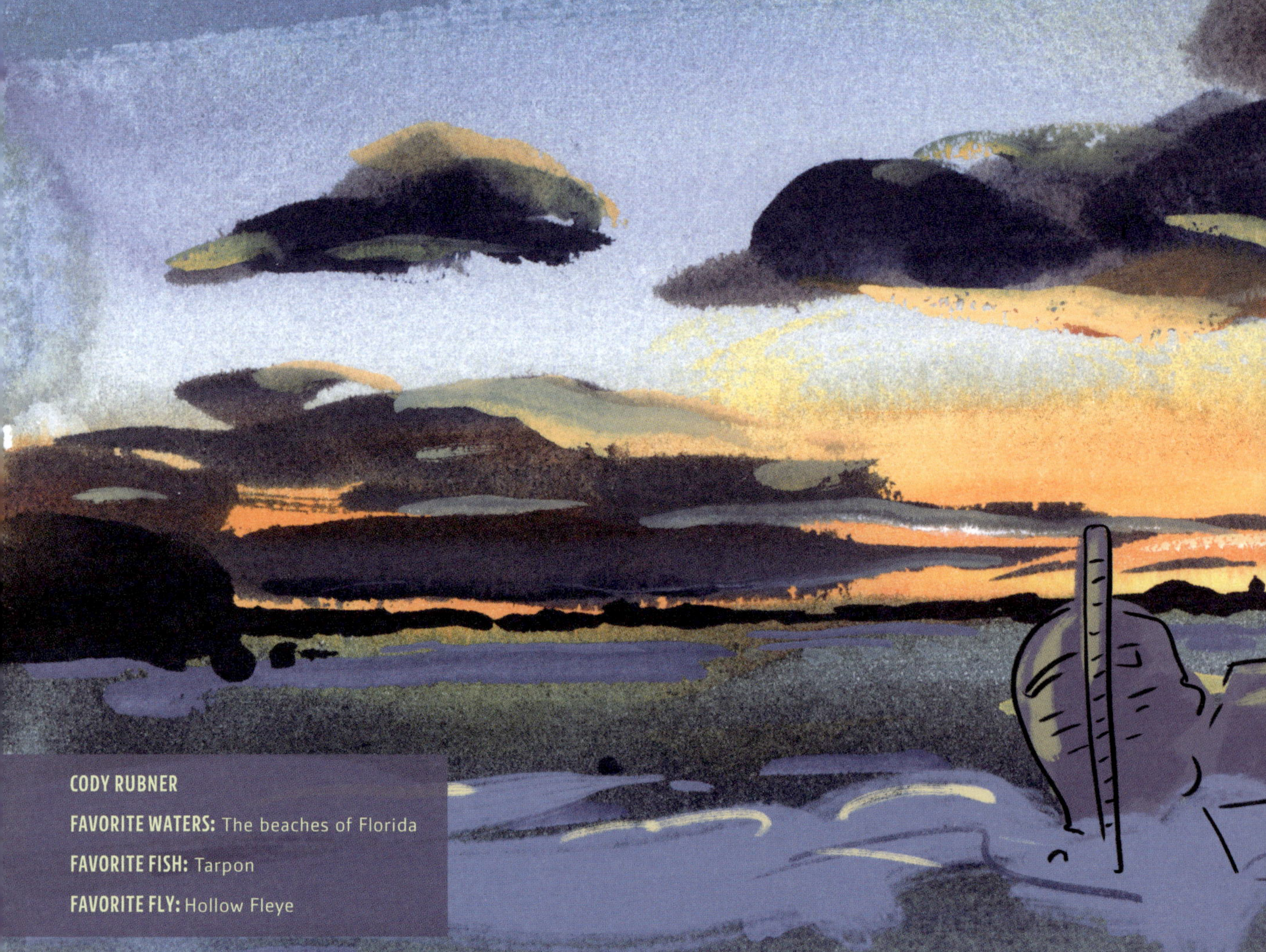

CODY RUBNER

FAVORITE WATERS: The beaches of Florida

FAVORITE FISH: Tarpon

FAVORITE FLY: Hollow Fleye

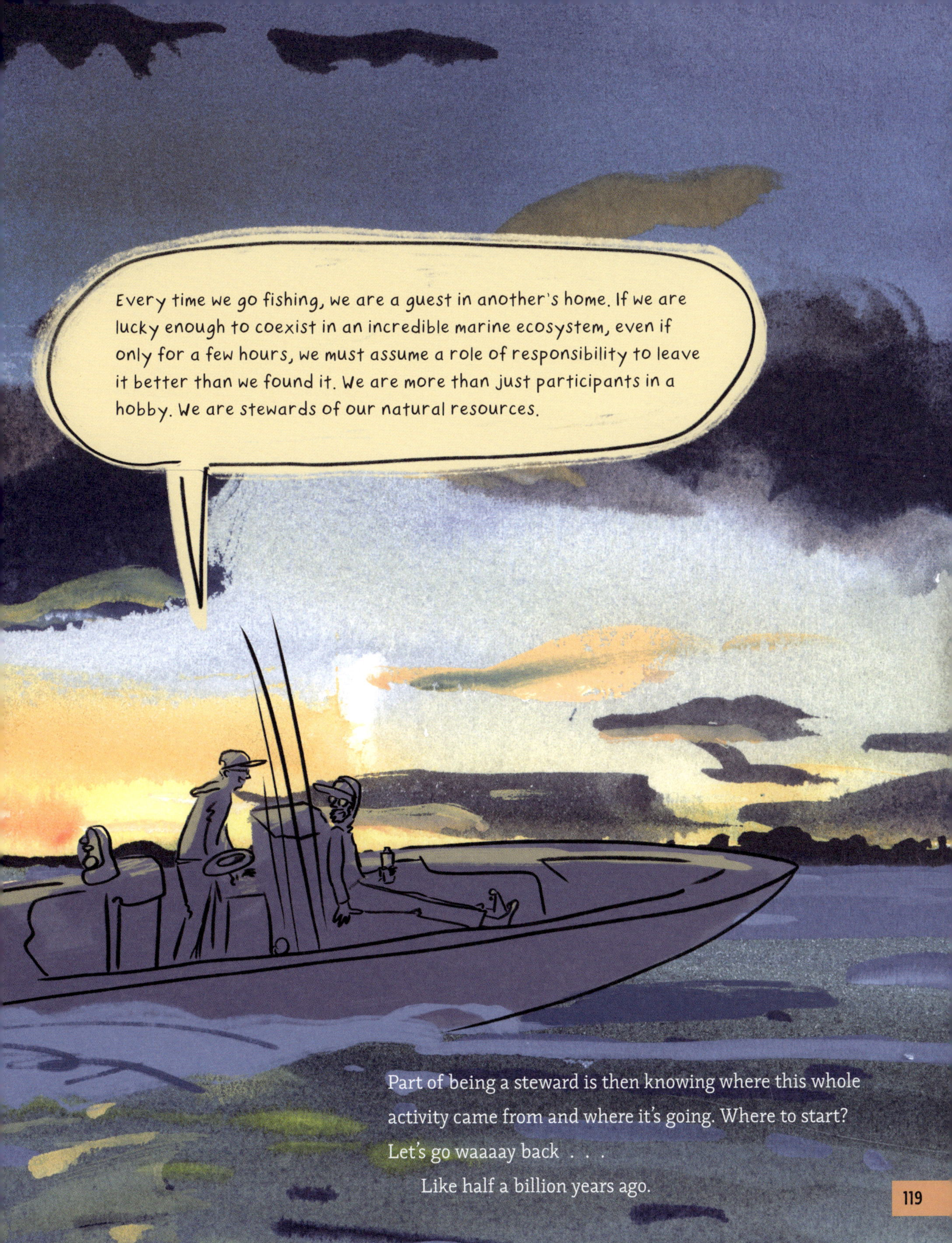

Part of being a steward is then knowing where this whole activity came from and where it's going. Where to start? Let's go waaaay back . . .

Like half a billion years ago.

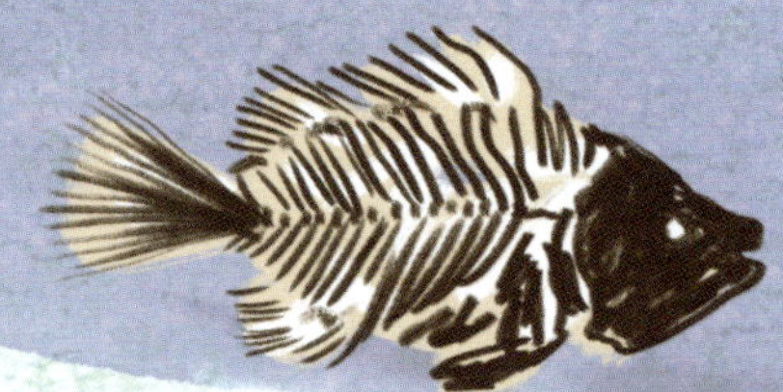

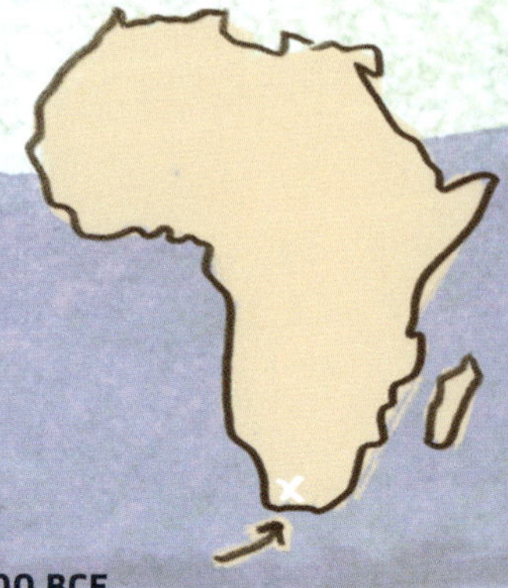

530 MILLION YEARS AGO

The first fish emerges in the fossil record. If someone invents time travel, I absolutely guarantee some fly fisher will go back and try to hook one of these.

138,000 BCE

Time travel aside, fish bones found in the Blombos Cave in South Africa are the oldest evidence of *Homo sapiens* fishing.

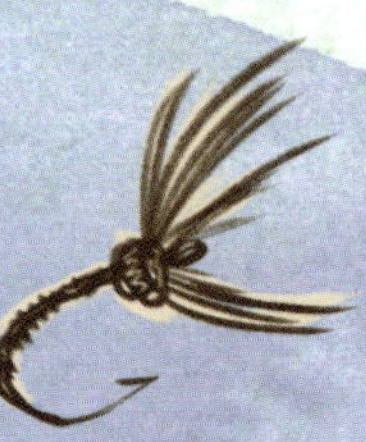

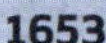

1653

Izaak Walton pens *The Compleat Angler,* considered by many to be the first book exclusively on fly fishing. Is it full of helpful tips? Not exactly . . . Full of lines you can drop on your next fishing trip? ABSOLUTELY.

1600(ISH)

Fly fishing in Japan, often called "tenkara," is usually cited to date back to this era. Likely, it's much older.

Oh the gallant Fisher's life,
It is the best of any;
'Tis full of pleasure, void of strife,
And 'tis belov'd of many

1791

Europeans describe the Seminole, Creek, Cherokee, and Choctaw peoples fly fishing in the Americas, suggesting that some sort of fly fishing was happening well before Europeans arrived. The fly is made from deer skin cured with the hair still on it and swung like a wet fly from a canoe.

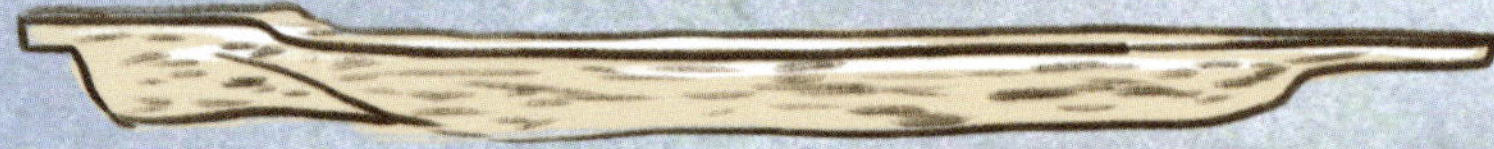

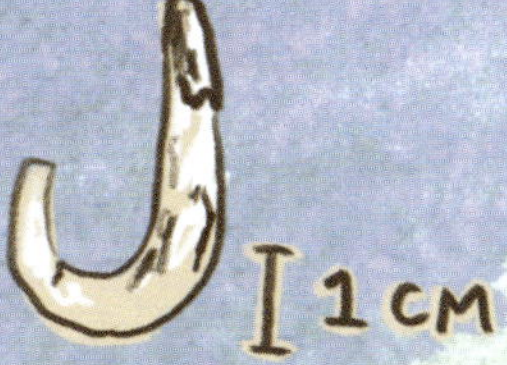

21,000 BCE

The oldest fishing hooks, made from shells and found in East Timor, date to around this time. I suspect previously attached feathers and fur have biodegraded over the millennia. Thus, this is indisputably the earliest example of fly fishing.

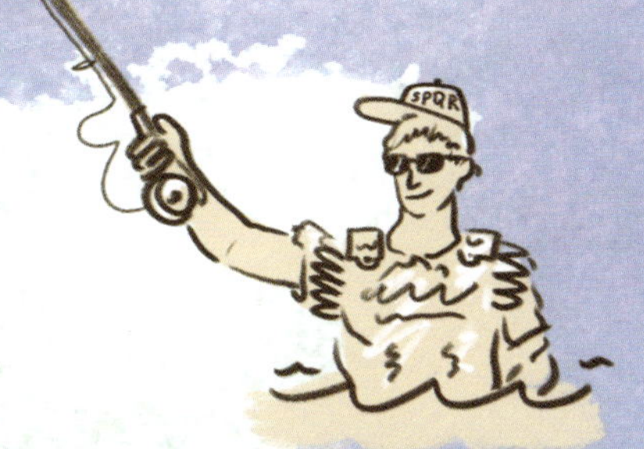

200(ISH) CE

The earliest written account of fly fishing, Claudius Aelianus's *De Natura Animalium*, mentions Macedonians using red wool and feather flies. Of course, the book also describes beavers cutting off their own testicles (with their teeth!) to foil would-be attackers . . . It's an honor joining this grand tradition of fly-fishing literature!

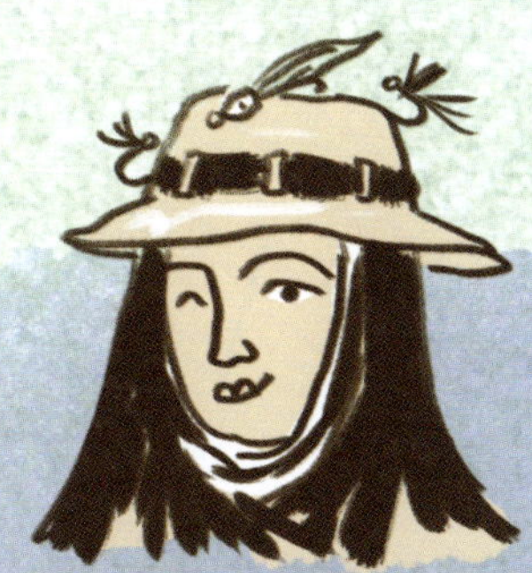

1486

The modern era of fly-fishing literature begins! A millennium or so after Aelianus and over in England, the *Book of Saint Albans* is written by Dame Juliana Berners. It covers a lot of the great outdoors—angling included.

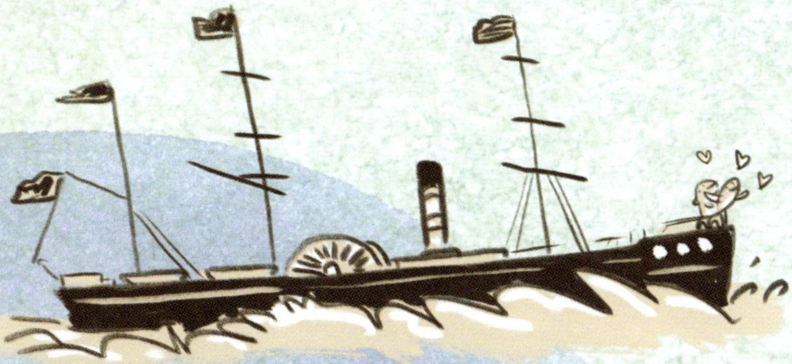

1850s

Europeans figure out how to transport fish eggs long-distance via steamship, bringing trout species all over the world. As befits the time period—environmental concerns about introducing invasive species globally were not deeply considered.

1890s
Catskills angler Theodore Gordon adapts English dry-fly styles to rougher North American waters. This spurs a whole new universe of fly tying. It's also why the Catskills are often seen as the birthplace of American fly fishing.

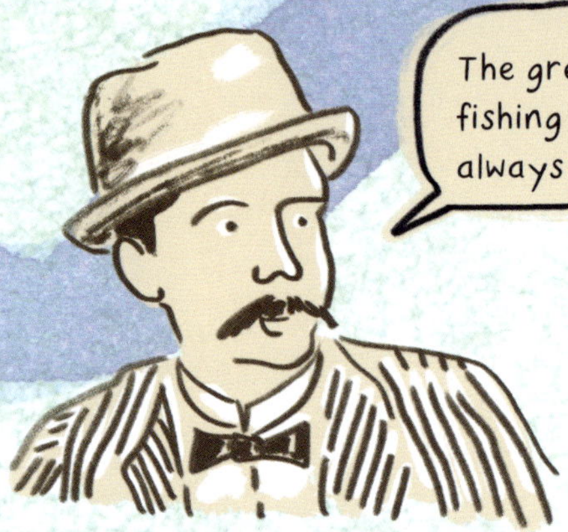

THEODORE GORDON

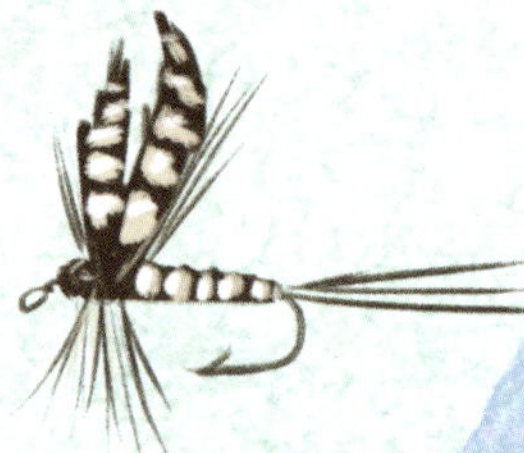

HIS "QUILL GORDON"

1920s
Ernest Hemingway's writing cements the image of fly fishing as something noble, done by men who'd rather not talk about their feelings. (Want to keep your feelings to yourself? Start with "Big Two-Hearted River.")

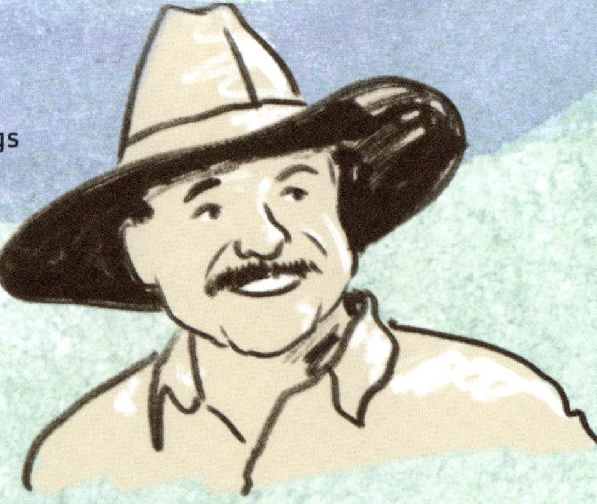

1920s AND ON
From here on, many of my favorite flies are invented. What I love about these flies is they're generalists and look all-around-buggy to trout.

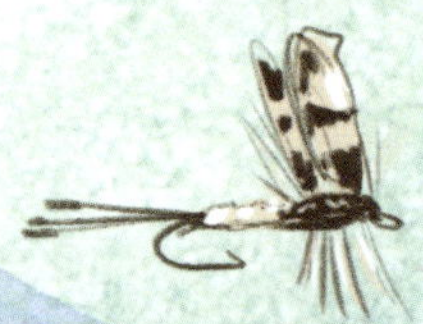

1922
The Adams

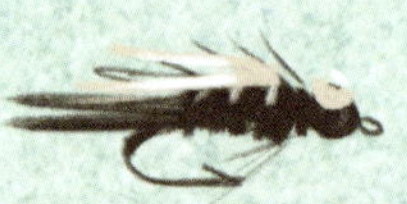

1930s
The Prince nymph

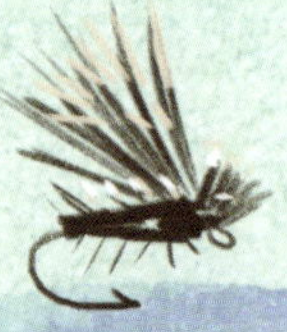

1957
The Elk Hair Caddis

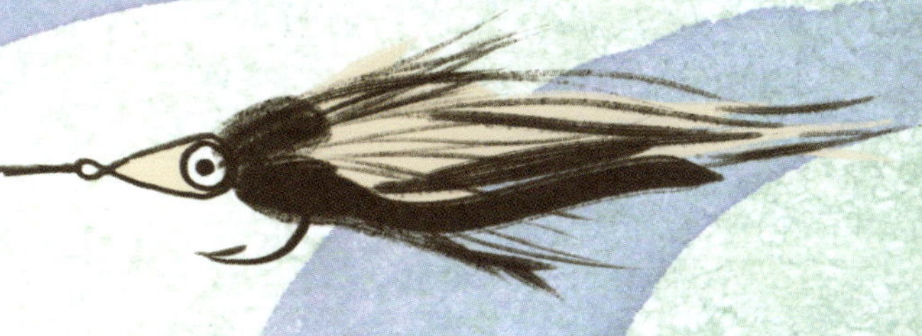

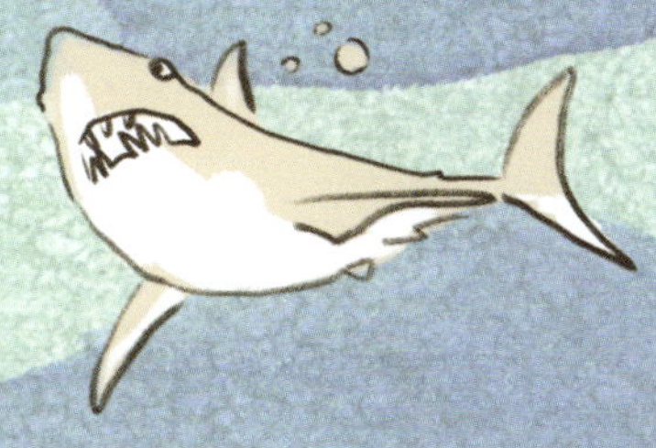

1960s AND '70s ON

Materials like carbon fiber, epoxy resin, foam, and other plastics revolutionize how and where we fly fish. This ushers in a new era of saltwater fly fishing and brings us flies for things like mako sharks!

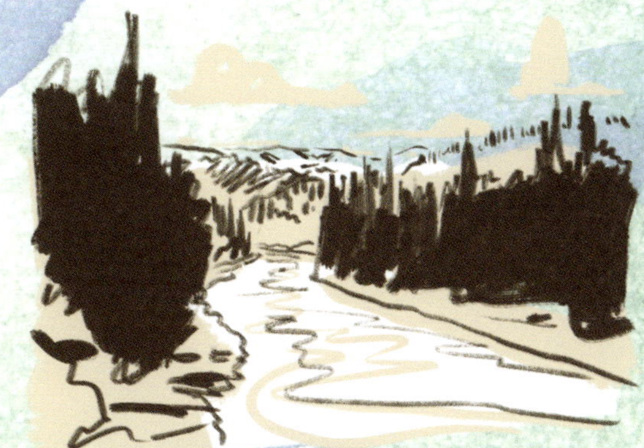

1976

Norman Maclean's masterpiece *A River Runs Through It* has always felt to me like the more emotionally mature version of Hemingway. The guys at least talk! Sometimes. And hey, it made me cry. Fourteen years later, the movie version will spur a renaissance of interest in fly fishing.

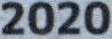

2020

Looking for safe activities during the COVID-19 pandemic, hordes of new anglers fall in love with fly fishing, starting a new boom.

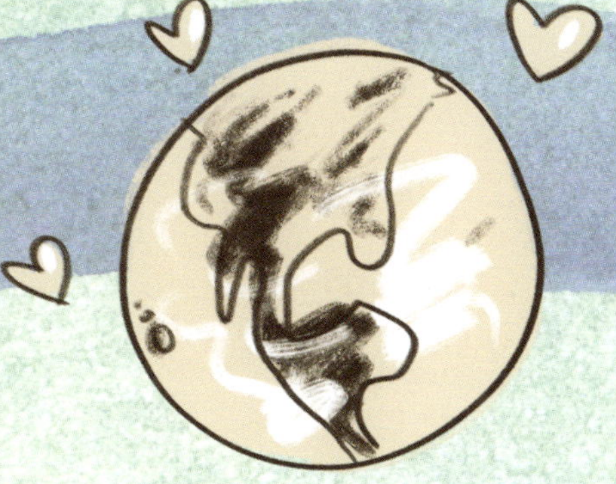

NOW (AND HOPEFULLY FOREVER)

Climate science, dam removal, and environmental advocacy? What inspires me the most about fly fishing is how it helps people to see the effect humans are having on the environment firsthand—and makes folks want to do something about it! (More on this on page 175.)

If the best way to learn how to fish is to fish, the best way to learn about fly fishing's history is to read. If this is your first book on fly fishing, strap in! There are plenty more. Here are some of the books* that informed and inspired me while becoming an angler and making this book.

HISTORY, TIPS & TECHNIQUE

Art Flick's New Streamside Guide to Naturals and Their Imitations by Art Flick

How to Read Water: Clues and Patterns from Puddles to the Sea by Tristan Gooley

Joan Wulff's New Fly-Casting Techniques by Joan Wulff

Longer Fly Casting by Lefty Kreh

Simple Fly Fishing Revised Second Edition: Techniques for Tenkara and Rod & Reel by Yvon Chouinard, Craig Mathews, and Mauro Mazzo

Tenkara by Daniel Galhardo

The Compleat Angler by Izaak Walton (and, later, Charles Cotton)

The Curtis Creek Manifesto: A Fully Illustrated Guide to the Strategy, Finesse, Tactics, and Paraphernalia of Fly Fishing by Sheridan Anderson

The History of Fly-Fishing in Fifty Flies by Ian Whitelaw

The Little Red Book of Fly Fishing by Kirk Deeter and Charlie Meyers

The Orvis Fly-Fishing Guide by Tom Rosenbauer (and everything else he's ever written)

The Unreasonable Virtue of Fly Fishing by Mark Kurlansky

Trout: An Illustrated History by James Prosek

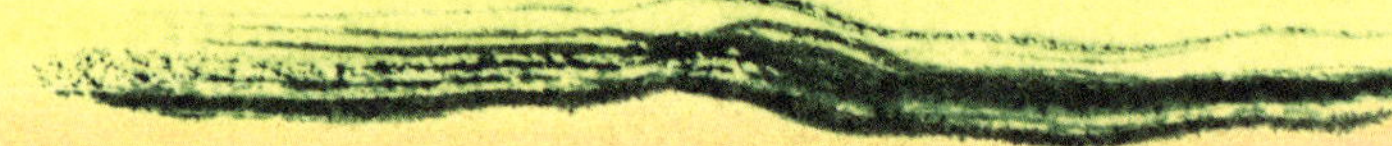

*Are you not an old white dude and thinking about writing a fly fishing book? PLEASE DO! In fact, look me up and I'd love to help you out. This genre desperately needs more voices.

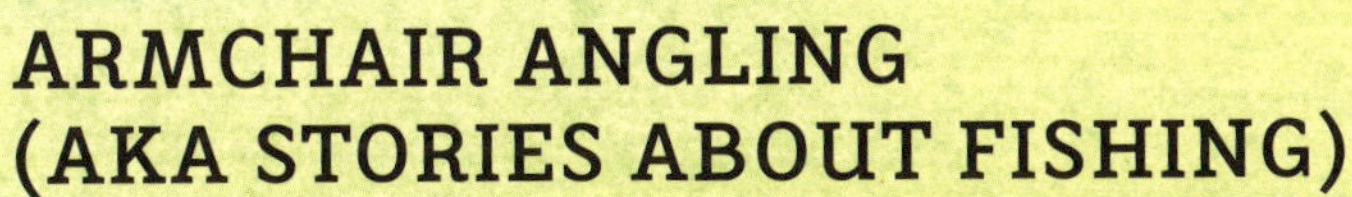

ARMCHAIR ANGLING (AKA STORIES ABOUT FISHING)

A River Runs Through It by Norman Maclean

Big Two-Hearted River by Ernest Hemingway

Cast, Catch, Release: Finding Serenity and Purpose through Fly Fishing by Marina Gibson

How to Think Like a Fish: And Other Lessons from a Lifetime in Angling by Jeremy Wade

Lords of The Fly: Madness, Obsession, and the Hunt for the World Record Tarpon by Monte Burke

The Art of Angling: Poems about Fishing (Everyman's Library Pocket Poets Series) edited by Henry Hughes

The Catch of a Lifetime: Moments of Flyfishing Glory by Peter Kaminsky, et al.

The Dog Stars by Peter Heller

The Longest Silence: A Life in Fishing by Thomas McGuane

The Optimist by David Coggins

Trout Bum by John Gierach

More of a magazine or blog reader? You're in luck! I'd start at Trout Unlimited's *Trout* Magazine, and then FlyLords.com online.

And from there . . . *Gray's Sporting Journal, The Drake, The American Fly Fisher, The Wading List, The Fly Fish Journal, Anglers Journal* . . . Delightfully, this list flows on and on!

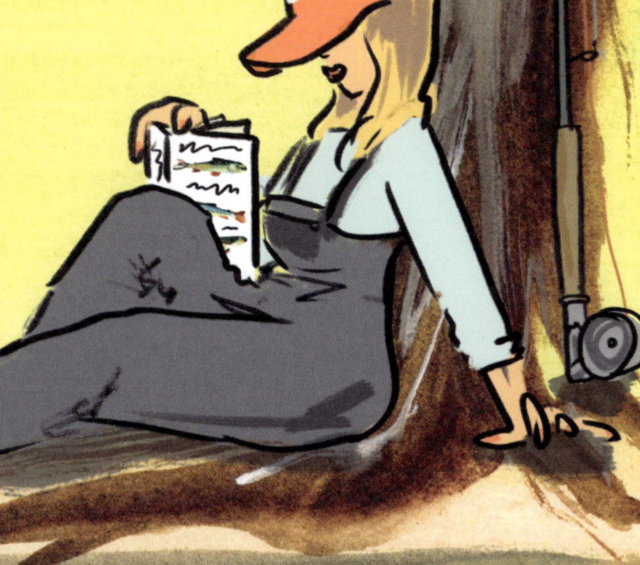

8 THINK LIKE A FISH

IT'S A PERFECT EARLY SUMMER DAY in New York City's Central Park. You know, that early part of summer where people are actually excited about it being warm, not feeling suffocated by the humidity and resenting everyone who's sneaking away to somewhere cooler.

I'm with Brandon Dale, my friend and fishing guide—IN NYC!—and we're fishing for carp. A warning, though: Brandon's the kind of person who makes you feel like you haven't done much with your life. Because at some point, while on the way to getting his MD/PhD at Mount Sinai, he realized he liked fly fishing for carp. How much? He thought, *"Why not become a licensed fishing guide too?"*

I'm very happy he did! I love his approach to fishing . . .

BRANDON DALE

FAVORITE WATERS: The Blackstone River

FAVORITE FISH: Carp

FAVORITE FLY: Mojo Mulberry

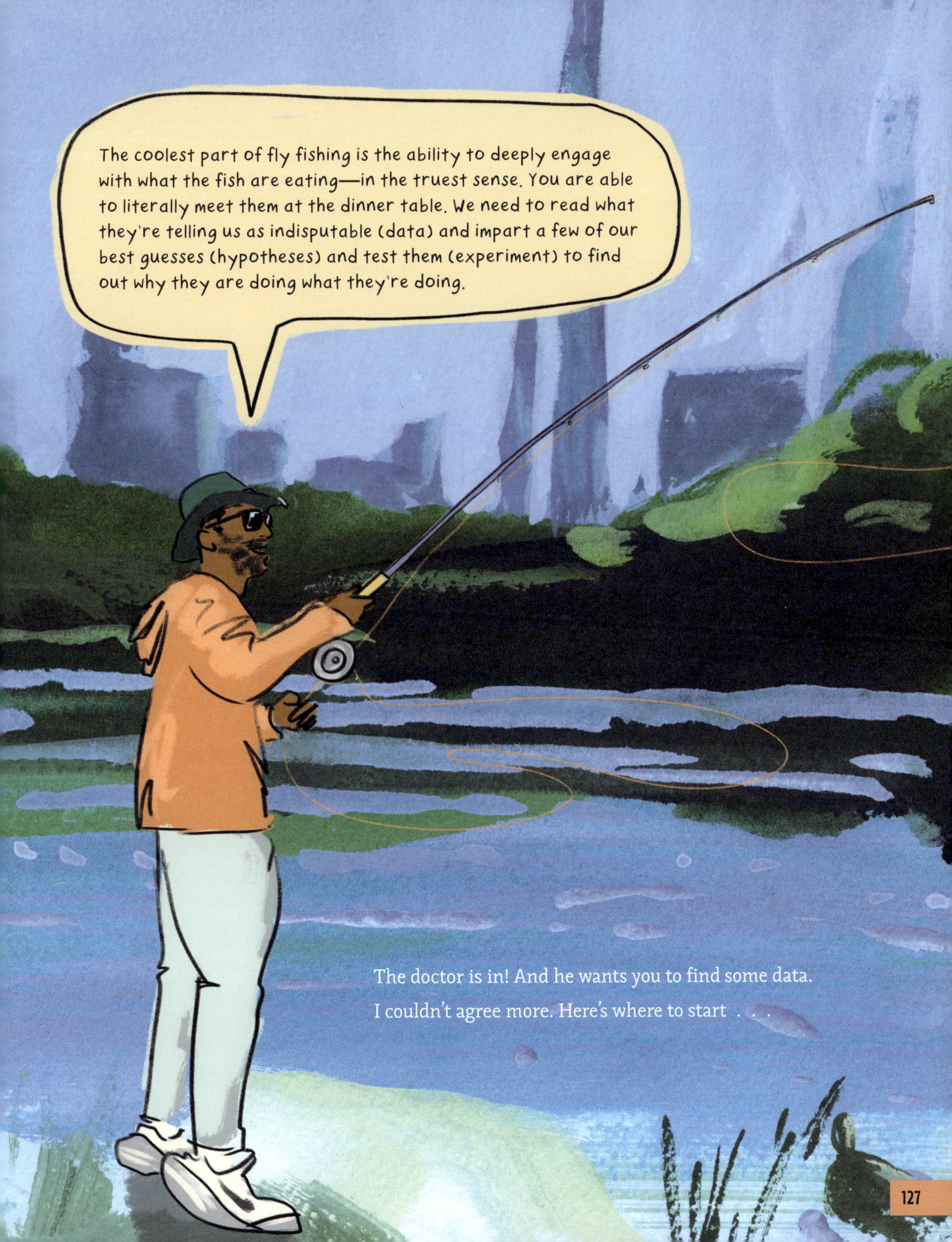

The doctor is in! And he wants you to find some data.

I couldn't agree more. Here's where to start . . .

TEMPERATURE

Temperature may be the biggest data point to consider before you head to any body of water. Fish are cold-blooded, which means that temperature regulation, metabolism, and overall energy (do they want to chase a fly?) are at the whim of water conditions. You need to know their Goldilocks zones, especially if you're catch-and-release fishing. If it's too warm, simply the act of hooking and fighting a fish can kill it.

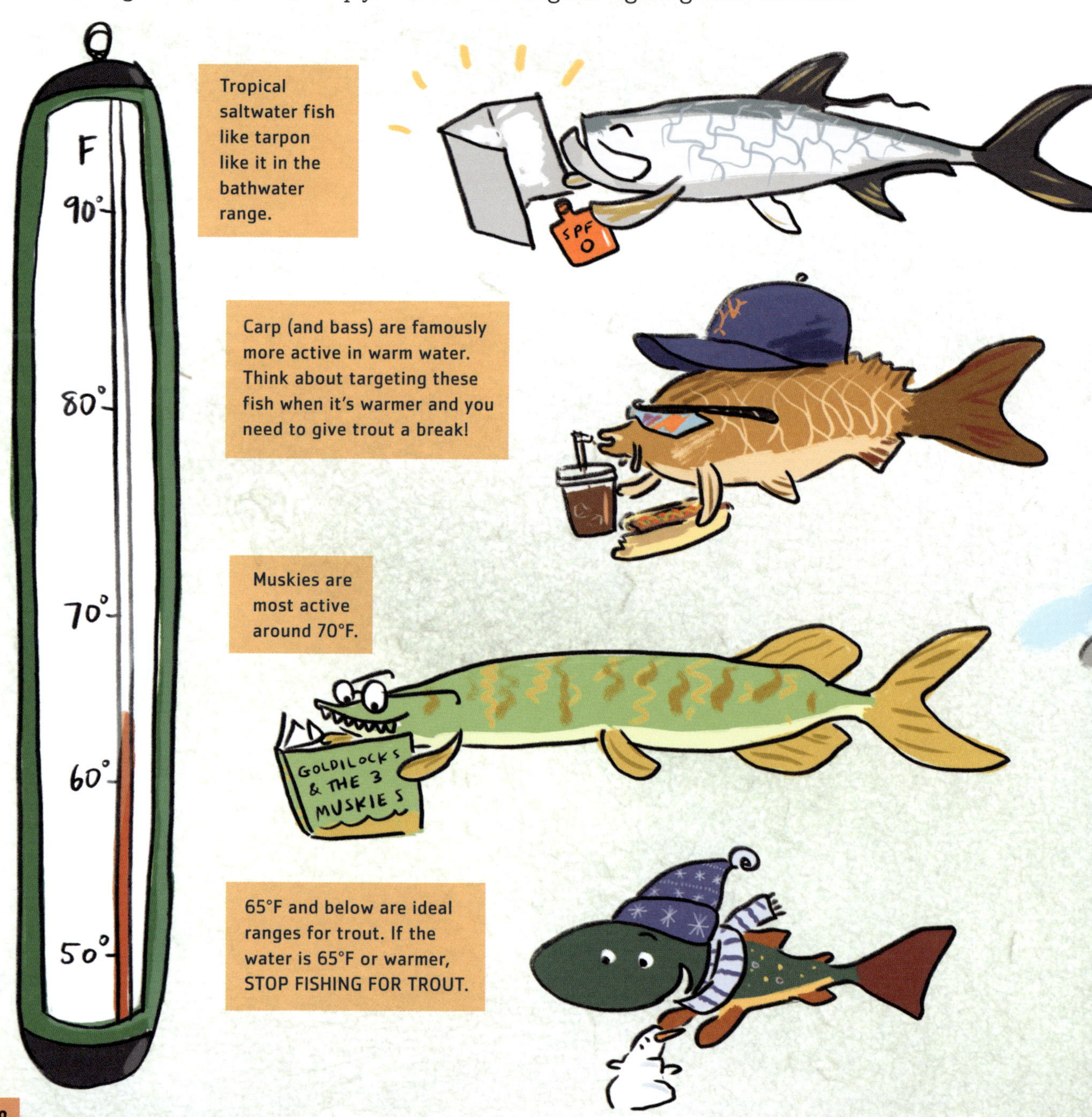

OXYGEN

Yes, fish breathe!

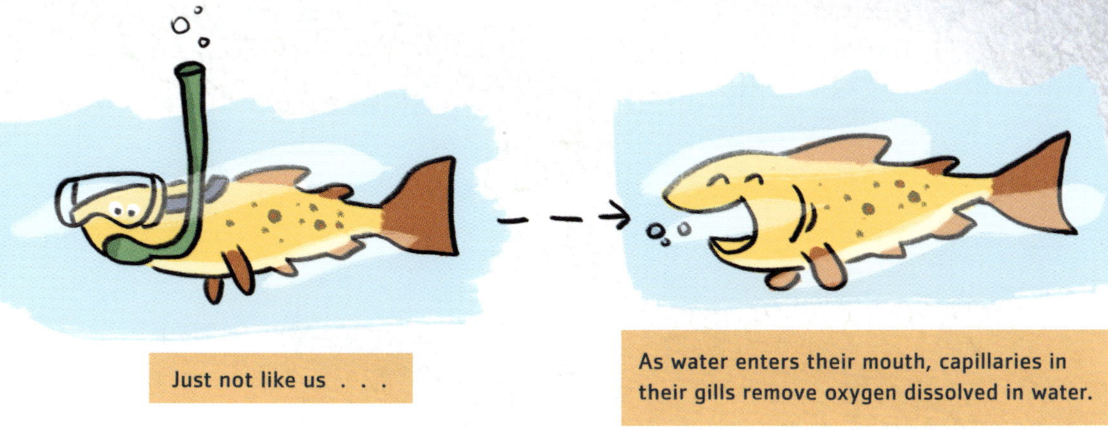

The important thing here is that there is essentially more oxygen (O_2) in some parts of the waterway than others. Trout like fast-moving cold water. But they also don't want to spend all day working against the current. So, ideally, they find a spot near moving water in an eddy.

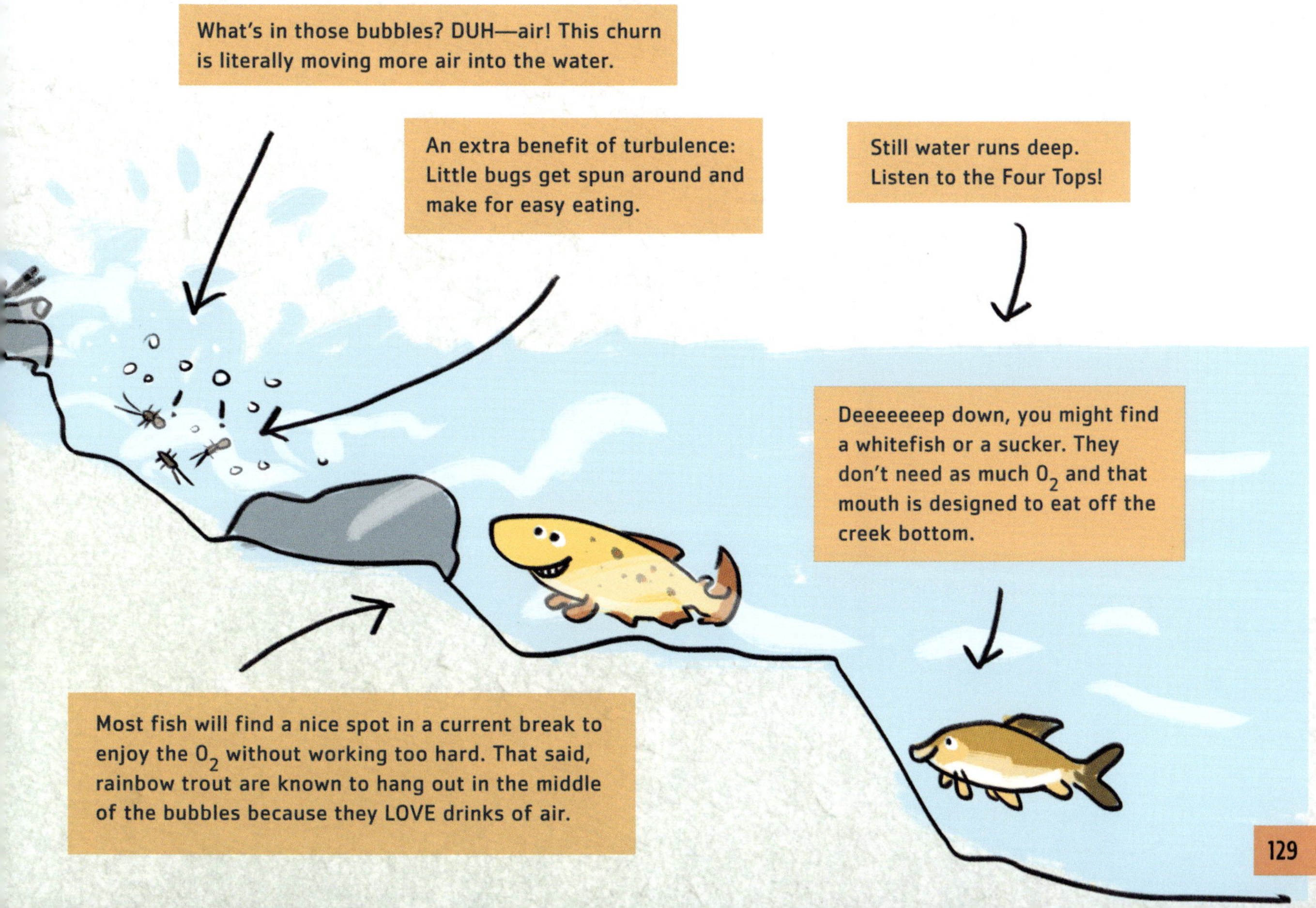

What's in those bubbles? DUH—air! This churn is literally moving more air into the water.

An extra benefit of turbulence: Little bugs get spun around and make for easy eating.

Still water runs deep. Listen to the Four Tops!

Deeeeeeep down, you might find a whitefish or a sucker. They don't need as much O_2 and that mouth is designed to eat off the creek bottom.

Most fish will find a nice spot in a current break to enjoy the O_2 without working too hard. That said, rainbow trout are known to hang out in the middle of the bubbles because they LOVE drinks of air.

And how do fish take this all in? Trout, and to various degrees other fish, rely mainly on three senses:

SIGHT

A trout's best vision is directly ahead, and it's described as telescopic, which I have never been able to ask trout about. But from experience, I believe it.

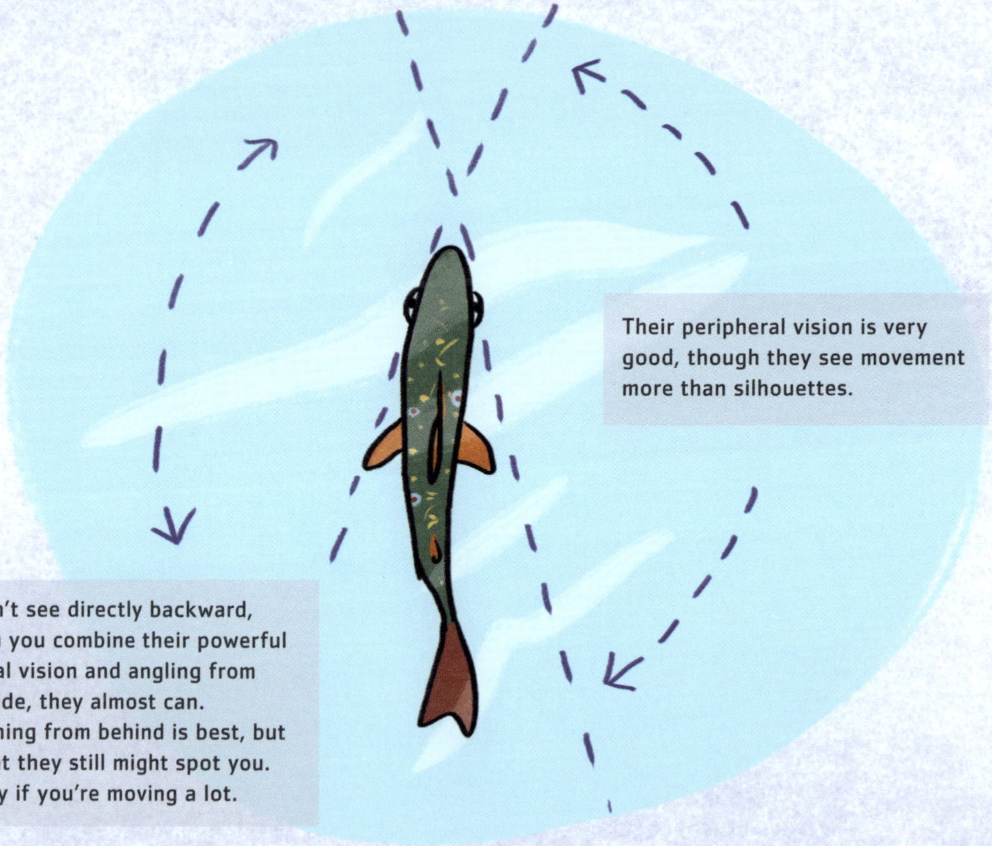

Their peripheral vision is very good, though they see movement more than silhouettes.

Trout can't see directly backward, but when you combine their powerful peripheral vision and angling from side to side, they almost can. Approaching from behind is best, but know that they still might spot you. Especially if you're moving a lot.

Trout can see in color too. This generally only makes a big difference in super-clean water and when they have time to check out your fly. Even then, many anglers swear the shape and presentation of the fly make a much bigger difference than the color.

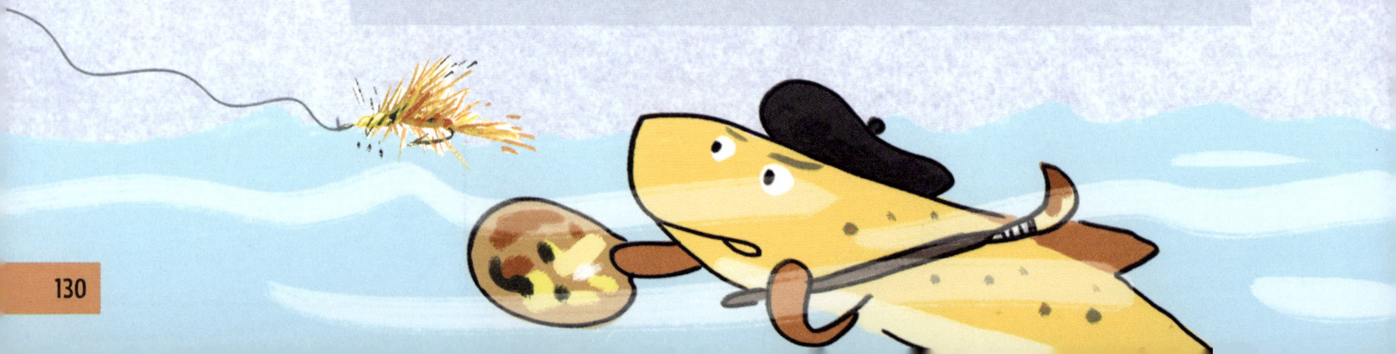

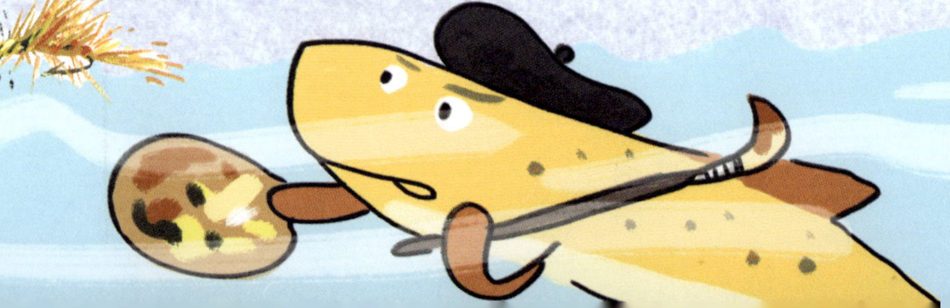

SOUND/FEEL

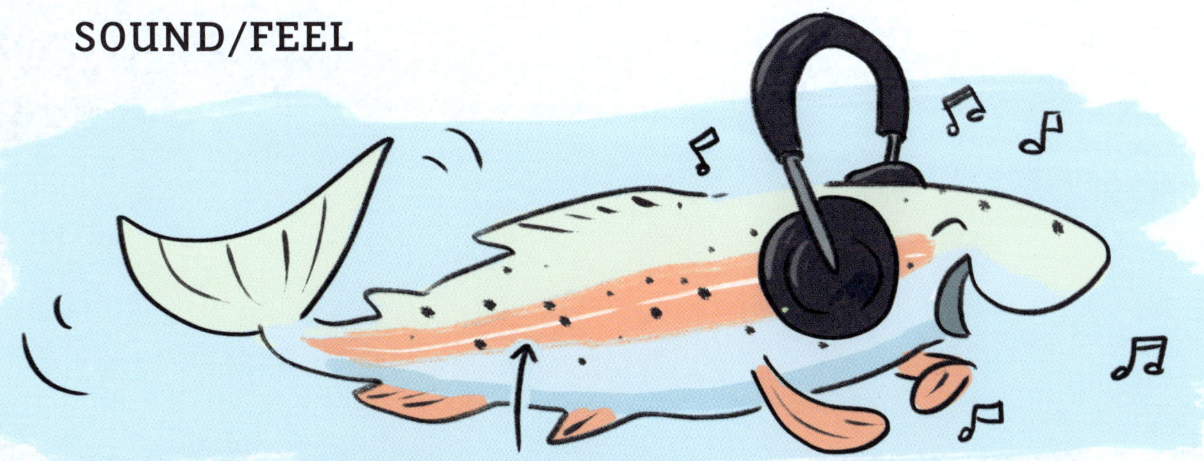

Trout hear sound (with their version of ears inside their body). And maybe more importantly, they FEEL it. They do this through very sensitive lateral lines across their bodies.

SMELL

Trout can smell too! But less so than some other fish (like carp—which is why you never want to use floatant when targeting carp). So, while you're not using something smelly like worms or cut bait to attract fish, it's good to think about any weird smells you might introduce into the water.

Sunblock, bug spray, and other smells not native to a stream can spook fish. My favorite move is to rub your hands in creek mud when you start fishing to cover whatever smells are there.

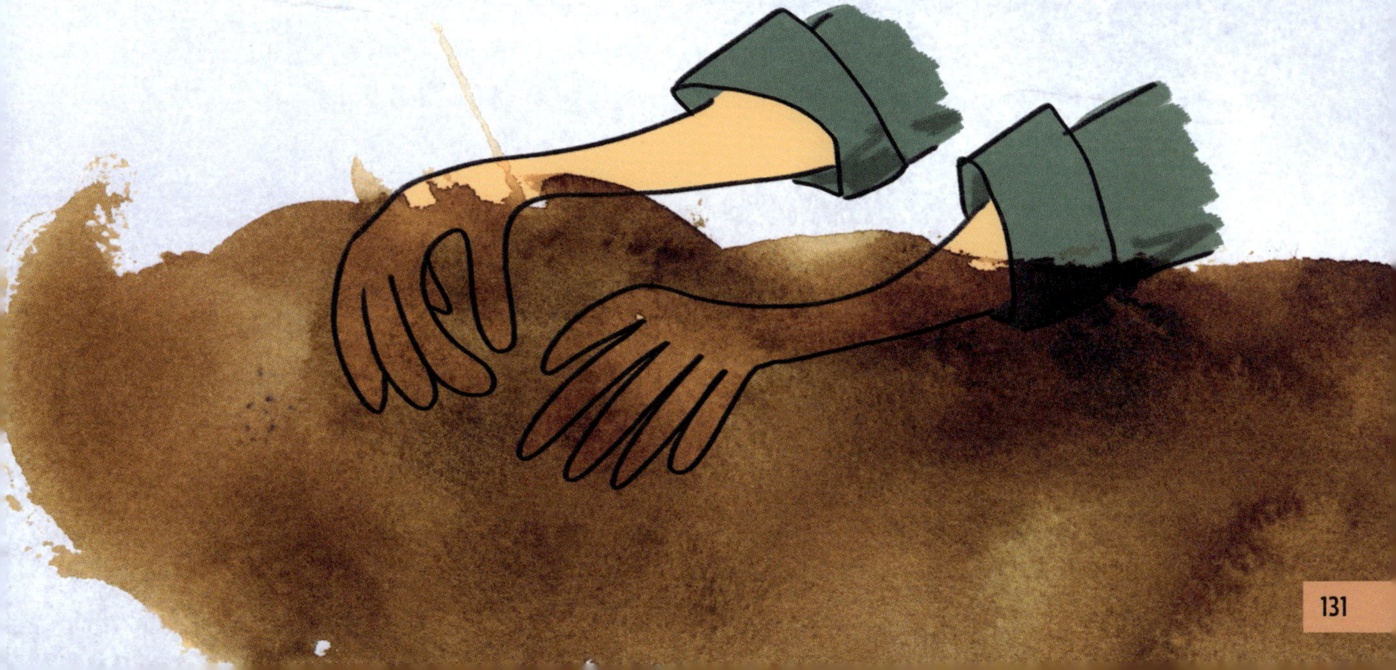

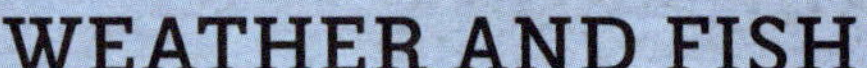

WEATHER AND FISH

Since temperature is so important to fish, weather obviously is too. Basically, SUPER bright and hot is bad. (Bad for trout—it's great for some saltwater angling.) Super cold is bad too. You want something right in between. Here's a perfect day for trout fishing:

No wind. This makes it easier to cast and easier for your fly to drift on the surface.

Lower light makes fish feel more hidden from predators. Their eyes also work well in this light.

AIR 70°F

IDEAL!

WATER 58°F

Bugs like mayflies tend to hatch out of the water more frequently and for longer periods when it's overcast . . .

Let's make some babies and then die, woooo-hooo!

Clear, medium-flow water. This generally means you're not in a drought (when fish will be stressed) or coming right after a huge storm (when the water is harder to fish).

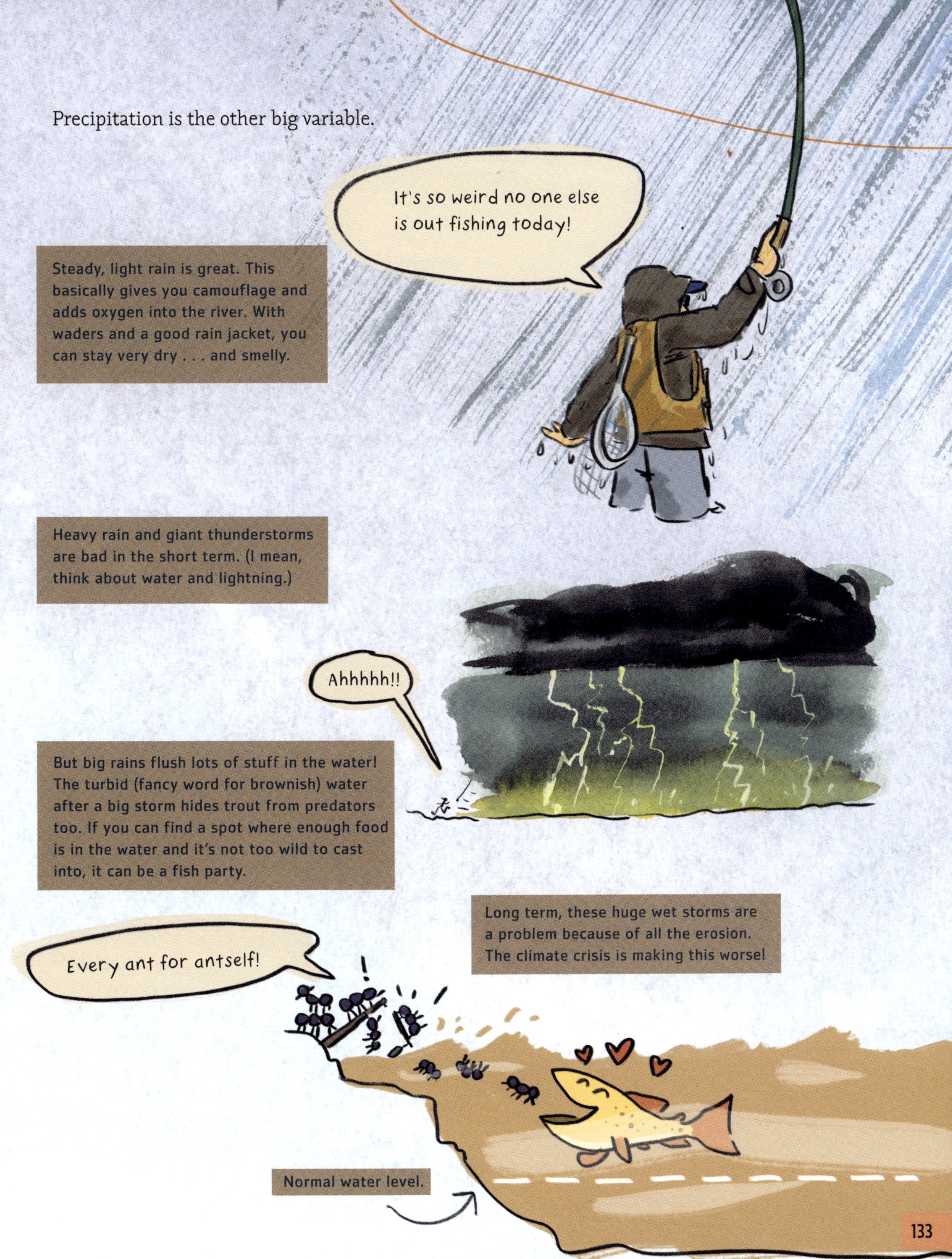
Precipitation is the other big variable.
It's so weird no one else is out fishing today!
Steady, light rain is great. This basically gives you camouflage and adds oxygen into the river. With waders and a good rain jacket, you can stay very dry . . . and smelly.
Heavy rain and giant thunderstorms are bad in the short term. (I mean, think about water and lightning.)
Ahhhhh!!
But big rains flush lots of stuff in the water! The turbid (fancy word for brownish) water after a big storm hides trout from predators too. If you can find a spot where enough food is in the water and it's not too wild to cast into, it can be a fish party.
Every ant for antself!
Long term, these huge wet storms are a problem because of all the erosion. The climate crisis is making this worse!
Normal water level.

TIDES!

The other big variation in water is tides! Mostly, this affects saltwater fishing—but you'll also see tidal effects in estuaries like the Hudson River. Here's a super simple way to think about how tides affect your fishing . . .

1. LOW TIDE

Often not the best for fishing . . . but take this as an opportunity to observe the fishing landscape without water.

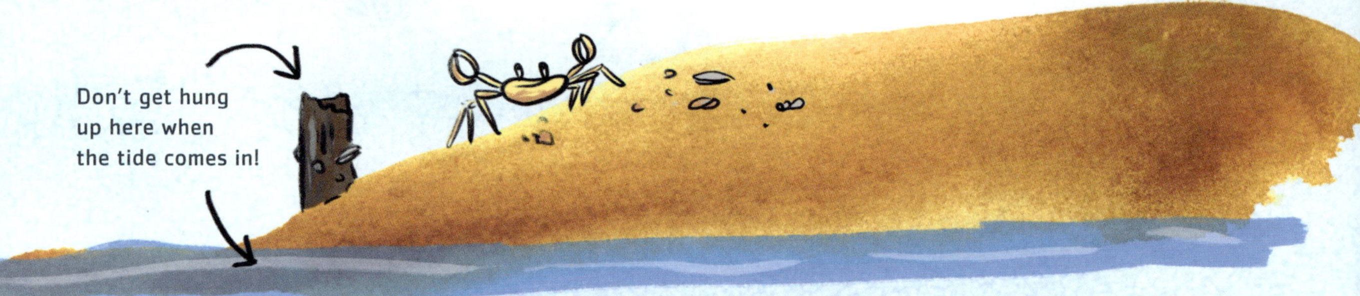

2. TIDE COMING IN (AKA FLOOD TIDE)

Where the action is! The water is pushing in more food from the deeper water, and fish are checking out the new real estate expanding by the second. It's pretty humbling to watch a tide come in and see the power of all this water on our planet.

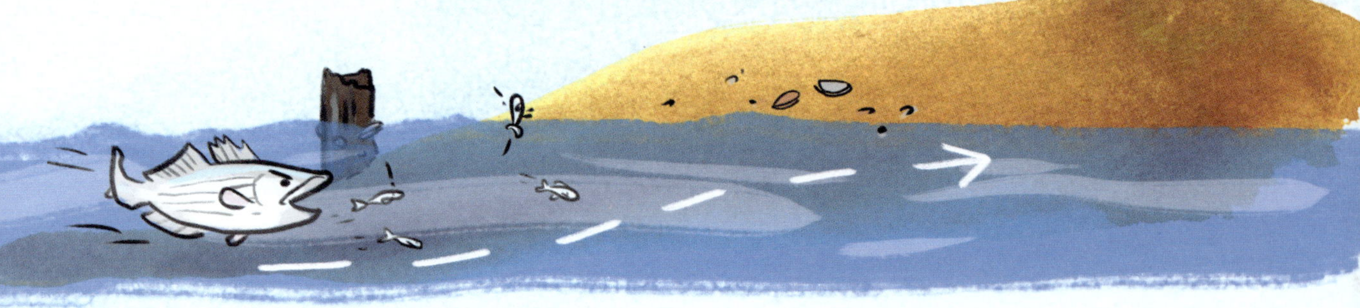

WE CAN MOSTLY THANK THE MOON FOR THE TIDES. HERE ARE THE BIG THINGS TO THINK ABOUT:

Moon phase! The fuller the moon, the bigger the tides. (Also, the more theories as to whether or not this helps fishing. I've heard them all and have no idea!)

Moon plus sun! When the moon and sun line up, the tide is stronger and called a spring tide. (Neap tide is the opposite.)

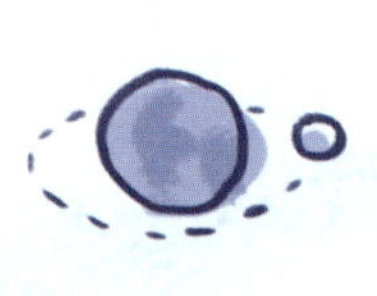

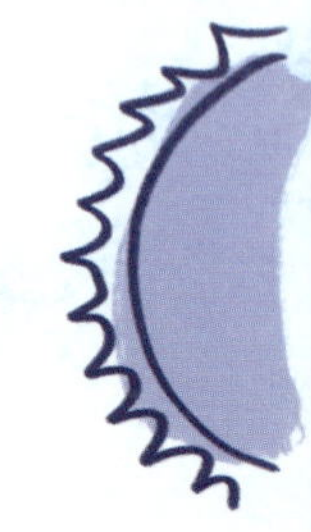

3. HIGH TIDE

When tides hit their high or low point, this is called the slack tide. The water moves a lot less during this time and fishing is often not great.

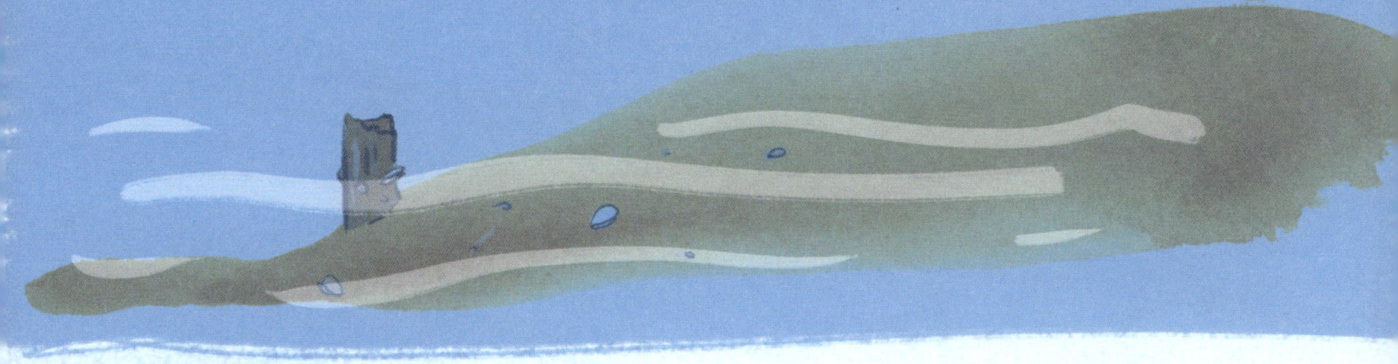

4. TIDE GOING OUT (AKA EBB TIDE)

Another great time to fish! Remember, no matter the water, always look to places of change to find fish.

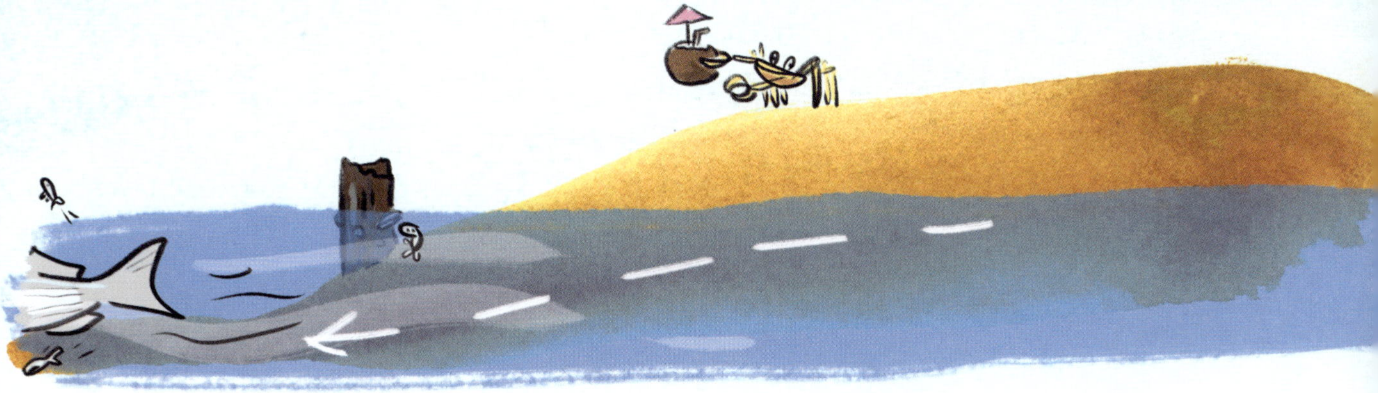

But most importantly, learn to enjoy tides! I like the attitude of saltwater expert—and author of my favorite history of saltwater fly fishing, *Lords of The Fly*—Monte Burke:

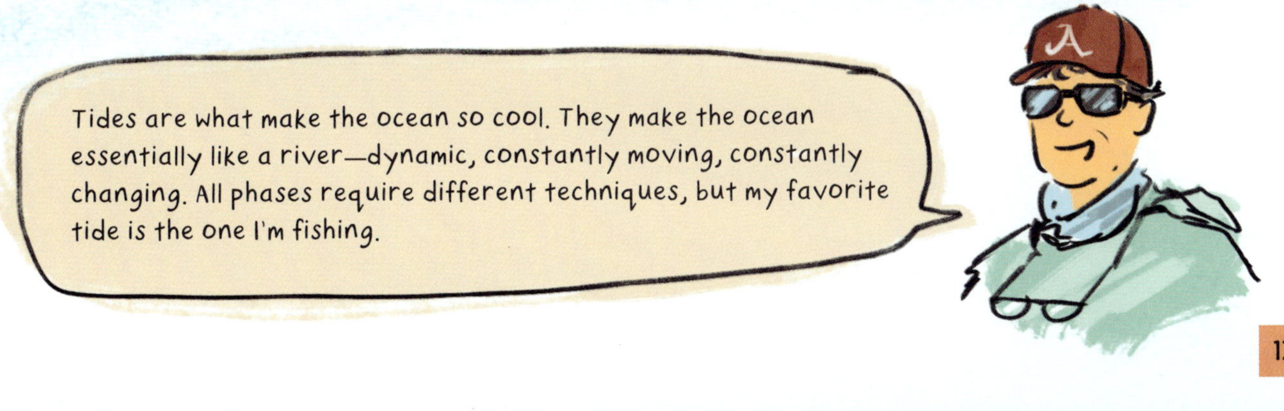

Tides are what make the ocean so cool. They make the ocean essentially like a river—dynamic, constantly moving, constantly changing. All phases require different techniques, but my favorite tide is the one I'm fishing.

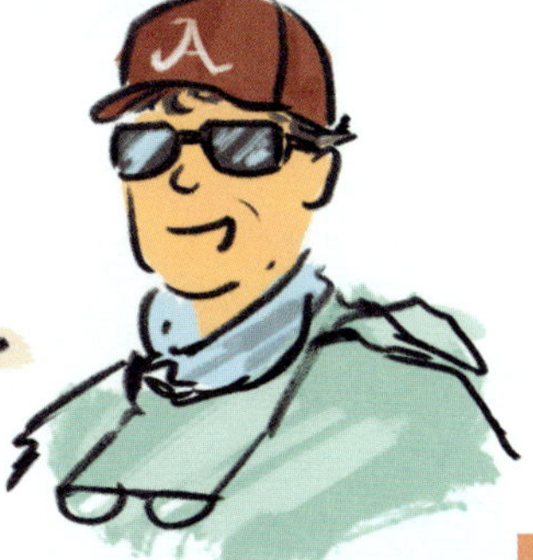

SEE IT ALL FOR YOURSELF!

Do you really want to think like a fish? Then maybe put away your rod and waders and pick up some snorkel gear. No, really—this is a thing!

Because, especially in the world of catch and release fishing, isn't the main idea to just see these beautiful creatures in action? Who needs a hook for that?

I first learned about this through Anna Le, a fisheries biologist and founder of the conservation consultancy Grayling Education. As an angler, snorkeling has helped her understand where fish school, how they investigate food with their mouths—you know, all the things we wonder about from the surface. But as a scientist, she really loves to focus on one thing . . .

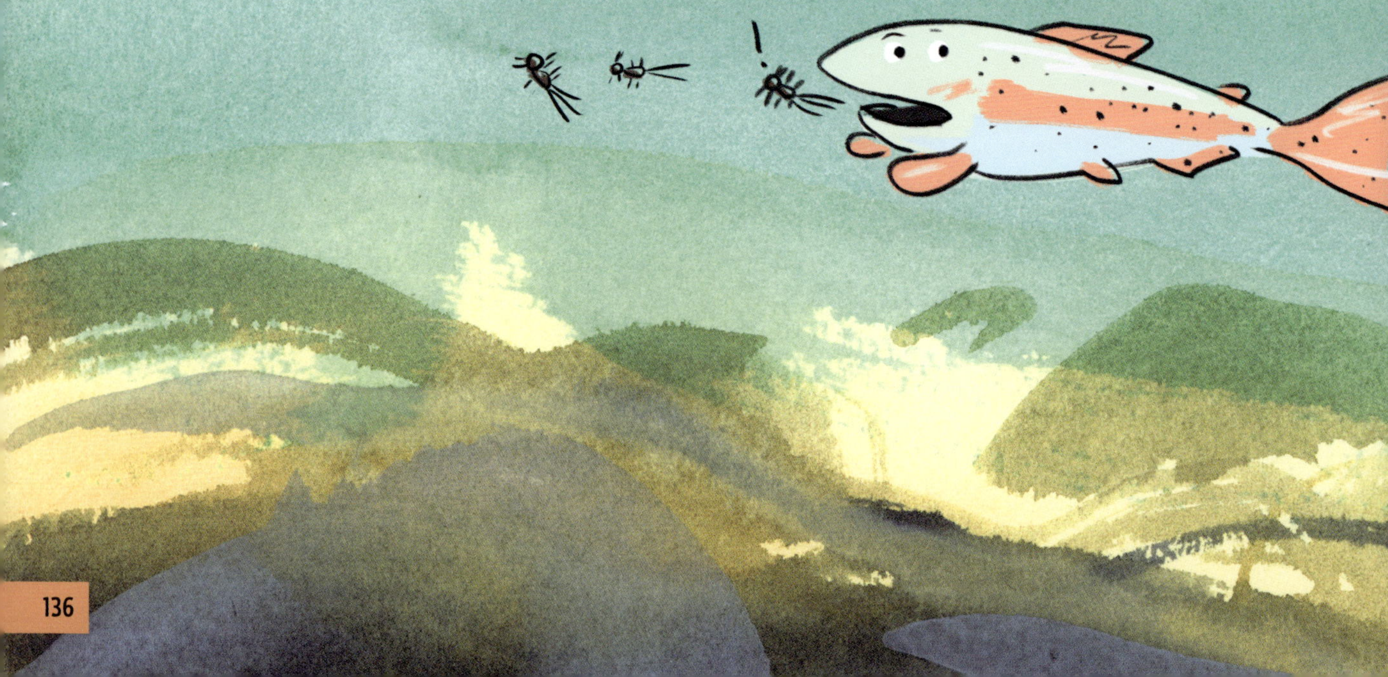

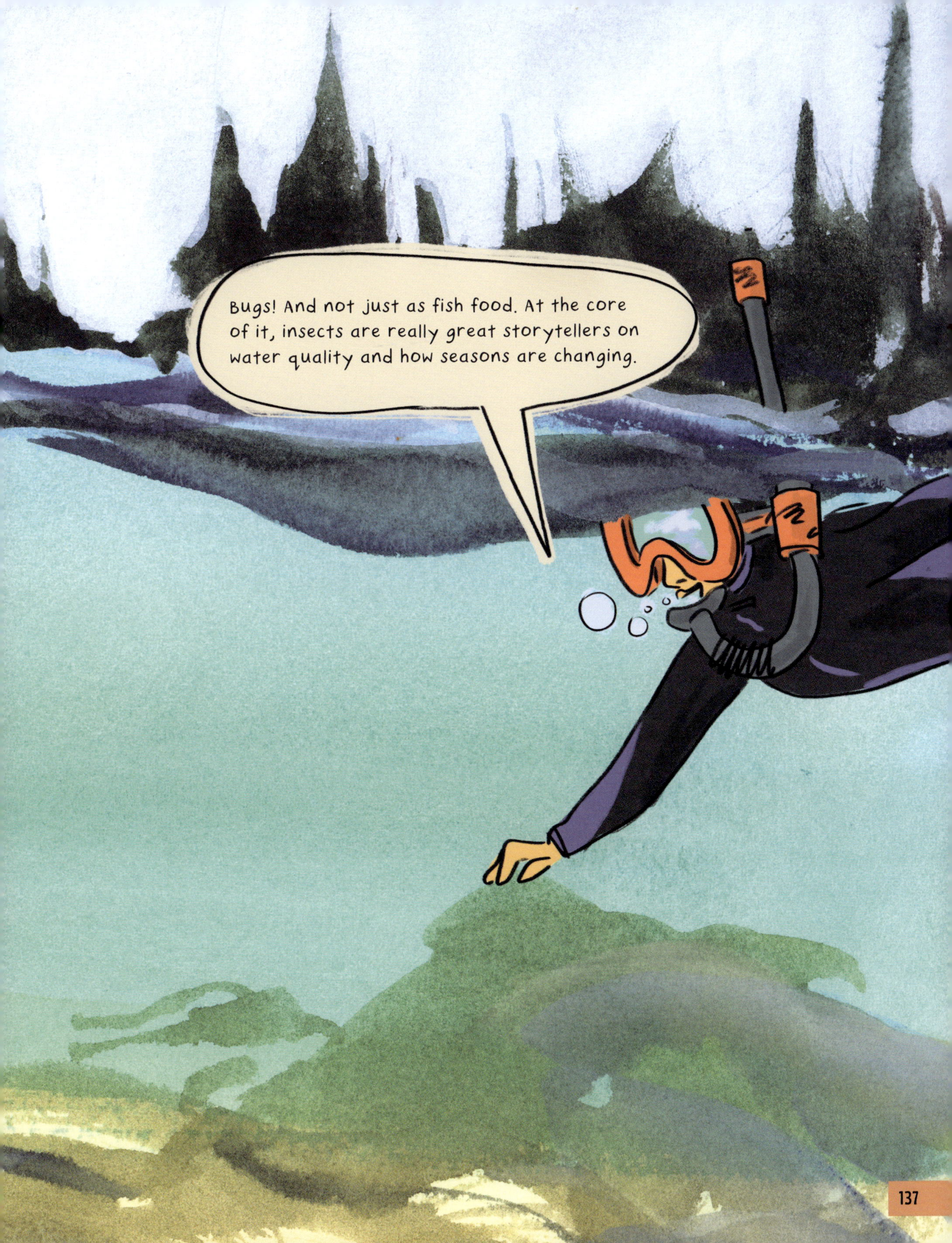
Bugs! And not just as fish food. At the core of it, insects are really great storytellers on water quality and how seasons are changing.

In terms of trout, the MOST important food you want to think about are water-born bugs like mayflies and caddis. Their life cycles are variations of the diagram below, which is featured constantly in anything mildly related to fly fishing.* I mean, don't get me wrong, the diagram is fine. It's just looking at things from the bugs' perspective.

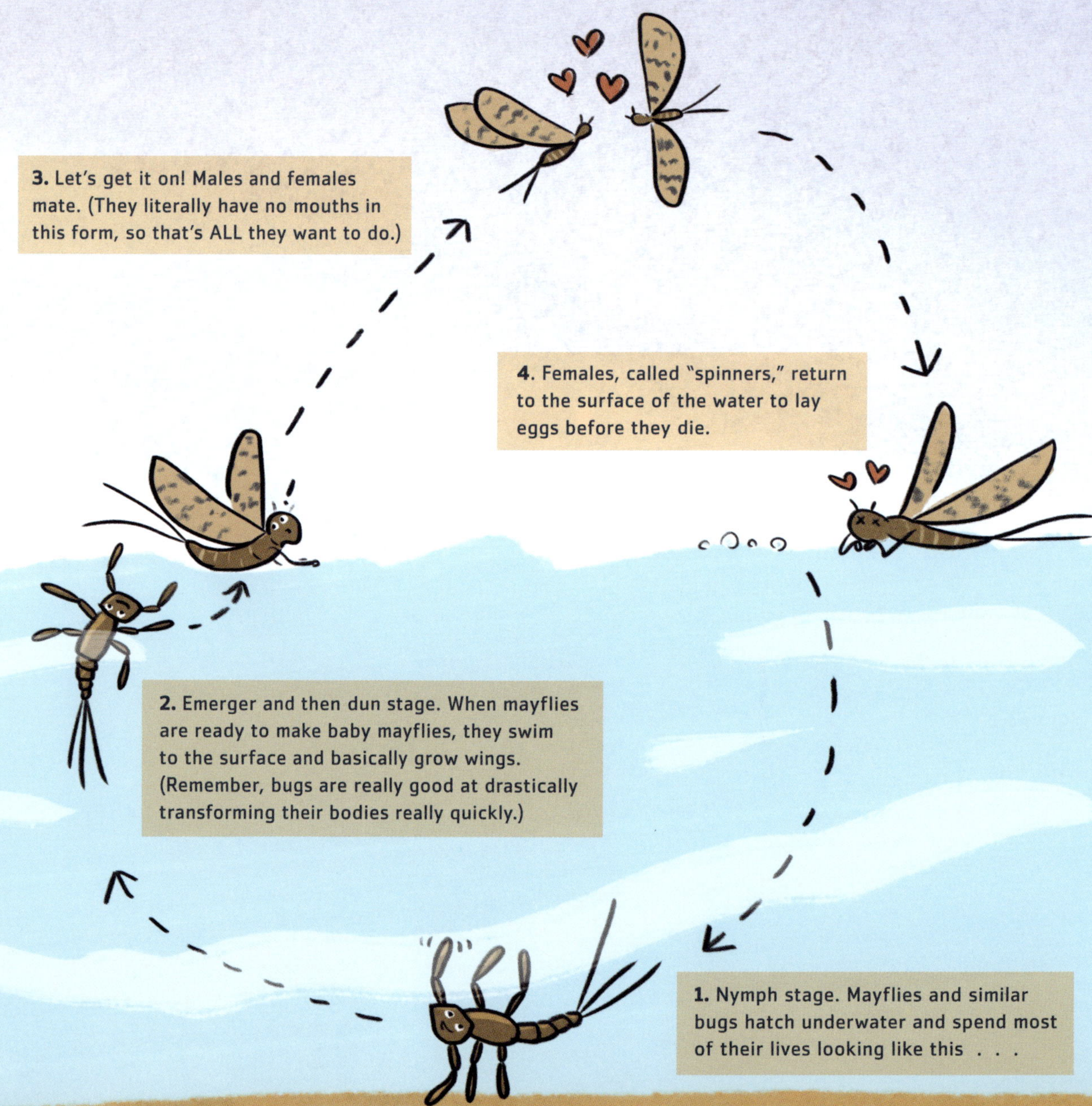

*Accompanying this diagram is often a "hatch calendar" that tells you the rough dates of when each species will hatch. I want to stress ROUGH, since so much depends on a deep knowledge of bug types and identification . . .

So here's my updated diagram from the fish's perspective. Because remember: The fish need to eat. Your job is to figure out where in the "water column" (the space between the creek bed and water's surface) they're chowing down. That's where you'll find fish!

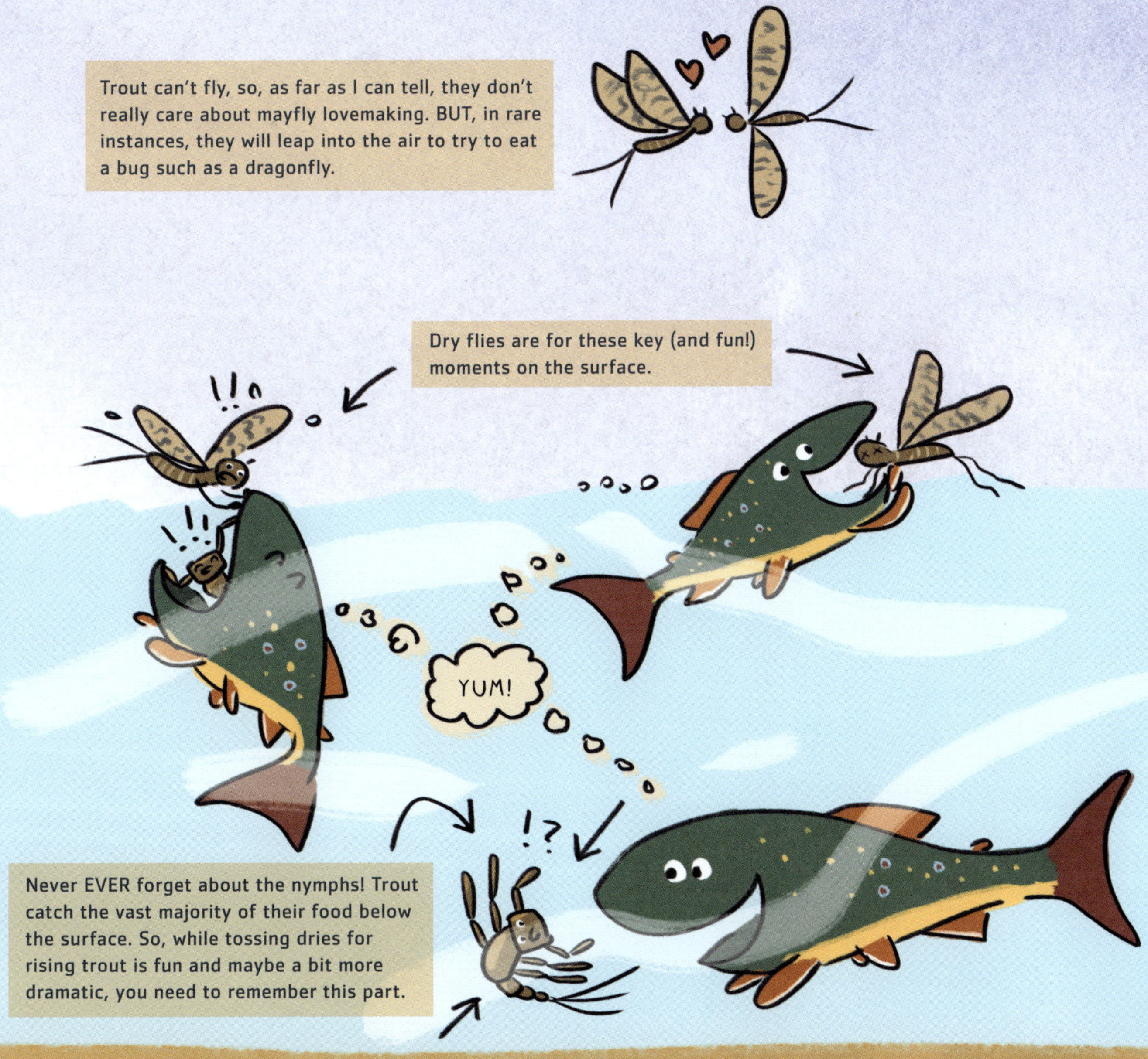

Trout can't fly, so, as far as I can tell, they don't really care about mayfly lovemaking. BUT, in rare instances, they will leap into the air to try to eat a bug such as a dragonfly.

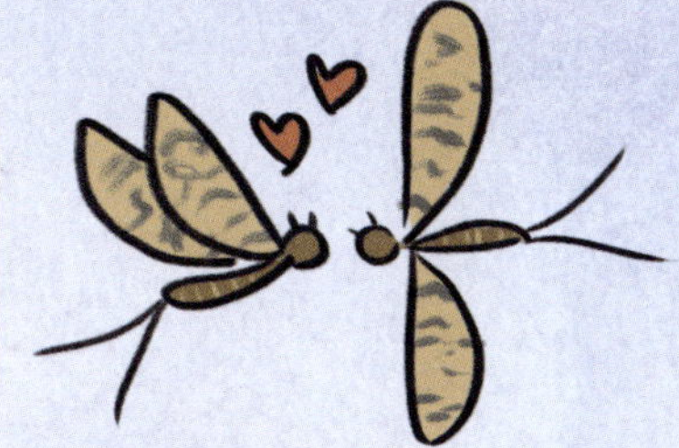

Dry flies are for these key (and fun!) moments on the surface.

Never EVER forget about the nymphs! Trout catch the vast majority of their food below the surface. So, while tossing dries for rising trout is fun and maybe a bit more dramatic, you need to remember this part.

. . . where exactly you are, and the steadily shifting weather patterns. So let's keep it simple for now: Mayflies generally are active in—can you guess it?—May.

Fish need to eat as much as possible, WHILE they're constantly being threatened by other predators. It's a busy world out there! Here are some of the animals you might see when you're fishing freshwater streams. Some have trout on their own menu and will spook the fish. Others the fish won't care about at all.

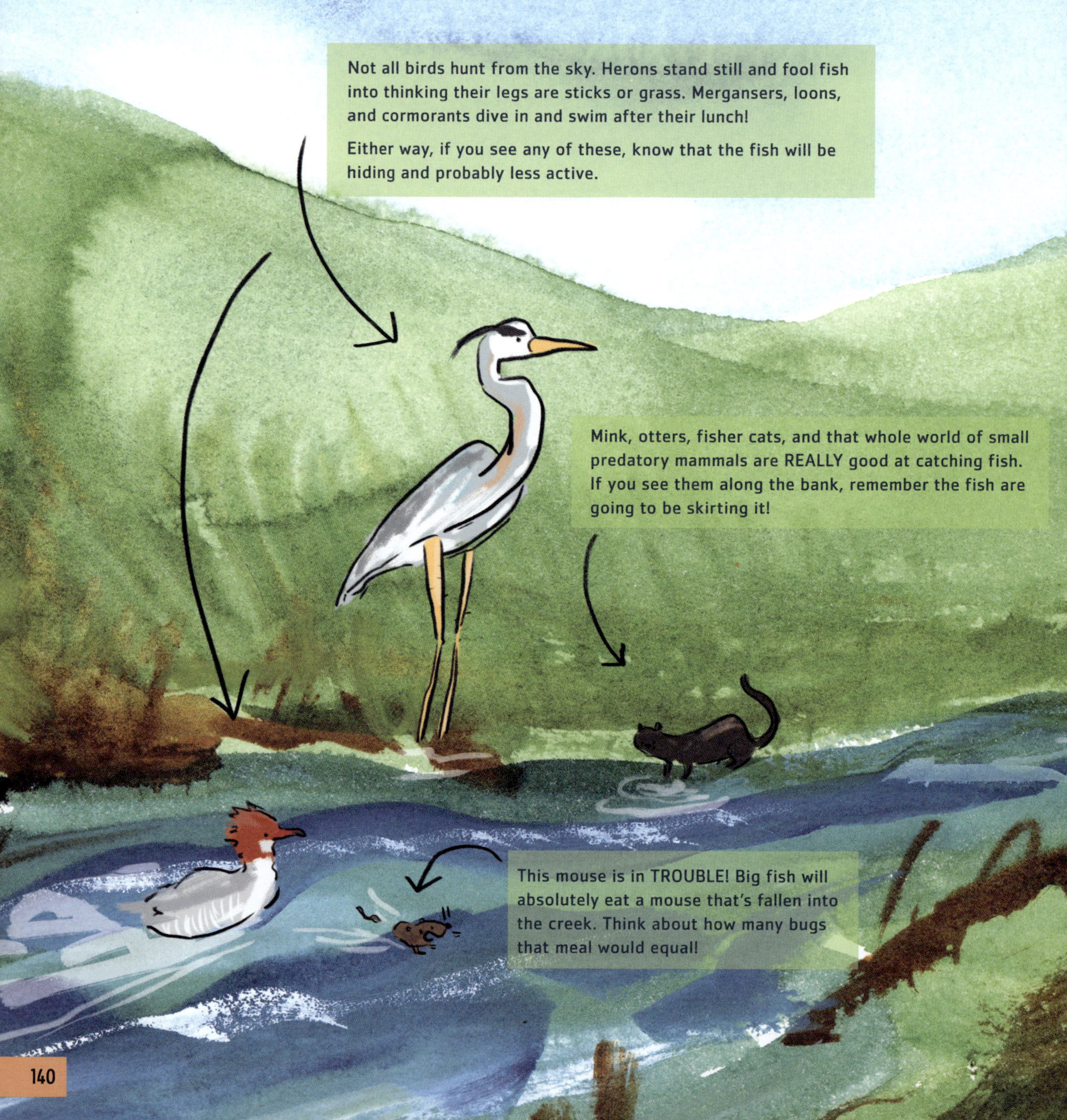

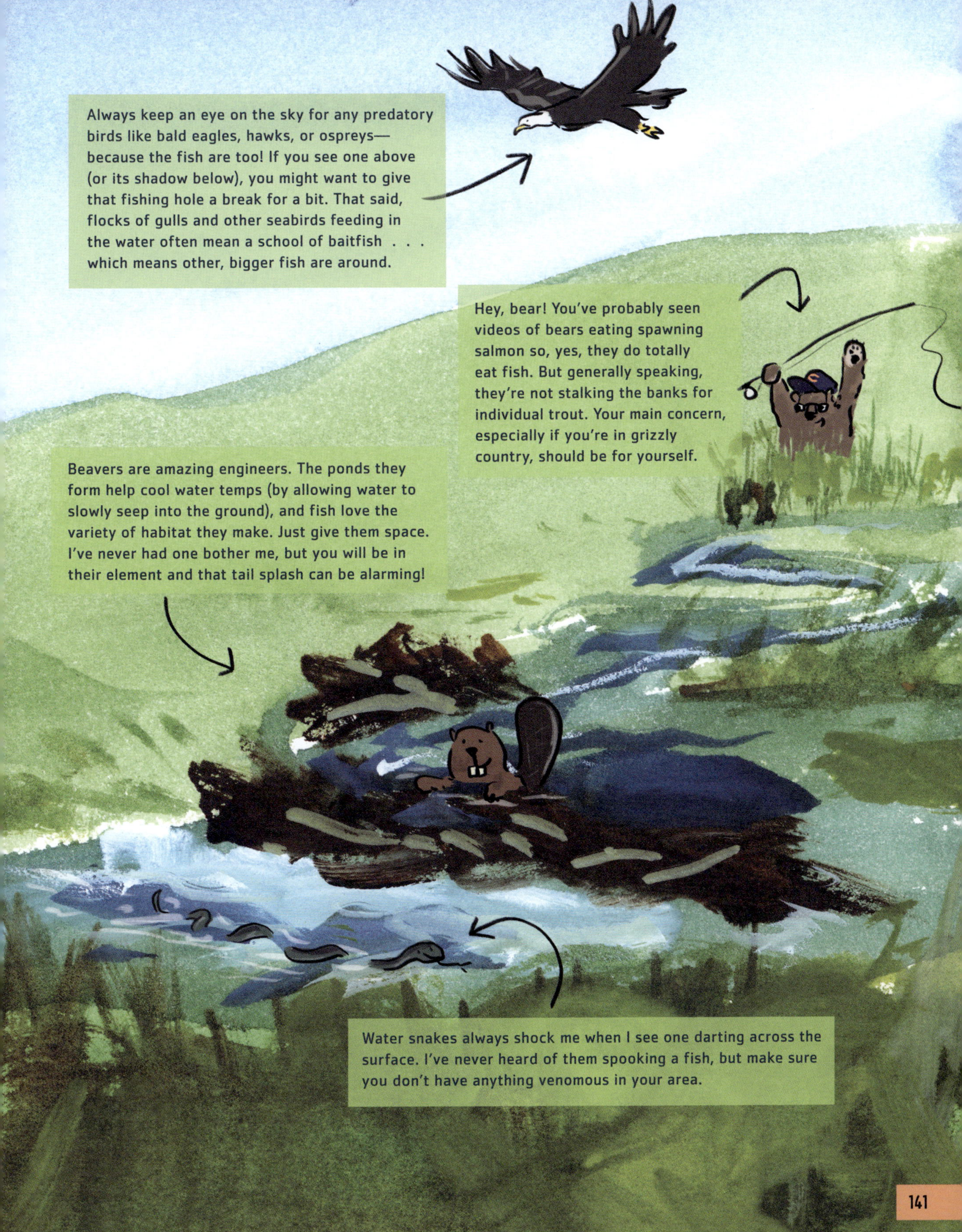
Always keep an eye on the sky for any predatory birds like bald eagles, hawks, or ospreys—because the fish are too! If you see one above (or its shadow below), you might want to give that fishing hole a break for a bit. That said, flocks of gulls and other seabirds feeding in the water often mean a school of baitfish . . . which means other, bigger fish are around.
Hey, bear! You've probably seen videos of bears eating spawning salmon so, yes, they do totally eat fish. But generally speaking, they're not stalking the banks for individual trout. Your main concern, especially if you're in grizzly country, should be for yourself.
Beavers are amazing engineers. The ponds they form help cool water temps (by allowing water to slowly seep into the ground), and fish love the variety of habitat they make. Just give them space. I've never had one bother me, but you will be in their element and that tail splash can be alarming!
Water snakes always shock me when I see one darting across the surface. I've never heard of them spooking a fish, but make sure you don't have anything venomous in your area.

9 FIND YOUR FISHING SPOT

WOW, YOU KNOW SO MUCH NOW! Casting! Knots! Flies! And yet there's still one question you're probably thinking: *BUT WHERE SHOULD I FISH??!*

I could give you some hot tips. And I'm sure I will if we ever meet in person. But for now, do yourself a favor and just start looking. Because my favorite places are ones I stumbled upon—often with this guy, Jamie Kennard. Besides being a great friend, he's the best kind of fishing buddy—organized, curious, and willing to share a hatch. I also love him because he's the kind of guy who doesn't bring a book to read on vacations. He brings maps—to plan out future trips, of course.

So, Jamie, how do we—ahem, I mean you—find the perfect spot?

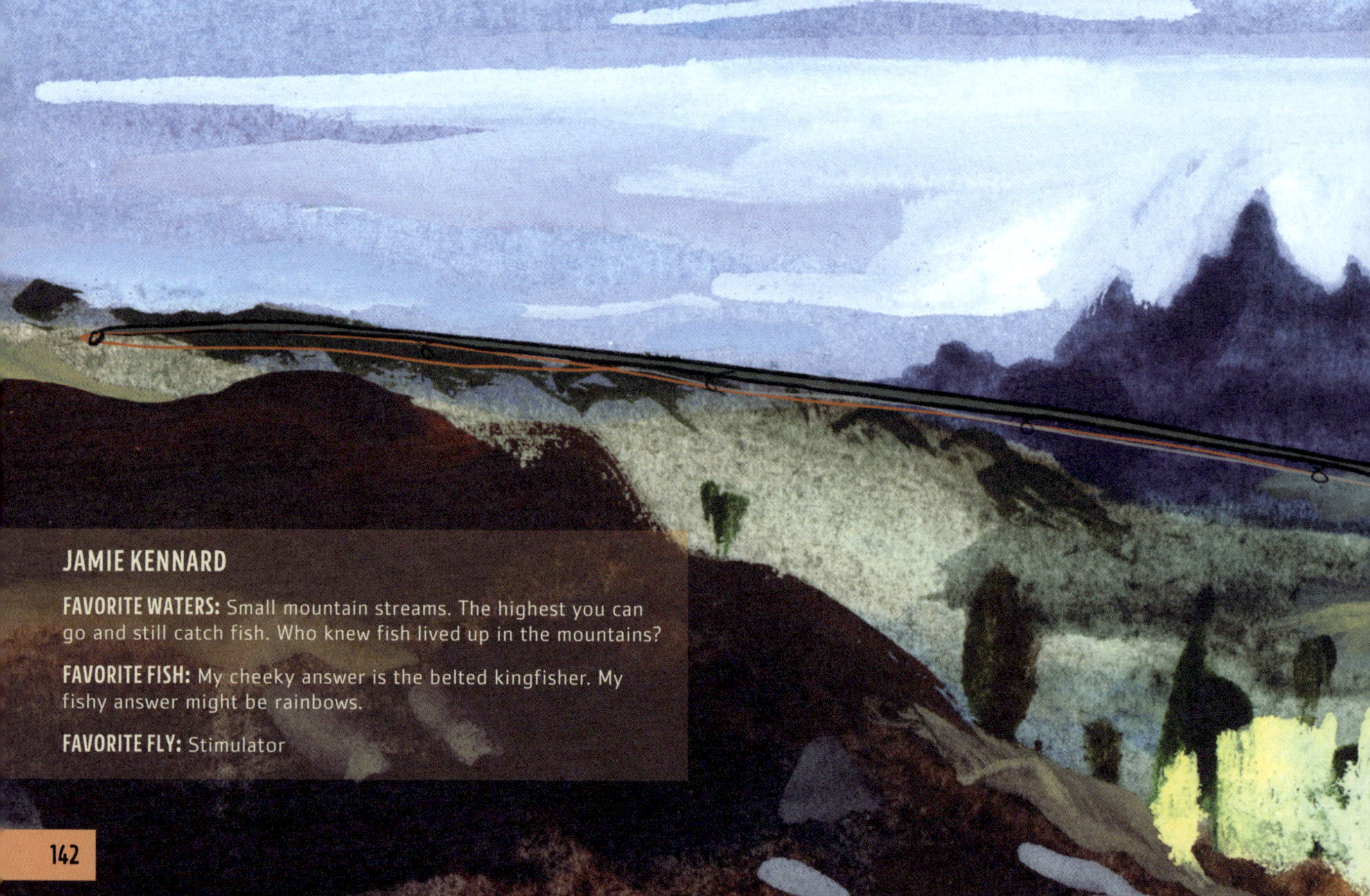

JAMIE KENNARD

FAVORITE WATERS: Small mountain streams. The highest you can go and still catch fish. Who knew fish lived up in the mountains?

FAVORITE FISH: My cheeky answer is the belted kingfisher. My fishy answer might be rainbows.

FAVORITE FLY: Stimulator

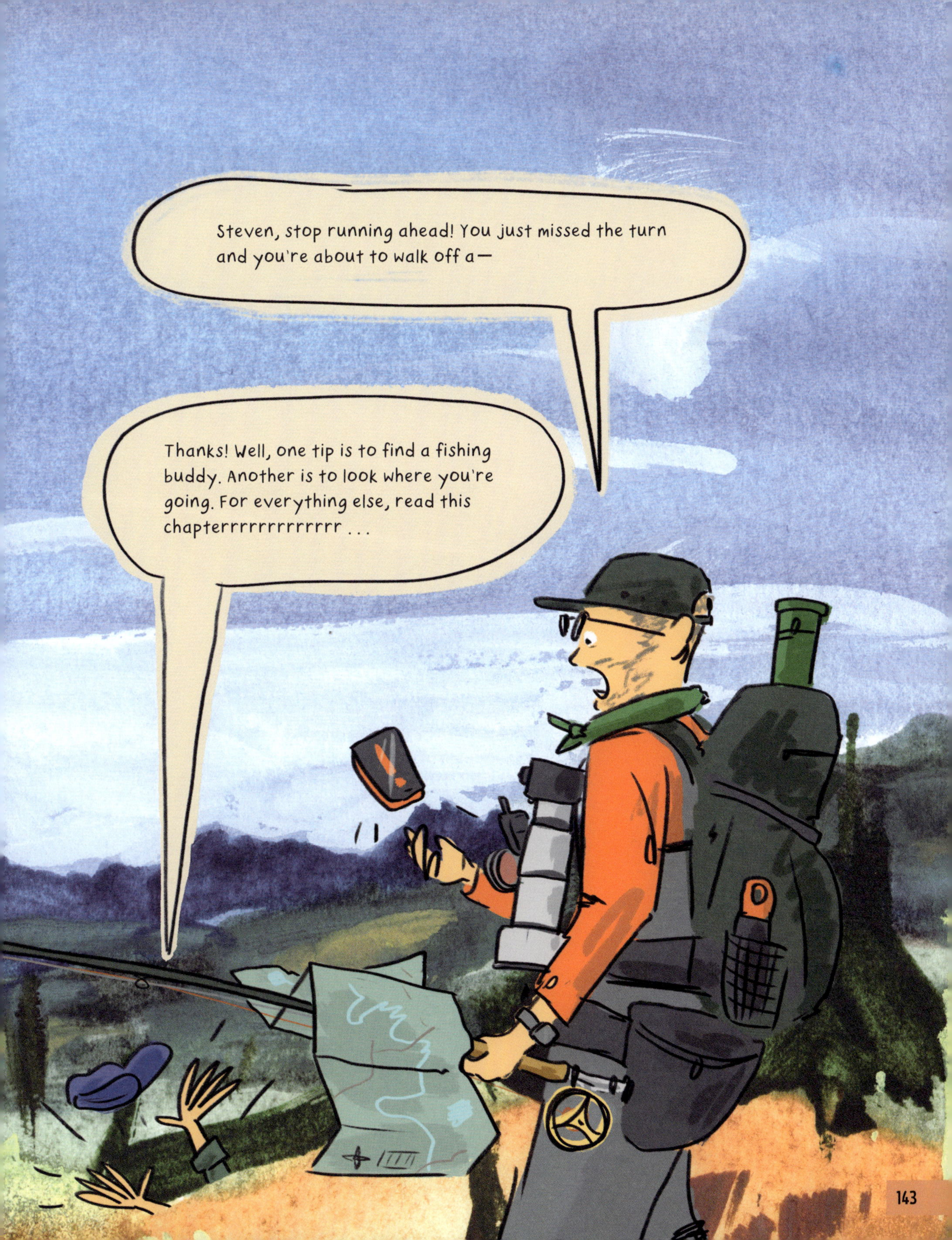
Steven, stop running ahead! You just missed the turn and you're about to walk off a—
Thanks! Well, one tip is to find a fishing buddy. Another is to look where you're going. For everything else, read this chapterrrrrrrrrrrr . . .

WHAT'S YOUR VIBE?

A CLASSIC FISHING STREAM?
Be careful what you wish for! The Beaverkill and Willowemoc rivers near me are the cradle of fly fishing in the US, so everyone wants to dip a line. And you can really feel that on weekends. If you can, think about hitting these kinds of creeks midweek or in the offseason.

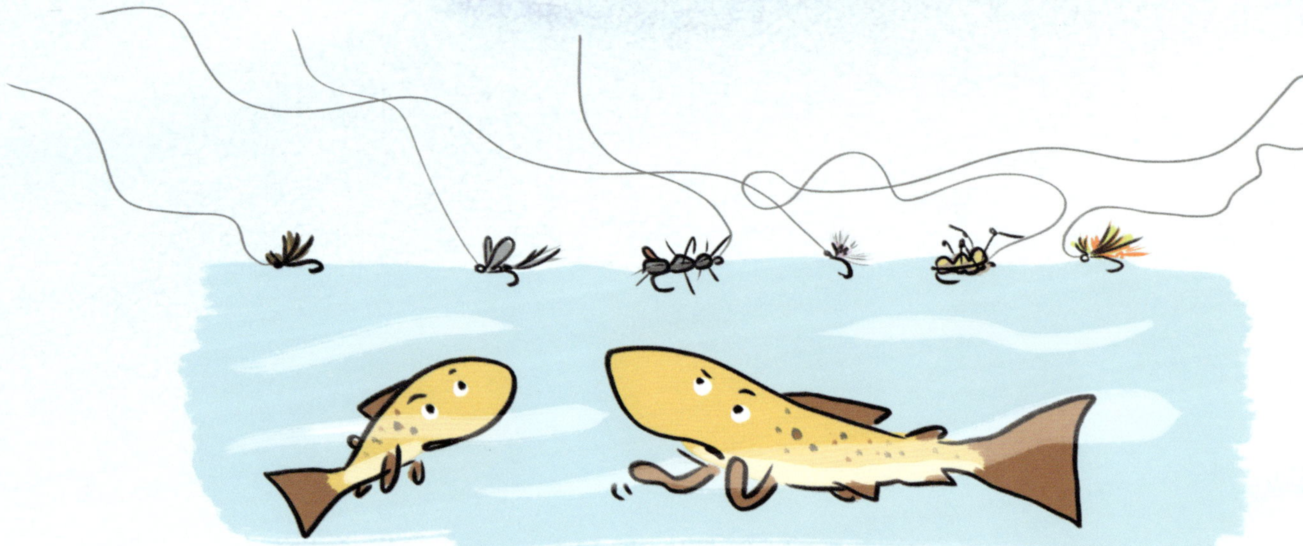

A TINY, REMOTE CREEK?
You'll hear this called "blue lining," as you're often following a blue line on a map up into the mountains.

The danger here is "One More Bend Syndrome." Because—hey, let's just keep . . . on . . . seeing . . . what's . . . next . . . Ooooh, look at that pool!

In other words, the danger is that you're probably heading into the backcountry. Plan ahead!

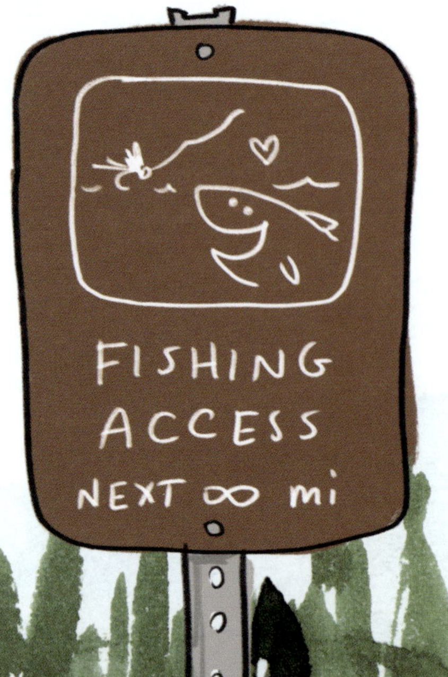

OVERLOOKED URBAN WATERWAY?

It's not just Central Park. There are plenty of carp in the Los Angeles River too!

Don't believe me? Take it from LA angler Lino Jubilado, who famously finds treasure where you'd least expect it.

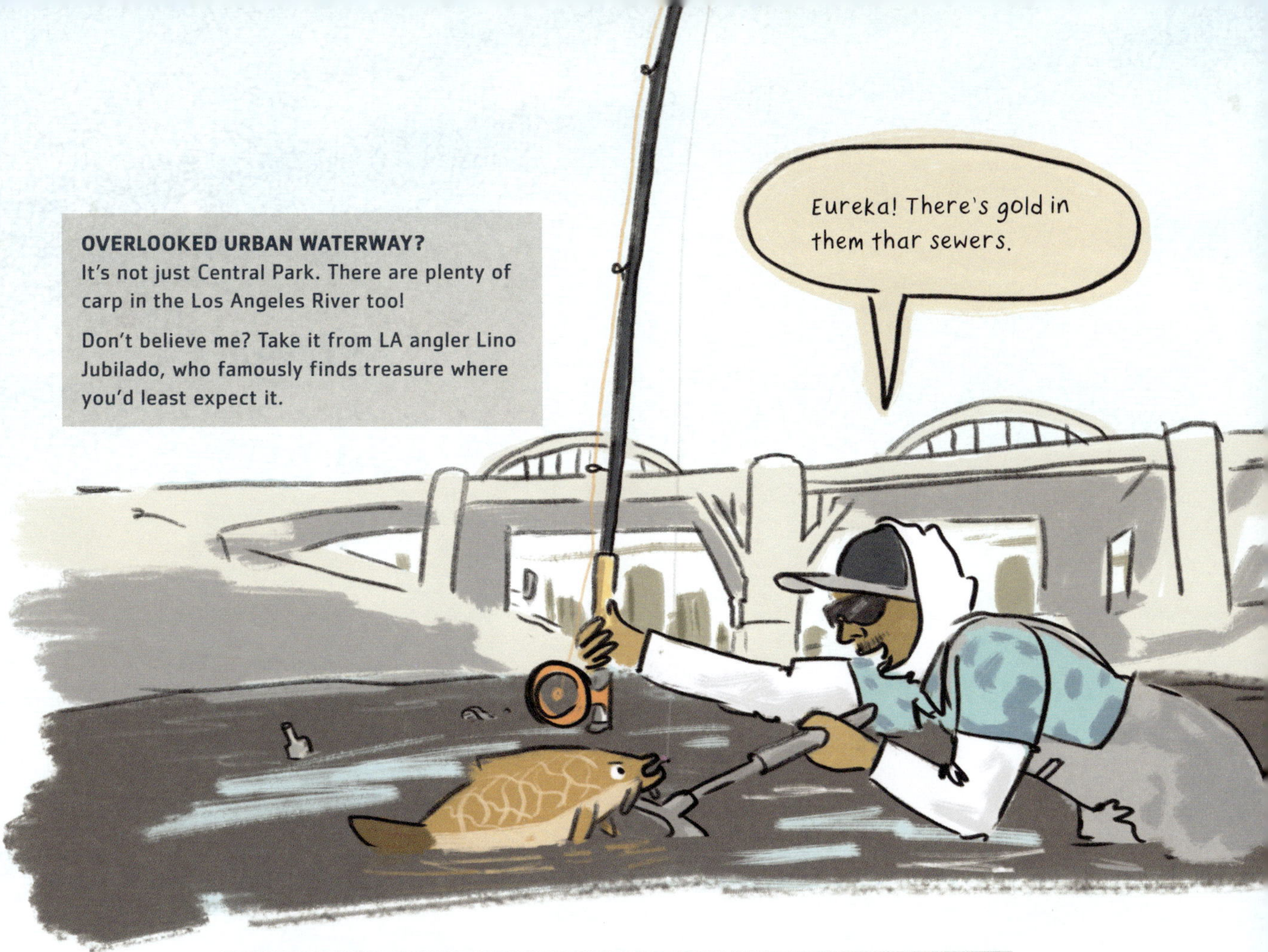

Eureka! There's gold in them thar sewers.

A GIANT DESTINATION TRIP—PATAGONIA? OMAN? BHUTAN?

Start dreaming. Start saving. Oh . . . and speaking of . . . did you want an artist to come along to paint your epic fish? I have a reasonable daily rate!

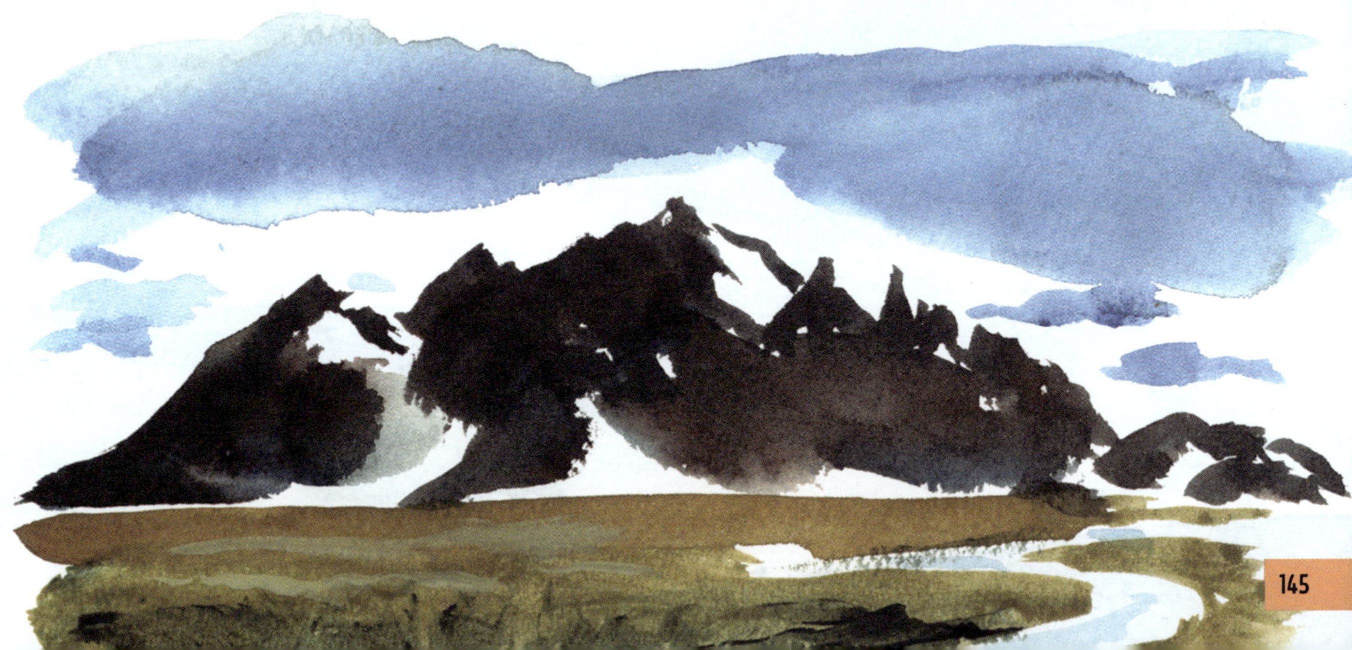

GUIDES!

What if there was a way you could just pay someone to show you the best fishing spots? Oh, wait—there is! Guides will always be your best teachers and your best critics. And, if you're lucky, it's like having a stand-up comedian in your boat. That said, beware. You are a captive audience! Here are some of my favorite bits of guide quotes, advice, and jokes, all told to me by different guides.

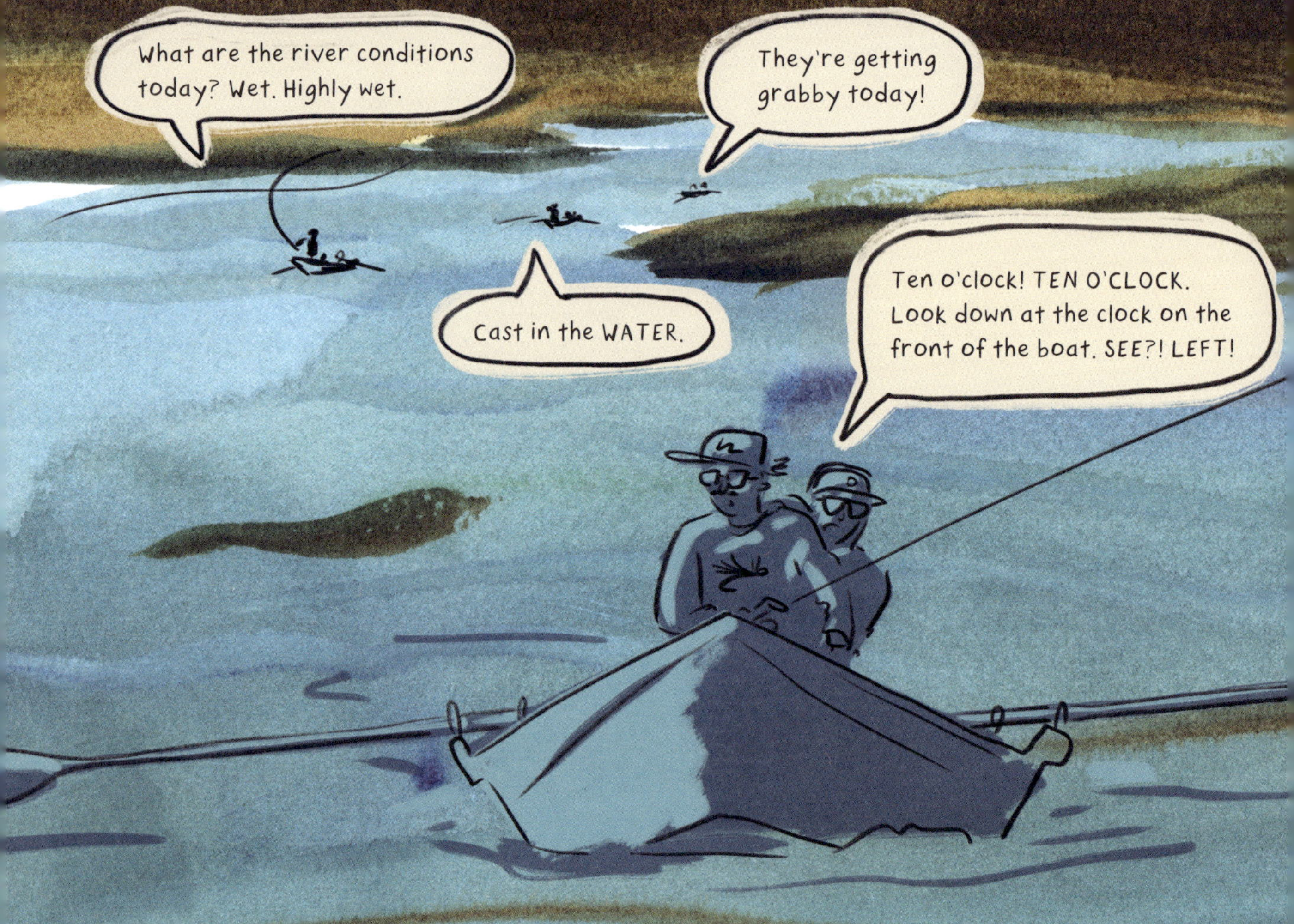

What are the river conditions today? Wet. Highly wet.

They're getting grabby today!

Cast in the WATER.

Ten o'clock! TEN O'CLOCK. Look down at the clock on the front of the boat. SEE?! LEFT!

TIPPING! It's a thing. Guiding services price out their costs assuming you'll tip. So just do it. (Even if you don't catch the fish of your dreams that day.) Generally speaking, twenty to twenty-five percent of the trip cost is a good tip, though some lodges and guides will specify preferred rates. It also never hurts to ask.

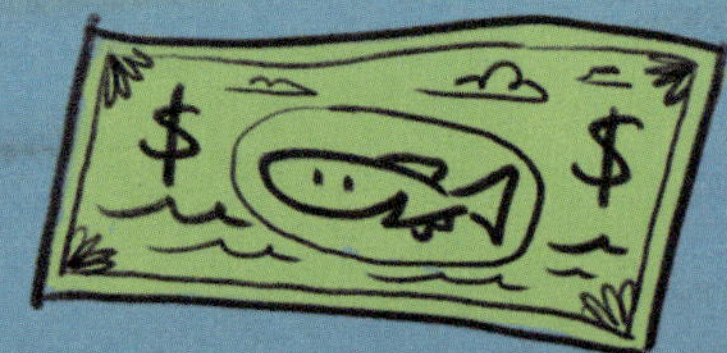

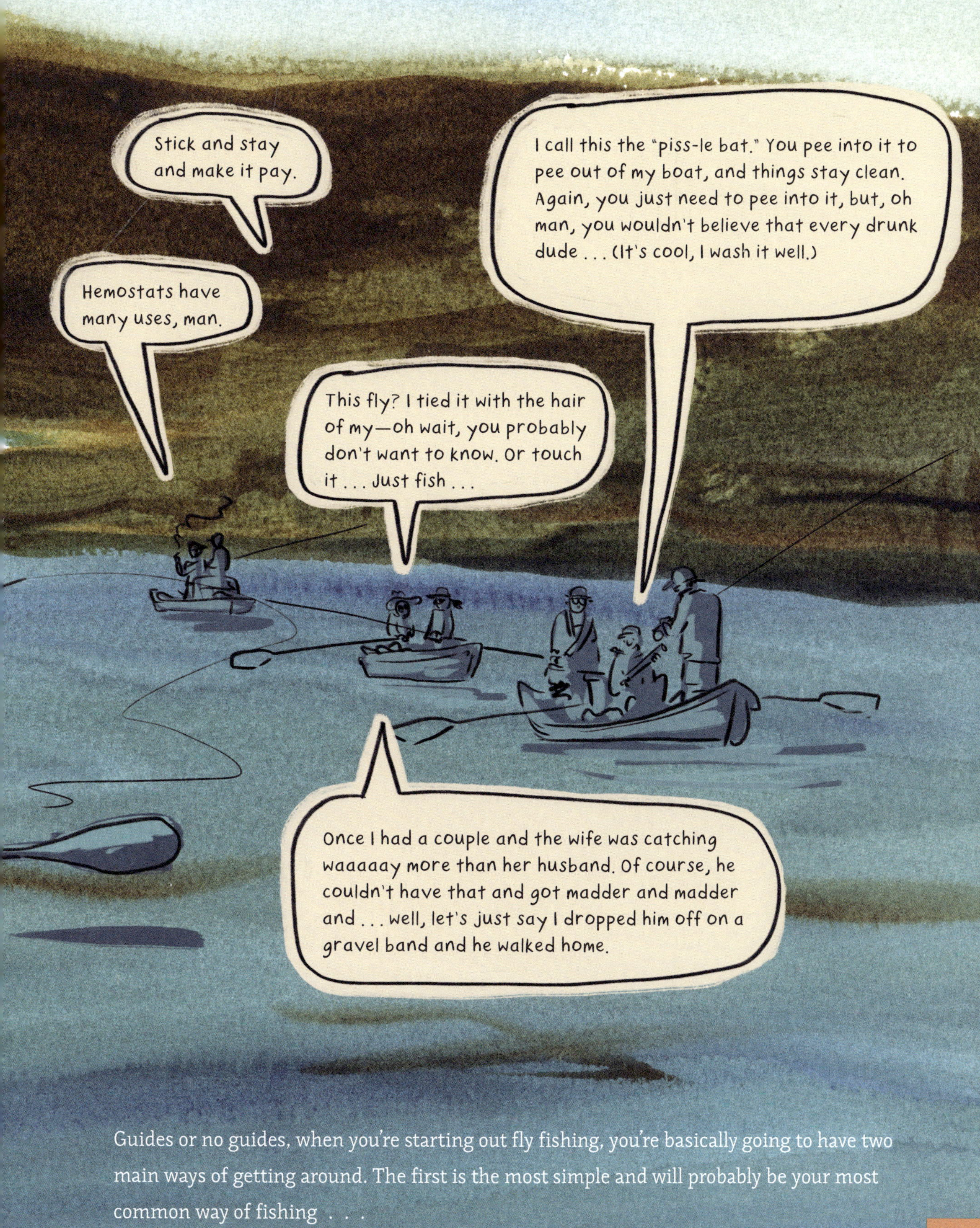

Guides or no guides, when you're starting out fly fishing, you're basically going to have two main ways of getting around. The first is the most simple and will probably be your most common way of fishing . . .

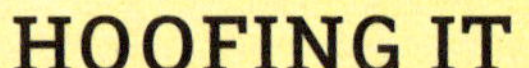HOOFING IT

The simplest (and cheapest) way to fish is on your own two feet. When you do this with a guide, they're often called "wading trips," but as discussed earlier, you don't always even need to wade. Or wear waders! Here are some things to watch out for:

Professional angler Kayla Lockhart shows the best way to use waders: Fishing from shore, but ready to go deeper if necessary, like when landing a fish.

And me? Well, I saw a fish splash and waded out too far and just slipped and now there's a giant waterfall downstream and WOW I'm getting tossed around in this chapter . . .

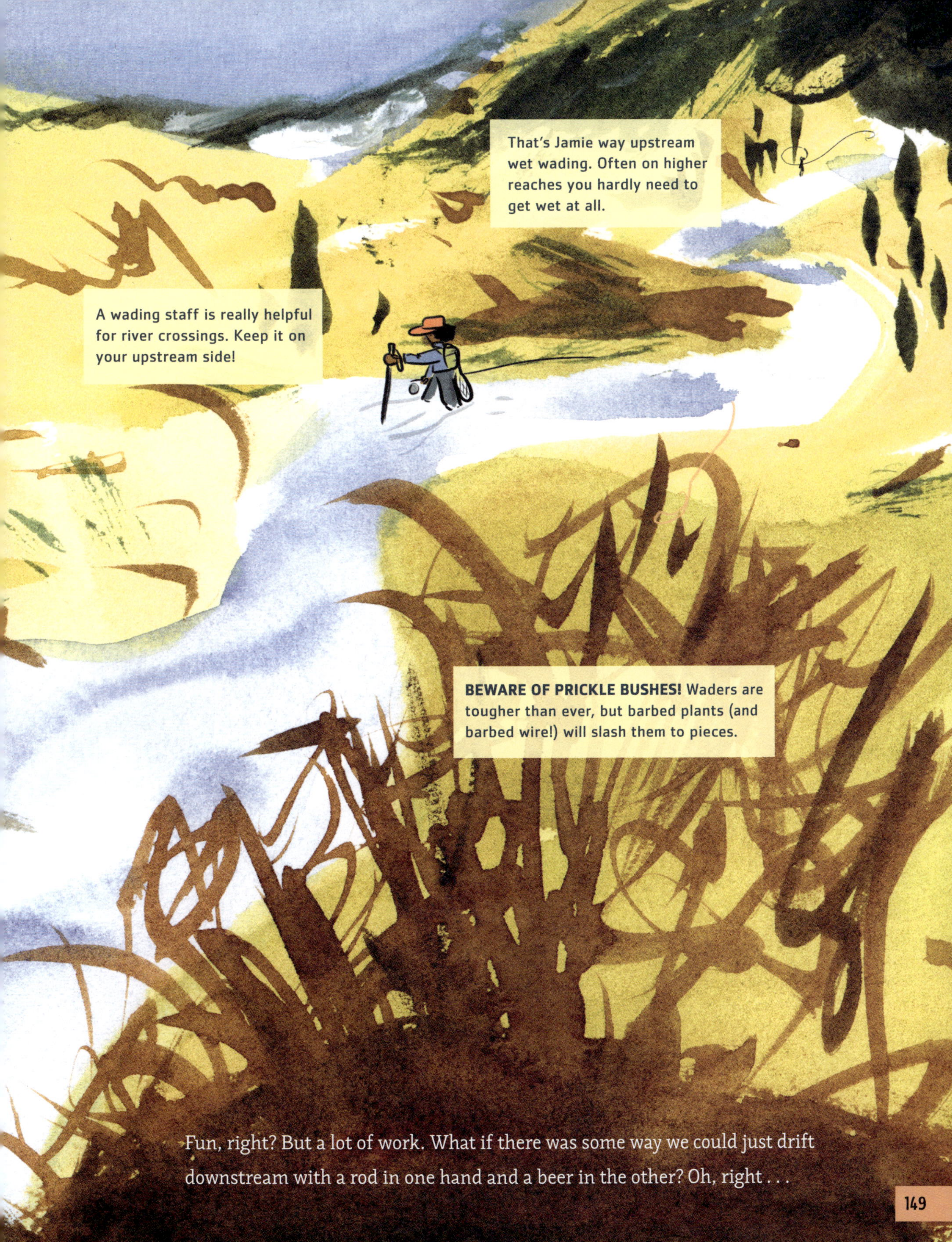

Fun, right? But a lot of work. What if there was some way we could just drift downstream with a rod in one hand and a beer in the other? Oh, right . . .

BOATS!

This is where guides really shine. Floating a river takes experience—and back muscles! Besides not having to schlep yourself and all your gear around, boats are also great at getting you places wading can't. You even fish differently—one cast can drift (and mend—mending is key here) for hundreds of feet at a time.

I highly recommend trying a drift boat with a guide. It'll basically be your own *Magic School Bus* field trip but with no homework at the end. They rig you. They teach you. Only sometimes will they scold you. Here's how a traditional drift boat works . . .

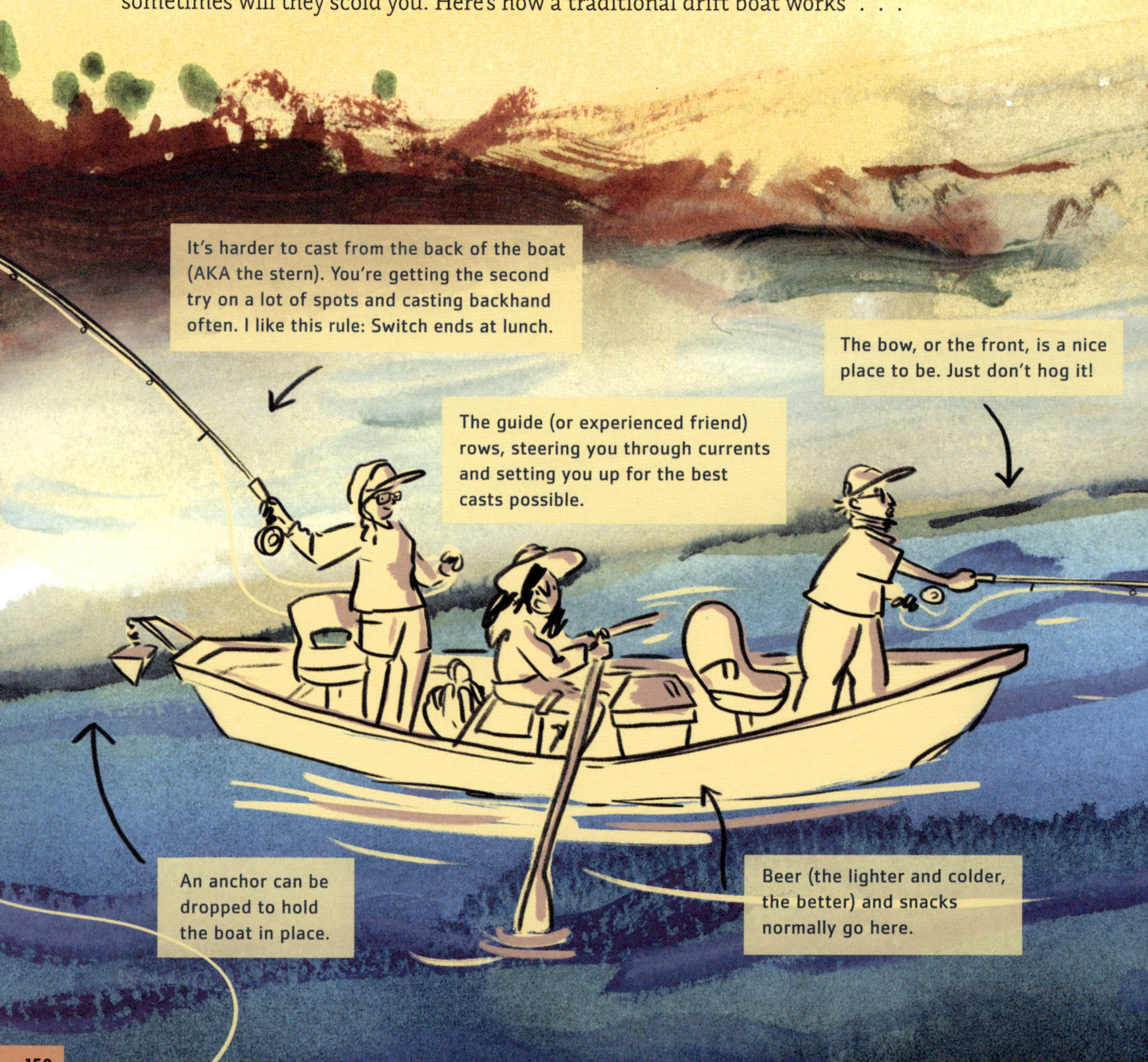

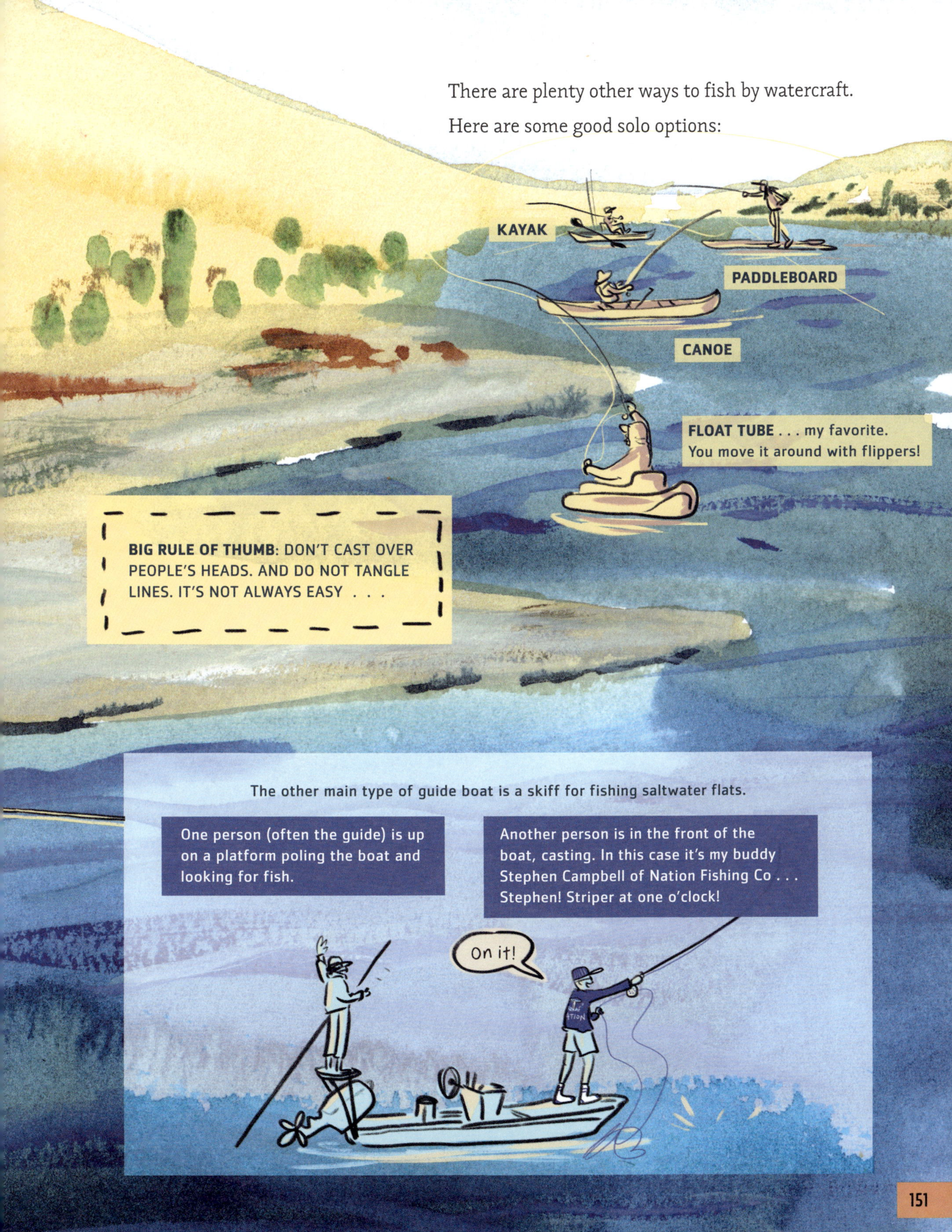
There are plenty other ways to fish by watercraft.
Here are some good solo options:
KAYAK
PADDLEBOARD
CANOE
FLOAT TUBE . . . my favorite. You move it around with flippers!
BIG RULE OF THUMB: DON'T CAST OVER PEOPLE'S HEADS. AND DO NOT TANGLE LINES. IT'S NOT ALWAYS EASY . . .
The other main type of guide boat is a skiff for fishing saltwater flats.
One person (often the guide) is up on a platform poling the boat and looking for fish.
Another person is in the front of the boat, casting. In this case it's my buddy Stephen Campbell of Nation Fishing Co . . . Stephen! Striper at one o'clock!
On it!

FINDING YOUR WAY . . .

Especially if you're self-catering, you need to know where you're going. To find new spots, I use an old technology but a good one: maps.

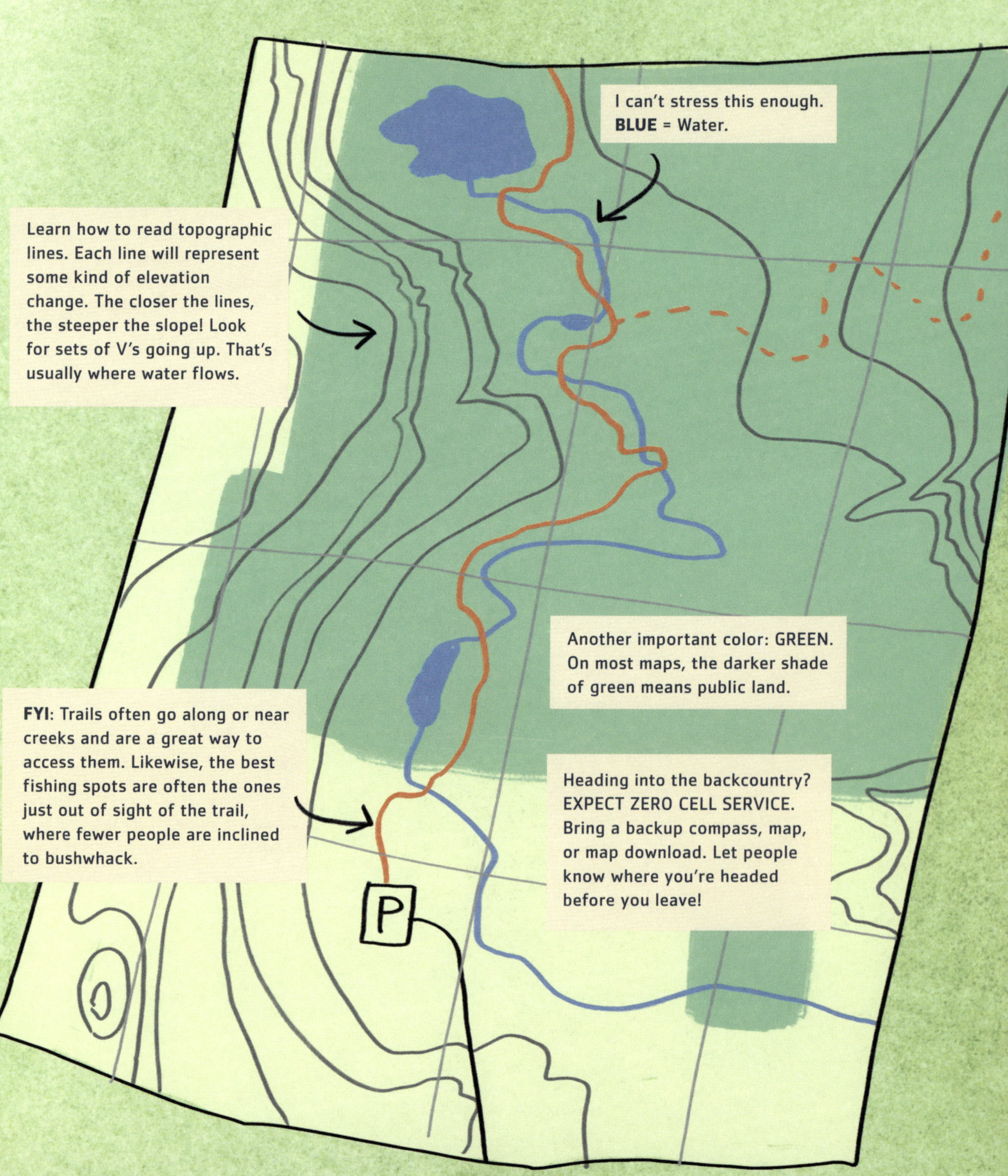

And don't forget about all the other high-tech (and low-tech) tools!

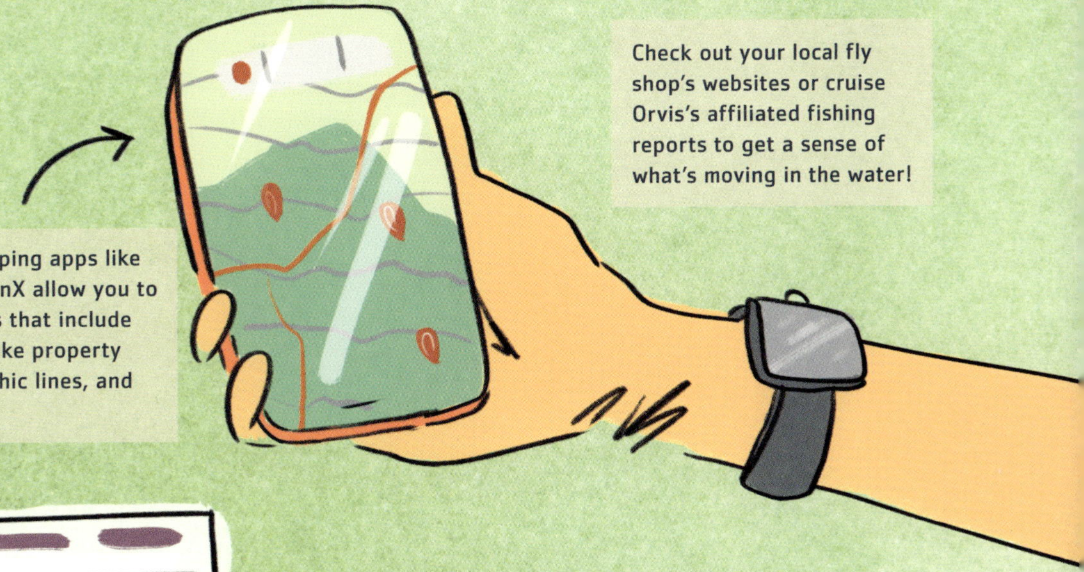

Check out your local fly shop's websites or cruise Orvis's affiliated fishing reports to get a sense of what's moving in the water!

Next-level mapping apps like Gaia GPS and onX allow you to download maps that include helpful layers like property lines, topographic lines, and trail markers.

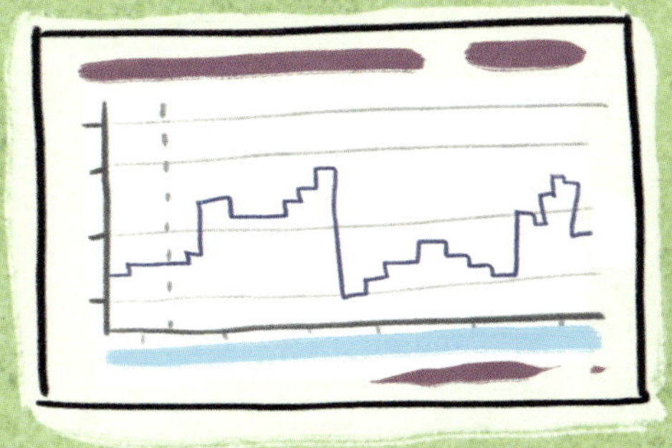

Tax dollars at work! The USGS has monitoring stations that track flow, water temperature, and more on waterways all over the country. These are SO helpful, posted online, and absolutely free to use!

Weather. I know—"Check the weather. Duh." But you will become your father/grandfather/elderly relative who checks the weather constantly.

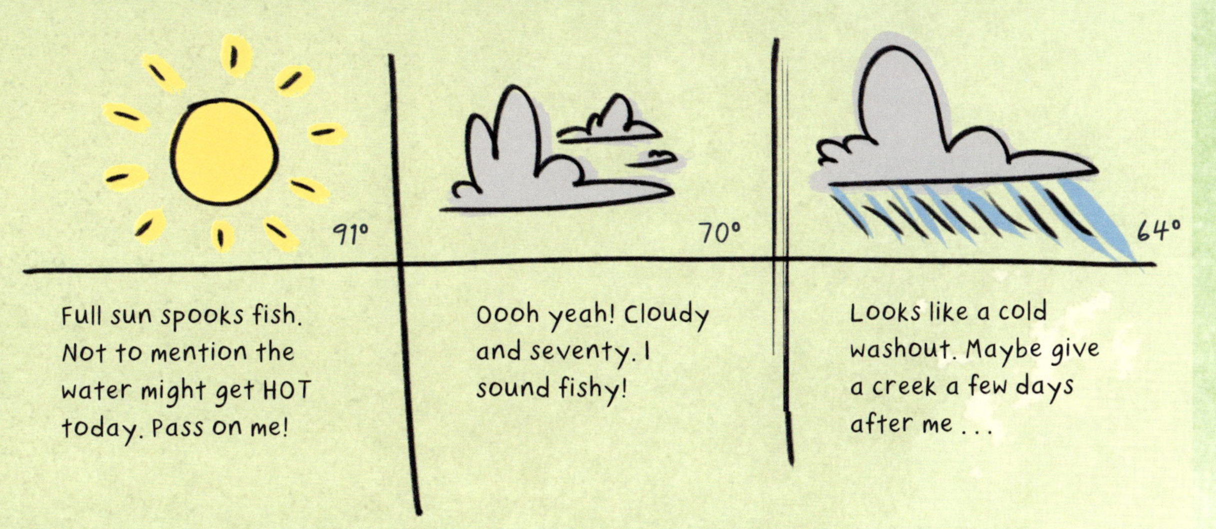

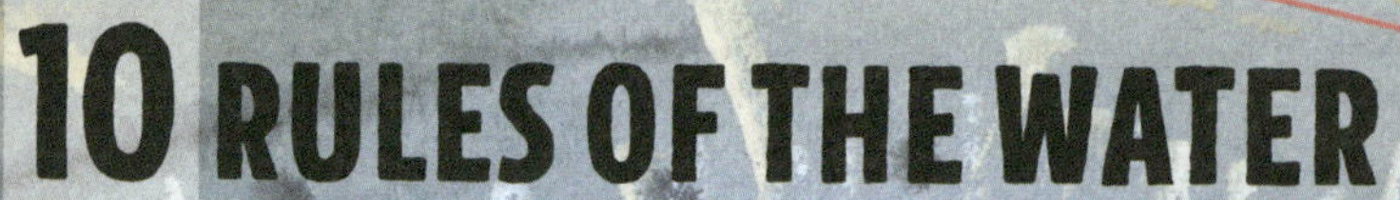

10 RULES OF THE WATER

SO FAR IN THIS BOOK we've covered everything you need to fly fish: the gear, the fish, even the bugs! But what about your fellow anglers?

Here's the good news: I absolutely LOVE the fly fishing community. Most of the time. We're supportive! We're secretive. We have really clear rules! We have unspoken ways of doing things. We . . . are like pretty much everything Homo sapiens have ever touched: complicated.

All of this brings me to Marina Gibson. She's a world famous angler, guide, and writer. And yet, while being one of the best in her field, she often receives compliments that begin with "You're pretty good for a . . . "

When I asked her about navigating the world of angling, she couldn't help but bring it first to salmon. She is British, after all . . .

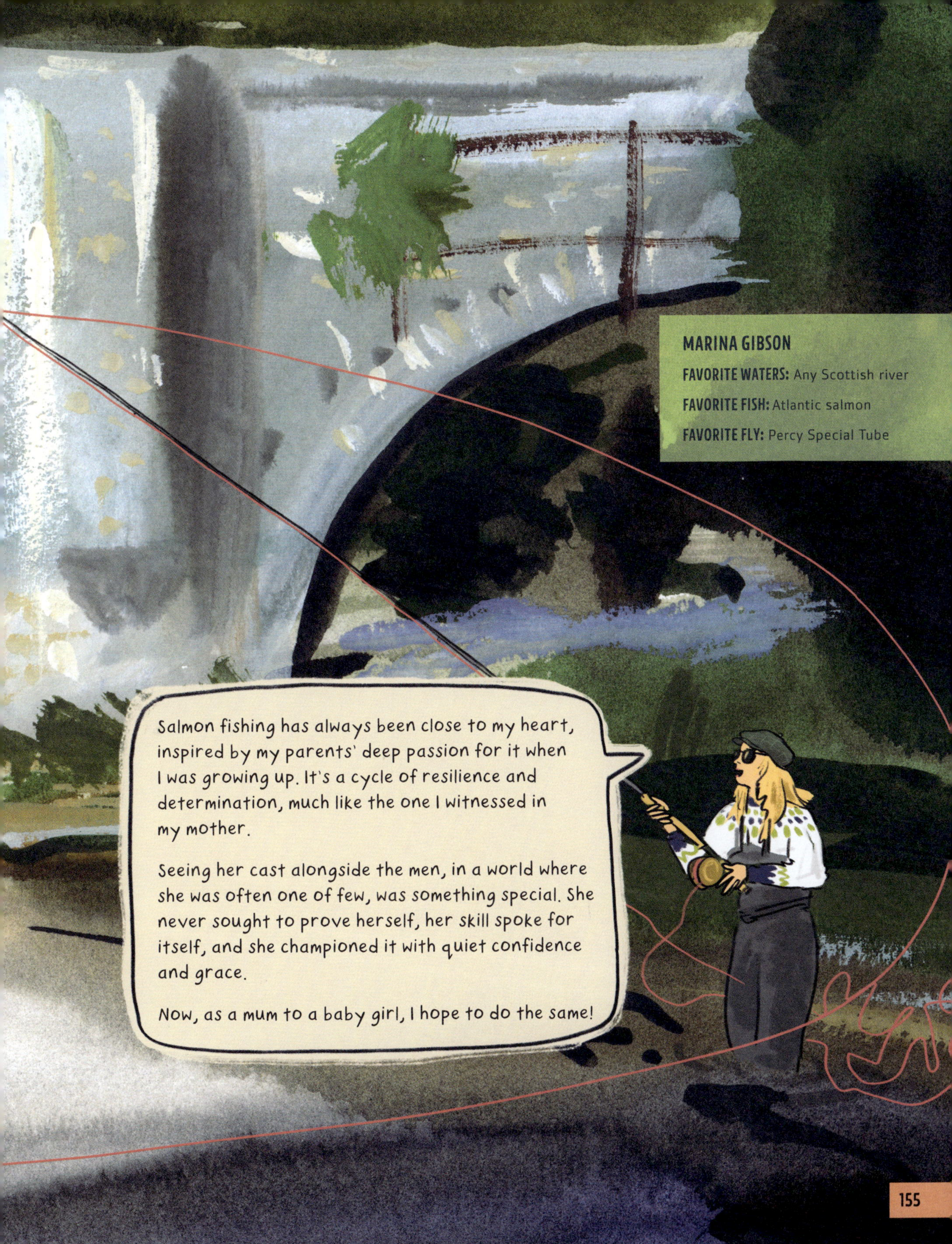
MARINA GIBSON
FAVORITE WATERS: Any Scottish river
FAVORITE FISH: Atlantic salmon
FAVORITE FLY: Percy Special Tube
Salmon fishing has always been close to my heart, inspired by my parents' deep passion for it when I was growing up. It's a cycle of resilience and determination, much like the one I witnessed in my mother.
Seeing her cast alongside the men, in a world where she was often one of few, was something special. She never sought to prove herself, her skill spoke for itself, and she championed it with quiet confidence and grace.
Now, as a mum to a baby girl, I hope to do the same!

FISHING LICENSES—AND MORE!

Just like you need a license to drive, you need one to fish. The good news is that, unlike driving, no test is required! There are usually two ways to get a license:

YE OLDE INTERNET. These are usually issued through US State/Canadian Provincial agencies. It's a lot of forms, but it's easy. This is a good way to go if you're getting a license from afar.

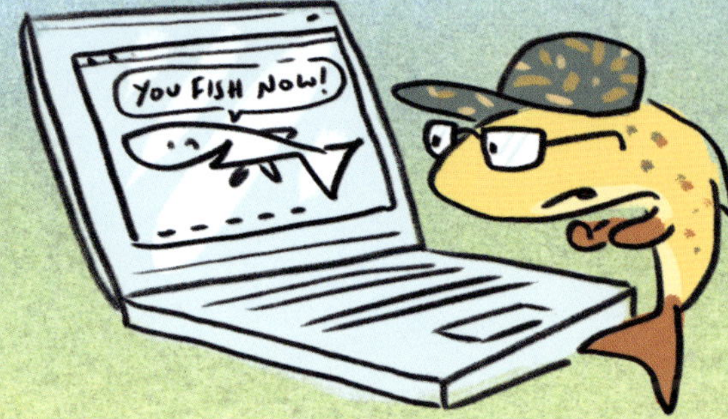

FISHING SHOP/GAS STATION/HARDWARE STORE. Honestly, licenses are sometimes sold in the weirdest places. I love doing this when I can, because you might overhear an amazing fishing tip or a fishing hole you haven't heard of.

But wait, why is someone telling me when I can and can't fish? I'll let my pal (and author of *The Shotgun Conservationist)* Brant MacDuff explain.

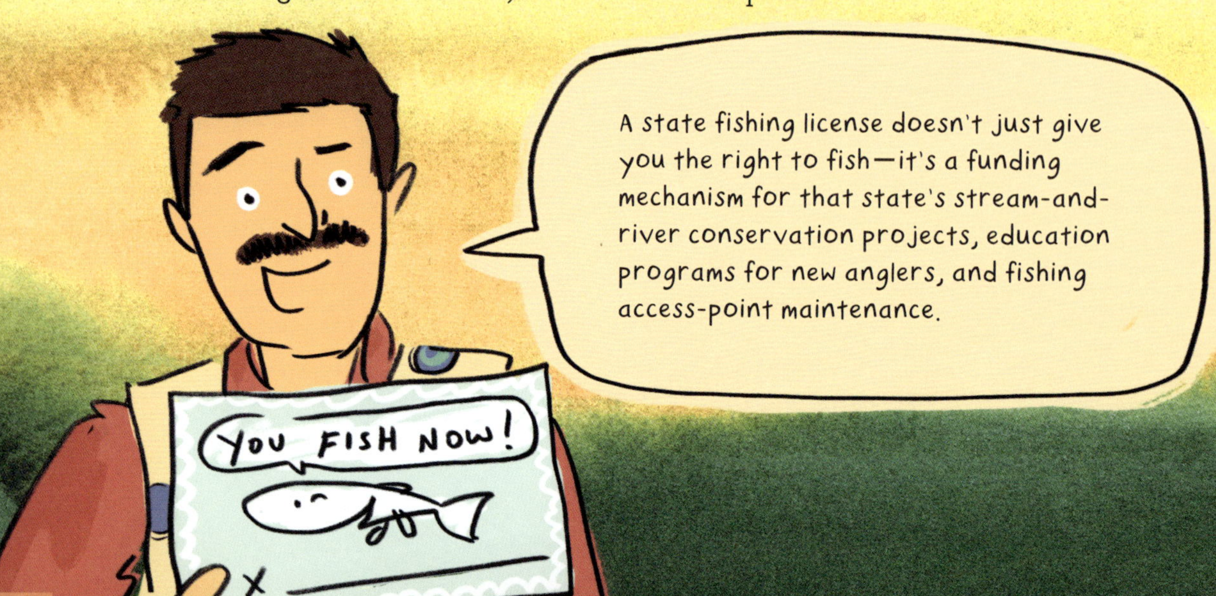

Your license helps fund . . .

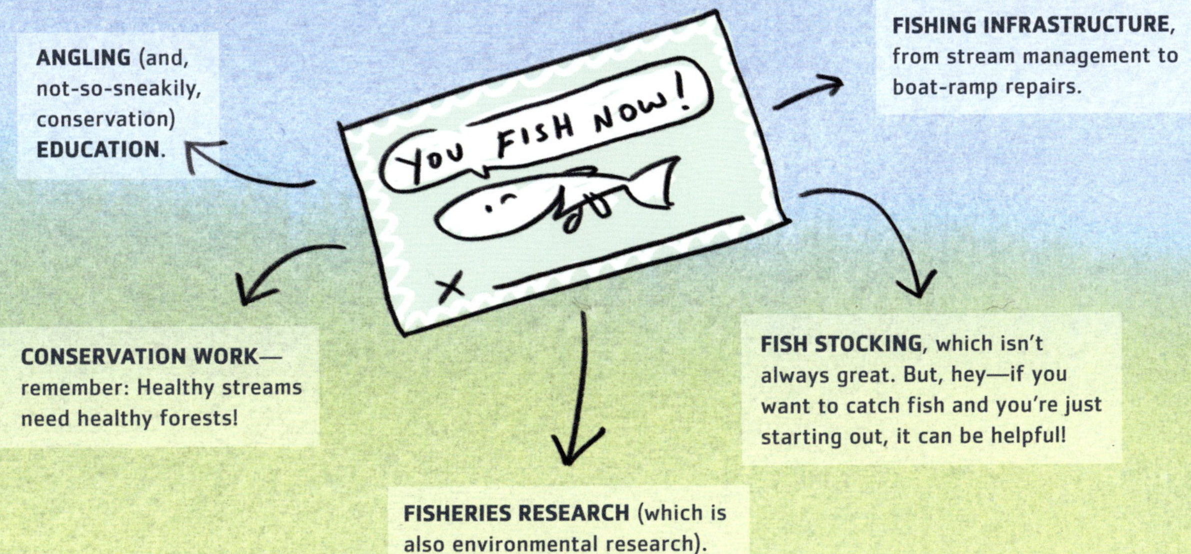

ANGLING (and, not-so-sneakily, conservation) **EDUCATION.**

FISHING INFRASTRUCTURE, from stream management to boat-ramp repairs.

CONSERVATION WORK—remember: Healthy streams need healthy forests!

FISH STOCKING, which isn't always great. But, hey—if you want to catch fish and you're just starting out, it can be helpful!

FISHERIES RESEARCH (which is also environmental research).

But wait—AGAIN—there's even more! Brant will explain . . .

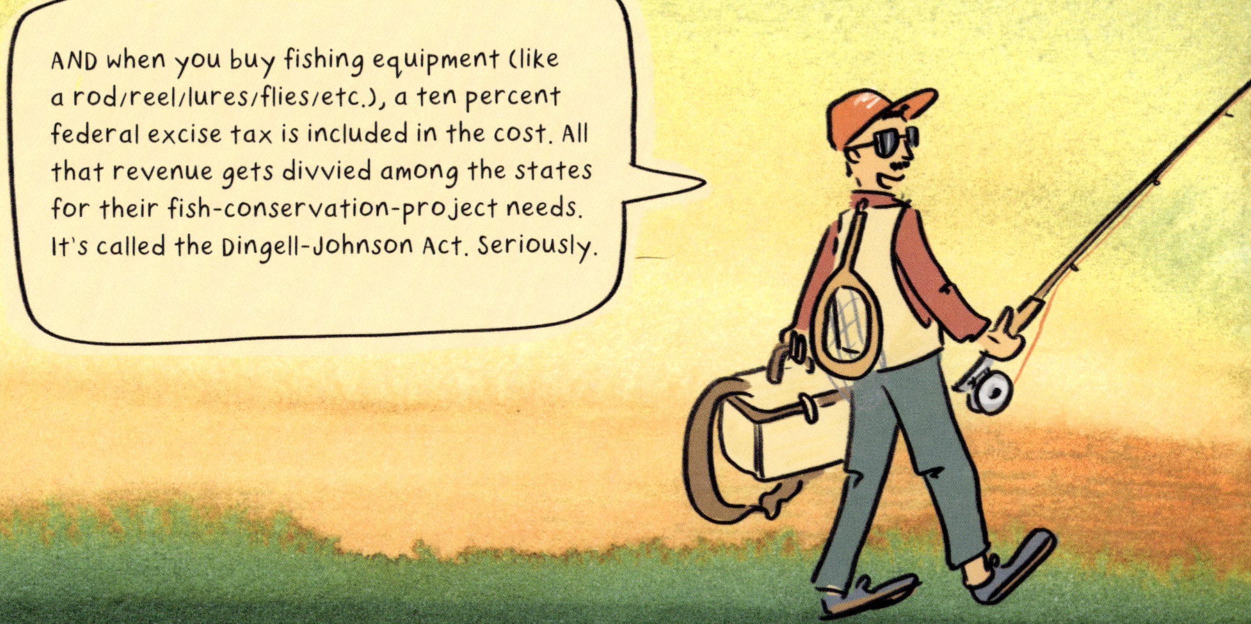

Thanks, Brant! And what a perfect segue to even more fishing rules . . .

MORE RULES!

Besides your license, there are three main sets of rules to research before you hit the water. They're different everywhere, and they're always changing, so it's worth double-checking them.

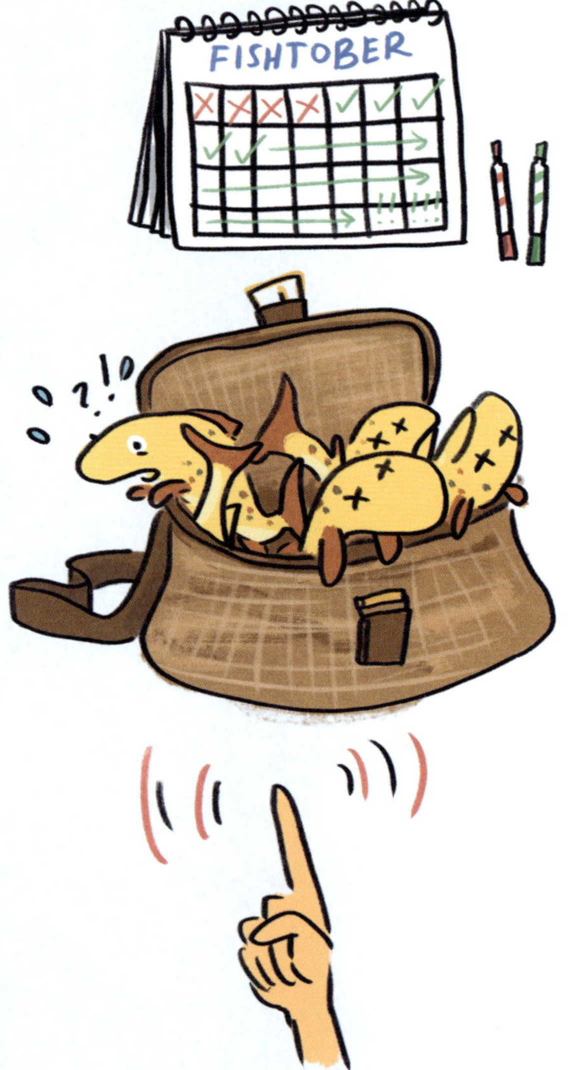

FISHING SEASON! Most fisheries have seasons when you can and can't fish. Often, this is to protect fish while they're spawning. So if you want to keep fishing in the future, follow the rules!

CREEL LIMITS. A creel is that old-fashioned wicker basket people used to (and some still do) carry caught fish in. Creel limits refer to how many fish you can take to eat and how big they have to be. Sometimes, these even specify whether or not you can use barbed hooks.

ACCESS! Is the water publicly accessible? Maybe it is, but it runs through private land so there's no way to get to it without wading up- or downstream for miles. Or maybe you can float a stream but not touch the banks—this is a real thing. Generally speaking, the rights here tilt toward landowners even when the rules might say otherwise. Check fisheries' websites. Ask at fly shops. I tread lightly here.

The big law that protects your ability to fish is called the Clean Water Act. Enacted back in 1972, it has been central to keeping American waterways clean. (They generally no longer do things like catch on fire.) It has also made fishing WAY better. So, regardless of how you vote, if you want to keep catching fish, you want a powerful Clean Water Act.

HERE'S A HYPOTHETICAL STREAM WITH RULES IN ACTION . . .

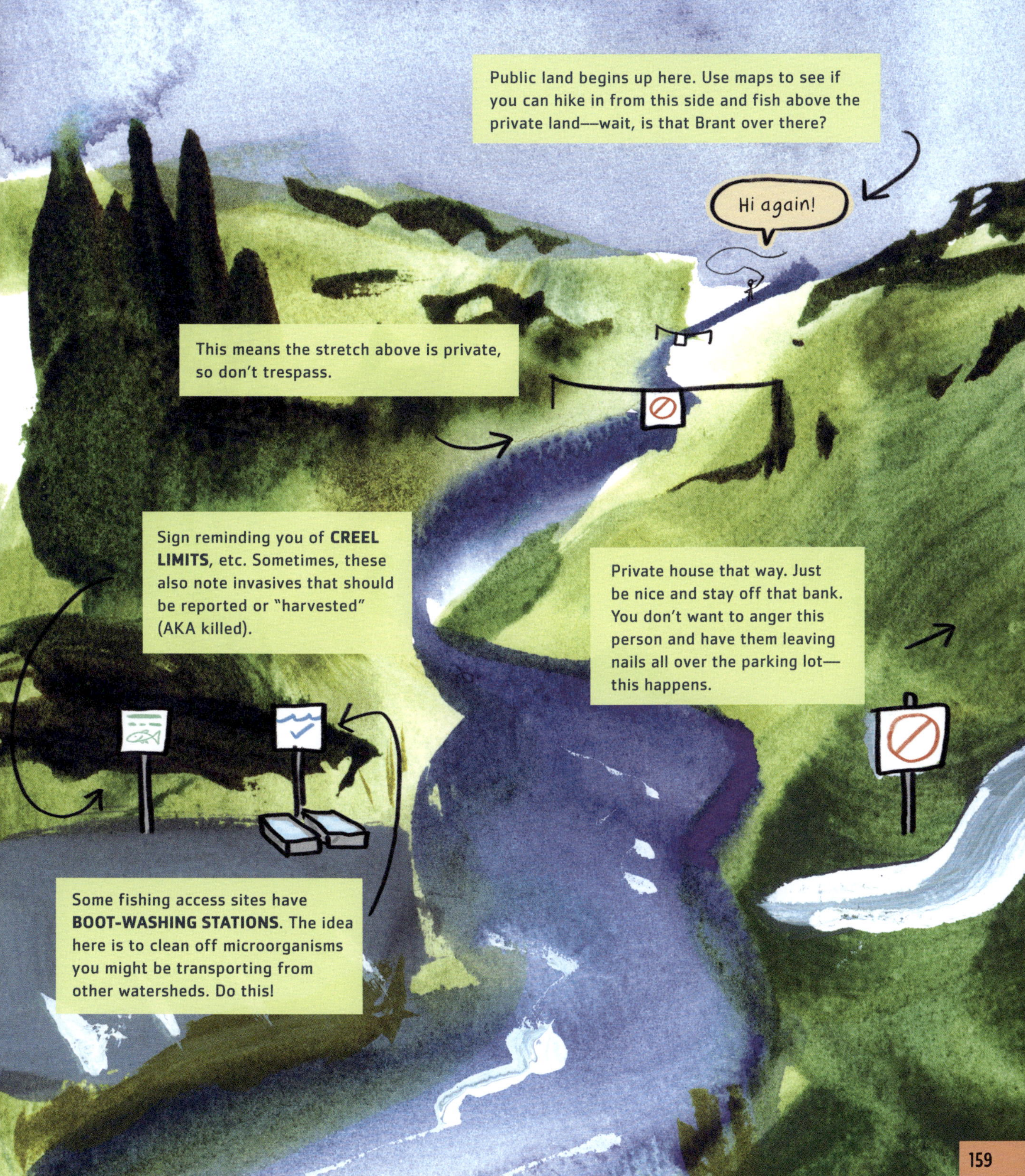

NON-LAW DO'S AND DON'TS . . .

It's not enough to look cool (see chapter 1). Fly fishing is all about acting cool. What does this mean? Generally speaking, be nice.

If you see someone else angling up- or downstream . . .

. . . **DO** give them space. Say "hi," but expect that they might be out looking for some quiet time.

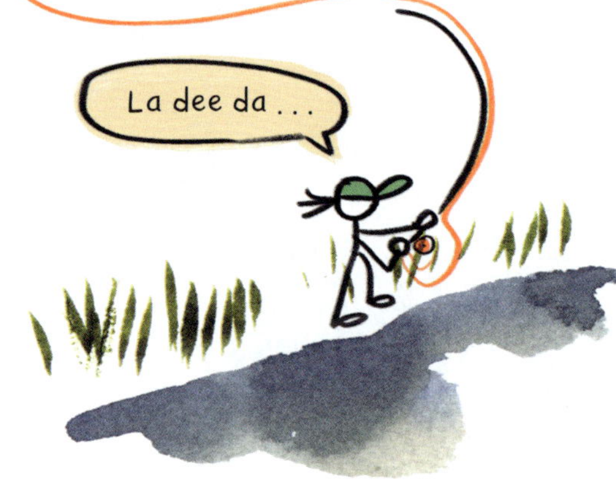

. . . **DON'T** fish all over the water they're about to fish, be loud (please . . . no portable speakers!), or ask a billion questions.

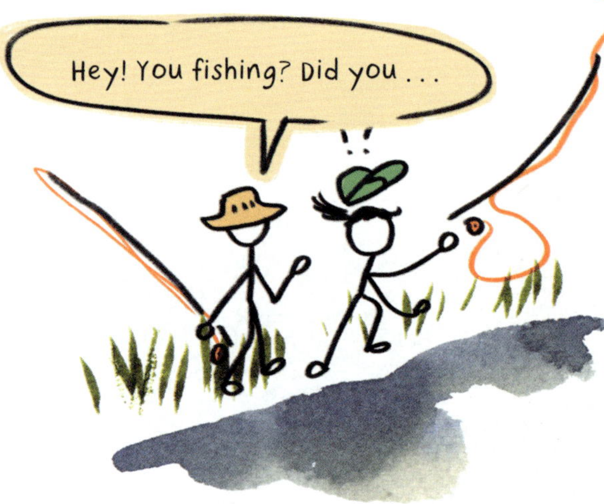

If you snag a fly on a tree branch . . .

. . . **DO** figure out a way to grab it! In fact, no matter what you do in the woods, follow the "Leave no trace, pack it in/pack it out" approach.

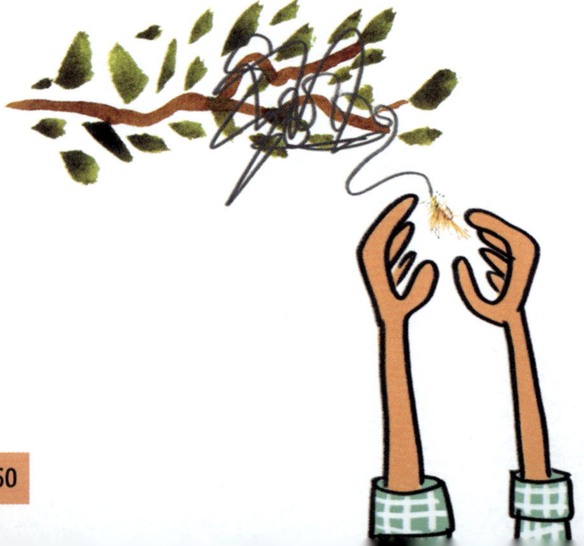

. . . **DON'T** just leave it there. Birds eat the same bugs your flies imitate. They will eat flies in trees, get hung up, and die.

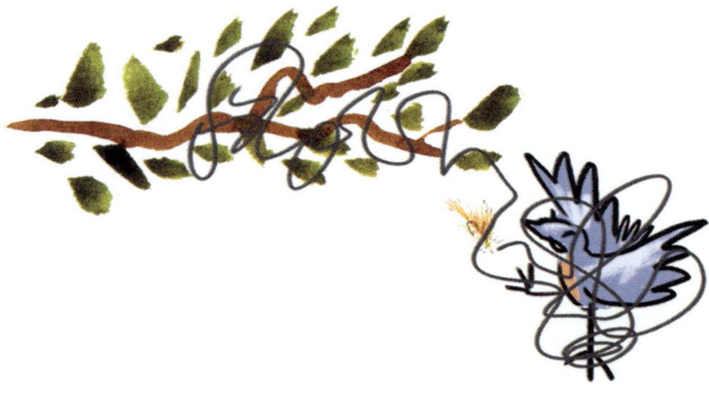

If you just found the most amazing fishing hole on a remote public stream . . .

. . . **GO AHEAD**, tell your friends. But know that for everyone you tell, that's probably one more person fishing there. That said, I love sharing cool, if hard-to-reach, spots with folks new to fishing. It's encouraging to be let in on a little secret knowledge!

. . . **DON'T** scream to the *entire* world about it. But at the same time, don't act like it's your personal piece of heaven to protect and police. I avoid geotagging. I also avoid getting into fights online about people "spot-burning." Remember the theme here: Be nice.

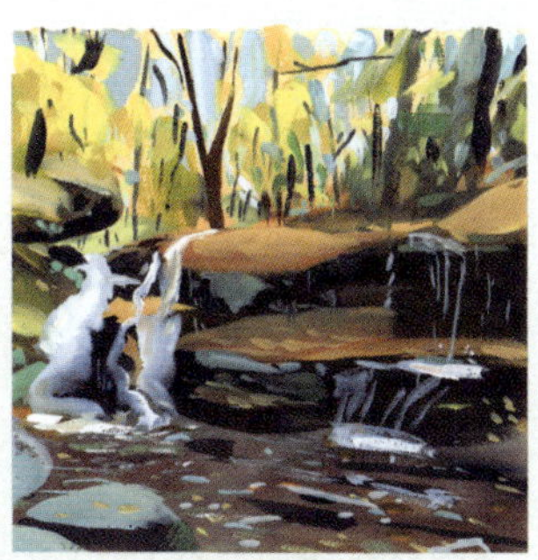

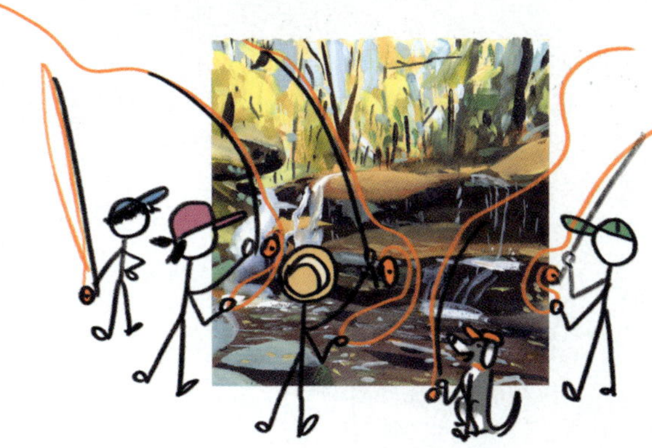

If—WHOA, BRAH! CHECK OUT THIS LUNKER! . . .

. . . **DO** take a photo and all that. Just, like I said on page 49, try to keep your catch wet. If you absolutely need that out-of-water shot, make it QUICK and GENTLE.

(Also, a warning: This is called a "grip and grin," and some anglers will make fun of you for it.)

. . . **DON'T** take a billion out-of-water shots of the fish. (You don't want to torture the fish, and you also don't want to bring on the "grip and grin" antagonists . . .)

One last time: Be nice!

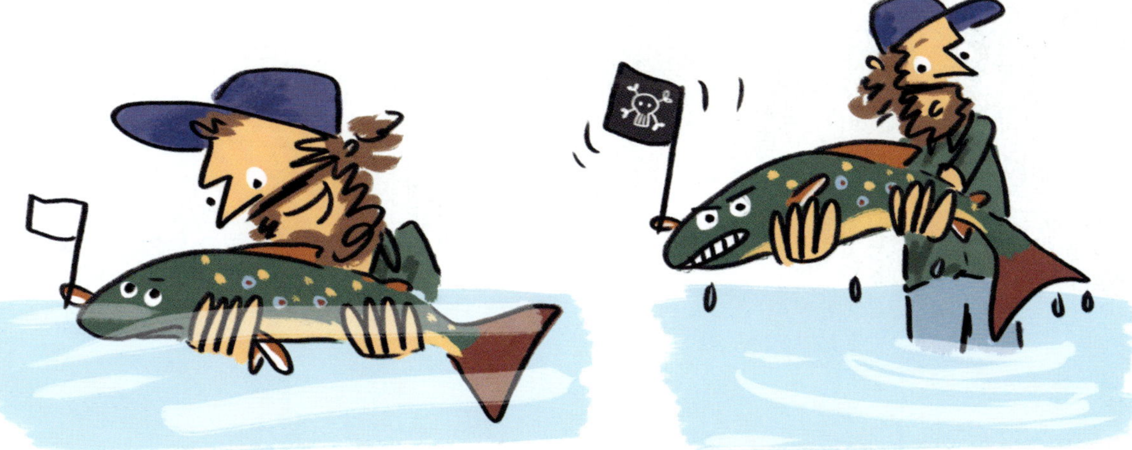

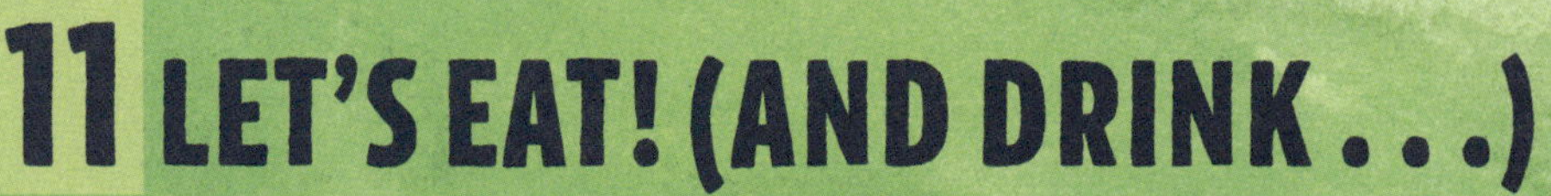

11 LET'S EAT! (AND DRINK . . .)

CATCH AND RELEASE—YES! Always? Well . . . sometimes there are enough fish, so it's OK to eat a few—or you're actually helping the environment by eating invasive species. If that's the case, you want to hang with these two neighbors of mine: chef Sohail Zandi of Brushland and brewer Mike Barcone of West Kill Brewing.

It takes little effort to make a freshly-caught fish delicious, which is why It's fun to bring a small grill right down to the river bank. With the help of some salt & pepper, a lemon, and a cooler of beers, it is the lunch everyone dreams about in deep winter . . .

. . . says the James Beard–nominated chef. He also fishes with a hook and worm, but I let it go because he's that good of a cook. Plus, we'll get him into a fly rod eventually.

SOHAIL ZANDI

FAVORITE WATERS: Little Delaware

FAVORITE FISH: Brown Trout

FAVORITE FLY: Hook & Worm all day, baby.

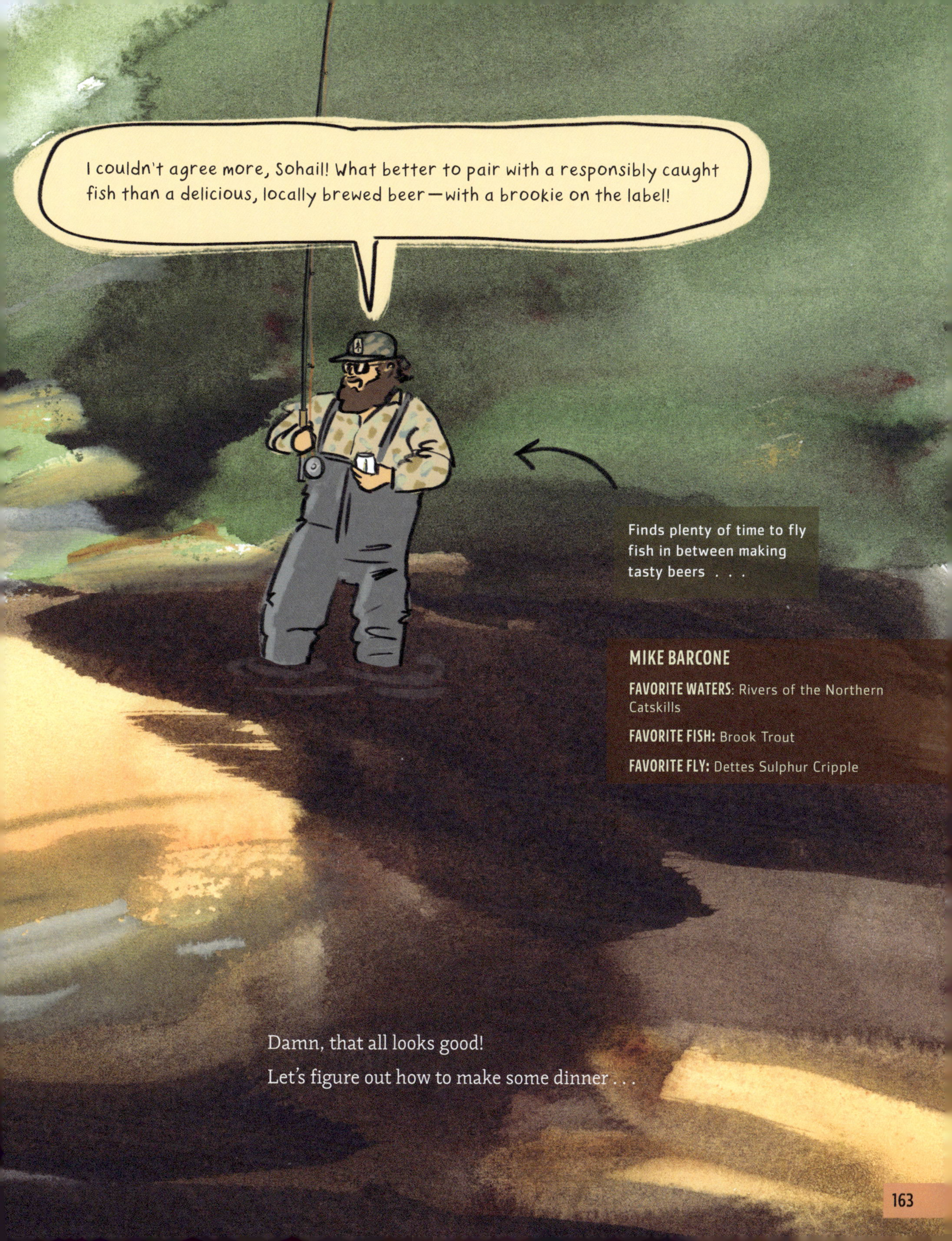

I couldn't agree more, Sohail! What better to pair with a responsibly caught fish than a delicious, locally brewed beer—with a brookie on the label!

Finds plenty of time to fly fish in between making tasty beers . . .

MIKE BARCONE

FAVORITE WATERS: Rivers of the Northern Catskills

FAVORITE FISH: Brook Trout

FAVORITE FLY: Dettes Sulphur Cripple

Damn, that all looks good!

Let's figure out how to make some dinner . . .

IMPORTANT: READ THIS BEFORE KILLING A FISH!

Laws about catching and killing fish (AKA "creel limits") are set up to please a lot of parties. Conservation is a concern. But recreation is too. So it's worth thinking a bit beyond what's technically legal and more toward what's best for the whole ecosystem. Here's how I decide if the fish I hooked would make a good dinner:*

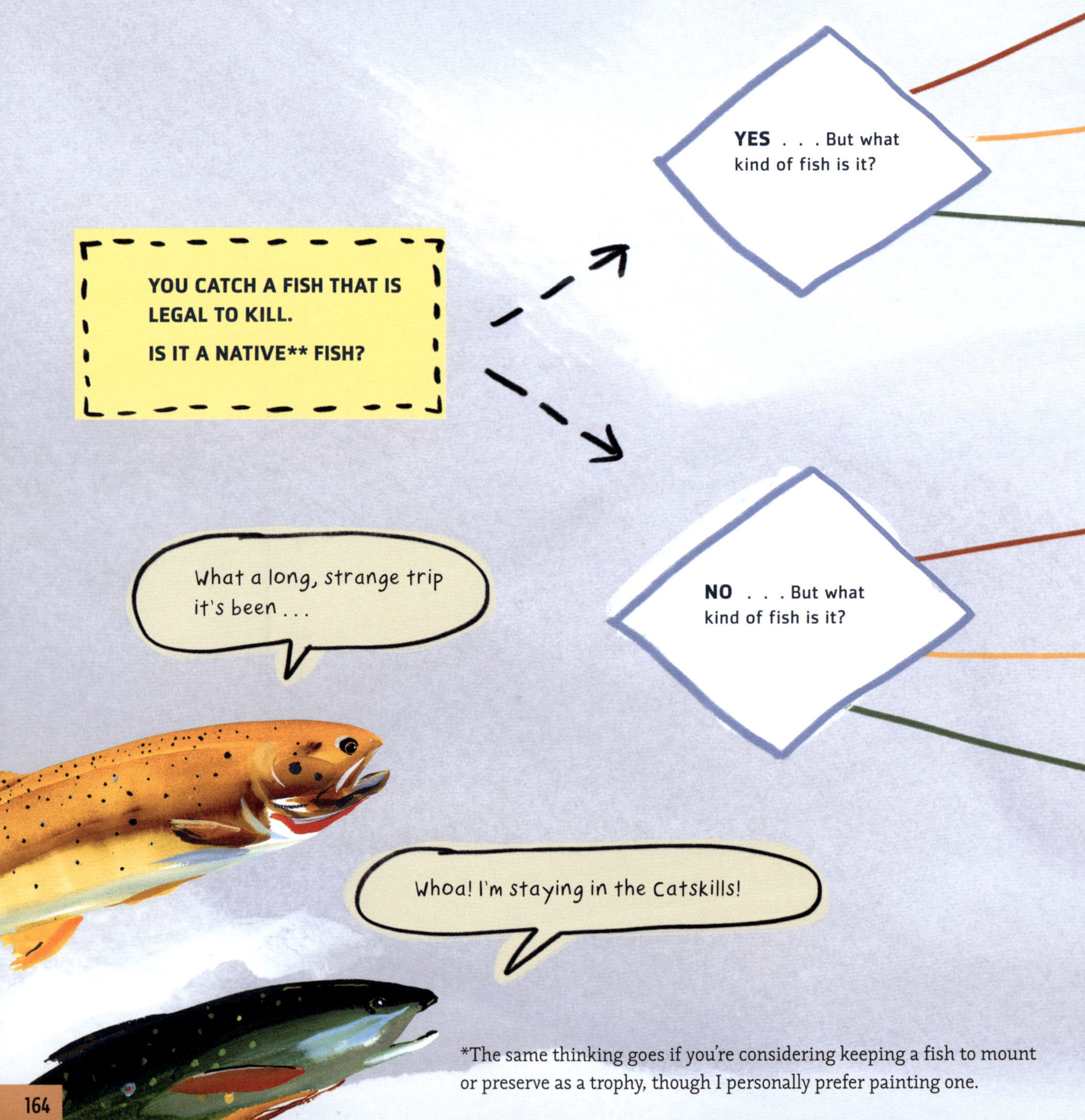

*The same thinking goes if you're considering keeping a fish to mount or preserve as a trophy, though I personally prefer painting one.

IT'S THREATENED—SEND IT BACK.

In the Catskills, brook trout are the native fish. Between the climate crisis, warming streams, and non-native fish intrusion, brookies have it rough! I send them back. Similar scenarios exist for species like cutthroat trout or striped bass. A little research done before fishing goes a long way.

IT'S STOCKED—THINK ABOUT IT.

Native fish are stocked too. Often, fisheries do this with the idea that people are going to catch and kill. Just remember: Every fish you keep is one you won't catch the next time.

IT'S ABUNDANT—OK, BUT STILL . . .

I'm fishing in New York three hours from NYC. There is a lot of population pressure. So, again: I do not eat my neighborhood brookies. Are you deep in the woods, away from big cities, where there's a ton of fish and very few anglers? By all means, go for it.

IT'S WILDISH—SEND IT BACK.

Remember, most of this species migration happened well over a century ago and we're in a new world. The Esopus Creek near me is a great example. Rainbows are "wild" here in the sense that, while they were first introduced in the 1880s, they're now a self-sustaining population of fish and not actively stocked. So I avoid eating these.

IT'S STOCKED—THINK ABOUT IT.

This is the bulk of the fish you'll see fly fishing: brown trout dumped into waterways, literally by the truckload. As with native stocked fish (and everything in life), moderation is the key here.

IT'S INVASIVE/DANGEROUS—GO FOR IT.

I WOULD eat a brookie out West. There, they're invasive and considered pests! Eating them can help preserve habitat for native cutthroats. THIS IS THE BEST-CASE SCENARIO FOR EATING WILD FISH.

** "Native," as in: Was it around in the area before the 1850s? (See timeline on page 120.)

HOW TO KILL AND GUT A FISH

Assuming it's legal and ethical, here's how I kill and prep a trout. You only need two things!

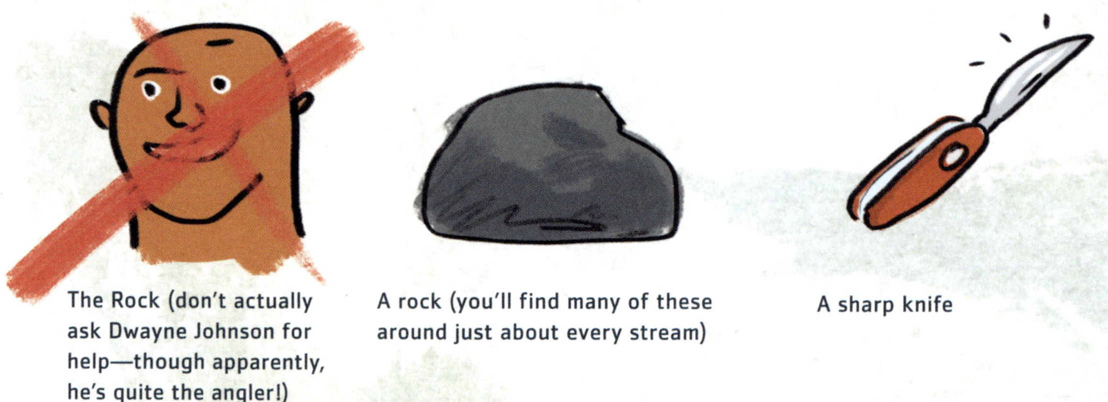

The Rock (don't actually ask Dwayne Johnson for help—though apparently, he's quite the angler!)

A rock (you'll find many of these around just about every stream)

A sharp knife

STEP 1. Hold the fish upright and below its head. Hit its head with the rock—hard. An eyeball might pop out. That's just how it goes. The important thing is to be as swift and painless as possible. Respect the fish!

Pro Tip: DON'T HIT YOUR HOLDING HAND. I've done this before. OUCH!

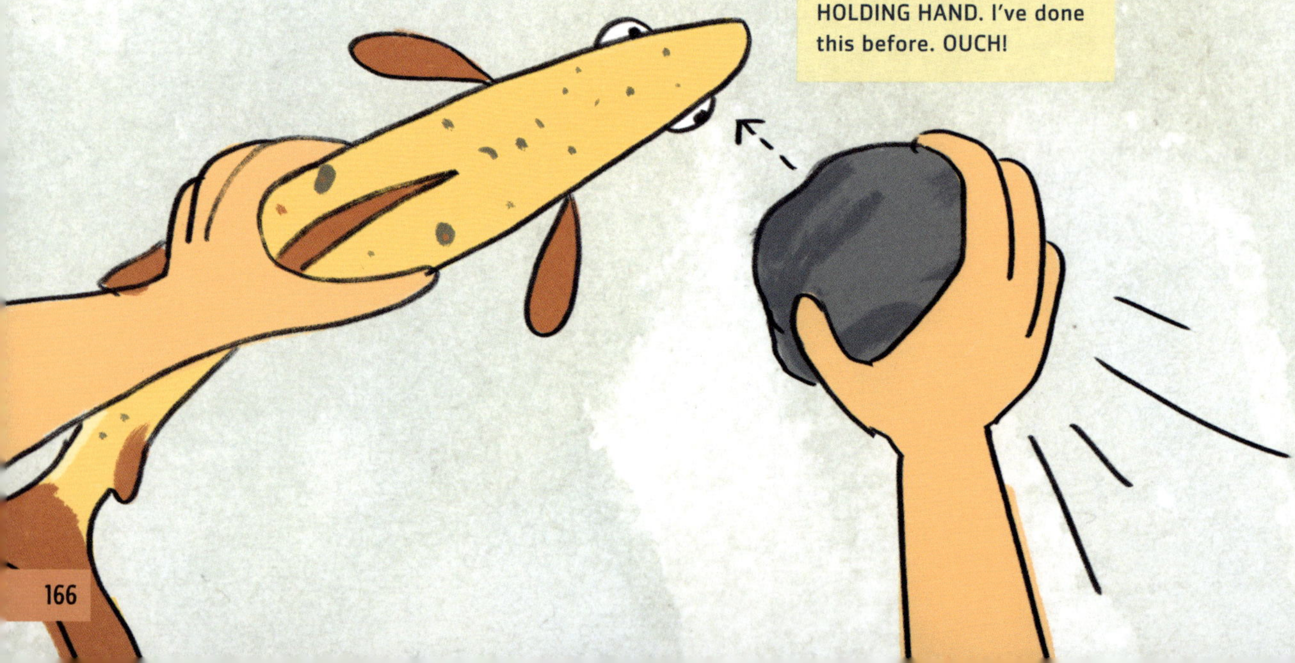

STEP 2. Flip the (now dead) fish over. Insert the knife into the fish's anus (the only hole on the bottom) and gently cut up, trying not to slice into the meat.

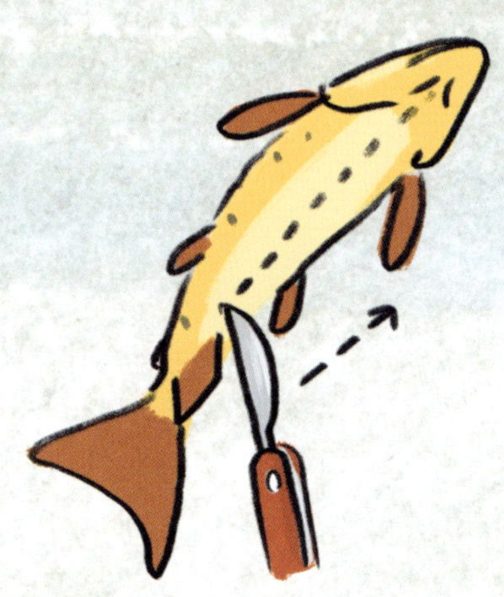

STEP 3. Gill move. Cut right under the triangle where the gills form a V under the head.

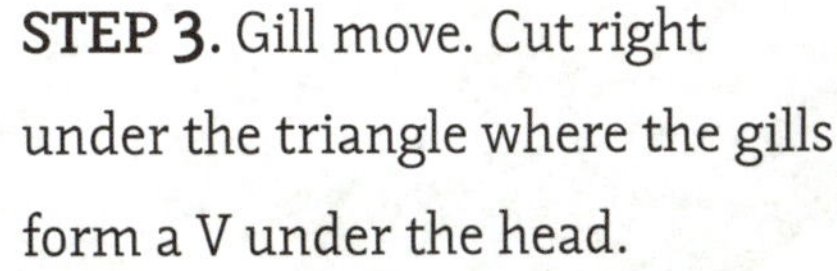

STEP 4. From the head back, pull out the guts and other organs. If you're inquisitive, look in the stomach. This is a great opportunity to learn EXACTLY what the fish was eating for future angling.

STEP 5. With your knife and fingers, get out the kidneys (all that black stuff) along the spine.

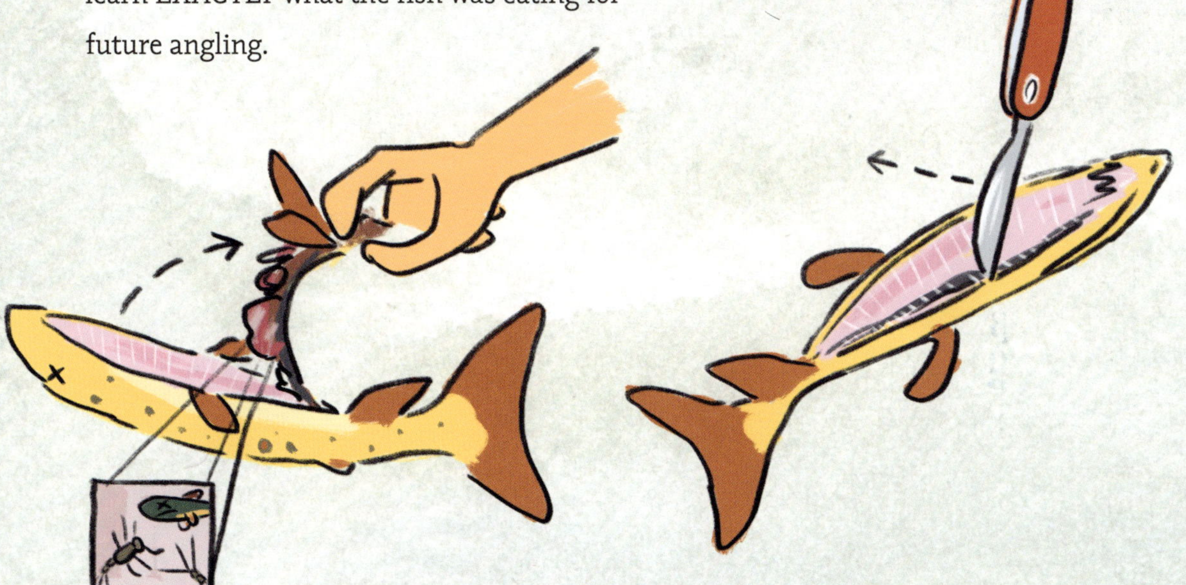

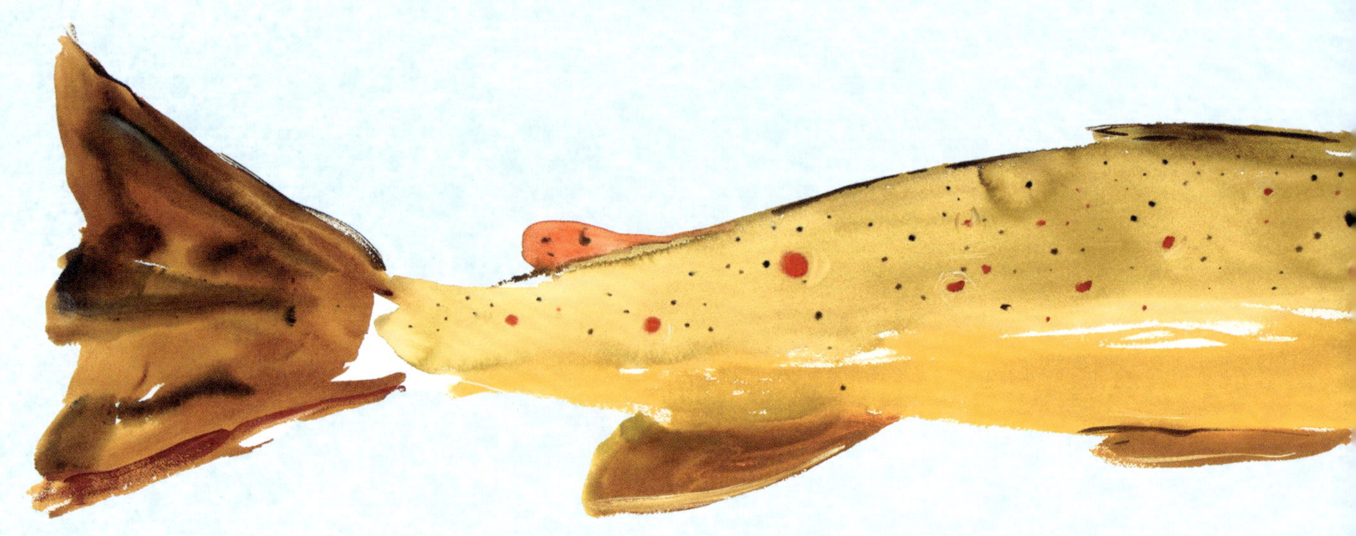

HOW TO COOK A TROUT

HERE'S A SECRET: This recipe is JUST AS DELICIOUS if you make it with trout from a local sustainable trout hatchery! (Maybe better, as they often do the gutting for you!) However I "catch" one, here's how I generally go about cooking a trout. Adjust as you'd like. This also works great on a stovetop, grill, or smoker!

Caviar is pickled sturgeon eggs. You can do the same thing with trout eggs. It's called roe.

1. Separate the eggs from the egg sac, gently and slowly. (Try not to break the eggs.)

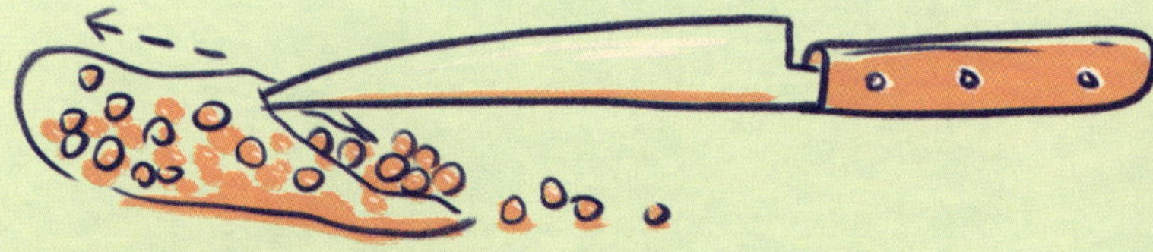

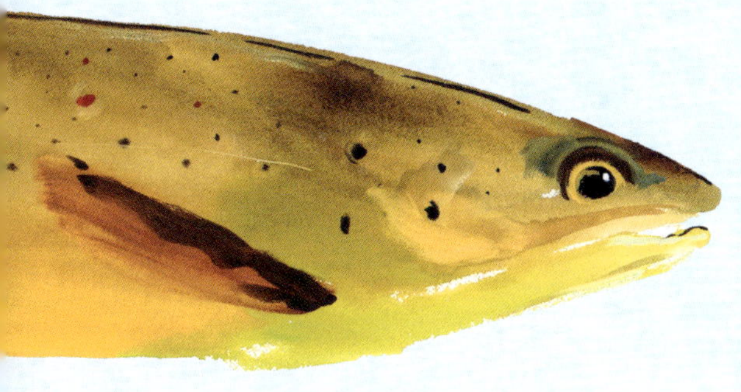

WHAT YOU NEED

- A few lemon slices
- Some fresh herbs (dill and parsley are my favorites)
- A bunch of salt
- Some olive oil
- A few pats of butter

DIRECTIONS

STEP 1. Preheat your oven to 400° F.

STEP 2. Pour some olive oil on the fish, then some salt. Rub it all around. Stuff the inside of the trout (where all the guts used to be) with lemon slices, herbs, and pats of butter. Maybe throw a pat or two of butter on top as well.

STEP 3. Put this on a roasting pan. Is your oven at 400° yet? Great! Put it in the oven.

STEP 4. Open a beer (or beverage of your choice) and recount the story of how you caught this fish to someone nearby.

STEP 5. In about 20 minutes (give or take 5–10 minutes depending on the size of the trout), it's done. You'll want crispy, browned skin on top and the flesh more opaque and firm than when you started.

STEP 6. Serve and eat immediately. Hot, fresh trout is the best! Don't forget to eat the cheeks too!

2. Rinse the eggs a few times in cold water until it runs clear.

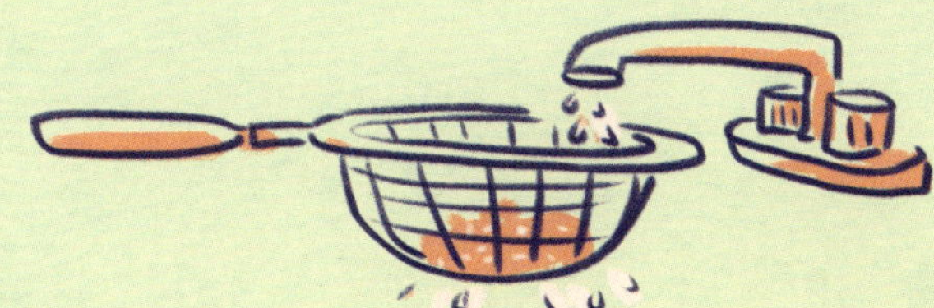

3. Salt the roe. The ratio of salt to roe should be about 1:10 by weight, and less is more. A scale is helpful here. Enjoy within a day or two.

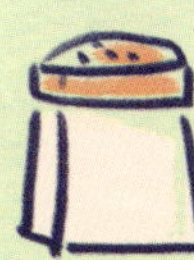

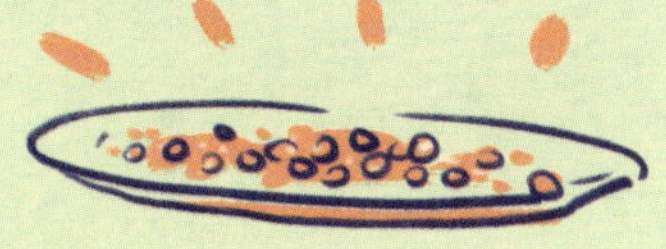

HOW ABOUT A DRINK WITH THAT?

Stay hydrated! Here are some options . . .

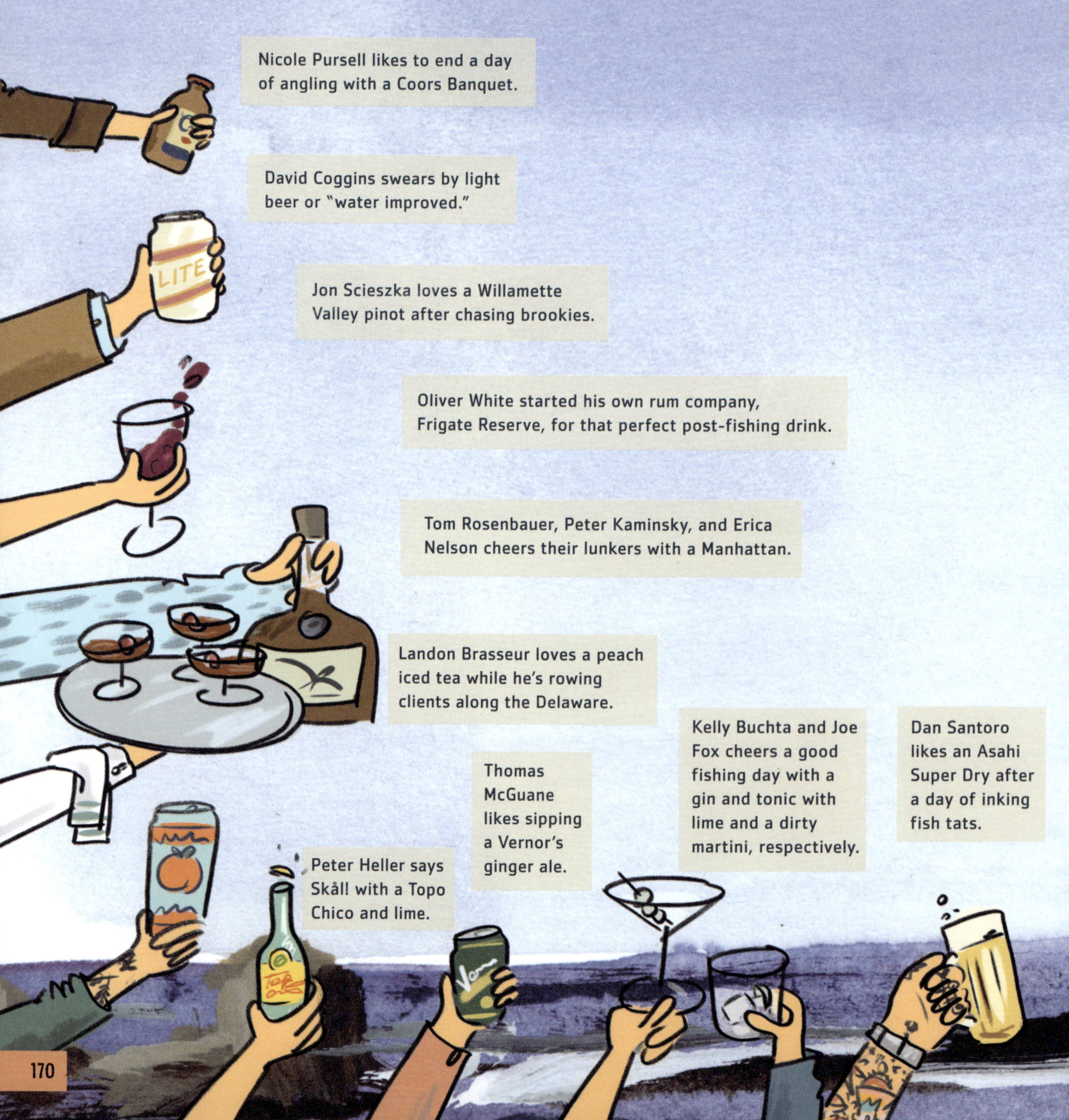

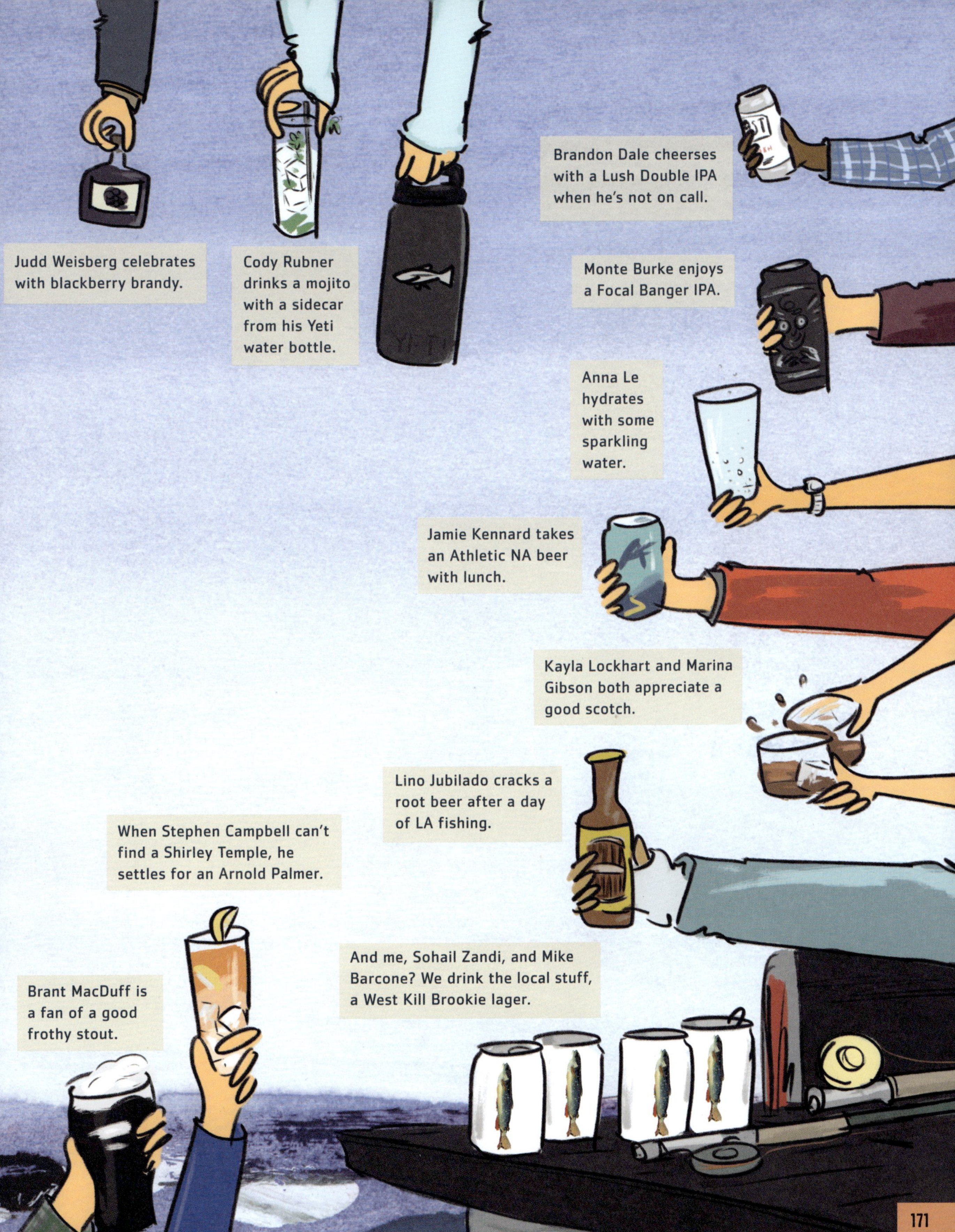
Judd Weisberg celebrates with blackberry brandy.
Cody Rubner drinks a mojito with a sidecar from his Yeti water bottle.
Brandon Dale cheerses with a Lush Double IPA when he's not on call.
Monte Burke enjoys a Focal Banger IPA.
Anna Le hydrates with some sparkling water.
Jamie Kennard takes an Athletic NA beer with lunch.
Kayla Lockhart and Marina Gibson both appreciate a good scotch.
Lino Jubilado cracks a root beer after a day of LA fishing.
When Stephen Campbell can't find a Shirley Temple, he settles for an Arnold Palmer.
Brant MacDuff is a fan of a good frothy stout.
And me, Sohail Zandi, and Mike Barcone? We drink the local stuff, a West Kill Brookie lager.

Oh, wow. Looks like my kids have something big on, so I'll make this quick . . . Now it's time for the best part of this book: Your turn!

Let your mind empty. Don't worry if your cast isn't perfect. (It'll never be—and that's OK.) Take a moment to appreciate the nature around you. And most importantly: Have fun. It's just fishing.

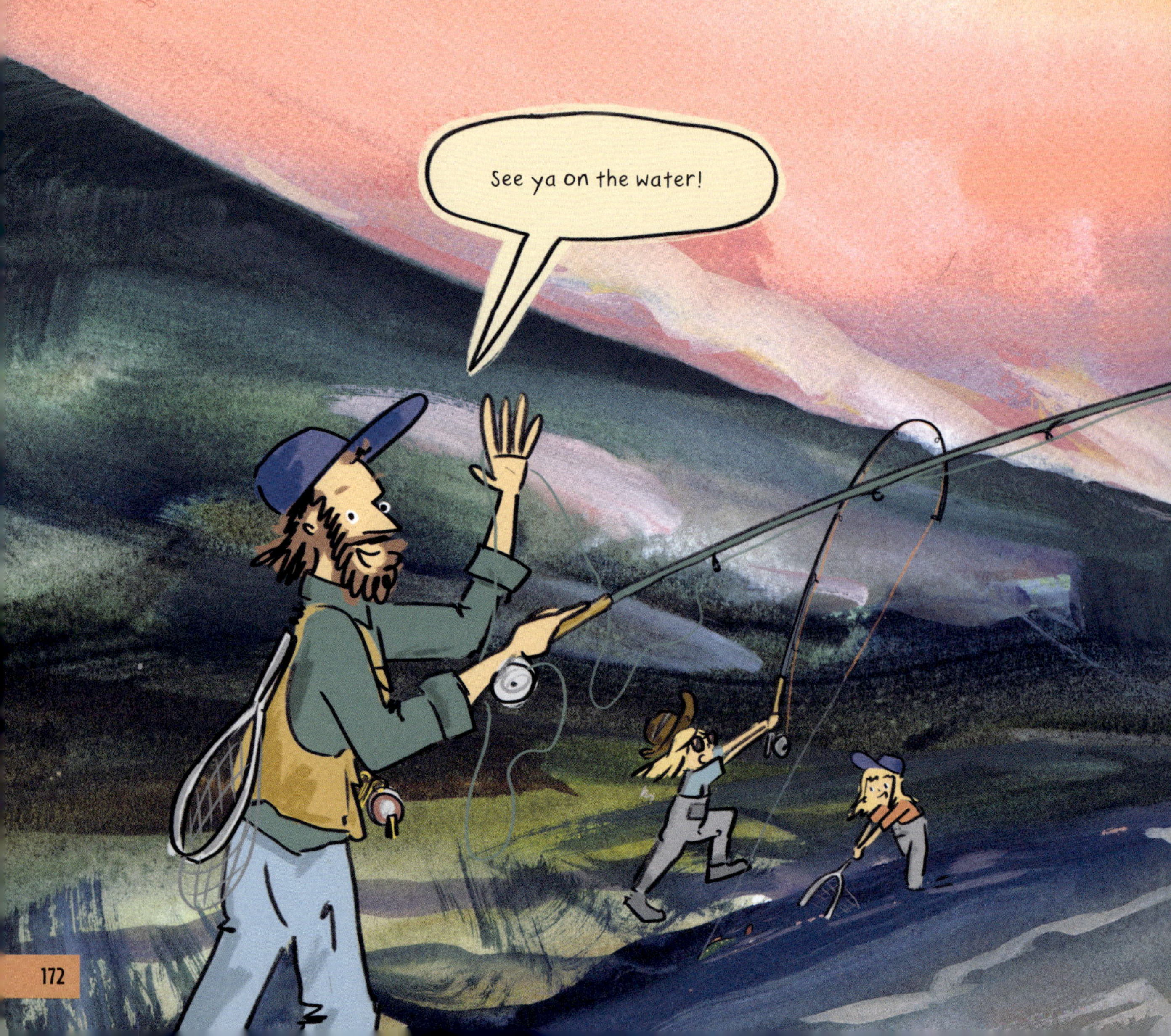

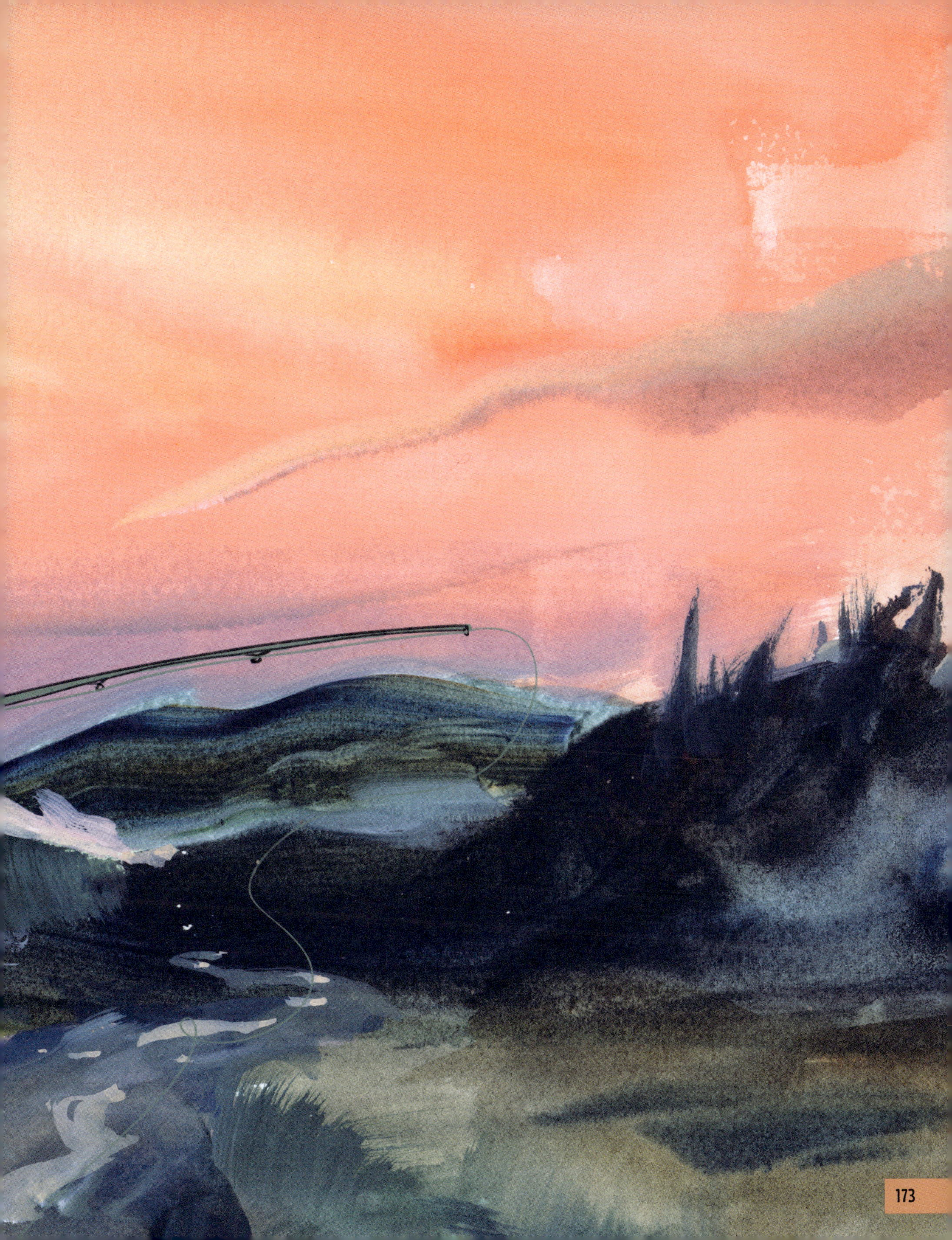

ACKNOWLEDGMENTS

To anyone I've ever met on some water, who has lent a fly or even the hint of a fishing hole, thank you. A book like this can only exist because I'm lucky enough to work in two fields full of encouraging, brilliant, and creative people: fly fishing and publishing. (Or maybe I'm just biased because fishing and books are some of my favorite things.)

In alphabetical order: Christian Anwander, Nick Aster, Mike Barcone, Kevin Boyer, Landon Brasseur, Kelly Buchta, Monte Burke, Amber Campbell, Stephen Campbell, Bruno A. Carullo, David Coggins, Brandon Dale, Kelly Farber, Isaac Fitzgerald, Joe Fox, Marina Gibson, Darrell Hartman, Graham Hiemstra, Lino Jubilado, Michael Kauffman, Jamie Kennard, George Kerchner, Jimmy Kimmel, Justin Krasner, Anna Le, Kayla Lockhart, everyone at the South Fork Lodge, everyone at West Kill Brewing, Brant MacDuff, Thomas McGuane, Kevin McIlravy, Kate Meltzer, Scott Neild, Erica Nelson, Jo Piazza, Nicole Pursell, Christina Quintero, Chuta Reyes, Tom Rosenbauer, Cody Rubner, Dan Santoro, Leonard Schoenberger, Jon Scieszka, Jeremy Shelhorn, Todd Spire, Eeland Stibling, Steven Swenson, Jesse Vadala, Judd Weisberg, Oliver White, Andrew Worthington, Joan Wulff, and Sohail Zandi.

Peter Kaminsky, thank you so much for your reads throughout.

A special thanks, too, to my agent, Marcia Wernick; editor, Deirdre Langeland; art director, Jen Keenan; publisher, Nathalie Le Du; senior production editor, Kathy Wielgosz; and proofreaders Desiree Guillermo, Peter Mavrikis, and Ellie Durham-Britton.

THANK YOU ALL SO MUCH!!!

And most importantly to my wife, Casey, and kids, Amina and Felix. See, I wasn't *just* fishing this whole time!

HOW TO HELP

Truly, the best way I can say thank you to everyone who's helped make fly fishing what it is today is by passing that on to future anglers.

Luckily, I'm not the only one trying to do this. AND no matter how you feel about everything else in society, there's probably a fishing or outdoor organization for you! Here are some of my favorites:

350:
350.org

American Museum of Fly Fishing:
amff.org

American Saltwater Guides Association:
saltwaterguidesassociation.com

Backcountry Hunters & Anglers:
backcountryhunters.org

Bonefish & Tarpon Trust:
bonefishtarpontrust.org

Captains for Clean Water:
captainsforcleanwater.org

Casting for Recovery:
castingforrecovery.org

Catskill Fly Fishing Center & Museum:
cffcm.org

National Park Foundation:
nationalparks.org

Natural Resources Defense Council:
nrdc.org

Outdoor Afro:
outdoorafro.org

Project Healing Waters:
projecthealingwaters.org

Sierra Club:
sierraclub.org

The Mayfly Project:
themayflyproject.com

Theodore Gordon Flyfishers:
tgf.org

Theodore Roosevelt Conservation Partnership:
TRCP.org

Trout Unlimited:
TU.org

Unlikely Hikers:
unlikelyhikers.org

The Cancer and Pisces Trust:
cancerandpiscestrust.org

Reel Recovery:
reelrecovery.org

ABOUT THE AUTHOR

When Steven Weinberg isn't fishing, he paints mountains and fish from his home in the Catskills, New York. His art has been featured in museums, galleries, the *New York Times*, and places like the cover of Thomas McGuane's Fly Fishing classic *The Longest Silence*, Jimmy Kimmel's fishing hotel The South Fork Lodge, and West Kill Brewing's Brookie Lager and Kaaterskill IPA beer cans. He's written and illustrated more than fifteen children's books including *What Is Color?*, a critically acclaimed journey into how color is made. He and his wife, Casey Scieszka, also own and operate the Spruceton Inn: a Catskills Bed and Bar. Their annual artist residency hosts world-renowned painters, bestselling authors, and Pulitzer Prize and National Book Award finalists.

For more of Steven's work, including original art and prints for sale, find him at **stevenweinbergstudio.com** and on Instagram as **@steven_draws**.

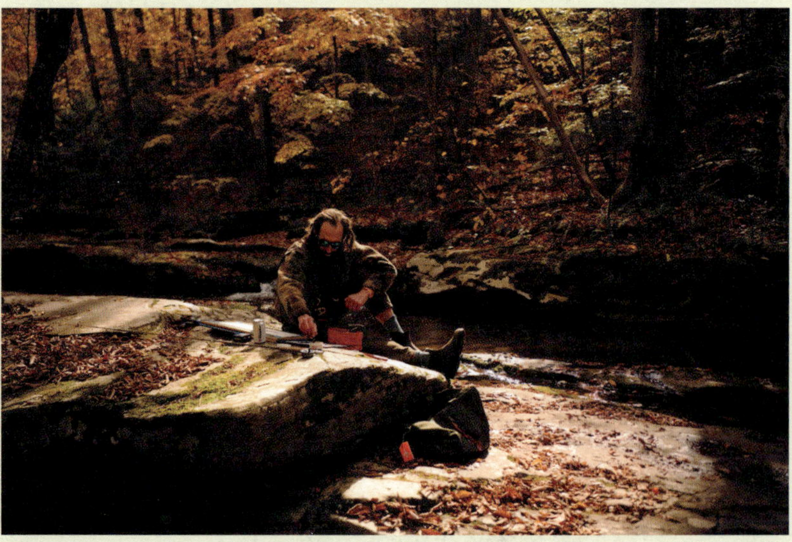

Photo © 2024 by Christian Anwander